T0311938

ECO-FRIENDLY TECHNOLOGY FOR POSTHARVEST PRODUCE QUALITY

ECO-FRIENDLY TECHNOLOGY FOR POSTHARVEST PRODUCE QUALITY

Edited by

MOHAMMED WASIM SIDDIQUI

Bihar Agricultural University, Department of Food Science and Postharvest Technology, Sabour, Bhagalpur, Bihar, India

AMSTERDAM • BOSTON • HEIDELBERG • LONDON • NEW YORK • OXFORD
PARIS • SAN DIEGO • SAN FRANCISCO • SINGAPORE • SYDNEY • TOKYO
Academic Press is an imprint of Elsevier

Academic Press is an imprint of Elsevier
125 London Wall, London EC2Y 5AS, UK
525 B Street, Suite 1800, San Diego, CA 92101-4495, USA
50 Hampshire Street, 5th Floor, Cambridge, MA 02139, USA
The Boulevard, Langford Lane, Kidlington, Oxford OX5 1GB, UK

Copyright © 2016 Elsevier Inc. All rights reserved.

No part of this publication may be reproduced or transmitted in any form or by any means, electronic or
mechanical, including photocopying, recording, or any information storage and retrieval system, without
permission in writing from the publisher. Details on how to seek permission, further information about the
Publisher's permissions policies and our arrangements with organizations such as the Copyright Clearance
Center and the Copyright Licensing Agency, can be found at our website: www.elsevier.com/permissions.

This book and the individual contributions contained in it are protected under copyright by the Publisher
(other than as may be noted herein).

Notices
Knowledge and best practice in this field are constantly changing. As new research and experience broaden
our understanding, changes in research methods, professional practices, or medical treatment may become
necessary.

Practitioners and researchers must always rely on their own experience and knowledge in evaluating and
using any information, methods, compounds, or experiments described herein. In using such information
or methods they should be mindful of their own safety and the safety of others, including parties for whom
they have a professional responsibility.

To the fullest extent of the law, neither the Publisher nor the authors, contributors, or editors, assume any
liability for any injury and/or damage to persons or property as a matter of products liability, negligence or
otherwise, or from any use or operation of any methods, products, instructions, or ideas contained in the
material herein.

British Library Cataloguing-in-Publication Data
A catalogue record for this book is available from the British Library

Library of Congress Cataloging-in-Publication Data
A catalog record for this book is available from the Library of Congress

ISBN: 978-0-12-804313-4

For information on all Academic Press publications
visit our website at http://store.elsevier.com/

Working together
to grow libraries in
developing countries

www.elsevier.com • www.bookaid.org

Publisher: Nikki Levy
Acquisition Editor: Patricia Osborn
Editorial Project Manager: Karen Miller
Production Project Manager: Caroline Johnson
Designer: Matthew Limbert

Typeset by Thomson Digital

Dedication

To my beloved sister "Asma" this book is affectionately dedicated.

TABLE OF CONTENTS

Chapter 3   Recent Trends in Active Packaging in Fruits and Vegetables 77

Samad Bodbodak, Zahra Rafiee

Chapter 4   Advances in Modified Atmosphere Packaging of Fruits and Vegetables 127

Samad Bodbodak, Mohammad Moshfeghifar

LIST OF CONTRIBUTORS

Mohammadreza Asghari
Urmia University, Department of Horticulture, Faculty of Agriculture, Urmia, Iran

Mohammad Ali Askari Sarcheshmeh
University of Tehran, Department of Horticultural Science, College of Agriculture and Natural Resource, Karaj, Iran

Mesbah Babalar
University of Tehran, Department of Horticultural Science, College of Agriculture and Natural Resource, Karaj, Iran

Kalyan Barman
Bihar Agricultural University, Department of Horticulture (Fruit and Fruit Technology), Sabour, Bhagalpur, Bihar, India

Samad Bodbodak
University of Tabriz, Department of Food Science and Technology, Faculty of Agriculture, Tabriz, Iran

Salvador Castillo
University Miguel Hernández, Department of Food Technology, Orihuela, Alicante, Spain

Huertas M. Díaz-Mula
University Miguel Hernández, Department of Food Technology, Orihuela, Alicante, Spain

Fabián Guillén
University Miguel Hernández, Department of Food Technology, Orihuela, Alicante, Spain

Endrit Kullaj
Agricultural University of Tirana, Department of Horticulture and Landscape Architecture, Faculty of Agriculture and Environment, Koder-Kamez, Tirana, Albania

Domingo Martínez-Romero
University Miguel Hernández, Department of Food Technology, Orihuela, Alicante, Spain

Mohammad Moshfeghifar
Islamic Azad University, Faculty of Food Sciences and Engineering (FFSE), Science & Research Branch Tehran, Tehran, Iran

Zahra Rafiee
Tarbiat Modares University, Department of Food Science and Technology, Faculty of Agriculture, Tehran, Iran

María Serrano
University Miguel Hernández, Department of Applied Biology, Orihuela, Alicante, Spain

Swati Sharma
ICAR–National Research Centre on Litchi, Muzaffarpur, Bihar, India

Morteza Soleimani Aghdam
University of Tehran, Department of Horticultural Science, College of Agriculture and Natural Resource, Karaj, Iran

Daniel Valero
University Miguel Hernández, Department of Food Technology, Orihuela, Alicante, Spain

Juan M. Valverde
University Miguel Hernández, Department of Food Technology, Orihuela, Alicante, Spain

Mohammed Wasim Siddiqui
Bihar Agricultural University, Department of Food Science and Postharvest Technology, Sabour, Bhagalpur, Bihar, India

Pedro J. Zapata
University Miguel Hernández, Department of Food Technology, Orihuela, Alicante, Spain

PREFACE

The horticultural sector is an important source of employment for developing countries. Global horticultural production has increased manyfold but still there is the need to work on the management of the huge production processes that facilitate safe and healthy produce to reach the consumer. Most of the developing countries have been losing about 35–40% of total production of fruits and vegetables due to inadequate postharvest handling and are facing huge monitory losses. Several methods have been developed to preserve the postharvest horticultural produce quality because of consumer concerns about the quality and safety of produce. Postharvest management technologies determine food quality and safety, competitiveness in the market, and the profits earned by producers.

There are many traditional technologies, with limited success, used in fresh product preservation. Although substantial research has been carried out to preserve the quality of fresh horticultural produce, further research on this topic is still required, since none of the methods reported can control all the parameters necessary to achieve produce with an extending shelf life and without compromising quality. The book *Eco-Friendly Technology for Postharvest Produce Quality* determines the scope of emerging eco-friendly technologies to maintain the postharvest quality of fresh produce in terms of safety and nutrition. The book covers an analysis of the alternative and traditional methodologies, pointing out the significant advantages and limitations of each technique. This book is comprised of nine chapters, which are written by experts from across the globe.

Chapter: New Insights on Postharvest Ecophysiology of Fresh Horticultural Crops discusses the new insights on postharvest ecophysiology of fresh horticultural crops. The chapter gives an in-depth understanding on postharvest physiology, which is an important issue in maintaining postharvest quality. Several advancements in storage systems of fresh produce have been made, in which controlled atmosphere storage is the most important. In this curriculum, chapter: Advances in Controlled Atmosphere Storage of Fruits and Vegetables broadly deals with the advances in controlled atmosphere storage of fruits and vegetables. Protection and communication during transportation of fresh produce are very important issues that could be achieved by appropriate packaging techniques. Two very important chapters are included to describe the recent trends in active packaging (chapter: Recent

Trends in Active Packaging in Fruits and Vegetables) and modified atmosphere packaging (chapter: Advances in Modified Atmosphere Packaging of Fruits and Vegetables) of fruits and vegetables. The regulation of ethylene production and its action in fresh harvested produce is of utmost importance to preserve shelf life. Among the different treatments for inhibiting effects of ethylene on produce quality, 1-methylcylopropane (1-MCP) has been identified as the most potent ecofriendly molecule for fresh fruits and vegetables. Recent developments of 1-MCP treatments on fruit quality are discussed in chapter: Recent Developments of 1-Methylciclopropene (1-MCP) Treatments on Fruit Quality Attributes.

The roles of ecofriendly molecules such as brassinosteroids, polyamines, and salicylic acid in regulating postharvest physiology and ultimately the postharvest quality of fresh commodities are described in chapters: Impact of Brassinosteroids on Postharvest Physiology of Fruits and Vegetables, Polyamines as an Ecofriendly Postharvest Tool to Maintain Fruit Quality, and Impact of Salicylic Acid on Postharvest Physiology of Fruits and Vegetables, respectively. The application of chitosan as a coating on horticultural commodities has shown immense potential to maintain the quality as well as extend the shelf life of several fresh fruits and vegetables. Chapter: Chitosan: Properties and Roles in Postharvest Quality Preservation of Horticultural Crops broadly discusses the different properties of chitosan and its roles in postharvest quality preservation of horticultural crops. This book is a standard reference work for professionals working in the postharvest industry, especially fresh produce management. In addition, this is a valuable textbook for higher-level undergraduate and graduate courses in the area of food processing, food preservation, and quality of fresh produce.

ABOUT THE EDITOR

Mohammed Wasim Siddiqui, PhD

Dr Mohammed Wasim Siddiqui is an Assistant Professor and Scientist in the Department of Food Science and Post-Harvest Technology, Bihar Agricultural University, Sabour, India and author or coauthor of 31 peer reviewed research articles, 26 book chapters, 02 manuals, and 18 conference papers. He has 10 edited and 01 authored books to his credit published by Elsevier, USA, CRC Press, USA, Springer, USA, & Apple Academic Press, USA.

Dr Siddiqui has established an international peer reviewed journal "Journal of Postharvest Technology." He has been honored to be the Editor-in-Chief of two book series entitled "Postharvest Biology and Technology" and "Innovations in Horticultural Science" being published from Apple Academic Press, New Jersey, USA. Dr Siddiqui is a Senior Acquisitions Editor in Apple Academic Press, New Jersey, USA for Horticultural Science. He has been serving as an editorial board member and active reviewer of several international journals such as LWT—Food Science and Technology (Elsevier), Food Science and Nutrition (Wiley), Acta Physiologiae Plantarum (Springer), Journal of Food Science and Technology (Springer), Indian Journal of Agricultural Science (ICAR), etc.

Recently, Dr Siddiqui is conferred with the Best Young Researcher Award—2015 by GRABS Educational Trust, Chennai, India and the Young Scientist Award—2015 by Venus International Foundation, Chennai, India. He was also a recipient of the Young Achiever Award—2014 for the outstanding research work by the Society for Advancement of Human and Nature (SADHNA), Nauni, Himachal Pradesh, India, where he is an Honorary Board Member and Life Time Author. He has been an active member of organizing committee of several national and international seminars/conferences/summits. He is one of key members in establishing the WORLD FOOD PRESERVATION CENTER (WFPC), LLC, USA. Presently, he is an active associate and supporter of WFPC, LLC, USA.

Dr Siddiqui acquired BSc (Agriculture) degree from Jawaharlal Nehru Krishi Vishwa Vidyalaya, Jabalpur, India. He received the MSc (Horticulture) and PhD (Horticulture) degrees from Bidhan Chandra Krishi Viswavidyalaya, Mohanpur, Nadia, India with specialization in the Postharvest Technology. He was awarded Maulana Azad National Fellowship Award from the University Grants Commission, New Delhi, India. He is a member of "Core

Research Group" at Bihar Agricultural University (BAU) and providing appropriate direction and assisting to sensitize priority of the research. He has received several grants from various funding agencies to carry out his research projects. Dr Siddiqui has been associated to postharvest technology and processing aspects of horticultural crops. He is dynamically indulged in teaching (graduate and doctorate students) and research, and he has proved himself as an active scientist in the area of Postharvest Technology.

ACKNOWLEDGMENTS

First of all, I ascribe all glory to the Gracious "Almighty Allah" from whom all blessings come. I would like to thank Him for His blessing to write this book.

I wish to extend my appreciation to and thank the Bihar Agricultural University, India, for providing me the opportunity and facilities to bring forth such an exciting book. I convey special thanks to my colleagues and other research team members for their support and encouragement for helping me to accomplish this venture.

I also would like to express my appreciation for Ms Patricia Osborn, Senior Acquisitions Editor, and Ms Karen Miller and Ms Jacky Truesdell, Editorial Project Managers, from Elsevier, USA, who offered considerable and valuable information during the preparation of this book.

My acknowledgments will not be complete without expressing indebtedness to my beloved parents and family members for their infinitive love, cordial affection, incessant inspiration, and silent prayer to "Allah" for my well-being and confidence.

1

NEW INSIGHTS ON POSTHARVEST ECOPHYSIOLOGY OF FRESH HORTICULTURAL CROPS

Endrit Kullaj

Agricultural University of Tirana, Department of Horticulture and Landscape Architecture, Faculty of Agriculture and Environment, Koder-Kamez, Tirana, Albania

1   Introduction

Scientists and technicians are increasingly aware that their main postharvest problems depend on preharvest conditions; in other words, the life of a horticultural product after harvest cannot be independent from its previous "history." Such a history is influenced by a multitude of factors such as mineral nutrition status and fertilization, rainfall and irrigation, susceptibility of crops to pests and their management, seasonal temperatures and light conditions, or maturity at the time of harvest. These factors can directly or indirectly affect postharvest quality and storability. Since preharvest and postharvest development is linked, knowledge of the interactions between the products' physiological development stages and the abiotic conditions to which they are exposed could permit a better understanding of their behavior in storage. Notwithstanding, postharvest objectives are not part of the farm planning process used for fertilization, pest control, irrigation, etc. This is also related to the fact that scientific interest devoted to the complex influence of preharvest factors on postharvest quality is insufficient. Further impetus of research on the control of preharvest factors is essential to quality retention and development of horticultural products. This is crucial for conceiving precise methods and strategies to identify the key attributes that influence quality retention.

With due consideration to the vast diversity of horticultural species and cultivars, genetic factors, bioregulators, or other similar

Eco-Friendly Technology for Postharvest Produce Quality. http://dx.doi.org/10.1016/B978-0-12-804313-4.00001-3
Copyright © 2016 Elsevier Inc. All rights reserved.

compounds as well as maturity at harvest and harvesting methods, we limit our discussion to environmental factors (climatic factors and cultural practices). Climatic changes are seriously threatening agricultural production, but even more so horticultural products, especially fresh fruits and vegetables. As most of the horticultural breeding programs, now armed with the tools of genetic engineering, are focused more on pest resistance and less on the response to abiotic stresses, there is an urgent need to adapt and adopt cultural practices to maintain quality under increasing pressure. Furthermore, the concept of quality has gone beyond attributes such as size, color, flavor, texture, and main nutrients; more and more consumers use fruits and vegetables for their nutraceutical values because of their constituents such as carotenoids, flavonoids and other polyphenols, phenolic acids, and other phytonutrients, which lower the risk of cancer (Doll, 1990; Dragsted et al., 1993), cardiovascular disease (Anderson et al., 2000), and other diseases (Ames et al., 1993). Although the breeding and biotechnology approaches are improving the gene pool for enhanced nutritional quality, climatic conditions, especially temperature and light intensity, have a strong effect on the expression of these genes. These phytonutrients are even more susceptible to variations in temperature, relative humidity, and/or concentrations of oxygen, carbon dioxide, and ethylene during the entire postharvest handling system and require new postharvest technologies.

Among the range of environmental factors affecting postharvest quality and storability of horticultural products, water, chemicals, temperature, and radiation are the most important and consequently have received more scientific interest. The tremendous diversity of fruits and vegetables that are produced commercially and the general lack of research relating preharvest factors to postharvest quality precludes generalizations about preharvest influences that uniformly apply to all horticultural products (Crisosto and Mitchell, 2002). Although the author has attempted to equally exemplify the main horticultural crop species, frequent reference to some of them is related to the level of scientific reports, which relates to their storability (pome fruits vs. stone fruits), short lifecycle (vegetables vs. fruits), and economic importance. An example of physiological mechanisms is climacteric (eg, tomato, apple, or banana) and nonclimacteric (eg, strawberry, citrus, and grape berries) fruits. Readers interested in specific crops or quality attributes can refer to other reviews (Arpaia, 1994; Crisosto et al., 1997; Ferguson et al., 1999; Goldman et al., 1999; Kader, 1988; Kays, 1999; Lee and Kader, 2000; Kullaj, 2013; Léchaudel and Joas, 2007; Mattheis and Fellman, 1999; Monselise and Goren, 1987; Prange and Dell, 1997; Sams, 1999; Silva, 2008; Shewfelt, 1990; Weston and Barth, 1997).

Optimum postharvest quality and storability can be achieved only by understanding and managing the various roles that preharvest factors play in postharvest quality (adapted from Crisosto and Mitchell, 2002). This requires knowledge of how the quality of a horticultural product changes in response to environmental conditions as a prerequisite to improve preharvest and postharvest protocols and technologies (Kullaj, 2013). The aim of this chapter is to describe and discuss the impact of environmental factors on postharvest life (storage and shelf life) of main horticultural products. The structure of the chapter is not orthodox, whereby we list the effects of the main abiotic stresses (nutrients and other chemicals, temperature, water, light, etc.); among the large spectrum of biochemical and structural modifications during growth and maturation of harvested plant parts, we chose those with a major impact on global quality and storability and discussed how abiotic stresses affect these. Thus we focus on the role of abiotic factors on processes related to structural modifications of the flesh due to depolymerization of principal components of cell walls and loss of cell turgor, which affect texture. These processes will be exemplified with various cases of preharvest treatments using sprays and dips of nutrients to avoid some typical physiological disorders. Other important processes involve modifications of nutritional and organoleptic value of fruits due to an increase in mono- and disaccharides following starch hydrolysis and/or de novo synthesis, biosynthesis of volatile compositions, and the degradation of organic acids. Here we try to underline how soil and climatic factors affect the enzymatic activity, particularly for horticultural professionals involved in production and postharvest to design appropriate technologies. Modifications of the color due to a degradation of chlorophyll and accumulation of carotenoids and/or flavonoids in relation to light and temperature levels at the farm level have received increased attention in recent research. Finally, we review how abiotic factors determine susceptibility to pathogens and the response of fruits, for instance, by accumulating defense proteins. This structure enables us to concentrate on the biological processes elucidated by the most recent scientific knowledge.

2 Effects on Texture

A factor of primary importance to determine consumer acceptance, quality, and storability of harvested plant organs is *texture*. Furthermore, it impacts organoleptic quality (see next section). In fact, one of the most obvious changes for consumers is fruit *softening*, which reduces quality and limits shelf life and storability of fresh horticultural products. Different horticultural fruits differ in terms of softening; for instance, apple, Asian pear, and watermelon do not soften to the same extent as tomato and strawberry but are still crisp when ripe (Harker et al., 1997). Shelf life duration of strawberries and peaches varies from a few days to a few weeks while for apples and pears it can be prolonged for months.

Atkinson et al. (2012) describes softening as a complex developmental program that involves the disassembly of various pectin and hemicellulose components of the primary cell wall, as well as alterations to cell turgor and fruit water status (Brummell, 2006; Ghiani et al., 2011; Saladié et al., 2007; Shackel et al., 1991) affecting texture. Soil, climatic, and agrotechnical factors (fertilization, irrigation, etc.) during the growing season of horticultural plants determine the synergistic actions of processes such as loss of cell turgor (accumulation of solutes such as carbohydrates, organic acids, ions, etc.), calcium levels, and particularly changes in architecture and composition of cell wall and middle lamella (modified from Costa et al., 2012) (interested readers can refer to Carpita and Gibeaut, 1993; Cosgrove, 1997; Braidwood et al., 2014; Reiter, 2002; Wolf et al., 2012). The middle lamella in fruit cell walls is rich in pectic polysaccharides (particularly homogalacturonan-rich pectin) (Caffall and Mohnen, 2009; Mohnen, 2008) with a major role in intercellular adhesion (Knox et al., 1990; Steele et al., 1997). Initially thought as filling material for the open space in cellulose/hemicellulose networks, pectins have important structural roles (Peaucelle et al., 2012). Polysaccharides represent 95% of the cell wall constituents and are composed of cellulose (30%), hemicellulose (30%), and pectins (35%). As it was discussed earlier, pectins in particular have crucial effects on softening following their depolymerization and solubilization. Cell wall changes associated with fruit softening are related to the expression of a number of hydrolase and transglycosylase genes (Huber, 1983). Among these genes the main player, but not sufficient alone to significantly alter texture (Giovannoni et al., 1989; Sheehy et al., 1988; Smith and Gross, 2000; Smith et al., 1988; Sun et al., 2012), is polygalacturonase (PG) as it has been observed that its activity and mRNA levels during fruit ripening increase (Kramer et al., 1990; Fischer and Bennett, 1991; Hadfield and Bennett, 1998; Murayama et al., 2009). The enzymes responsible for such modifications are the wall hydrolases, among which endo-β-(1,4) glucanase (Lashbrook et al., 1998), xyloglucan endotransglycosylase, pectin methylesterase (Tieman et al., 1992), pectate lyase, PG, both as exo- and endo- forms) and β-galactosidase (β-GAL), to which expansins (EXP) (Brummell et al., 1999b; Civello et al., 1999; Cosgrove, 2000a, 2000b; Rose et al., 1997) are added, are involved in the relaxation of the wall. In apple fruits, for instance, softening has been associated with the increase in the expression of cell wall hydrolase genes such as *PG1*, *β-GAL*, and *XET1* (Atkinson, 1994; Goulao and Oliveira, 2007). The activity of PG enzymes was observed only after the flesh of the fruit had reached a certain consistency (about 20 Newton in peach) and corresponding to the peak of ethylene production. The latest plays a crucial role in regulating the expression of enzyme activity of different wall hydrolases (Brummell and Harpster, 2001). This is confirmed either by biotechnological approaches aiming to alter the biosynthesis and/or perception of the hormone or through treatments with specific inhibitors of its action (see chapter: Recent Developments of 1-Methylciclopropene (1-MCP) Treatments on Fruit Quality Attributes). Sun et al. (2012) elucidated also the role of abscisic acid (ABA) in fruit ripening of tomato, which was known to enhance the production of several metabolites involved in fruit ripening when applied exogenously to grape (*Vitis vinifera*) at the véraison stage (Ban et al., 2003; Cakir et al., 2003; Chernys and Zeevaart, 2000; Deluc et al., 2007; Giribaldi et al., 2010; Jeong et al., 2004; Lacampagne et al., 2009; Wheeler et al., 2009). Such a role of ABA, which is known to induce a complex reprogramming of plant metabolism and particularly affects genes involved in responses against stress and in stress-dependent signaling networks (Hoth et al., 2002; Seki et al., 2007; Suzuki et al., 2003), can explain the role of water stress in quality indicators, as we will see later.

2.1 Nutrient Stress

Calcium is involved in the synthesis of new cell walls, by binding with the polygalacturonic acid in middle lamellae, forming pectates that separate new divided cells and enabling a higher cohesion between them (Taiz and Zeiger, 2010). Thus it has a fundamental role in firmness, the physical component of texture. Homogalacturonic acid, a polymer of galacturonic acid, is ionically cross-linked by Ca^{2+}, when the carboxy group is not methylated. In ripe fruit, Ca cross-links between stretches of demethylesterified GalA residues of homogalacturonan provide the main bonding between adjacent cells (Peña and Carpita, 2004; Thompson et al., 1999). The cross-bonding of cell wall pectates by Ca^{2+} is directly related to fruit firmness, thus during softening, wall Ca is reduced, resulting in weaker cell–cell binding (Huber, 1983; Stow, 1993; Wallner, 1978). During fruit ripening, homogalacturonan can be depolymerized by endo-PGs, cell wall-localized enzymes that cleave stretches of unesterified GalA residues and weaken the middle lamella (Brummell and Harpster, 2001).

Early knowledge that Ca levels are positively correlated to the maintenance of wall integrity and therefore compactness has led to the application of Ca treatments to fruits (Fallahi et al., 1997; Ferguson et al., 1999; Sams, 1999). Although it has improved fruit firmness and reduced the incidence and severity of physiological disorders during and after storage, there are frequent situations leading to chemical stress from excessive doses (significantly higher than 1000 µg g^{-1}) resulting in surface injury to the fruit (Crisosto and Mitchell, 2002).

Many other disorders of considerable economic importance, such as apple bitter pit and cork spot (Shear, 1975), lenticel rupturing, water core, splitting, breakdown, lenticel blotch pit and confluent pit or crinkle (Bramlage et al., 1980; Perring, 1984; Perring et al., 1985; Sharples, 1980), pear black end (Woodbridge, 1971), blackheart in celery (Shear, 1975), tomato blossom end rot (Shear, 1975), cavity spot and cracking in carrot, and tipburn of lettuce, are associated with low Ca concentrations (Crisosto and Mitchell, 2002; Kays, 1999). The same authors (Crisosto et al., 1997) call for caution on the use of preharvest Ca sprays of calcium chloride on peaches and nectarines because their heavy metal (Fe, Al, Cu, etc.) content may contribute to skin discoloration (inking). Even postharvest vacuum infiltrations of solutions into mature peaches did not show a reduction in decay incidence, although they maintained higher fruit flesh firmness during cold storage, but the latest benefit was negated by skin injury and sanitation problems (Crisosto and Mitchell, 2002). This practice in apples soon after harvest or after 3 months' cold storage greatly reduces subsequent fruit softening. Electron micrographs of treated fruits show well-structured, darkly staining middle lamellae indicative of tightly packed polyuronides even after prolonged storage, whereas the corresponding untreated controls show the middle lamella to have degraded to the point of cell wall separation (Poovaiah et al., 1988; Siddiqui and Bangerth, 1993). This infiltration into Ca significantly reduces ethylene production (Poovaiah et al., 1988) and it has been suggested that microsomal membranes are the sites of interaction of Ca, and that ethylene biosynthesis is modulated through its binding with the membrane (Ben-Arie et al., 1982).

As respiration rates of untreated apples are inversely related to flesh Ca content (Bramlage et al., 1974; Faust and Shear, 1972), Ca dips have been used to reduce respiration too (Watkins et al., 1982). Accelerated respiration of Ca-deficient apples might be linked to effects of Ca on ADP/ATP ratios in the cell (Bramlage et al., 1980) because Ca ions are essential for the activity of a number of enzymes including the membrane-associated,

Ca-dependent ATPases, and Ca movement across the membrane can directly drive ATP synthesis. Calcium chloride sprays reduce the activity of pyruvate kinase, which exerts considerable control of respiration (Meli and Bygrave, 1972) leading to incidence of bitter pit (Witney and Kushad, 1990). Individual cells and their middle lamellae remain active as sinks for Ca well into their postharvest life. This supports the concept that the decline in Ca importation into the fruit in the later stages of their growth in the orchard is a function of an impaired transport system through the stalk, not simply to a decline in demand with the cessation of cell division (Jackson, 2003).

Another important quality indicator for fruits and vegetables, *juiciness*, requires a cohesive network of large, turgid, thin-walled cells. Cohesion of middle lamella depends on ionic bonds involving Ca ions and uronic acids (Bartley and Knee, 1982). If the middle lamella is stronger than the cell walls, the cells fracture on biting and juice is released; if it is weaker, then the fracture is between cells, the juice is not released, and the fruit is perceived as nonjuicy (Boulton et al., 1997; Szczesniak and Ilker, 1988; Tu et al., 1997). A typical example are apples; cell separation proceeds until they develop a dry or mealy texture when the consumer's teeth pass between cells without breaking them, so that they fail to release juice (Knee, 1993).

Calcium is also required for the normal functioning of plant membranes by regulating their microviscosity or fluidity. Cellular senescence is accompanied by increases in microviscosity and the proportion of gel-phase lipid of membranes, and Ca may diminish these trends (Ferguson, 1984). The earliest pertinent evidence related to storability of apples (Fuller, 1976) has demonstrated that Ca retards breakdown cell membranes; while high-Ca fruits in mid-Dec. had intact membranes, mitochondria, plastids, and nuclei in most of the epidermal and hypodermal cells and in many outer cortical cells, low-Ca fruits had much disorganization of the cytoplasm and separation of the plasma membrane from the cell wall. Elevated Ca concentrations retard the solute leakage from tissue discs during ripening (Ferguson and Watkins, 1989; Sharples and Johnson, 1977).

The role of *boron* for cell walls required for cross-linking side chains of pectic polymer rhamnogalacturonan II (RGII) was observed a long time ago (Lee and Aronoff, 1966). It forms diesters between apiose residues (Ishii et al., 1999), the first sugar of some RGII side chains and thereby stabilizes the pectic network and the cell wall itself (Tenhaken, 2015). Boron deficiency is associated with an increase in thickness of the cell walls caused by an increase of the pore size of the cell wall (Fleischer et al., 1999).

Imbalances of boron in the soil can be an important abiotic stress factor affecting plant cell walls (Wimmer and Eichert, 2013).

Many of the adverse effects of high *nitrogen* are associated with its effect in increasing fruit size and vigor of shoot growth, which adversely affect Ca concentrations, and also with the direct effect of the ammonium ion on Ca uptake (Jackson, 2003). The postharvest fruit water loss from peach/nectarine fruit from the highest N rate tested (3.6% leaf N) was greater than that from the lowest rate (2.6% leaf N) (Crisosto and Mitchell, 2002). Similarly, optimal fruit quality in nectarines in the Eastern Po Valley area (Italy) was obtained in trials having 3.0% leaf N concentration (Scudellari et al., 1999; Tagliavini et al., 1997). High N fertilizer rates can also reduce the concentration of alcohol-insoluble solids and malate but increase the concentration of sugar in apples (Richardson, 1986).

Low nitrogen increases susceptibility to breakdown, especially if Ca levels are also low (Sharples, 1980). This knowledge has led to calcium nitrate late sprays, which were found beneficial on texture associated with an increase in the ratio of N:C, rather than of Ca:C, in the primary cell wall and middle lamella (Johnson et al., 2001).

Nitrogen can indirectly affect the velocity of the softening process because of its role in the structural characteristics and composition of cuticle, the latter playing a fundamental role in the regulation of water losses through transpiration.

Phosphorus is an integral component of important compounds of plant cells, including the sugar phosphate intermediates of respiration and photosynthesis as well as the phospholipids that make up plant membranes. Low phosphorous stress leads to increased senescent breakdown and low-temperature breakdown (Jackson, 2003) and this could be alleviated using phosphorous sprays (Yogaratnam and Sharples, 1982).

Potassium plays an important role in the regulation of the osmotic potential of plant cells (osmosis and ionic balance) and can impact texture. Potassium deficiency in citrus reduces fruit size (Chapman, 1968a,b; Du Plessis and Koen, 1988; Embleton et al., 1979) and K sprays are used to strengthen the peel (Embleton et al., 1979).

Growth of plant organs is based on cell division in the meristematic zones followed by a tremendous expansion of new cells in a complex turgor-driven process (Schopfer, 2006). Therefore it is obvious that any reduction in cell turgor, caused by osmotic stress, also reduces the mechanical power of the cell to expand the polysaccharide network. Here we mainly refer to *sodium* as salt stress, comprising osmotic and ionic components. Uptake of Na^+ across the plasma membrane is very fast resulting in physiological effects on extracellular as well as intracellular sites. Sodium reduces binding of Ca^{2+} to the plasma membrane, inhibits influx while increasing efflux of Ca^{2+}, and depletes the internal stores of Ca^{2+} from endomembranes (Rengel, 1992).

2.2 Water Stress

The effect of water supply during fruit growth is an important factor for postharvest texture. Drought conditions affect both architecture and biology of cell walls. Under such conditions, pectins are modified; there is an increase in side chains of the pectic polymers RGI and II, possibly because the pectins form hydrated gels that limit damage to cells (Leucci et al., 2008). Furthermore, drought stress, likewise osmotic or salt stress, causes a loosening of cell wall polysaccharides to maintain the possibility for cell expansion. Such effects will alter the shape and firmness of harvested plant parts.

Moderate water stress has generally no major effects on cell demography for grape berries, pear, or olives but when imposed under severe stress, the induced carbon starvation may negatively regulate cell division, as it has been observed in tomato fruit at the gene and tissue level (modified from Urban et al., 2014). On the contrary, cell expansion is clearly restricted, affecting tissue expansion via its effects on the biophysical, metabolic, and hormonal processes involved in the regulation of cell turgor and osmotic pressures as well as cell wall extension (modified from Urban et al., 2014). The effects on the biology of cell walls are also related to an increase in peroxidase activity (Ranjan et al., 2012) and/or the formation of reactive oxygen species (ROS) (Miller et al., 2010). If both occur in the same tissue the cross-linking of cell wall components might strengthen the mechanical properties of the wall (Kieffer et al., 2000; Passardi et al., 2005; Wakabayashi et al., 2012). The other face of ROS is the formation of OH· radicals, which are capable of cleaving sugar bonds in plant polysaccharides (Fry, 1998; Schopfer, 2001; Renew et al., 2005), causing a cell wall loosening similar to the action of classical loosening enzymes such as EXP or xyloglucan modifying enzymes (Renew et al., 2005). The oxidative stress-induced accumulation of antioxidant compounds, which prevents oxidative damage, may also affect texture (modified from Urban et al., 2014). For example, ascorbate has been shown in vitro to solubilize tomato pectins, a response that may explain the positive correlation between fruit firmness and reduced ascorbate content observed in tomato in response to postharvest chilling injury (Dumville and Fry, 2003).

The broad range of water management and irrigation practices, combined with the multitude of horticultural crops under a wide spectrum of climates, makes it difficult to generalize on the effects of water stress on texture. Kiwifruit, apple, and pear fruit grown under water deficit have been shown to have a better shelf life after harvest, but no effect of growth conditions on postharvest firmness has been reported for apricot or kiwifruit (modified from Urban et al., 2014).

It is acknowledged that water deficit has negative effects on plant growth and fruit yield, but when it comes to many horticultural crops what matters more is quality and not yield, as would be the case for grain crops. There are frequent reports in the literature on the negative effects of deficit irrigation on the size of fruits and vegetative growth, as explained in earlier paragraphs.

Many descriptive studies have reported significant but contrasting variations of water stress on fruit firmness; increasing in pears but not in apricots, kiwifruit, and apples (modified from Urban et al., 2014). Water stress may or not impact cell demography but it definitely impacts cell turgor, solute transport, and accumulation of osmotically active solutes at the cell level.

Peach fruits from 50% ethylene were small in size (Johnson et al., 1992) while Lepaja et al. (2015a) did not find a significant effect of regulated deficit irrigation on the diameter of Williams pears, even if combined with mulching (Lepaja et al., 2015b). In Bartlett pears, tree water stress was associated with increases in fruit firmness (Crisosto and Mitchell, 2002). A positive link between dry matter or total soluble solids and firmness was reported for tomato (modified from Urban et al., 2014). In strawberries, reduction of water stress by natural rainfall or irrigation during maturation and ripening decreases firmness and sugar content and provides more favorable conditions for mechanical fruit injury and rot (Crisosto and Mitchell, 2002). Lepaja et al. (2015a) found changes in mineral content of strawberries under partial root drying, in combination or not with mulching. On the contrary, if strawberries are overirrigated, especially at harvest, the fruit is softer and more susceptible to bruising and decay (Crisosto and Mitchell, 2002). Overirrigation can result in low soluble solids concentration (SSC) in melons (Mayberry et al., 1996).

3   Effects on Organoleptic and Nutritional Phytochemicals

The nutritional and organoleptic qualities of horticultural products depend on a multitude of phytochemicals, many yet to be determined, and most of them under both endogenous and exogenous control. They are responsible for flavor, aroma, perception, storability, and transportability. Taste and flavor of fruits are characterized by important sensorial qualities mainly defined (but not exclusively) by the entire processes that regulate the metabolism of sugars and organic acids (Costa et al., 2012). Sugars are among the most important compounds that determine the fruit flavors. Abiotic stresses greatly affect starch hydrolysis followed by sucrose hydrolysis to form more glucose and fructose responsible for sugar content in fruits. Acidity is a fundamental component of flavor and it develops during the first phase of fruit growth, following common metabolic pathways of diverse fruit typologies that result in the biosynthesis of malic and citric acids, quantitatively the most important organic acids (Costa et al., 2012). During maturation, malate is used as a respiratory substrate, decreasing the level of organic acidity (with some exceptions such as banana or mango) and forming a carbon skeleton for the synthesis of other compounds. Abiotic stresses affect the catalysis of reproductive decarboxylation of malate to pyruvate by malic enzymes. In apples the metabolism of malate by tissue slices increases as they pass through the climacteric (Hulme and Rhodes, 1971; Knee, 1993). During the maturation of grapes, increased quantities of malic acid are released from vacuoles and directed toward the mitochondria to feed the Krebs cycle, maintain the respiration, and sustain the production of ATP. Environmental conditions play a crucial role in these processes and their outcome. The utilization of organic acids during the postharvest period is the main reason for the increase in sweetness in originally high-sugar, high-acid apples or insipidity and blandness when sugar and acid concentrations are initially low (Lott, 1965).

Among phytochemicals, anthocyanin accumulation is controlled by various abiotic factors, such as nutrients (nitrogen and phosphate), sucrose, methyl jasmonate, water stress, and ultraviolet, visible, and far-red light (Chalker-Scott, 1999; Dixon and Paiva, 1995).

3.1 Temperature Stress

Exposure to low temperature stimulates ethylene synthesis in pears even when detached (Jackson, 2003) and it has been found to differ between genotypes (El-Sharkawy et al., 2004). Similarly in "Golden Delicious" apples, low temperatures simultaneously increase 1-aminocyclopropane-1-carboxylic acid (ACC), ethylene concentration in the gas spaces in the fruit, and total ethylene production (Knee et al., 1983). "Royal Gala" apples produce ethylene without prolonged cold exposure (Larrigaudiere et al., 1997) while other cultivars such as "Cox's Orange Pippin" and "Bramley's

Seedling" do not show this effect (Jackson, 2003). Leliévre et al. (1995) induced the production of ACC oxidase, in addition to ACC synthase, by chilling preclimateric "Granny Smith" apples (Leliévre et al., 1995). A short period of cold stimulates ethylene biosynthesis in "Royal Gala" and "Starking Delicious" as well as "Granny Smith" (Larrigaudiere et al., 1997). Research has hypothesized a possible synergistic molecular mechanism for the cold- and ethylene-regulated control of fruit softening (Tacken et al., 2010).

Transcriptional regulation of PG1 through the ethylene pathway is likely to be through an ETHYLENE-INSENSITIVE3-like transcription factor, which increases in expression during apple fruit development and transactivates the PG1 promoter in transient assays in the presence of ethylene. A cold-related gene that resembles a COLD BINDING FACTOR (CBF) class of gene also transactivates the PG1 promoter. The transactivation by the CBF-like gene is greatly enhanced by the addition of exogenous ethylene. Downregulation of PG1 expression in tomato had little effect on fruit firmness (Sheehy et al., 1988; Smith et al., 1988), while in strawberry, suppression of PG led to firmer fruit (Quesada et al., 2009). In apple, PG1 expression levels have been associated with softening patterns in a range of cultivars (Wakasa et al., 2006). Transgenic apple plants overexpressing PG1 have reduced cell-to-cell adhesion in the leaves (Atkinson et al., 2002), and suppression of PG1 results in firmer fruit. While these PG-suppressed apples were firmer than the controls, they were significantly softer than the ACC OXIDASE1 (ACO1)-suppressed apples, suggesting that also in apples a suite of enzymes is required for fruit softening. Fusions of the PG1 promoter to the GUS reporter gene were cloned into tomato, and the first 1.6 kb was found to have an expression pattern corresponding to tomato ethylene fruit ripening, while a larger 2.6-kb promoter did not and was hypothesized to contain an element that caused inhibition of expression (Atkinson et al., 1998).

Li et al. (2012) has demonstrated that cold acclimation treatment of peach fruits increases PG enzyme activity, retarding woolliness and promoting normal fruit ripening and fruit quality retention during low-temperature storage and shelf life. The activity of this suite of cell wall-related enzymes will determine the loss of flesh firmness in fleshy fruit (Goulao and Oliveira, 2008). Reduction in the levels of a single enzyme often has only minor effects on the maintenance of fruit firmness (Sheehy et al., 1988; Smith et al., 1988).

The environmental conditions present during maturation strongly influence the concentration of organic acids, in particular that of malic acid. Besides increasing the velocity of respiration and therefore the consumption of different substrates utilized (including organic acids), elevated temperatures induce an increase in the activity of cytoplasmic malic enzyme (nicotinamide adenine dinucleotide phosphate-malic enzyme), responsible of the decarboxylation of malic acid and pyruvate (Costa et al., 2012).

Temperature regimes other than during fruit ripening have major effects on fruit composition (Mullins et al., 1992). Thus Brix increases slightly with increasing temperature up to about 30°C and malate concentration is strongly dependent on temperature throughout the range 15–40°C, being lower at the higher temperatures. pH is positively correlated to ambient temperature and titratable acids (TA) and malate concentration of juice are negatively correlated with temperature (Kliewer and Lider, 1970; Kliewer, 1973). Accumulation of proline is greatly affected by night temperatures (Kliewer, 1973). Day/night temperature regime influences whole plant growth, color, SSC, TA, SSC/TA ratio, and ascorbic acid content in the fruit, fructose, glucose, and total carbohydrates in fruits of strawberries (Wang and Camp, 2000).

Acclimation by low (<7°C) preharvest temperatures increases the rate of SSC accumulation and reduces the susceptibility of kiwifruit to low-temperature breakdown disorder (Burdon et al., 2007).

Pome fruit disorders associated with high-temperature growing seasons are cork spot and mealy breakdown of pear, and bitter pit and water core of apple (Westwood, 1993). This is particularly the case in hot climates with mean temperatures near the critical temperature for high-temperature disorders. Similarly, where climate is considered cool for a given horticultural crop, low-temperature disorders are more likely to occur because the mean is close to the critical temperature inducing them. This is the case in scald in pears and internal browning and brown core of apples (Hansen, 1961).

Heat waves prior to harvest in plums and prunes cause drought spot, heat spot, or heat injury similar to pit burn on apricots (Westwood, 1993). As a result of high respiration, the internal O_2 level is depressed, which in turn results in abnormal (anaerobic) respiration deep in the tissue, leading to tissue breakdown, browning, and death (Maxie and Claypool, 1957).

In terms of the role of abiotic stressors on the synthesis of phytochemicals, Lin-Wang et al. (2011) cite some examples of temperature control on anthocyanin synthesis in a diverse range of horticultural species, including grape (*V. vinifera*) (Mori et al., 2007), petunia (*Petunia hybrida*) (Shvarts et al., 1997), red orange (*Citrus sinensis*) (Lo Piero et al., 2005), and rose (*Rosa hybrida*) (Dela et al., 2003). In *Arabidopsis*, anthocyanins are induced by low temperatures (Leyva et al., 1995) and reduced by high temperatures (Rowan et al., 2009). Other publications have elucidated the biosynthesis of anthocyanin pigments (Grotewold, 2006), gene networks that regulate synthesis (Allan et al., 2008), transcription factor complex (Zhang et al., 2003; Gonzalez et al., 2008), especially the first isolated MYB member of this complex the *PRODUCTION OF ANTHOCYANIN PIGMENTS 1* (*PAP1*) gene (Borevitz et al., 2000; Tohge et al., 2005; Dare et al., 2008), the expression of which is induced by light (Cominelli et al., 2007), sugars (Pourtau et al., 2006; Solfanelli et al., 2006; Teng et al., 2007), and nutrient deficiencies (Lillo et al., 2008).

3.2 Water Stress

In the case of water stress, we should start by underlining that its effects on horticultural products' quality are highly variable, species specific because of different responses and sensitivities, and therefore occasionally conflicting. Such highly variable responses depend on the length and intensity of the deficit, the plant/fruit development stage affected by water stress (Vallverdu et al., 2012), the genotype, and combination with other stress factors. Moreover, there is a large number of underlying processes that interact during development and the timing and intensity of water stress (Ripoll et al., 2014).

Water stress may hasten fruit ripening in many horticultural crops, for instance, peach, apple, and detached avocado, brought by stress-induced increase in endogenous ethylene, which plays an important role in the coordination of fruit ripening processes in many horticultural crop species, including climacteric and nonclimacteric (modified from Urban et al., 2014).

While it can be generalized that under water stress soluble sugars increase, response of organic acid content (primarily malic and citric acids) is more conflicting in the literature. Such variations in soluble sugar and acid accumulation in response to water stress, often reported on the basis of fresh weight, may result from dilution/dehydration effects, from active solute accumulation, or from starch breakdown (Urban et al., 2014).

Under water deficit, sugar content increased in tomato fruit depending upon the cultivar and timing of stress with the greatest positive impact when water deficit is applied near ripening (Ripoll et al., 2014). Crisosto and Mitchell (2002) comment that the effects of water stress at the end of the season may markedly improve SSC in tomatoes. In this species, invertases, whether alone or combined with plant hormones, have been recognized as key metabolic enzymes involved in plant responses to environmental stimuli due to their role in sugar signaling and sensing (Ruan et al., 2010). For instance, the reduction in apoplastic invertase activity has been suggested as an early step in the signal transduction cascade induced by water stress that leads to irreversible fruit abortion (Zanor et al., 2009). Water stress increases sucrose synthase activity. Vallverdu et al. (2012) found that water stress-induced ABA stimulates sugar accumulation by increasing the activity of sorbitol oxidase in peach fruits, an effect observed under moderate water stress but not under severe water stress. Urban et al. (2014) report the results of a study with transformed tomato lines that revealed a negative link between malate accumulation and levels of transitory starch and final soluble sugar content, and suggested the regulation of AGPase activity by the cellular redox status in developing fruit.

Contrasting evidence from what is stated in the preceding paragraphs is the case of water stress-induced starvation, which is thought to decrease fruit sugar content, as has been observed in grape berries, peaches, tomatoes, mangoes, and clementines, whereas organic acids typically show the opposite trend (Urban et al., 2014).

Consumer acceptance correlates not only with individual concentrations of sugars and acids but also with the sugar/acid ratio, the variations of which under water stress are difficult to anticipate and depend on season, plant fruit load, and carbon status (Poiroux-Gonord et al., 2013).

Great varieties of volatile organic compounds (VOC) are contained and released by horticultural crops conferring their typical aroma. The majority of plant VOCs can be assigned to the biochemical classes of terpenoids, lipoxygenase products, and phenylpropanoids (over 400 VOC identified in tomatoes). Many VOC produced and released by fruits accumulate in fruit tissues at nondetectable levels. Together with sugars and acids many of these VOC affect consumer taste perception (Baldwin et al., 1998). Water stress enhances the aroma of horticultural fruits although such a statement should be cautiously considered because in many studies the gain in aroma content was accompanied by a loss in fruit size (Song et al., 2012); therefore it could be due to a dilution/concentration effect. Apart from methodological aspects various serious studies have reported significant positive effects of water stress on the concentration of aroma compounds in grapevine (Deluc et al., 2009; Song et al., 2012), apples (van Hooijdonk et al., 2007), strawberries (Modise et al., 2006), and tomatoes (Veit-Köhler et al., 1999). In the case of grapes, water deficit increases carotenoid breakdown volatiles (so-called norisoprenoids) in relation to an increased abundance of carotenoid cleavage enzyme transcripts (Deluc et al., 2009; Song et al., 2012).

Many horticultural products supply a wide range of health-promoting phytochemicals such as terpenoids (carotenoids, ABA, and others) and phenolic compounds, along with ascorbate (modified from Urban et al., 2014). Although investigations in relation to the effects of water stress on the accumulation of such phytochemicals are limited, controlled drought causing a moderate stress appears promising (Poiroux-Gonord et al., 2010). Urban et al. (2014) generalize the relation of water stress to phenolic compound content as generally positive with peaks at +40%, that for carotenoids ranging from negative to highly positive (+150%), and similarly for vitamin C, with many reports showing positive effects of water deficit. Such variability depends on genetic and seasonal factors or the intensity and duration of treatment. Drought typically induces a decrease in leaf stomatal conductance, resulting in a decrease in net photosynthesis. The decrease in net photosynthesis results in a reduced transport of primary metabolites to the fruits that are the major source of precursors for the biosynthesis of phenolic compounds, carotenoids, and ascorbate. Drought may exacerbate oxidative stress/oxidative signaling. Oxidative stress is known to directly or indirectly influence the biosynthetic pathways of these compounds. Both major mechanisms are not mutually exclusive and appear closely linked because the accumulation of carbohydrates may exacerbate photooxidative stress in photosynthetic organs, such as leaves, whereas the latter mechanism may influence primary metabolism in nearby fruits. Moreover, water stress may influence the metabolism of health-promoting phytochemicals by hastening fruit development. Photooxidative stress stimulates the accumulation of antioxidant compounds, therefore these plants have a higher health value (Nora et al., 2012), sometimes at the cost of taste (Wang and Frei, 2011). Deficit irrigation has been found to improve the antioxidant capacity in fresh basil (Bekhradi et al., 2015).

There is strong evidence showing that the unbalanced cellular redox state, resulting from the stress-induced production of ROS, ROS regulatory processes, and the accumulation of reducing power, tightly controls the synthesis of carotenoids in leaves and fruits. Similarly, the entire biosynthetic pathway of phenolic compounds is under ROX/redox control and is consistent with knowledge of the gene-controlling role of redox-sensitive systems.

Moisture stress in hot dry seasons, which reduces fruit Ca needed for normal respiration (Faust, 1975) and normal ethylene production (Vaz and Richardson, 1984), induces bitter pit of apples and cork spot of pears (Westwood, 1993). The use of sprinklers to reduce the effects of heat waves is a possible method to modify the microclimate, especially in pears, which suffer water stress from heat and low relative humidity even with ample soil moisture (Aldrich et al., 1940).

It has been demonstrated that water stress can reduce the occurrence of various physiological disorders of horticultural products. Thus withholding irrigation from 14 weeks after full bloom (WAFB) until commercial harvest (26 WAFB) of "Pacific Rose" apples reduced calyx-end splitting (Opara and Tadesse, 2000). Irrigation cutoff 1 week before harvest can reduce splitting in radish (*Raphanus sativus*) (Monaghan et al., 2012). Preharvest water stress lowers membrane integrity of carrot roots, and this may enhance moisture loss during storage (Shibairo et al., 1998).

Variable levels of irrigation cause a differential ripening process, and in fruits susceptible to cracking like persimmon increases alternaria black spot development during storage, especially by increased maturity at the stem end (Biton et al., 2014).

3.3 Nutrient Stress

As a constituent of amino acids, proteins, enzymes, coenzymes, nucleic acids, nucleotides, chlorophyll, and other pigments present in the leaves and fruits (anthocyanins), *nitrogen* stress has a great effect on organoleptic quality (Crisosto et al., 1997; Crisosto et al., 1995; Daane et al., 1995). Despite the visible and measurable effects on vegetative growth, excess N does not increase fruit size, production, or SSC (Crisosto and Mitchell, 2002). On the contrary, increased availability reduces fruit storability and increases breakdown of apples during storage (Sharples, 1973) and susceptibility to some storage disorders, especially those associated with low Ca concentrations (Jackson, 2003), such as cork spot and bitter pit, scald, internal browning, and internal breakdown after storage (Bramlage et al., 1980; Daane et al., 1995). High N fertilizer rates can also reduce the concentration of alcohol-insoluble solids and malate but increase the concentration of sugar in apples (Richardson, 1986). High N can result in composition changes such as reduced ascorbic acid (vitamin C) content, lower sugar content, lower acidity, and altered ratios of essential amino acids (Crisosto and Mitchell, 2002). These authors list a series of deleterious effects of high N in the quality indices of vegetable crops such as lower SSC in potatoes and weight loss during storage of sweet potatoes, as well as physiological disorders such as internal browning and soft rot in tomato, fruit spot in peppers, hollow stem and hollow heart in broccoli, and growth cracks in cauliflower. They even report a reduction of volatile production and the characteristic flavor in celery and increased glutamine levels that result in off-flavors in processed beet purée. Low N also increases susceptibility to breakdown, especially if Ca levels are also low (Sharples, 1980).

Potassium activates many enzymes involved in respiration and photosynthesis. Although high K concentrations have a strong positive effect on fruit acidity (Wilkinson, 1958; Johnson, 2000) and therefore the taste of apples, excessive K increases suscepti-bility to breakdown, bitter pit, and other disorders associated with low Ca status because of K–Ca interactions in cells whereby high K induces Ca deficiency (Jackson, 2003).

Similar to K, *magnesium* ions have a specific role in the acti-vation of enzymes involved in respiration, photosynthesis, and the synthesis of DNA and RNA. Mg concentrations in apple fruits tend to be proportional to those of K and have similar associations with fruit acidity, bitter pit, etc. (Jackson, 2003). Mg salt sprays or dips can greatly increase bitter pit incidence, which can be attrib-uted to direct competition with Ca at the cellular level (Sharples et al., 1979). In the case of bitter pit this could be due to a localized Mg toxicity (Hopfinger and Poovaiah, 1979). According to Fergu-son and Watkins (1989) this Mg-induced pitting differs from true bitter pit but Burmeister and Dilley (1994) found a correlation of bitter pit on Northern Spy apples with bitter pit-like symptoms in-duced by Mg^{2+} salt infiltration.

There is mounting evidence that *soil cation balance* directly impacts the postharvest quality of several vegetables. Research (Hartz et al., 1998) has demonstrated that the incidence of yellow eye and white core, two color defects in tomato, are correlated with soil cation balance. Several Ca-related storage disorders are sometimes closely correlated to the ratio of Ca to K or K + Mg than to Ca alone (Holland, 1980; Waller, 1980). Furthermore, imbalance of nutrients in the soil strongly influences Ca uptake. In synergetic terms, it is known that sprays with zinc sulfate, especially early in the season, increase fruit Ca content in apples, possibly by releas-ing bound Ca from various chelating and complexing agents such as lignin, organic acids, and proteins for transport to the shoot (Shear, 1980). Copper can have similar effects (Jackson, 2003).

3.4 Light Stress

The concentration of various plant pigments such as antho-cyanins, chlorophylls, and carotenoids, essential for plant per-formance but also considered as phytonutrients (Harborne and Williams, 2000; Kirsh et al., 2006; Mayne, 1996), is affected by the environment, and light in particular, via several photoreceptors (Reinbothe and Reinbothe, 1996).

Shading of harvested parts of horticultural plants has pronounced effects on their eating quality and storability. In grapes, low light intensity decreases sugar accumulation, anthocyanins, total phenols, ammonia, pH, and the concentration of proline, and increases TA and the concentration of malate and arginine (Kliewer and Lider, 1970; Smart et al., 1985). Some of these effects are explained by the effects on photochrome-regulated enzymes important in fruit ripening, for example, phenylalanine ammonia lyase or malic enzymes. Phytochromes and cryptochromes have been reported to be involved in fruit pigmentation in grape berries (González et al., 2015), tomato (Azari et al., 2009), and apple fruits (Li et al., 2013; Toledo-Ortiz et al., 2010). Variation in the level of light incident on a grape cluster may have an effect on berry carotenoids in experiments comparing sun-exposed and shaded grape bunches (Bindon, 2004; Bureau et al., 1998, 2000; Oliveira et al., 2004; Razungles et al., 1998).

Broccoli florets harvested at the end of the day, after which starch degradation produces single sugars, have a delayed postharvest senescence with less loss of color and chlorophyll degradation and more total soluble and reducing sugars, antioxidants, and phenolic compounds during storage (Hasperué et al., 2011). In leafy green vegetables grown under low light, this can result in the accumulation of nitrates in plant tissues to unhealthy levels (Crisosto and Mitchell, 2002).

Increase in norisoprenoids (carotenoid breakdown volatiles) in fruits may be associated with metabolic responses to excess light energy. From a series of experiments (Baumes et al., 2002; Bindon, 2004; Bureau et al., 1998, 2000; Downey et al., 2004; Düring and Davtyan, 2002; Marais, 1992; Razungles et al., 1998; Ristic et al., 2007; Steel and Keller, 2000; Tevini and Teramura, 1989) it seems clear that sunlight may influence the formation and degradation of carotenoids and C^{13}-norisoprenoids (a group of potent aroma compounds) in grape berries, mainly when extremes in the levels of sun exposure are evaluated.

4 Effects on Color

The most visible and frequent change in maturing fruits is the loss of green color following chlorophyll degradation due to both nonenzymatic processes (changes in pH) and to the action of specific enzymes such as chlorophyllase, activated during maturation, which oxidizes chlorophyll molecules (modified from Costa et al., 2012). Less chlorophyll would be expected in shaded fruit since chlorophyll synthesis is light induced (Raven et al., 1992; Zucker, 1972). Ethylene accelerates the chlorophyll destruction through the enhancement of chlorophyllase activity (Shimokawa et al., 1978). Chlorophyll degradation unmasks preexisting pigments and makes evident the results of their synthesis ex novo (Costa et al., 2012). The other important change related to fruit coloration during maturation is the synthesis of new pigments belonging to two large biochemical categories, carotenoids and anthocyanins (Costa et al., 2012), which have a critical role in human nutrition and health. Anthocyanins are hydrosoluble phenolic compounds that accumulate in the vacuoles and belong to the category of flavonoids. For a review on the genetics and biochemistry of these pigments refer to Grotewold (2006). Intensity of the anthocyaninic coloration of fruits during maturation is strongly influenced by environmental conditions. The biosynthesis of anthocyanins, responsible for the superficial coloration ranging from pale-intensive rose to blue/violet is highly regulated under the genetic profile, is tissue specific, depends on the development stage, and is strongly influenced by environmental factors (Costa et al., 2012).

4.1 Light Stress

Shading of harvested parts of horticultural plants has pronounced effects on their color development. For instance, immediately postharvest red color development is also controlled by effects of light on anthocyanin formation. The concentration of anthocyanin in the most highly colored skin areas is also a function of the light intensity under which the fruit is grown (Jackson et al., 1977). High amplitudes of temperatures between day and night during maturation accompanied by elevated light intensities result in fruits with more anthocyanin coloration. In grapes, low light intensity decreases anthocyanins (Kliewer and Lider, 1970; Smart et al., 1985). Anthocyanin synthesis occurs during fruit growth whereas color changes during ripening depend mainly on the disappearance of chlorophylls a and b. A number of enzymes involved in anthocyanin synthesis, including dihydroflavonal reductase and phenylalanine ammonia-lyase, are correlated to light levels (Lister et al., 1996; Ju et al., 1997). An important catalyst in these reactions is uridine diphosphate (UDP)-glucose:flavanone-7–O-glucosyltransferase, the expression of which is strongly regulated by endogenous (development) and exogenous (growing environment) factors.

Carotenoids, responsible for yellow/orange coloration (indicated as ground color), are isoprenoids synthesized in chromoplasts starting from isopentenyl-diphosphate. Besides genetic control and ethylene, a number of abiotic stresses affect the accumulation of various carotenoids (lycopene, β-carotene, xanthophylls) in the mature fruit because these stress factors affect specific biosynthetic stages. It is known that some isoprenoids play roles in protection against environmental stresses, especially light stress. In particular, to protect the photosynthetic apparatus the quantity and composition of carotenoid compounds, particularly xanthophylls, are increased to detoxificate free radical and active oxygen caused by high light stress (Demmig-Adams and Adams, 1996; Niyogi et al., 1997). Zeaxanthin, an important component of the xanthophyll cycle, is epoxidated by zeaxanthin epoxidase to produce violaxanthin, and this reaction can be reversed by violaxanthin deepoxidase to increase the xanthophyll cycle for plants to adapt to high light stress (Johnson et al., 2008).

4.2 Temperature Stress

A vast literature can be found on the optimal day–night temperature regime for fruit color related to pigment intensity. Temperatures must be high enough, but not too high, and of sufficient duration in daylight hours to catalyze anthocyanin biosynthesis. A period of cold temperatures stimulates anthocyanin production. In red apples, for instance, a series of a few nights with temperatures in the range 2–5°C followed by warm sunny days promotes red color development (Jackson, 2003). High daytime temperatures (31°C) inhibit anthocyanin formation even when the nights are cool (Creasy, 1966), although different apple genotypes have various temperature optima and preference for daily temperature amplitudes (Curry, 1997; Proctor, 1974). Other research has found that in apples and pears, low temperatures increase both anthocyanin content and the expression of genes of the anthocyanin biosynthetic pathway (Steyn et al., 2005, 2009; Ubi et al., 2006). On the contrary, high temperatures prevent the accumulation of cyanidin and UDP-sugars (Ban et al., 2009), resulting in a rapid reduction in anthocyanins, followed by renewed synthesis with cooler temperatures, causing fluctuations in skin color (Steyn et al., 2005). This response to fluctuating daily temperatures has been postulated to protect the sensitive fruit skin from light stress-induced photoinhibition by acting as a screen to shade chloroplasts from blue/green light (Steyn et al., 2009). Hot temperatures in apples result in a downregulation of the transcriptional activator complex with a primary effect on the expression of the genes of the activation complex, rather than by induction of repressors (Lin-Wang et al., 2011). Higher temperature causes reduction of total anthocyanin concentration in pears (Steyn et al., 2005) and grapes (Mori et al., 2007).

Practices such as fruit bagging in Japan manipulate chlorophyll synthesis, therefore reducing the quantity to be degraded during the climacteric phase and increasing the synthesis of anthocyanin resulting in a unique pink or red color (Proctor and Lougheed, 1976), particularly for apple cultivars such as "Mutsu," which produce very little anthocyanin if not bagged (Jackson, 2003).

Lycopene, a product of the carotenoid biosynthetic pathway, is responsible for the red coloration of tomatoes where it accumulates in the mature fruit. Prestorage heat treatment of mature green tomatoes inhibits lycopene synthesis (including ethylene production and chlorophyll and cell wall degradation) and enhances respiration (Lurie and Klein, 1992), with a redder color, higher SSC, and less chilling injury (Lurie and Klein, 1992). Prestorage heating of apples at 38–40°C supresses softening during subsequent storage at 0° to –1° chastening chlorophyll loss (Liu, 1978; Porrit and Lidster, 1978). In other types of fruits (eg, stonefruits), lycopene does not accumulate, but through the action of cyclasis is more or less rapidly transformed into α-carotene and especially β-carotene (Costa et al., 2012). The introduction of the oxygen molecule in the cyclic structure of β-carotene determines the synthesis of xanthophylls (neoxantine, violaxantine, and cyptoxantine), pigments mainly responsible for the yellow coloration of peaches and apricots (Costa et al., 2012).

Fruit ripening in tomatoes is reversibly inhibited by short exposures to temperatures above 35°C (Biggs et al., 1988; Lurie and Klein, 1990) similar to what has been observed in apples (Lurie and Klein, 1990) due to inhibition of ethylene synthesis (Biggs et al., 1988), PG accumulation (Yoshida et al., 1984), and interference with lycopene synthesis (Ogura et al., 1975). Some of these effects have been attributed to temperature disruption of enzyme activities (Ogura et al., 1975), particularly ACC oxidase synthesis, but and Grierson et al. (1986) demonstrated that inhibition also occurred at the level of gene expression, decreasing the abundance of mRNA (Lurie et al., 1996).

4.3 Nutrient Stress

As a constituent of chlorophyll and other pigments present in the leaves and fruits (anthocyanin), *nitrogen* stress has a great effect on the color of horticultural products. Increased availability reduces coloration (Daane et al., 1995). In apples, excessive N content reduces the area and intensity of red color on red cultivars (Sharples, 1973). Saure (1990) found that high levels of N usually reduce the percentage of well-colored apple fruits at harvest time, partly due to the shading effect of the extra foliage but primarily through a direct effect of N, mainly attributed to effects on fruit maturity and pigment development (Marsh et al., 1996). Excessive nitrogen concentrations were found to have the most significant role in determining the severity of mesocarp discoloration in "Pinkerton" avocado, a disorder to which low concentrations of copper, manganese, and boron contribute (Van Rooyen and Bower, 2005). Low K:N ratios cause discoloration of cut lettuce but this can be reduced with Ca applications (Hilton et al., 2009).

Increasing levels of soil *potassium* (expressed as ppm extractable or as a percentage of base exchange) decrease color disorders, while higher soil magnesium levels increase them (Crisosto and Mitchell, 2002). Applications of gypsum and K amendments may be helpful in reducing the incidence of these color defects, but they may not be economically practical in soils that tightly fix K, causing K to be available at such low levels that the treatment may result in little benefit for tomatoes grown in those locations (Crisosto and Mitchell, 2002).

Magnesium is part of the ring structure of the chlorophyll molecule, therefore any imbalance in its levels in horticultural products may affect its color.

Chloroplasts are the most sensitive organelles affected by *salinity*, which affects the chloroplast ultrastructure and inhibits photochemical activity (Boyer, 1976). Lower chlorophyll content has been found in susceptible crops such as tomato (Lapina and Popov, 1970), potato (Abdullah and Ahmed, 1990), pea (Hamada and El-Enany, 1994), and beans (Seemann and Critchley, 1985). Natrium has been found to reduce chlorophyll content by inhibiting synthesis of 5-aminolaevulinic acid, a precursor of chlorophyll (Santos, 2004).

5 Effects on Resistance to Biotic Stresses

Horticultural crops are continuously under the attack of plant parasites or pests, which are referred to here as biotic stresses. As previously discussed, abiotic stresses may *affect the structural component of horticultural products* making them physical less susceptible to pest attack. For instance, increased availability of N reduces cuticle thickness of fruits resulting in increased vulnerability to pathogen attack (Daane et al., 1995). The relationship between fruit N concentration and fruit susceptibility to decay caused by brown rot (*Monilinia fructicola* [Wint.] Honey) has been extensively studied on stored nectarines (Daane et al., 1995). Wounded and brown rot-inoculated fruit from "Fantasia" and "Flavortop" nectarine trees having more than 2.6% leaf N were more susceptible to brown rot than fruit from trees with 2.6% or less leaf N. Anatomical observations and cuticle density measurements on the fruit indicated differences in cuticle thickness among "Fantasia" fruit from the low, middle, and high N treatments, but this can only partially explain the differences in fruit susceptibility to this disease (Crisosto and Mitchell, 2002). Similarly, Ca deficiency increases fruit decay caused by postharvest wound pathogens such as *Gloeosporium* spp. (Sharples, 1980).

As horticultural crops are simultaneously exposed to both abiotic and biotic stresses, it is important to elucidate the *interaction among stress factors*. To understand this interaction we should refer to the role of endogenous phytohormones, which act as signals to combat many abiotic (ABA) and biotic stresses (salicylic acid, jasmonic acid, and ethylene). Urban et al. (2014) notices that while interactions among abiotic stress factors, such as a combination of very high temperatures and water stress, induce more deleterious effects for plant health than individual factors (Mittler and Blumwald, 2010), in contrast, interactions between biotic and abiotic stresses often show beneficial effects of one or both stressors. In the case of diseases he gives the example of *Botrytis cinerea* infection, which triggers the expression of genes involved in pathogen resistance. In tomato, the co-occurrence of *B. cinerea* and abiotic stresses (water stress, osmotic stress, and oxidative stress) reduces the susceptibility to the pathogen and induces tolerance to the abiotic stress (AbuQamar et al., 2008). In the case of pests he chooses the beneficial interactions between pests and drought reported in *Citrus latifolia* (Quiros-Gonzales, 2000) and in apple (Gutbrodt et al., 2012), independent of stress intensity. Fruit quality may be impacted by interactions between sensors (Urban et al., 2014) as in the case of nematode attack on tomato combined with water stress, which was found to promote sugar and flavonoid levels compared to control and stressors alone (Atkinson et al., 2011). As we have mentioned before, in the case of horticultural crops we are more interested in the quality rather than quantity (biomass), as the latest, important for arable crops, may be reduced by such a stress combination like the case of soybean (Grinnan et al., 2013).

Another more interesting aspect of abiotic–biotic stress interactions is related to the biochemical modifications during the maturation of horticultural fruits in response to pathogen attack by *accumulating defense proteins*, responsible in some cases for allergic reactions to humans.

References

Abdullah, Z., Ahmed, R., 1990. Effect of pre and post kinetin treatment on salt tolerance of different potato cultivars growing on saline soils. J. Agron. Crop Sci. 165, 94–102.

AbuQamar, S., Chai, M.-F., Luo, H., Song, F., Mengiste, T., 2008. Tomato protein kinase 1b mediates signalling of plant responses to necrotrophic fungi and insect herbivory. Plant Cell Online 20, 1964–1983.

Aldrich, W.W., Lewis, M.R., Work, R.A., Lloyd Ryall, A., Reimer, F.C., 1940. Anjou pear responses to irrigation in a clay adobe soil. Oregon State Coll. Agr. Expt. Sta. Bull. 374.

Allan, A.C., Hellens, R.P., Laing, W.A., 2008. MYB transcription factors that colour our fruit. Trends Plant Sci. 13, 99–102.

Ames, B.N., Shigenaga, M.K., Hagen, T.M., 1993. Oxidants, antioxidants and the degenerative diseases of aging. Proc. Natl. Acad. Sci. USA 90, 7915–7922.

Anderson, J.W., Allgood, L.D., Lawrence, A., Altringer, L.A., Jerdack, G.R., Hengehold, D.A., Morel, J.G., 2000. Cholesterol-lowering effects of psyllium intake adjunctive to diet therapy in men and women with hypercholesterolemia: meta-analysis of 8 controlled trials. Am. J. Clin. Nutr. 71, 472–479.

Arpaia, M.L., 1994. Preharvest factors influencing postharvest quality of tropical and subtropical fruit. HortScience 29, 982–985.

Atkinson, R.G., 1994. A cDNA clone for endopolygalacturonase from apple. Plant Physiol. 105, 1437–1438.

Atkinson, R.G., Bolitho, K.M., Wright, M.A., Iturriagagoitia–Bueno, T., Reid, S.J., Ross, G.S., 1998. Apple ACC-oxidase and polygalacturonase: ripening-specific gene expression and promoter analysis in transgenic tomato. Plant Molec. Biol. 38 (3), 449–460.

Atkinson, R.G., Schröder, R., Hallett, I.C., Cohen, D., MacRae, E.A., 2002. Overexpression of polygalacturonase in transgenic apple trees leads to a range of novel phenotypes involving changes in cell adhesion. Plant Physiol. 129 (1), 122–133.

Atkinson, R.G., Gunaseelan, K., Wang, M.Y., Luo, L., Wang, T., Norling, C.L., Johnston, S.L., Maddumage, R., Schröder, R., Schaffer, R.J., 2011. Dissecting the role of climacteric ethylene in kiwifruit (*Actinidia chinensis*) ripening using a 1-aminocyclopropane-1-carboxylic acid oxidase knockdown line. J. Experimen. Bot. 62 (11), 3821–3835.

Atkinson, R.G., Sutherland, P.W., Johnston, S.L., Gunaseelan, K., Hallett, I.C., Mitra, D., Brummell, D.A., Schröder, R., Johnston, J.W., Schaffer, R.J., 2012. Down-regulation of POLYGALACTURONASE1 alters firmness, tensile strength and water loss in apple (*Malus* x *domestica*) fruit. BMC Plant Biol. 12, 129.

Azari, R., Tadmor, Y., Meir, A., Reuveni, M., Evenor, D., Nahon, S., Shlomo, H., Chen, L., Levin, I., 2009. Light signaling genes and their manipulation towards modulation of phytonutrient content in tomato fruits. Biotechnol. Adv. 28, 108–118.

Baldwin, E.A., Scott, J.W., Einstein, M.A., Malundo, T.M.M., Carr, B.T., Shewfelt, R.L., Tandon, K.S., 1998. Relationship between sensory and instrumental analysis for tomato flavour. J. Am. Soc. Hortic. Sci. 123, 906–915.

Ban, T., Ishimaru, M., Kobayashi, S.N., Goto-Yamamoto, S., Horiuchi, S., 2003. Abscisic acid and 2,4-dichlorophenoxyacetic acid affect the expression of anthocyanin biosynthesic pathway genes in "Kyoho" grape berries. J. Hortic. Sci. Biotechnol. 78, 586–589.

Ban, Y., Kondo, S., Ubi, B.E., Honda, C., Bessho, H., Moriguchi, T., 2009. UDP-sugar biosynthetic pathway: contribution to cyanidin 3-galactoside biosynthesis in apple skin. Planta 230, 871–881.

Bartley, I.M., Knee, M., 1982. The chemistry of textural changes in fruit during storage. Food Chem. 9 (1), 47–58.

Baumes, R., Wirth, J., Bureau, S., Gunata, Y., Razungles, A., 2002. Bio-generation of C^{13}-norisoprenoid compounds: experiments supportive for an apocarotenoid pathway in grapevines. Anal. Chim. Acta 458, 3–14.

Bekhradi, F., Luna, M.C., Delshad, M., Jordan, M.J., Sotomayor, J.A., Martínez-Conesa, C., Gil, M.I., 2015. Effect of deficit irrigation on the postharvest quality of different genotypes of basil including purple and green Iranian cultivars and a Genovese variety. Postharvest Biol. Technol. 100, 127–135.

Ben-Arie, R., Lurie, S., Mattoo, A.K., 1982. Temperature-dependent inhibitory effects of calcium and spermine on ethylene biosynthesis in apple discs correlate with changes in microsomal membrane microviscosity. Plant Sci. Lett. 24, 239–247.

Biggs, M.S., Woodson, W.R., Handa, A.K., 1988. Biochemical basis of high temperature inhibition of ethylene biosynthesis in ripening tomato fruits. Physiol. Plant. 72, 572–578.

Bindon, K., 2004. Influence of Partial Rootzone Drying on Aspects of Grape and Wine Quality. University of Adelaide, Adelaide, 182–204.

Biton, E., Kobiler, I., Feygenberg, O., Yaari, M., Kaplunov, T., Ackerman, M., Prusky, D., 2014. The mechanism of differential susceptibility to alternaria black spot, caused by *Alternaria alternata*, of stem- and bottom-end tissues of persimmon fruit. Postharvest Biol. Technol. 94, 74–81.

Borevitz, J.O., Xia, Y., Blount, J., Dixon, R.A., Lamb, C., 2000. Activation tagging identifies a conserved MYB regulator of phenylpropanoid biosynthesis. Plant Cell 12, 2383–2393.

Boulton, G., Corrigan, V., Lill, R., 1997. Objective method for estimating sensory response to juiciness in apples. N. Z. J. Crop Hortic. Sci. 25, 283–289.

Boyer, J.S., 1976. Water deficits and photosynthesis. Kozlowsky, T.T. (Ed.), Water Deficit and Plant Growth, 4, Academic Press, New York, pp. 153–190.

Braidwood, L., Breuer, C., Sugimoto, K., 2014. My body is a cage: mechanisms and modulation of plant cell growth. New Phytol. 201, 388–402.

Bramlage, W.J., Drake, M., Baker, J.H., 1974. Relationships of calcium content to respiration and postharvest condition of apples. J. Am. Soc. Hortic. Sci. 99, 376–378.

Bramlage, W.J., Drake, M., Lord, W.J., 1980. The influence of mineral nutrition on the quality and storage performance of pome fruit grown in North America. In: Atkinson, D., Jackson, J.E., Sharples, R.O., Waller, W.M. (Eds.), Mineral Nutrition of Fruit Trees. London, Butterworths, pp. 29–39.

Brummell, D.A., 2006. Cell wall disassembly in ripening fruit. Funct. Plant Biol. 33, 103–119.

Brummell, D.A., Harpster, M.H., 2001. Cell wall metabolism in fruit softening and quality and its manipulation in transgenic plants. Plant Mol. Biol. 47, 311–340.

Brummell, D.A., Harpster, M.H., Civello, P.M., Palys, J.M., Bennett, A.B., Dunsmuir, P., 1999b. Modification of expansin protein abundance in tomato fruit alters softening and cell wall polymer metabolism during ripening. Plant Cell 11, 2203–2216.

Burdon, J., Lallu, N., Francis, K., Boldingh, H., 2007. The susceptibility of kiwifruit to low temperature breakdown is associated with pre-harvest temperatures and at-harvest soluble solids content. Postharvest Biol. Technol. 43 (3), 283–290.

Bureau, S.M., Razungles, A.J., Baumes, R.L., Bayonove, C.L., 1998. Effect of qualitative modification of light on the carotenoid contents in *Vitis vinifera* L. cv Syrah berries. Sci. Aliment. 18, 485–495.

Bureau, S., Baumes, R., Razungles, A., 2000. Effects of vine or bunch shading on the glycosylated flavor precursors of *Vitis vinifera* L. cv. Syrah. J. Agric. Food Chem. 48, 1290–1297.

Burmeister, D.M., Dilley, D.R., 1994. Correlation of bitter pit on Northern Spy apples with bitter pit-like symptoms induced by Mg^{2+} salt infiltration. Postharvest Biol. Technol. 4 (4), 301–308.

Caffall, K.H., Mohnen, D., 2009. The structure, function, and biosynthesis of plant cell wall pectic polysaccharides. Carbohydr. Res. 344, 1879–1900.

Cakir, B., Agasse, A., Gaillard, C., Saumonneau, A., Delrot, S., Atanassova S.R., 2003. A grape ASR protein involved in sugar and abscisic acid signaling. Plant Cell 15, 2165–2180.

Carpita, N.C., Gibeaut, D.M., 1993. Structural models of primary-cell walls in flowering plants—consistency of molecular-structure with the physical-properties of the walls during growth. Plant J. 3, 1–30.

Chalker-Scott, L., 1999. Environmental significance of anthocyanins in plant stress responses. Photochem. Photobiol. 70, 1–9.

Chapman, H.D., 1968a. The mineral nutrition of citrus. Reuther, W. (Ed.), The Citrus Industry, vol. 3, second ed. Berkeley, University of California Press, pp. 127–289.

Chapman, H.D., 1968b. The mineral nutrition of citrus. Reuther, W., Batchelor, L.D., Webber, H.J. (Eds.), The Citrus Industry, vol. II, second ed. Berkeley, University of California Press, pp. 127–289.

Chernys, J.T., Zeevaart, J.A.D., 2000. Characterization of the 9-cis-epoxycarotenoid dioxygenase gene family and the regulation of abscisic acid biosynthesis in avocado. Plant Physiol. 124, 343–353.

Civello, P.M., Powell, A.L.T., Sabehat, A., Bennett, A.B., 1999. An expansin gene expressed in ripening strawberry fruit. Plant Physiol. 121, 1273–1280.

Cominelli, E., Gusmaroli, G., Allegra, D., Galbiati, M., Wade, H.K., Jenkins, G.I., Tonelli, C., 2007. Expression analysis of anthocyanin regulatory genes in response to different light qualities in *Arabidopsis thaliana*. J. Plant Physiol. 165, 886–894.

Cosgrove, D.J., 1997. Assembly and enlargement of the primary cell wall in plants. Annu. Rev. Cell Dev. Biol. 13, 171–201.

Cosgrove, D.J., 2000a. New genes and new biological roles for expansins. Curr. Opin. Plant Biol. 3, 73–78.

Cosgrove, D.J., 2000b. Loosening of plant cell walls by expansins. Nature 407, 321–326.

Costa, G., Ramina, A., Bassi, D., Bonghi, C., Botta, R., Fabbri, A., Massai, R., Morini, S., Sansavini, S., Tonutti, P., Vizzotto, G., 2012. Ciclo ontogenetico dell'albero. Sansavini, S., Costa, G., Inglese, P., Ramina, A., Xiloyannis, C. (Eds.), Arboricoltura Generale Pátron Editore, Bologna, pp. 129–186.

Creasy, L.L., 1966. The effect of temperature on anthocyanin synthesis in McIntosh apple skin. Proc. New York State Hortic. Soc. 111, 93–96.

Crisosto, C.H., Mitchell, J.P., 2002. Preharvest factors affecting fruit and vegetable quality. In: Kader, A.A. (Ed.), Postharvest Technology of Horticultural Crops. University of California, Agriculture and Natural Resources Publication, p. 3311.

Crisosto, C.H., Mitchell, F.G., Johnson, R.S., 1995. Factors in fresh market stone fruit quality. Postharvest News Inform. 6, 17N–21N.

Crisosto, C.H., Johnson, R.S., Dejong, T., Dar, K.R., 1997. Orchard factors affecting postharvest stone fruit quality. HortScience 32, 820–823.

Curry, E.A., 1997. Temperatures for optimum anthocyanin accumulation in apple tissue. J. Hortic. Sci. 72, 723–729.

Daane, K.M., Johnson, R.S., Michailides, T.J., Crisosto, C.H., Dlott, J.W., Ramirez, H.T., Yokota, G.T., Morgan, D.E., 1995. Excess nitrogen raises nectarine susceptibility to disease and insects. Calif. Agric. 49 (4), 13–17.

Dare, A.P., Schaffer, R.J., Lin-Wang, K., Allan, A.C., Hellens, R.P., 2008. Identification of a cis-regulatory element by transient analysis of co-ordinately regulated genes. Plant Meth. 4, 17.

Dela, G., Or, E., Ovadia, R., Nissim-Levi, A., Weiss, D., Oren-Shamir, M., 2003. Changes in anthocyanin concentration and composition in "Jaguar" rose flowers due to transient high-temperature conditions. Plant Sci. 164, 333–340.

Deluc, L.G., Grimplet, J., Wheatley, M.D., Tillett, R.L., Quilici, D.R., Osborne, C., Schooley, D.A., Schlauch, K.A., Cushman, J.C., Cramer, G.R., 2007. Transcriptomic and metabolite analyses of Cabernet Sauvignon grape berry development. BMC Genom. 8, 429–471.

Deluc, L.G., Quilici, D., Decendit, A., Grimplet, J., Wheatley, M., Schlauch, K., Merillon, J.-M., Cushman, J., Cramer, G., 2009. Water deficit alters differentially metabolic pathways affecting important flavour and quality traits in grape berries of Cabernet Sauvignon and Chardonay. BMC Genom. 10, 212.

Demmig-Adams, B., Adams, III, W.W., 1996. The role of xanthophyll cycle carotenoids in the protection of photosynthesis. Trends Plant Sci. 1, 21–26.

Dixon, R.A., Paiva, N.L., 1995. Stress-induced phenylpropanoid metabolism. Plant Cell 7, 1085–1097.

Doll, R., 1990. An overview of the epidemiological evidence linking diet and cancer. Proc. Nutr. Soc. 49, 119–131.

Downey, M.O., Harvey, J.S., Robinson, S.P., 2004. The effect of bunch shading on berry development and flavonoid accumulation in Shiraz grapes. Aust. J. Grape Wine Res., 55–73.

Dragsted, L.O., Strube, M., Larsen, J.C., 1993. Cancer-protective factors in fruit and vegetables: biochemical and biological background. Pharmacol. Toxicol. 72, 116–135.

Du Plessis, S.F., Koen, T.J., 1988. The effect of N and K fertilization on yield and fruit size of Valencia. In: Goren, R., Mendel, K. (Eds.), Proceedings of the International Citrus Congress, vol. 2. Balaban Publishers, Philadelphia/Rehovot; Margraf Scientific Books, Weikersheim, Germany, pp. 663–672.

Dumville, J.C., Fry, S.C., 2003. Solubilisation of tomato fruit pectins by ascorbate: a possible non-enzymic mechanism of fruit softening. Planta 217 (6), 951–961.

Düring, H., Davtyan, A., 2002. Developmental changes of primary processes of photosynthesis in sun and shade-adapted berries of two grapevine cultivars. Vitis 41, 63–67.

El-Sharkawy, I., Jones, B., Gentzbittel, L., Lelievre, J.M., Pech, J.C., Latch, A., 2004. Differential regulation of ACC SYNTHASE genes in cold-dependent and -independent ripening in pear fruit. Plant Cell Environ. 27, 1197–1210.

Embleton, T.W., Reitz, H.J., Jones, W.W., 1979. Citrus fertilization. Reuther, W. (Ed.), The Citrus Industry, vol. 3, second ed. Berkeley, University of California Press, pp. 122–182.

Fallahi, E., Conway, W.S., Hickey, K.D., Sams, C.E., 1997. The role of calcium and nitrogen in postharvest quality and disease resistance of apples. HortScience 32, 831–835.

Faust, M., 1975. The role of calcium in the respiratory mechanism and senescence of apples. Colloques International du CNRS 238, 84–92.

Faust, M., Shear, C.B., 1972. The effect of calcium on respiration of apples. J. Am. Soc. Hortic. Sci. 97, 69–72.

Ferguson, I.B., 1984. Calcium in plant senescence and fruit ripening. Plant Cell Environ. 7, 477–489.

Ferguson, I.B., Watkins, C.B., 1989. Bitter pit in apple fruit. Hortic. Rev. 11, 289–355.

Ferguson, I., Volz, R., Woolf, A., 1999. Preharvest factors affecting physiological disorders of fruit. Postharvest Biol. Technol. 15, 255–262.

Fischer, R.L., Bennett, A.B., 1991. Role of cell wall hydrolases in fruit ripening. Annu. Rev. Plant Physiol. Plant Mol. Biol. 42, 675–703.

Fleischer, A., O'Neill, M.A., Ehwald, R., 1999. The pore size of non-graminaceous plant cell walls is rapidly decreased by borate ester cross-linking of the pectic polysaccharide rhamnogalacturonan I. Plant Physiol. 121, 829–838.

Fry, S.C., 1998. Oxidative scission of plant cell wall polysaccharides by ascorbate-induced hydroxyl radicals. Biochem. J. 332, 507–515.

Fuller, M.M., 1976. The ultrastructure of the outer tissues of cold–stored apple fruit of high and low calcium content in relation to cell breakdown. Ann. Appl. Biol. 83, 229–304.

Ghiani, A., Onelli, E., Aina, R., Cocucci, M., Citterio, S., 2011. A comparative study of melting and non-melting flesh peach cultivars reveals that during fruit ripening endo-polygalacturonase (endo-PG) is mainly involved in pericarp textural changes, not in firmness reduction. J. Exp. Bot. 62, 4043–4054.

Giovannoni, J.J., DellaPenna, D., Bennett, A.B., Fischer, R.L., 1989. Expression of a chimeric polygalacturonase gene in transgenic rin (ripening inhibitor) tomato fruit results in polyuronide degradation but not fruit softening. Plant Cell 1, 53–63.

Giribaldi, M., Gény, L., Delrot, S., Schubert, A., 2010. Proteomic analysis of the effects of ABA treatments on ripening Vitis vinifera berries. J. Exp. Bot. 61, 2447–2458.

Goldman, I.L., Kader, A.A., Heintz, C., 1999. Influence of production, handling and storage on phytonutrient content of foods. Nutr. Rev. 57 (9), S46–S52.

Gonzalez, A., Zhao, M., Leavitt, J.M., Lloyd, A.M., 2008. Regulation of the anthocyanin biosynthetic pathway by the TTG1/bHLH/Myb transcriptional complex in Arabidopsis seedlings. Plant J. 53, 814–827.

González, C.V., Franzone, M. L., Cortés, L.E., et al., 2015. Fruit-localized photoreceptors increase phenolic compounds in berry skins of field-grown Vitis vinifera L. cv. Malbec. Phytochemistry 110, 46–57.

Goulao, L.F., Oliveira, C.M., 2007. Molecular identification of novel differentially expressed mRNAs up-regulated during ripening of apples. Plant Sci. 172, 306–318.

Goulao, L.F., Oliveira, C.M., 2008. Cell wall modifications during fruit ripening: when a fruit is not the fruit. Trends Food Sci. Technol. 19, 4–25.

Grierson, D., Tucker, G.A., Keen, J., Ray, J., Bird, C.R., Schuch, W., 1986. Sequencing and identification of a cDNA clone for tomato polygalacturonase. Nucleic Acids Res. 14, 8595–8603.

Grinnan, R., Carter, Jr., T.E., Johnson, M.T.J., 2013. Effects of drought, temperature, herbivory, and genotype on plant–insect interactions in soybean (Glycine max). Arthropod–Plant Interact. 7, 201–215.

Grotewold, E., 2006. The genetics and biochemistry of floral pigments. Annu. Rev. Plant Biol. 57, 761–780.

Gutbrodt, B., Dorn, S., Mody, K., 2012. Drought stress affects constitutive but not induced herbivore resistance in apple plants. Arthropod–Plant Interact. 6, 171–179.

Hadfield, K.A., Bennett, A.B., 1998. Polygalacturonases: many genes in search of a function. Plant Physiol. 117, 337–343.

Hamada, A.M., El-Enany, A.E., 1994. Effect of NaCl salinity on growth, pigment and mineral elements contents, and gas exchange of broad bean and pea plants. Biol. Plant. 36, 75–81.

Hansen, E., 1961. Climate in relation to postharvest physiological disorders of apples and pears. Proc. Oregon Hortic. Soc. 53, 54–58.

Harborne, J.B., Williams, C.A., 2000. Advances in flavonoid research since 1992. Phytochemistry 55, 481–504.

Harker, F.R., Redgwell, R.J., Hallett, I.C., Murray, S.H., Carter, G., 1997. Texture of fresh fruit. Hortic. Rev. 20, 121–224.

Hartz, T.K., Giannini, C., Miyao, G., Valencia, J., Cahn, M., Mullen, R., Brittan, K., 1998. Soil cation balance affects tomato fruit color disorders. HortScience 33, 445–446.

Hasperué, J.H., Chaves, A.R., Martínez, G.A., 2011. End of day harvest delays postharvest senescence of broccoli florets. Postharvest Biol. Technol. 59 (1), 64–70.

Hilton, H.W., Clifford, S.C., Wurr, D.C.E., Burton, K.S., 2009. The influence of agronomic factors on the visual quality of field-grown, minimally-processed lettuce. J. Hortic. Sci. Biotechnol. 84 (2), 193–198.

Holland, D.A., 1980. The prediction of bitter pit. In: Atkinson, D., Jackson, J.E., Sharples, R.O., Waller, W.M. (Eds.), Mineral Nutrition of Fruit Trees. London, Butterworths, pp. 380–381.

van Hooijdonk, B.M., Dorji, K., Behboudian, M.H., 2007. Fruit quality of "Pacific Rose"™ apple grown under partial rootzone drying and deficit irrigation. J. Food Agric. Environ. 5, 173–178.

Hopfinger, J.A., Poovaiah, B.W., 1979. Calcium and magnesium gradients in apples with bitterpit. Commun. Soil Sci. Plant Anal. 10, 57–65.

Hoth, S., Morgante, M., Sanchez, J.P., Hanafey, M.K., Tingey, S.V., Chua, N.H., 2002. Genome-wide gene expression profiling in *Arabidopsis thaliana* reveals new targets of abscisic acid and largely impaired gene regulation in the abi1-1 mutant. J. Cell Sci. 115, 4891–4900.

Huber, D.J., 1983. The role of cell wall hydrolases in fruit softening. Hortic. Rev. 5, 169–219.

Hulme, A.C., Rhodes, M.J.C., 1971. Pome fruits. Hulme, A.C. (Ed.), The Biochemistry of Fruits and Their Products, vol. 2, Academic Press, London, pp. 333–373.

Ishii, T., Matsunaga, T., Pellerin, P., O'Neill, M.A., Darvill, A., Albersheim, P., 1999. The plant cell wall polysaccharide rhamnogalacturonan II self-assembles into a covalently cross-linked dimer. J. Biol. Chem. 274, 13098–13104.

Jackson, J.E., 2003. Biology of Apples and Pears. Cambridge University Press, Cambridge, UK.

Jackson, J.E., Palmer, J.W., Perring, M.A., Sharples, R.O., 1977. Effects of shade on tdhe growth and cropping of apple trees III. Effects on fruit growth, chemical composition and quality at harvest and after storage. J. Hortic. Sci. 52, 267–282.

Jeong, S.T., Goto-Yamamoto, N., Kobayashi, S., Esaka, M., 2004. Effects of plant hormones and shading on the accumulation of anthocyanins and the expression of anthocyanin biosynthetic genes in grape berry skins. Plant Sci. 167, 247–252.

Johnson, D.S., 2000. Mineral composition, harvest maturity and storage quality of 'Red Pippin', 'Gala' and 'Jonagold' apples. J. Horticult. Sci. Biotechnol. 75, 697–704.

Johnson, R.S., Handley, D.E., Dejong, T., 1992. Long-term response of early maturing peach trees to postharvest water deficit. J. Am. Soc. Hortic. Sci. 69, 1035–1041.

Johnson, D.S., Dover, C.J., Samuelson, T.J., Huxham, I.M., Jarvis, M.C., Knox, J.P., Shakespeare, L., Seymour, G.B., 2001. Nitrogen, cell walls and texture of stored "Cox's Orange Pippin" apples. Acta Hortic. (ISHS) 564, 105–112.

Johnson, M.P., Davison, P.A., Ruban, A.V., Horton P., 2008. The xanthophyll cycle pool size controls the kinetics of non-photochemical quenching in *Arabidopsis thaliana*. FEBS Lett. 582, 262–266.

Ju, Z., Yuan, Y., Liu, C., Wang, Y., Tian, X., 1997. Dihydroflavonol reductase activity and anthocyanin accumulation in "Delicious," "Golden Delicious" and "Indo" apples. Sci. Hortic. 70, 31–43.

Kader, A.A., 1988. Influence of preharvest and postharvest environment on nutritional composition of fruits and vegetables. In: Quebedeaux, B., Bliss, E.A. (Eds.), Horticulture and Human Health – Contributions of Fruits and Vegetables. Englewood Cliffs, NJ, Prentice Hall, pp. 18–22.

Kays, S.J., 1999. Preharvest factors affecting appearance. Postharvest Biol. Technol. 15, 233–247.

Kieffer, F., Lherminier, J., Simon-Plas, F., Nicole, M., Paynot, M., Elmayan, T., et al., 2000. The fungal elicitor cryptogein induces cell wall modifications on tobacco cell suspension. J. Exp. Bot. 51, 1799–1811.

Kirsh, V.A., Hayes, R.B., Mayne, S.T., Chatterjee, N., Subar, A.F., Dixon, L.B., Albanes, D., Andriole, G.L., Urban, D.A., Peters, U., 2006. Supplemental and dietary vitamin E, beta-carotene, and vitamin C intakes and prostate cancer risk. J. Natl. Cancer Inst. 98, 245–254.

Kliewer, W.M., 1973. Berry composition of *Vitis vinifera* cultivars as influenced by photo- and nyco-temperatures during maturation. J. Am. Soc. Hortic. Sci. 98, 153–159.

Kliewer, W.M., Lider, L.A., 1970. Effects of day temperature and light intensity on growth and composition of *Vitis vinifera* L. fruits. J. Am. Soc. Hortic. Sci. 95, 766–769.

Knee, M., Looney, N.E., Hatfield, S.G.S., Smith, S.M., 1983. Initiation of rapid ethylene synthesis by apple and pear fruits in relation to storage temperature. J. Exp. Bot. 34, 1207–1212.

Knee, M., 1993. Pome fruits. In: Seymour, G., Taylor, J., Tucker, G. (Eds.), Biochemistry of Fruit Ripening. Chapmen and Hall, London, pp. 325–346.

Knox, J.P., Linstead, P.J., King, J., Cooper, C., Roberts, K., 1990. Pectin esterification is spatially regulated both within cell walls and between developing tissues of root apices. Planta 181, 512–521.

Kramer, M., Sanders, R., Sheehy, R., Melis, M., Kuehn, M., Hiatt, W., 1990. Field evaluation of tomatoes with reduced polygalacturonase by antisense RNA. In: Bennett, A., O'Neill, S. (Eds.), Hortic. Biotechnol. Liss, New York, pp. 347–355.

Kullaj, E., 2013. Apple Harvest and Post-Harvest Protocols. SNV–Promali, Albanian.

Lacampagne, S., Gagne, S., Geny, L., 2009. Involvement of abscisic acid in controlling the proanthocyanidin biosynthesis pathway in grape skin: new elements regarding the regulation of tanning composition and leucoanthocyanidin reductase (LAR) and anthocyanidin reductase (ANR) activities and expression. J. Plant Growth Regul. 29, 81–90.

Lapina, L.P., Popov, B.A., 1970. Effect of sodium chloride on the photosynthetic apparatus of tomatoes. Soviet Plant Physiol. 17, 477–481, (in Russian).

Larrigaudiere, C., Graell, J., Salas, J., Vendrell, M., 1997. Cultivar differences in the influence of a short period of cold storage on ethylene biosynthesis in apples. Postharvest Biol. Technol. 10, 21–27.

Lashbrook, C.C., Giovannoni, J.J., Hall, B.D., Fischer, R.L., Bennett, A.B., 1998. Transgenic analysis of tomato endo-beta-1,4-glucanase gene function: role of cel1 in floral abscission. Plant J. 13, 303–310.

Léchaudel, M., Joas, J., 2007. An overview of preharvest factors influencing mango fruit growth, quality and postharvest behaviour. Brazilian J. Plant Physiol. 19 (4), 287–298.

Lee, S.G., Aronoff, S., 1966. Investigations on role of boron in plants. 3. Anatomical observation. Plant Physiol. 41, 1570.

Lee, S.K., Kader, A.A., 2000. Preharvest and postharvest factors influencing vitamin C content of horticultural crops. Postharvest Biol. Technol. 20 (3), 207–220.

Leliévre, J.M., Tichit, L., Fillion, L., Larrigaudiere, C., Vendrell, M., Pech, J.C., 1995. Cold-induced accumulation of 1-aminocyclopropane-carboxylate oxidase protein in "Granny Smith" apples. Postharvest Biol. Technol. 5, 11–17.

Lepaja, K., Lepaja, L., Kullaj, E., Krasniqi, N., Shehaj, M., 2015a. Effect of partial rootzone drying (PRD) on fruit quality and nutrient contents of "Albion" strawberry. Proceedings of 50th Croatian & 10th International Symposium on Agriculture, Opatija, Croatia, 16-20/02/2015, pp. 600–604.

Lepaja, L., Kullaj, E., Lepaja, K., Zajmi, A., 2015b. Effects of regulated deficit irrigation, mulching and their combination on fruit diameter growth of young "William" pears. Proceedings of 50th Croatian & 10th International Symposium on Agriculture, Opatija, Croatia, 16-20/02/2015, pp. 580–584.

Leucci, M.R., Lenucci, M.S., Piro, G., Dalessandro, G., 2008. Water stress and cell wall polysaccharides in the apical root zone of wheat cultivars varying in drought tolerance. J. Plant Physiol. 165, 1168–1180.

Leyva, A., Jarillo, J.A., Salinas, J., Martinez-Zapater, J.M., 1995. Low temperature induces the accumulation of phenylalanine ammonia-lyase and chalcone synthase mRNAs of *Arabidopsis thaliana* in a light-dependent manner. Plant Physiol. 108, 39–46.

Li, Y.X., Wang, G.X., Liang, L.S., 2012. Effect of cold acclimation treatment and exogenous ethylene treatment on woolliness related enzymes on "Okubo" peach fruits during low temperature storage. Acta Hortic. (ISHS) 934, 1103–1109.

Li, Y.-Y., Mao, K., Zhao, C., Zhang, R.-F., Zhao, X.-Y., Zhang, H.-L., Shu, H.-R., Zhao, Y.-J., 2013. Molecular cloning of cryptochrome 1 from apple and its functional characterization in *Arabidopsis*. Plant Physiol. Biochem. 67, 169–177.

Lillo, C., Lea, U.S., Ruoff, P., 2008. Nutrient depletion as a key factor for manipulating gene expression and product formation in different branches of the flavonoid pathway. Plant Cell Environ. 31, 587–601.

Lin-Wang, K.U.I., Micheletti, D., Palmer, J., Volz, R., Lozano, L., Espley, R., Allan, A.C., 2011. High temperature reduces apple fruit colour via modulation of the anthocyanin regulatory complex. Plant Cell Environ. 34 (7), 1176–1190.

Lister, C.E., Lancaster, J.E., Walker, J.R.L., 1996. Phenylalanine ammonia-lyase (PAL) activity and its relationship to anthocyanin and flavonoid levels in New Zealand-grown apple cultivars. J. Am. Soc. Hortic. Sci. 121, 281–285.

Liu, F.W., 1978. Modification of apple quality by high temperature. J. Am. Soc. Horticult. Sci. 103, 730–732.

Lo Piero, A.R., Puglisi, I., Rapisarda, P., Petrone, G., 2005. Anthocyanins accumulation and related gene expression in red orange fruit induced by low temperature storage. J. Agric. Food Chem. 53, 9083–9088.

Lott, R.V., 1965. The quality, color and keepability characteristics of a low-acid Jonared apple sport. Proc. Am. Soc. Horticult. Sci. 87, 47–54.

Lurie, S., Klein, J.D., 1990. Heat treatment of ripening apples: differential effects on physiology and biochemistry. Physiol. Plant. 78, 181–186.

Lurie, S., Klein, J.D., 1992. Ripening characteristics of tomatoes stored at 12°C and 2°C following a prestorage heat treatment. Sci. Hortic. 51 (1), 55–64.

Lurie, S., Handros, A., Fallik, E., Shapira, R., 1996. Reversible inhibition of tomato fruit gene expression at high temperature (effects on tomato fruit ripening). Plant Physiol. 110 (4), 1207–1214.

Marais, J., 1992. 1,1,6–Trimethyl-1,2-dihydronaphthalene (TDN): a possible degradation product of lutein and beta-carotene. S. Afr. J. Enol. Vitic. 13, 52–55.

Marsh, K.B., Volz, R.K., Cashmore, W., Reay, P., 1996. Fruit colour, leaf nitrogen level, and tree vigour in "Fuji" apples. New Zealand J. Crop Hortic. Sci. 24, 393–399.

Mattheis, J.P., Fellman, J.K., 1999. Preharvest factors influencing flavor of fresh fruits and vegetables. Postharvest Biol. Technol. 15, 227–232.

Maxie, E.C., Claypool, L.L., 1957. Heat injury in prunes. Proc. Am. Soc. Hortic. Sci. 69, 116–121.

Mayberry, K.S., Hartz, T.K., Valencia, J., 1996. Mixed melon production in California. Oakland: University of California, Devision of Agriculture, Narural Resource Publications 7209, p. 3. Available from: http://anrcatalog.ucdavis.edu.

Mayne, S.T., 1996. Beta-carotene, carotenoids, and disease prevention in humans. FASEB J. 10, 690–701.

Meli, J., Bygrave, E., 1972. The role of mitochondria in modifying calcium-sensitive cytoplasmicmetabolic activities: modification of pyruvate kinase activity. Biochem. J. 128, 415–420.

Miller, G., Suzuki, N., Ciftci-Yilmaz, S., Mittler, R., 2010. Reactive oxygen species homeostasis and signalling during drought and salinity stresses. Plant Cell Environ. 33, 453–467.

Mittler, R., Blumwald, E., 2010. Genetic engineering for modern agriculture: challenges and perspectives. Annu. Rev. Plant Biol. 61, 443–462.

Modise, D., Wright, C., Atherton, J., 2006. Changes in strawberry aroma in response to water stress. Boston J. Agric. Appl. Sci. 2.

Mohnen, D., 2008. Pectin structure and biosynthesis. Curr. Opin. Plant Biol. 11, 266–277.

Monaghan, J.M., Chiramba, T., Mogren, L.M., 2012. Effect of pre- and postharvest factors on splitting in radish (*Raphanus sativus*). Acta Hortic. (ISHS) 934, 1347–1351.

Monselise, S.P., Goren, R., 1987. Preharvest growing conditions and postharvest behaviour of subtropical and temperate-zone fruits. HortScience 22, 1185–1189.

Mori, K., Goto-Yamamoto, N., Kitayama, M., Hashizume, K., 2007. Loss of anthocyanins in red-wine grape under high temperatures. J. Exp. Bot. 58, 1935–1945.

Mullins, M.G., Bouquet, A., Williams, L.E., 1992. Biology of the Grapevine. Cambridge University Press, Cambridge, UK.

Murayama, H., Arikawa, M., Sasaki, Y., Dal Cin, Y., Mitauhashi, W., Toyomasu, T., 2009. Effect of ethylene treatment on expression of polyuronide-modifying genes and solubilization of polyuronides during ripening in two peach cultivars having different softening characteristics. Postharvest Biol. Technol. 52, 196–201.

Niyogi, K.K., Björkman, O., Grossman, A.R., 1997. The roles of specific xanthophylls in photoprotection. Proc. Natl. Acad. Sci. 94 (25), 14162–14167.

Nora, L., Dalmazo, G.O., Nora, F.R., Rombaldi, C.V., 2012. Controlled water stress to improve fruit and vegetable postharvest quality. In: Mofizur Rahman, I.M. (Ed.), Water Stress. InTech, Croatia, pp. 59–72.

Ogura, N., Nakagawa, H., Takenhana, H., 1975. Effect of high temperature short term storage of mature green tomato fruits on changes in their chemical composition after ripening at room temperature. J. Agric. Chemi. Soc. Japan 49, 189–196.

Oliveira, C., Ferreira, A.C., Costa, A., Guerra, J., De Pinho, P.G., 2004. Effect of some viticultural parameters on the grape carotenoids profile. J. Agric. Food Chem. 52, 4178–4184.

Opara, L.U., Tadesse, T., 2000. Calyx-end splitting and physico-chemical properties of "Pacific Rose"™ apple as affected by orchard management factors. J. Hortic. Sci. Biotechnol. 75 (5), 581–585.

Passardi, F., Cosio, C., Penel, C., Dunand, C., 2005. Peroxidases have more functions than a Swiss army knife. Plant Cell Rep. 24, 255–265.

Peaucelle, A., Braybrook, S., Hoefte, H., 2012. Cell wall mechanics and growth control in plants: the role of pectins revisited. Front.Plant Sci. 3, 121.

Peña, M.J., Carpita, N.C., 2004. Loss of highly branched arabinans and debranching of rhamnogalacturonan I accompany loss of firm texture and cell separation during prolonged storage of apple. Plant Physiol. 135, 1305–1313.

Perring, M.A., 1984. Indirect influences on apple fruit mineral composition and storage quality. Proceedings VIth International Colloquium for Optimization of Plant Nutrition 1984, Montpellier, France 4, 1199–1206.

Perring, M.A., Samuelson, T.J., Caverly, D.J., Marks, M.J., 1985. Boron and calcium deficiency symptoms in apple. Report of the East Malling Research Station for 1984, pp. 223–224.

Poiroux-Gonord, F., Bidel, L.P.R., Fanciullino, A.-L., Gautier, H., Lauri-Lopez, F., Urban, L., 2010. Health benefits of vitamins and secondary metabolites of fruits and vegetables and prospects to increase their concentrations by agronomic approaches. J. Agric. Food Chem. 58, 12065–12082.

Poiroux-Gonord, F., Fanciullino, A.-L., Poggi, I., Urban, L., 2013. Carbohydrate control over carotenoid build-up is conditional on fruit ontogeny in clementine fruits. Physiol. Plant. 147, 417–431.

Poovaiah, B.W., Glenn, G.M., Reddy, A.S.N., 1988. Calcium and fruit softening: physiology and biochemistry. Hortic. Rev. 10, 107–152.

Porritt, S., Lidster, P., 1978. The effect of prestorage heating on ripening and senescence of apples during cold storage. J. Am. Soc. Horticult. Sci. 103, 584–587.

Pourtau, N., Jennings, R., Pelzer, E., Pallas, J., Wingler, A., 2006. Effect of sugar-induced senescence on gene expression and implications for the regulation of senescence in *Arabidopsis*. Planta 224, 556–568.

Prange, R., Dell, J.R., 1997. Preharvest factors affecting quality of berry crops. HortScience 32, 824–830.

Proctor, J.T.A., 1974. Color stimulation in attached apples with supplementary light. Canadian J. Plant Sci. 54, 499–503.

Proctor, J.T.A., Lougheed, E.C., 1976. The effect of covering apples during development. HortScience 11, 108–109.

Quesada, M.A., Blanco-Portales, R., Posé, S., García-Gago, J.A., Jiménez-Bermúdez, S., Muñoz-Serrano, A., Caballero, J.L., Pliego-Alfaro, F., Mercado, J.A., Muñoz-Blanco, J., 2009. Antisense down-regulation of the FaPG1 gene reveals an unexpected central role for polygalacturonase in strawberry fruit softening. Plant Physiol. 150 (2), 1022–1032.

Quiros-Gonzales, M., 2000. Phytophagous mite populations on Tahiti lime, *Citrus latifolia*, under induced drought conditions. Exp. Appl. Acarol. 24, 897–904.

Ranjan, A., Pandey, N., Lakhwani, D., Dubey, N.K., Pathre, U.V., Sawant, S.V., 2012. Comparative transcriptomic analysis of roots of contrasting *Gossypium herbaceum* genotypes revealing adaptation to drought. BMC Genom. 13, 680.

Raven, P.H., Evert, R.F., Eichhorn, S.E., 1992. Biology of Plants. Worth Publishers, New York.

Razungles, A.J., Baumes, R.L., Dufour, C., Sznaper, C.N., Bayonove, C.L., 1998. Effect of sun exposure on carotenoids and C^{13}-norisoprenoid glycosides in Syrah berries (*Vitis vinifera* L.). Sci. Aliment. 18, 361–373.

Reinbothe, S., Reinbothe, C., 1996. Regulation of chlorophyll biosynthesis in angiosperms. Plant Physiol. 111, 1–7.

Reiter, W.D., 2002. Biosynthesis and properties of the plant cell wall. Curr. Opin. Plant Biol. 5, 536–542.

Renew, S., Heyno, E., Schopfer, P., Liszkay, A., 2005. Sensitive detection and localization of hydroxyl radical production in cucumber roots and *Arabidopsis* seedlings by spin trapping electron paramagnetic resonance spectroscopy. Plant J. 44, 342–347.

Rengel, Z., 1992. The role of calcium in salt toxicity. Plant Cell Environ. 15, 625–632.

Richardson, A., 1986. The effect of herbicide soil management systems and nitrogen fertilizer on the eating quality of "Cox's Orange Pippin" apples. J. Hortic. Sci. 61, 447–456.

Ripoll, J., Urban, L., Staudt, M., Lopez-Lauri, F., Bidel, L.P.R., Bertin, N., 2014. Water shortage and quality of fleshy fruits, making the most of the unavoidable. J. Exp. Bot. 65 (15), 4097–4117.

Ristic, R., Downey, M.O., Iland, P.G., Bindon, K., Francis, I.L., Herderich, M., Robinson, S.P., 2007. Exclusion of sunlight from Shiraz grapes alters wine colour, tannin and sensory properties. Aust. J. Grape Wine Res. 13, 53–65.

Rose, J.K.C., Lee, H.H., Bennett, A.B., 1997. Expression of a divergent expansin gene is fruit-specific and ripening-regulated. Proc. Natl. Acad. Sci. USA 94, 5955–5960.

Rowan, D.D., Cao, M., Lin-Wang, K., et al., 2009. Environmental regulation of leaf colour in red 35S:PAP1 *Arabidopsis thaliana*. New Phytol. 182, 102–115.

Ruan, Y., Jin, Y., Li, G., Boyer, J.S., 2010. Sugar input, metabolism, and signalling mediated by invertase: roles in development, yield potential, and response to drought and heat. Mol. Plant 3, 942–955.

Saladié, M., Matas, A.J., Isaacson, T., Jenks, M.A., Goodwin, S.M., Niklas, K.J., Xiaolin, R., Labavitch, J.M., Shackel, K.A., Fernie, A.R., 2007. A re-evaluation of the key factors that influence tomato fruit softening and integrity. Plant Physiol. 144, 1012–1028.

Sams, C.E., 1999. Preharvest factors affecting postharvest texture. Postharvest Biol. Technol. 15, 249–254.

Santos, C.V., 2004. Regulation of chlorophyll biosynthesis and degradation by salt stress in sunflower leaves. Sci. Hortic. 103 (1), 93–99.

Saure, M.C., 1990. External control of anthocyanin formation in apple. Sci. Hortic. 42, 181–218.

Schopfer, P., 2001. Hydroxyl radical-induced cell-wall loosening in vitro and in vivo: implications for the control of elongation growth. Plant J. 28, 679–688.

Schopfer, P., 2006. Biomechanics of plant growth. Am. J. Bot. 93 (10), 1415–1425.

Scudellari, D., Toselli, M., Marangoni, B., Tagliavini, M., 1999. La diagnostica fogliare nelle piante arboree da frutto a foglia caduca. Bollettino della Società Italiana di Scienza del Suolo 48, 829–842.

Seemann, J.R., Critchley, C., 1985. Effects of salt stress on the growth, ion content, stomatal behaviour and photosynthetic capacity of a salt sensitive species *Phaseolus vulgaris* L. Planta 164, 151–162.

Seki, M., Umezawa, T., Urano, K., Shinozaki, K., 2007. Regulatory metabolic networks in drought stress responses. Curr. Opin. Plant Biol. 10, 296–302.

Shackel, K.A., Greve, C., Labavitch, J.M., Ahmadi, H., 1991. Cell turgor changes associated with ripening in tomato pericarp tissue. Plant Physiol. 97, 814–816, 1991.

Sharples, R.O., 1973. Orchard and climatic factors, Part IV. In: Fidler, J.C., Wilkinson, B.G., Edney, K.L., Sharples, R.O. (Eds.), The Biology of Apple and Pear Storage. Research Review Commonwealth Bureau of Horticulture and Plantation Crops No. 3. CAB, Farnham Royal, UK, pp. 175–225.

Sharples, R.O., 1980. The influence of orchard nutrition on the storage quality of apples and pears grown in the United Kingdom. In: Atkinson, D., Jackson, J.E., Sharples, R.O., Waller, W.M. (Eds.), Mineral Nutrition of Fruit Trees. London, Butterworths, pp. 17–28.

Sharples, R.O., Johnson, D.S., 1977. The influence of calcium on senescence changes in apple. Ann. Appl. Biol. 85, 450–453.

Sharples, R.O., Reid, M.S., Turner, N.A., 1979. The effects of post harvest mineral element and lecithin treatments on the storage disorders of apples. J. Hortic. Sci. 54, 299–304.

Shear, C.B., 1975. Calcium-related disorders of fruit and vegetables. HortScience 10, 361–365.

Shear, C.B., 1980. Interaction of nutrition and environment on mineral composition of fruits. In: Atkinson, D., Jackson, J.E., Sharples, R.O., Waller, W.M. (Eds.), Mineral Nutrition of Fruit Trees. Butterworths, London, pp. 41–50.

Sheehy, R.E., Kramer, M.K., Hiatt, W.R., 1988. Reduction of polygalacturonase activity in tomato fruit by antisense RNA. Proc. Natl. Acad. Sci. USA 85, 8805–8809.

Shewfelt, R., 1990. Sources of variation in the nutrient content of agricultural commodities from the farms to the consumer. J. Food Qual. 13, 37–54.

Shibairo, S.I., Upadhyaya, M.K., Toivonen, P.M.A., 1998. Influence of preharvest water stress on postharvest moisture loss of carrots (*Daucus carota* L.). J. Hortic. Sci. Biotechnol. 73 (3), 347–352.

Shimokawa, K., Shimada, S., Yaeo, K., 1978. Ethylene-enhanced chlorophyllase activity during degreening of *Citrus unshiu* Marc. Sci. Hortic. 8 (2), 129–135.

Shvarts, M., Borochov, A., Weiss, D., 1997. Low temperature enhances petunia flower pigmentation and induces chalcone synthase gene expression. Physiol. Plant. 99, 67–72.

Siddiqui, S., Bangerth, F., 1993. Studies on cell wall-mediated changes during storage of calcium-infiltrated apples. Acta Hortic. 326, 105–113.

Silva, E., 2008. Influence of preharvest factors on postharvest quality. Wholesale Success: A Farmer's Guide to Selling, Postharvest Handling, and Packing Produce, Midwest edition. Available from: http://www.familyfarmed.org/wholesale-success/

Smart, R.E., Robinson, J.B., Due, G.R., Brien, C.J., 1985. Canopy microclimate modification for the cultivar Shiraz. II. Effects on must and wine composition. Vitis 24, 119–128.

Smith, D.L., Gross, K.C., 2000. A family of at least seven β-galactosidase genes is expressed during tomato fruit development. Plant Physiol. 123, 1173–1183.

Smith, C.J.S., Watson, C.F., Ray, J., Bird, C.R., Morris, P.C., Schuch, W., Grierson, D., 1988. Antisense RNA inhibition of polygalacturonase gene expression in transgenic tomatoes. Nature 334, 724–726.

Solfanelli, C., Poggi, A., Loreti, E., Alpi, A., Perata, P., 2006. Sucrose-specific induction of the anthocyanin biosynthetic pathway in *Arabidopsis*. Plant Physiol. 140, 637–646.

Song, J., Shellie, K.C., Wang, H., Qian, M.C., 2012. Influence of deficit irrigation and kaolin particle film on grape composition and volatile compounds in Merlot grape (*Vitis vinifera* L.). Food Chem. 134, 841–850.

Steel, C.C., Keller, M., 2000. Influence of UV-B radiation on the carotenoid content of *Vitis vinifera* tissues. Biochem. Soc. Trans. 28, 883–885.

Steele, N.M., McCann, M.C., Roberts, K., 1997. Pectin modification in cell walls of ripening tomatoes occurs in distinct domains. Plant Physiol. 114, 373–381.

Steyn, W., Holcroft, D., Wand, S., Jacobs, G., 2005. Red colour development and loss in pears. Acta Hortic. 671, 79–85.

Steyn, W.J., Wand, S.J., Jacobs, G., Rosecrance, R.C., Roberts, S.C., 2009. Evidence for a photoprotective function of low-temperature-induced anthocyanin accumulation in apple and pear peel. Physiol. Plant. 136, 461–472.

Stow, J.R., 1993. Effect of calcium ions on apple fruit softening during storage and ripening. Postharvest Biol. Technol. 3, 1–9.

Sun, L., Sun, Y., Zhang, M., Wang, L., Ren, J., Cui, M., Leng, P., 2012. Suppression of 9-cis-epoxycarotenoid dioxygenase, which encodes a key enzyme in abscisic acid biosynthesis, alters fruit texture in transgenic tomato. Plant Physiol. 158 (1), 283–298.

Suzuki, M., Ketterling, M.G., Li, Q.B., McCarty, D.R., 2003. Viviparous1 alters global gene expression patterns through regulation of abscisic acid signaling. Plant Physiol. 132, 1664–1677.

Szczesniak, A.S., Ilker, R., 1988. The meaning of textural characteristics – juiciness in plant foodstuffs. J. Text. Stud. 19, 61–78.

Tacken, E., Ireland, H., Gunaseelan, K., Karunairetnam, S., Wang, D., Schultz, K., Bowen, J., Atkinson, R.G., Johnston, J.W., Putterill, J., 2010. The role of ethylene and cold temperature in the regulation of the apple POLYGALACTURONASE 1 gene and fruit softening. Plant Physiol. 153, 294–305.

Taiz, L., Zeiger, E., 2010. Plant Physiology, 5th edn Sinauer Associates, Inc., Sunderland, MA.

Tagliavini, M., Scudellari, D., Corelli Grappadelli, L., Pelliconi, F., 1997. Valutazione di metodi rapidi per stimare il livello azotato del pescheto. Atti XXII Convegno Peschicolo, Cesena, Italy, October 5–7, 1995, pp. 141–150.

Teng, S., Keurentjes, J., Bentsink, L., Koorneet, M., Smeekens, S., 2007. Sucrose-specific induction of anthocyanin biosynthesis in *Arabidopsis* requires the MYB75/PAP1 gene. Plant Physiol. 139, 1840–1852.

Tenhaken, R., 2015. Cell wall remodeling under abiotic stress. Front. Plant Sci. 5, 771.

Tevini, M., Teramura, A.H., 1989. UV-B effects on terrestrial plants. Phytochem. Photobiol. 4, 479–487.

Thompson, A.J., Tor, M., Barry, C.S., Vrebalov, J., Orfila, C., Jarvis, M.C., Giovannoni, J.J., Grierson, D., Seymour, G.B., 1999. Molecular and genetic characterization of a novel pleiotropic tomato-ripening mutant. Plant Physiol. 120, 383–389.

Tieman, D.M., Harriman, R.W., Ramamohan, G., Handa, A.K., 1992. An antisense pectin methylesterase gene alters pectin chemistry and soluble solids in tomato fruit. Plant Cell 4, 667–679.

Tohge, T., Nishiyama, Y., Hirai, M.Y., et al., 2005. Functional genomics by integrated analysis of metabolome and transcriptome of *Arabidopsis* plants over-expressing an MYB transcription factor. Plant J. 42, 218–235.

Toledo-Ortiz, G., Huq, E., Rodríguez-Concepción, M., 2010. Direct regulation of phytoene synthase gene expression and carotenoid biosynthesis by phytochrome-interacting factors. Proc. Natl. Acad. Sci. 107, 11626–11631.

Tu, K., Waldron, K., Ingham, L., DeBarsy, T., De Baerdemaeker, J., 1997. Effect of picking time and storage conditions on "Cox's Orange Pippin" apple texture in relation to cell wall changes. J. Hortic. Sci. 72, 971–980.

Ubi, B., Honda, C., Bessho, H., Kondo, S., Wada, M., Kobayashi, S., Moriguchi, T., 2006. Expression analysis of anthocyanin biosynthetic genes in apple skin: effect of UV-B and temperature. Plant Sci. 170, 571–578.

Urban, L., Staudt, M., Ripoll, J., Lopez-Lauri, F., Bertin, N., 2014. Less can make more—revisting fleshy fruit quality and irrigation in horticulture. Chron. Hortic. 54 (4), 24–30.

Vallverdu, X., Girona, J., Echeverria, G., Marsal, J., Behboudian, M.H., Lopez, G., 2012. Sensory quality and consumer acceptance of "Tardibelle" peach are improved by deficit irrigation applied during stage II of fruit development. HortScience 47 (5), 656–659.

Van Rooyen, Z., Bower, J.P., 2005. The role of fruit mineral composition on fruit softness and mesocarp discolouration in "Pinkerton" avocado (*Persea americana* Mill.). J. Hortic. Sci. Biotechnol. 80 (6), 793–799.

Vaz, R.L., Richardson, D.G., 1984. Effect of calcium on respiration rate, ethylene production and occurrence of cork spot in Anjou pears (*Pyrus communis* L.). Acta Hortic. (ISHS) 157, 227–236.

Veit-Köhler, U., Krumbein, A., Kosegarten, H., 1999. Effect of different water supply on plant growth and fruit quality of *Lycopersicon esculentum*. J. Plant Nutr. Soil Sci. 162, 583–588.

Wakabayashi, K., Soga, K., Hoson, T., 2012. Phenylalanine ammonia-lyase and cell wall peroxidase are cooperatively involved in the extensive formation of ferulate network in cell walls of developing rice shoots. J. Plant Physiol. 169, 262–267.

Wakasa, Y., Kudo, H., Ishikawa, R., Akada, S., Senda, M., Niizeki, M., Harada, T., 2006. Low expression of an endopolygalacturonase gene in apple fruit with long-term storage potential. Postharv. Biol. Technol. 39, 193–198.

Waller, W.M., 1980. Use of apple analysis. In: Atkinson, D., Jackson, J.E., Sharples, R.O., Waller, W.M. (Eds.), Mineral Nutrition of Fruit Trees. London, Butterworths, pp. 383–394.

Wallner, S.J., 1978. Apple fruit β-galactosidase and softening in storage. J. Am. Soc. Hortic. Sci. 103, 364–366.

Wang, S.Y., Camp, M.J., 2000. Temperatures after bloom affect plant growth and fruit quality of strawberry. Sci. Hortic. 85 (3), 183–199.

Wang, Y., Frei, M., 2011. Stressed food – the impact of abiotic environmental stresses on crop quality. Agric. Ecosyst. Environ. 141, 271–286.

Watkins, C.B., Harman, J.E., Ferguson, I.B., Reid, M.S., 1982. The action of lecithin and calcium dips in the control of bitter pit in apple fruit. J. Am. Soc. Hortic. Sci. 107, 262–265.

Weston, L.A., Barth, M.M., 1997. Preharvest factors affecting postharvest quality of vegetables. HortScience 32, 812–816.

Westwood, M.N., 1993. Temperate-Zone Pomology: Physiology and Culture, third ed. Timber Press, Portland, OR.

Wheeler, S., Loveys, B., Ford, C., Davies, C., 2009. The relationship between the expression of abscisic acid biosynthesis genes, accumulation of abscisic acid and the promotion of *Vitis vinifera* L. berry ripening by abscisic acid. Aust. J. Grape Wine Res. 15, 195–204.

Wilkinson, B.G., 1958. The effect of orchard factors on the chemical composition of apples. II. The relationship between potassium and total titrateable acidity, and between potassium and magnesium, in the fruit. J. Horticult. Sci. 33, 49–57.

Wimmer, M.A., Eichert, T., 2013. Review: mechanisms for boron deficiency-mediated changes in plant water relations. Plant Sci. 203, 25–32.

Witney, G.W., Kushad, M.M., 1990. Correlation of pyruvate kinase activity with bitter pit development in apple fruit. Sci. Hortic. 43, 247–253.

Wolf, S., Hematy, K., Hoefte, H., 2012. Growth control and cell wall signaling in plants. Annu. Rev. Plant Biol. 63, 381–407.

Woodbridge, C.G., 1971. Calcium level of pear tissues affected with cork and black end. HortScience 6, 451–453.

Yogaratnam, N., Sharples, R.O., 1982. Supplementing the nutrition of Bramley's Seedling apple with phosphorus sprays II. Effects on fruit composition and storage quality. J. Hortic. Sci. 57, 53–59.

Yoshida, O., Nakagawa, H., Ogura, N., Sato, T., 1984. Effect of heat treatment on the development of polygalacturonase activity in tomato fruit during ripening. Plant Cell Physiol. 25 (3), 505–509.

Zanor, M.I., Osorio, S., Nunes-Nesi, A., Carrari, F., Lohse, M., Usadel, B., Kühn, C., Bleiss, W., Giavalisco, P., Willmitzer, L., Sulpice, R., Zhou, Y.-H., Fernie, A.R., 2009. RNA interference of LIN5 in tomato confirms its role in controlling Brix content, uncovers the influence of sugars on the levels of fruit hormones, and demonstrates the importance of sucrose cleavage for normal fruit development and fertility. Plant Physiol. 150, 1204–1218.

Zhang, F., Gonzalez, A., Zhao, M., Payne, C.T., Lloyd, A., 2003. A network of redundant bHLH proteins functions in all TTG1-dependent pathways of *Arabidopsis*. Development 130, 4859–4869.

Zucker, M, 1972. Light and enzymes. Annu. Rev. Plant Physiol. 23, 133–156.

2

ADVANCES IN CONTROLLED ATMOSPHERE STORAGE OF FRUITS AND VEGETABLES

Samad Bodbodak*, Mohammad Moshfeghifar**

*University of Tabriz, Department of Food Science and Technology, Faculty of Agriculture, Tabriz, Iran; **Islamic Azad University, Faculty of Food Sciences and Engineering (FFSE), Science & Research Branch Tehran, Tehran, Iran

1 Introduction

Controlled atmosphere (CA) storage is probably the most successful technology introduced to the fruit and vegetable industry in the 20th century. CA storage commonly uses low oxygen (O_2) levels and high carbon dioxide (CO_2) levels in the storage atmosphere combined with refrigeration. Even very early storage practices may have utilized a modified atmosphere enriched with CO_2 and depleted O_2 levels to extend storage life of fruits, vegetables, cereals, and other commodities (Dilley, 2006). CA storage was studied for first time in France by Jacques Etienne Berard in the early 1800s in France (Dalrymple, 1969). He observed that fruits did not ripen in an atmosphere depleted of O_2 (Dalrymple, 1969). Other studies also investigated the effects of low levels of O_2 and of high levels of CO_2 on ripening, but the basis for commercial application of CA storage was established by Kidd and West (1927) who studied the effects of O_2, CO_2, and C_2H_4 on respiration and ripening in pome fruits and berries. However, after the 1950s when CA technology improved, its usage became more common and further developments and technical innovations during the 1990s expanded its use worldwide (Prange et al., 2005).

In CA storage, inside a food storage room is the gas composition that is continually monitored and adapted to maintain the optimum concentration within completely close tolerances. Because CA storage is capital intensive and expensive to operate, it is more appropriate for those foods that are agreeable to long-term storage such as apples, kiwifruit, and pears. The reason for

Eco-Friendly Technology for Postharvest Produce Quality. http://dx.doi.org/10.1016/B978-0-12-804313-4.00002-5
Copyright © 2016 Elsevier Inc. All rights reserved.

the exclusive application of CA storage to apples was related to its incomparable advantages over refrigeration for this specific produce. CA storage is beneficial for alleviating certain storage disorders and diseases of apples while other disorders may be aggravated or induced by CA storage, but generally its benefits prevail (Prange et al., 2006). However, research has investigated the application of CA storage for other commodities, which led to the commercial use and recommendation of CA conditions for storage of other fruits, vegetables, fresh cut fruits and vegetables, as well as cut flowers and ornamentals (Brecht, 2006; Kader, 2003; Saltveit, 2003). Also, CA storage has specific applications such as insect control and disinfection (Mitcham et al., 2003).

CA packaging is the enclosure of food in a gas impermeable package inside which the gaseous environment with respect to CO_2, O_2, N_2 (nitrogen gas), water vapor, and other trace gases has been changed and is selectively controlled to increase shelf life. Using this explanation, there are no CA packaging systems in commercial use. However, using the combination of O_2 and C_2H_4 absorbers, together with CO_2 release agents in packaging, at least during the early stages of storage life the packaged product could be classified as CA packaging.

An associated technique that consists of placing the food in an environment in which pressure, humidity, and air temperature are exactly controlled, and the rate at which air in the storage environment is changed and closely regulated, is called hypobaric storage (Burg, 2004). Unlike CA storage and modified atmosphere storage, no gases other than air are required. The total pressure within the hypobaric chamber is important because the O_2 concentration is directly proportional to that pressure. Although much research has been carried out into the use of hypobaric conditions for refrigerated storage of flesh foods and horticultural products, it has not been employed commercially to any great extent for the storage or transportation of foods. However, it is used commercially by growers of cut flowers.

2 Controlled Atmosphere Storage of Fruits and Vegetables

2.1 Generation of Controlled Atmosphere

There are some functions for the generation and maintaining of CA including O_2 removal, excess CO_2 removal, addition of air to replace O_2 consumed by respiration, removal of C_2H_4, and in some cases addition of CO_2. Selection of the appropriate functions and devices for generating and maintaining CA depends on what horticultural produce is stored and the storage conditions required for each produce.

2.1.1 Oxygen (O_2) Removal

There are several methods for oxygen removal from CA storage, such as reduction of O_2 levels by natural respiration of the horticultural produce in early stage of CA, rapid pulldown of O_2 levels in CA rooms (Allen, 1998; Malcolm, 2005), and rapid reduction of O_2 levels by flushing with N_2.

Flushing with N_2 is common practice to reduce O_2 levels to 3–5 kPa and respiration can be used for reduction to the final level. It should be mention that care must be taken to ensure that N_2 is discharged slowly to prevent low-temperature structural damage to produce.

Until about 1990 propane burners were used to convert O_2 to CO_2 by burning with propane ($C_3H_8 + 5O_2 \rightarrow 3CO_2 + 4H_2O$). These gas generators operated on the "open-flame" or catalytic burner principle and reduced O_2 levels to 3–5 kPa.

Nevertheless, incomplete burning of propane causes safety problems. It is necessary to install an explosive gas detector and CO_2 scrubber for removing the large amounts of produced CO_2 from the atmosphere in the storage room. Also, burning of propane produces C_2H_4, which leads to increased levels of C_2H_4 in the storage room. Therefore application of this equipment has been abandoned in new CA storage rooms (Coquinot and Chapon, 1992). An alternative system is operated based on cracking ammonia (NH_3) at high temperature to N_2 and H_2 ($2NH_3 \rightarrow N_2 + 3H_2$) and then further by consuming O_2 from the storage room to convert H_2 to water ($2N_2 + 6H_2 + 3O_2 \rightarrow 6H_2O + 2N_2$). In comparison with the propane burner the system has some advantages such as no production of CO_2 and C_2H_4; additionally any C_2H_4 present in atmosphere of the storage room is destroyed.

The other method of rapidly removing O_2 is flushing N_2 in the atmosphere in the CA storage room. N_2 can be supplied as a gas or liquid; alternatively, N_2 generators (gas separator systems) are used to produce N_2 on site as use of liquid N_2 is expensive. The capital costs for installation of N_2 generators are low but on-site storage of the N_2 is required. N_2 generators separate air into O_2 and N_2 (Malcolm, 2005; Dilley, 2006). There are two types of commercial N_2 generators: one is based on membrane technology and uses the hollow fiber membrane (HFM) system (Fig. 2.1). The other one is based on adsorption technology and is known as a pressure swing adsorber (PSA) (Fig. 2.2). A compressed air feed stream in the range of 800–1300 kPa is required in both the HFM and PSA

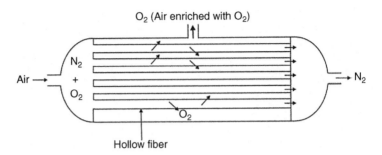

Figure 2.1 Scheme of hollow fiber membrane (HFM) nitrogen generator.

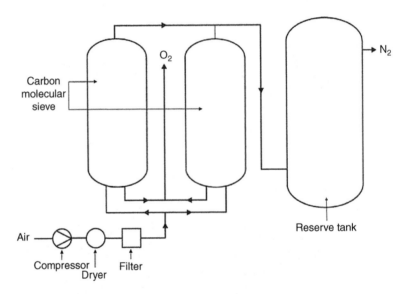

Figure 2.2 Scheme of pressure swing adsorber (PSA) nitrogen generator.

systems. In the HFM system, the driving force for gases to permeate across the fiber wall is the pressure differential between the inside of the membrane fiber and the outside of the fiber. The gas permeation rate from membrane fiber is based on gas separation because O_2, H_2O, and CO_2 are "fast" gases and diffuse at fast rates, whereas N_2 is a "slow" gas and diffuses at a slow rate. In HFM systems, N_2 is continuously separated from O_2 and other gases.

On the contrary, PSA systems for N_2 generation operate in a discontinuous mode and use completely different physical properties. PSA systems are composed of two beds of carbon molecular sieve that adsorb stream gases such as O_2 and CO_2 at the high pressure of compressed air. These gases are released by the molecular sieves as the pressure is reduced, which are then regenerated. The vacuum is commercially used in PSA systems during regeneration (Malcolm, 2005).

2.1.2 Carbon Dioxide (CO_2) Removal

Scrubber systems are generally used to control and remove CO_2 from the storage atmosphere. One of the first reagents used in the CO_2 scrubber (Fig. 2.3) for commercial CA storage is an aqueous solution of caustic soda (NaOH). The caustic soda solution is circulated in open tubes and absorbed CO_2 is produced ($2NaOH + CO_2 \rightarrow Na_2CO_3 + H_2O$) (Raghavan et al., 2005). The use of NaOH and potash (Osterloh, 1996) was discontinued due to their corrosiveness and potential danger in handling and disposal, which led to the use of lime in place of caustic soda. This method of CO_2 removal is based on utilizing hydrated lime [$Ca(OH)_2$] becoming limestone ($CaCO_3$) in the absorption process [$Ca(OH)_2 + CO_2 \rightarrow CaCO_3 + H_2O$].

Lime is used in scrubber systems or other scrubbing methods by placing it directly inside the CA storage room. Although lime scrubbing is still in use, activated charcoal scrubbers are gradually replacing lime scrubber systems.

Air from the storage room is circulated through an activated charcoal scrubber, which consists of two cylindrical beds or

Figure 2.3 Carbon dioxide scrubber.

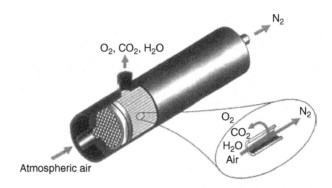

Figure 2.4 Semipermeable membrane that separates other gases from N$_2$ in Carrier's EverFresh controlled atmosphere (CA) system. From Carrier Corporation (2008).

chambers filled with activated charcoal; this process absorbs CO_2. For regeneration of saturated charcoal, outside air is circulated through the activated charcoal and back to the outside. This method can introduce O_2 into the CA rooms, which is a drawback for ultralow oxygen (ULO) storage. To overcome this problem it has been recommend to use air from the CA storage room, held in a breather bag, or N_2 from a gas generator to flush the scrubbers after regeneration (Bishop, 1996).

Other molecular sieve scrubbers such as sodium or aluminum silicate zeolites have also been used to adsorb CO_2. For regeneration of these porous materials, a heating process is required. Use of these types of scrubbers is limited because of high-energy demand for regeneration.

Flushing with N_2 is another method for controlling CO_2 levels (Bishop, 1996). In this method, N_2 generator is used to control both CO_2 and O_2 levels independently. However, by considering energy requirements, this method is less efficient than a CO_2 scrubber.

Yet another method for removing CO_2 is a system that uses water to control CO_2 levels. Water scrubbers have high demand for water because of their low CO_2 adsorption capacity (20 L of CO_2 m^{-3} of water).

Finally, Marcellin and Leteinturier (1967) proposed diffusion units as a new method for removing CO_2 from storage atmosphere. The system consists of gas diffusion panels (equipped with semipermeable membranes made of silicon rubber) in an airtight container with two separate airflow paths (Fig. 2.4).

2.1.3 Ethylene (C$_2$H$_4$) Removal

C_2H_4 removal is critical because a very low concentration of C_2H_4 (<0.1 ppm) may induce ripening or cause physiological disorders in some horticultural produce. There are two commercial types of C_2H_4 scrubbers: (1) catalytic oxidation of C_2H_4 to water and CO_2 and (2) use of C_2H_4 absorbing beads (Wojciechowski, 1989). Some of CO_2 scrubbers also absorb C_2H_4, for example, N_2 flushing systems that are used to remove the CO_2, also decrease the C_2H_4 concentration.

C_2H_4 could be oxidized by using ultraviolet radiation or ozone gas techniques. Because of limited success in refrigerated storage, the methods have not gained acceptance in commercial CA storage operations. Wojciechowski (1989) reported that C_2H_4 level in apple CA storage rooms was about 200 ppm but were much lower in storage rooms containing apples treated with 1-methylcyclopropene (1-MCP). This is in contrast with C_2H_4 levels in conventional cold storage rooms, wholesale markets, distribution centers, supermarket storage rooms, and even in domestic refrigerators (ranging from 20 up to 1500 ppm) (Wills et al., 2000).

Wills et al. (2000) designed C_2H_4-absorbing bead scrubbers, which consist of small spherical particles impregnated with potassium permanganate. They also utilized several porous inert matrix materials such as silica gel, zeolite, alumina, and others in the scrubbers. The air from the storage room is circulated through a sealed cartridge that is loaded with beads. It is not possible to regenerate beads and therefore bead scrubbers should be checked regularly to replace spent beads with new beads. However, use of this technology is limited because of the relatively high cost of potassium permanganate.

2.2 CA Methods

Essentially, CA storage comprises controlled gas composition and refrigerated storage of fruit or vegetables. Storage facilities (Fig. 2.5) are composed of airtight and thermally insulated rooms or enclosures, machinery, refrigeration systems, equipment for creating and maintaining the desired gas concentrations in a specific environment, and systems for measurement and control of storage factors (Hoehn et al., 2009). Table 2.1 illustrates different CA storage regimes such as LO (low O_2) storage or ULO storage, and more recently dynamic control of CA (DCA) or dynamic control system (DCS) (Prange et al., 2005).

2.2.1 Controlled Ventilation

Controlled ventilation is the most basic type of CA. In this method, CA is generated via accumulation of CO_2 created from respiration of the fruit or vegetable stored in an airtight room. Typically CO_2 levels in CA storage rooms are adjusted on 5–10 kPa

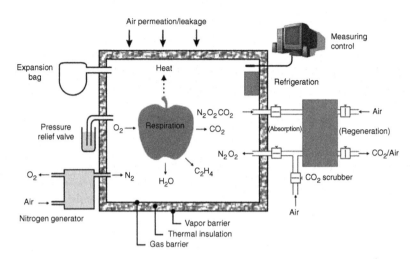

Figure 2.5 Scheme of a controlled atmosphere (CA) room (Hoehn et al., 2009).

(about 5–10% of the total gas composition, which is ~ 100 kPa) or even higher and excessive amounts are controlled by ventilation with outside air. Chapon and Westercamp (1996) implied that the sum of CO_2 and O_2 concentrations of such atmospheres was normally equal to 20–21%. Therefore O_2 levels in this condition range from about 10–16 kPa, which are not low enough to exert a sufficient decreasing effect on respiration.

However, some types of fruits such as many apple cultivars and pears are more sensitive to raised CO_2 concentrations and show CO_2-related storage disorders. It was suggested that in these

Table 2.1 CA Methods and Gas Compositions of Storage Atmosphere (Hoehn et al., 2009).

CA Methods	O_2 (kPa)	CO_2 (kPa)	N_2 (kPa)
Refrigerated storage (normal atmosphere)	21	0.03	79
Controlled ventilation	6–18	3–15	79
Conventional CA	2–5	2–5	90–92
LO	1.5–2	1–3	95–97.5
ULO	0.8–1.2	0.5–2	96.8–98.7
DCA or DCS	<0.8	<1.5	>98

cases, CO_2 should be maintained at levels below 3 kPa and accordingly O_2 levels of 18 kPa. But fruits such as cherries and berries tolerate high levels of CO_2. In these cases, ventilated CA storage is suggested for prolonging shelf life and retaining quality using optimal CA storage conditions but at low cost (Gasser and Höhn, 2004). Requirements for developing controlled ventilation storage are gastight rooms or pallet package systems, a device to monitor CO_2 level, and an installation that allows ventilation with outside air.

2.2.2 Conventional CA

It was proved that it is unachievable to maintain simultaneously low CO_2 (2–3 kPa) and LO levels (2–3 kPa) by ventilation with outside air since CO_2 created from respiration of the fruits or vegetables stored in an airtight room could accumulate to unacceptably high levels. In order to remove excessive CO_2 from the storage atmosphere, scrubbers are required. Furthermore, appropriate measuring systems are required for monitoring and controlling of CO_2 and O_2 levels in the storage rooms. Also the CA room should be gastight and equipped with reliable remote temperature control with an accuracy of ±0.5°C. The CO_2 as well as O_2 levels must be controlled within ±0.5 kPa of the set values for maintaining the right gas compositions (Markarian et al., 2003).

2.2.3 Low O_2 Storage and Ultralow O_2 Storage

The lowest recommended level of O_2 for CA storage was O_2 < 2 kPa. But researchers found that in lower O_2 levels, storability of various horticultural produce and preservation of their quality improves without detrimental effects. Consequently, storage of Cox apples at <1 kPa CO_2 and 1.25 kPa O_2 showed acceptable quality maintenance (Jameson, 1993; Peppelenbos, 2003). Furthermore, LO (1.5–2 kPa) or ULO (0.8–1.2 kPa) conditions have been successfully implemented for storage of different apple cultivars throughout the world (Dilley, 2006). The recommended O_2 concentration for recent static CA is lowest at about 1 kPa. Several studies of chlorophyll fluorescence application have indicated that the O_2 threshold concentrations (anaerobic compensation point) for tested apples ranged from 0.4 to 0.8 kPa (Table 2.2) (Gasser et al., 2005, 2007; DeLong et al., 2004). It was also demonstrated that ULO could be implemented for other commodities such as kiwifruit, grapefruit, nectarine, pear, onion, lettuce, and others (Ekman et al., 2005). Thus more airtight rooms, compared with common CA rooms, are required to maintain such low levels of O_2. Furthermore, CO_2 as well as O_2 levels must be controlled within ±0.5 kPa every 4–6 h and the gas concentration adjusted

Table 2.2 LO Threshold of Apple Cultivars Determined by Chlorophyll Fluorescence and Range of O_2 Employed in Storage

Cultivar	LO Threshold (kPa)	O_2 Settings for Storage (kPa)
Braeburn[a]	0.4	0.5–0.6
Cortland[b]	0.5	0.6–0.8
Delicious[b]	0.4	0.5–0.8
Elstar[a]	0.3	0.3–0.6
Golden Delicious[b]	0.5	0.5–0.8
Golden Delicious[b]	0.3	0.3–0.6
Honeycrisp[b]	0.4	0.5–0.8
Idared[c]	0.4	0.5–0.8
Jonagold[b]	0.5	0.5–0.8
Maigold[a]	0.3	0.4–0.6
McIntosh[b]	0.8	0.9–1.0

[a]*Gasser et al. (2007).*
[b]*DeLong et al. (2004).*
[c]*Gasser et al. (2005).*

frequently (every 30 min) to maintain the gas concentration with acceptable precision (Markarian et al., 2003).

2.2.4 Rapid CA

It was demonstrated that an accelerated reduction of O_2 in a CA storage room could retard ripening of apple more efficiently than reduction of O_2 solely through respiration. The technique of accelerated reduction of O_2 in a CA storage room has some advantages, such as LO levels, reduction in C_2H_4 synthesis, and increase of CO_2 levels, which lead to decreased sensitivity of plant tissue to C_2H_4 (Dilley, 2006). Studies have demonstrated that ripening of climacteric fruit such as apple could be delayed by LO levels when they are harvested in a preclimacteric stage because there is not sufficient O_2 for C_2H_4 synthesis (Yang and Hoffmann, 1984). Therefore purging rooms with N_2 to reduce O_2 levels within 1 or 2 days instead of 1–3 weeks is considered to be rapid CA (RCA). In RCA, O_2 levels are reduced to ≤ 5 kPa by purging rooms with N_2 and then achieving further reduction by respiration. Generally, room cooling is implemented in the postharvest storage of apple, which is relatively slow compared with forced air or hydrocooling. Vigneault and Artés Hernández (2007) reported that commercially precooling apple with cool water and storing within <24 h after harvest generated important benefits in fruit quality, mainly firmness.

2.2.5 Initial Low O_2 Stress

Initial low O_2 stress (ILOS) is a process of exposing produce at very LO levels of <0.5 kPa for a limited period of time, up to 2 weeks. Treatment with ILOS could generate a positive stress effect on fresh horticultural produce. ILOS is an alternative to treatment of apples with the chemical 1-MCP or diphenylamine (DPA) for inhibition of superficial scald (Matté et al., 2005). It was recommended that after ILOS treatment, fruits are stored under ULO conditions. It could efficiently control superficial scald of several apple cultivars (Wang and Dilley, 2000).

2.2.6 Delayed CA

It was observed that RCA storage of some apple cultivars (Fuji, Braeburn) or pears (Conference) caused disorders such as cavities and internal browning (Braeburn browning disorder). Saquet et al. (2003) found that delaying establishment of CA conditions by 3 weeks inhibited or reduced the development of internal browning. They also suggested that fruits could be adapted to lower O_2 levels during the early stages of the storage period when maintained at regular atmosphere. Saquet et al. (2003) attributed higher resistant for browning disorders to higher adenosine triphosphate concentration in the fruit tissue throughout the entire storage period in delayed CA fruit.

2.2.7 Low Ethylene

C_2H_4 removal from storage rooms could prolong storage life of climacteric and nonclimacteric horticultural produce. The aim of using CA, ULO, and RCA techniques, which were described before, is to minimize C_2H_4 effects. It was clearly demonstrated that logarithmic decrease in C_2H_4 concentrations from 10 to <0.005 mL L^{-1} could linearly increase the storage life of many fruits and vegetables (Wills et al., 2000). There are different systems for removing C_2H_4 such as burning, ozone destruction, using zeolite nanoabsorbers, and chemical compounds, for example, 1-MCP; nevertheless, it was quite difficult and costly to maintain C_2H_4 levels below 0.1 mL L^{-1}. It was demonstrated that 1-MCP could be used as a postharvest C_2H_4 inhibitor during storage of different fruits (Prange and DeLong, 2003).

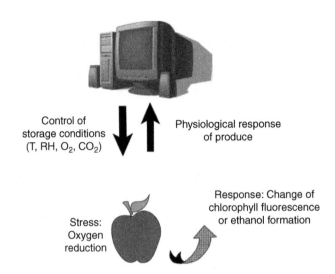

Control of
storage conditions
(T, RH, O_2, CO_2)

Physiological response
of produce

Response: Change of
chlorophyll fluorescence
or ethanol formation

Stress:
Oxygen
reduction

Figure 2.6 Concept of dynamic controlled atmosphere (CA) (Gasser et al., 2008).

2.2.8 Dynamic Control of CA or Dynamic Control System

The DCA storage consists of different stages: (1) monitoring the levels of gases according to the physiology of the fruit or vegetable, (2) processing data in the control system, and then (3) adjusting the atmosphere in the store (Fig. 2.6). It was reported that in some apple CA stores with 1% O_2, an alcohol detector was installed to detect ethanol fumes due to anaerobic (fermentation) respiration (Thompson, 1996). When the detector sounded an alarm, the store operator would increase the O_2 level to inhibit damage of fruits. Subsequently, dynamic control of ULO storage was introduced by Schouten (1997), which could analyze and maintain headspace ethanol and O_2 levels at less than 1 ppm and 0.3–0.7%, respectively, in order to adjust O_2 levels above the threshold for fermentation. Recently, other stress-associated metabolic responses of fruits and vegetables to LO were implemented as monitors of dynamic CA store atmosphere, and usually a computer program adjusts the level of O_2 at slightly above the stress level. Harvest-Watch™ is a patented and commercialized technology for measurement of chlorophyll fluorescence stress, which occurs when the O_2 level is insufficient for aerobic metabolism. It was demonstrated by DeLong et al. (2004) that in a HarvestWatch-facilitated an LO CA store, apple quality was retained at the highest possible level for some time without the use of scald controlling or other chemicals before storage. In another study on DCA storage using a chlorophyll fluorescence stress monitor, Burdon et al. (2008) indicated that Hass avocados ripened in 4.6 days at 20°C compared with 4.8 days for fruit stored in air and 7.2 days for "static" CA-stored fruit. They also compared Hass storage in DCA ($<3\%$ O_2 + 0.5% CO_2) for 6 weeks at 5°C with static CA in 5% O_2 + 5% CO_2. They indicated that chlorophyll fluorescence remained constant at 0.8 at 6°C in O_2 levels down to 1%, but below that it rapidly dropped to 0.68 within 24 h, and after 6 days' storage the fruits were returned to a nonstressed atmosphere and chlorophyll fluorescence rapidly returned to 0.8. They also reported that storage of Hass in DCA with CO_2 above 5% at 6°C resulted in a slight reduction in chlorophyll fluorescence, but when the fruits were returned to CO_2 levels below 5%, chlorophyll fluorescence rapidly returned to 0.8.

2.2.9 Sealed Plastic Tents

Sealed plastic tents tent may be used for the CA storage of small quantities of fruit and vegetables. A plastic tent was designed and constructed by Leyte and Forney (1999), which could hold two standard pallets stacked 1.8 m high and sealed with two airtight zippers and a small water trough to develop a maintained airtight chamber for the CA storage environment. Huang et al. (2002) used a $2 \times 2 \times 2$ m sealed plastic tent made of LDPE inside a cold storage room, at 0–1°C and 2–6% O_2 (mostly at 3%) and 3–5% CO_2 (mostly at 5%) atmosphere within tent. Ethylene scrubber was controlled at a concentration below 0.1 ppm inside the tent but the temperature inside the tent was about 0.7°C higher than the temperature in the rest of the room as there was no ventilation system.

2.2.10 Hypobaric/Hyperbaric Storage

Low-pressure or hypobaric storage is based on reducing pressure by using a vacuum pump to evacuate air from the store. This technique has been used for several decades to lower partial pressure of O_2 in fruit and vegetable stores. The vacuum pump continually introduces fresh air from the outside atmosphere and removes gases given out by the crop, thus constantly changing the store atmosphere. Air inlet and evacuation from the store should be balanced in order to achieve the required low pressure within the store. The O_2 level in a hypobaric store can be very accurately and simply controlled by measuring the pressure inside the store with a vacuum gauge. Stores should be sturdily designed and constructed of thick steel plate, normally with a curved interior to withstand low pressures without imploding. Another advantage of hypobaric storage is that it constantly removes C_2H_4 from the store to prevent C_2H_4 accumulating to a detrimental level in storage room. However, humidity should be controlled and adjusted at a high level in hypobaric storage in order to prevent excessive moisture loss from fruits or vegetables, as lower atmospheric pressure can lower the boiling point of water and rapidly evaporate water from the fruits or vegetables. Therefore the moisture in the air being introduced into the store should be close to saturation (100% relative humidity [RH]) to prevent serious dehydration of the crop.

Many researchers have investigated the effects of hypobaric storage on fruits and vegetables. Salunkhe and Wu (1975) showed that hypobaric storage combined with refrigeration significantly extended the storage life of a wide range of crops, but Hughes et al. (1981) stated that hypobaric conditions could not extend storage life of fruits and vegetables. They reported that the storage life of capsicums stored at hypobaric conditions combined with refrigeration (8.8°C in 152, 76, or 38 mm Hg) was not significantly different from those stored in air under the same conditions. They also found that hypobaric-stored capsicums had a significantly higher weight loss during storage than those stored in air. Burg (2004) implemented a system of hypobaric storage that controlled water loss from roses stored at 2°C and a reduced pressure of 3.33×10^3 Nm^2 for 21 days without humidifying the inlet air. In this system, the evacuation rate of air from the storage chamber reduced to a level so that the water evaporated from fruits and vegetables through transpiration and respiration exceeded the amount of water required to saturate the incoming air. The results showed that the vase life of treated roses was not significantly different from that of freshly harvested roses.

It was observed that pretreatment of Changhowon and Yumyung peaches stored in 6% O_2 + 18% CO_2 in hypobaric conditions (pressure ranging from 0 to 294.2 kPa) improved the retention of firmness in both cultivars, but did not affect any other quality parameter during subsequent storage in air at 7 or 10°C for 3 weeks (Lee et al., 2009). Studies have indicated that hypobaric storage of fruits and vegetables has considerable influence on the development of physiological disorders. It was demonstrated by Wang and Dilley (2000) that Granny Smith, Mutsu, Law Rome, Golden Delicious, and Red Delicious apples in hypobaric storage of 0.05 atm at 1°C for up to 8 months within 1 month of harvest prevented scald from developing, but after a 3-month delay, scald development was similar to that of fruits stored continuously at normal pressures. They also found that scald did not develop on any cultivars in hypobaric storage, while it developed on all cultivars except Golden Delicious stored at normal pressures. They attributed this to elimination of a scald-related volatile substance through hypobaric ventilation, which accumulates and partitions into the epicuticular wax of fruits stored in normal air pressure.

Hyperbaric storage is a technique used to control and inhibit microorganism growths and involves exposure for only brief periods. This technique was used originally in the medical and related industries but some researchers have studied exposing food products such as fresh fruits and vegetables to high-pressure storage (up to 9000 atm). Robitaille and Badenhop (1981) used a completely autonomous hyperbaric storage with CO_2 removal and automatic O_2 replenishment for the treatment of mushrooms. They reported that hyperbaric storage significantly reduced moisture loss and cap browning but did not affect mushroom respiration rate compared with storage at normal pressure. They also found that pressurization and subsequently gradual depressurization over 6 h did not damage the mushrooms. Romanazzi et al. (2008) studied hyperbaric (in pressures of 1.5 atm) storage of Ferrovia sweet cherries for 4 h and Italia table grapes for 24 h and compared them with storage of the fruits at normal atmospheric pressure. They stored cherries at $0 \pm 1°C$ for 14 days, followed by 7 days at $20 \pm 1°C$, and grapes at $20 \pm 1°C$ for 3 days and observed that the incidence of gray mold, brown rot, and blue mold in the cherries was reduced in hyperbaric storage compared with those stored at normal pressure. They also found that hyperbaric storage significantly reduced lesion diameter and percentage of *Botrytis cinerea* in grapes. They attributed decay reductions to induced resistance.

2.3 Control of Operational Parameters

2.3.1 Temperature Control

Refrigeration is the main and most effective way of preserving fruits and vegetables in storage or during long-distance transport, and modified atmosphere packaging and controlled atmosphere are considered supplements to enhance the effect of refrigeration. CA storage is only successful when applied at low temperatures. Therefore refrigeration units are integral components of CA stores. The main parts of a simple refrigeration unit are evaporator, compressor, condenser and expansion valve, and refrigerant that circulates in these parts. The common refrigerants are ammonia or chlorofluorocarbons R-12 and R-22 (the R-number denotes an industry standard specification), but because of the harmful effects of R-12 and R-22 on depletion of the ozone layer, a new generation of refrigerants has been introduced, for example, R410A (which is a 50:50 blend of R-32 and R-125), which is used as a substitute for R-22, with potentially less detrimental effects on the environment.

The evaporator is the part of the system that is placed inside the store and the liquid refrigerant at low temperature and low pressure is circulated and vaporized in evaporator pipes to absorb heat. The store air is passed over the coiled pipes containing the refrigerant by using fan to cool the air quickly and distribute it evenly throughout the store. The formed vapor moves through the compressor via pipes and is compressed into a hot, high-pressure vapor. Subsequently, the high-pressure gas is pumped through a condenser and is cooled and changed to high-pressure liquid. An expansion controls the flow of liquid refrigerant and reduces its pressure in order to vaporize and reduce the temperature of the refrigerant. Finally the refrigeration cycle completes by passing a cooled mixture of vapor and liquid refrigerant into the evaporator.

2.3.2 Humidity Control

High RH is required to maintain quality of most fruits and vegetables in store. It was recommended that RH must be closer to saturation to prevent moisture condensation on the fruits or vegetables. If the store air temperature is higher than the refrigerant temperature, water will condense on the evaporator, and when the refrigerant temperature is below the freezing point of water, then moisture will freeze on the cooling coils of the evaporator and reduce the efficiency of the cooling system. The stored crop loses moisture by vapor transpiration when moisture is removed from the store air. If the refrigerant temperature is kept close to the store air temperature, it will reduce crop desiccation. Also the crop temperature should be maintained by balancing the refrigerant temperature with the removal of the respiratory heat from the crop, heat generated by fans, and temperature leakage through the store insulation and doors. Hellickson et al. (1995) compared evaporator coil refrigerant temperature, room humidity, cool-down, and mass loss rates in commercial 1200-bin apple storage rooms. They found that in stores with computer-controlled evaporator coil temperatures, a shorter time is needed to achieve the desired humidity levels than in stores with dictating evaporator coil refrigerant temperatures by cooling demand. Also the mass loss rate of apples stored in rooms with controlled refrigerant temperature at approximately 1°C during the cool-down period was lower than in rooms with dictated cooling load by refrigerant temperature. Different humidifying devices such as spinning-disc humidifiers are used to compensate the moisture in the air that is condensed on the cooling coils of refrigeration units.

Dijkink et al. (2004) described a hollow-fiber membrane contactor system that could maintain RH very precisely in 500 L containers at 90.5 ± 0.1% RH through adequate transfer of water vapor between the air in the storage room and a liquid desiccant. The fiber membrane was made of polyetherimide, which was coated with a thin nonporous silicone layer on the inside. They used aqueous dilute glycerol solution as a desiccant, which was pumped through the hollow fibers at a low flow rate.

Secondary cooling is a technique for retaining high humidity within the store. In this system cooling coils do not have direct contact with the store air such as the "jacketed store" and refrigeration pipes cool the air between the space of metal inner wall and the outer insulated wall. Thus the temperature of cooling pipes is maintained at a low level without causing crop desiccation, and the whole wall of the store acts as a cooling surface.

The other method of secondary cooling is ice-bank cooling. In this method, the refrigerant pipes are immersed in a tank of water so that the water is frozen and used to cool the water; the cool water, after converting to a fine mist, is used to cool and humidify the store air (Neale et al., 1981). RH should be maintained at about 70% when crops such as onions are stored under CA conditions by creating a large differential between air temperature and the refrigerant of about 9–10°C for forced air circulation by fan and 11–12°C for natural air circulation.

2.3.3 Gas Control Equipment

The atmosphere should be controlled in CA storage to achieve target gas concentrations. O_2 and CO_2 concentrations in CA storerooms can be adjusted independently from one another. The composition of atmosphere in the storage room should be maintained at a stable state to achieve successful CA storage. However, constantly changing conditions of CA storage rooms make it difficult to achieve stable composition of atmosphere. Some parameters such as CO_2 and O_2 regulating equipment, cyclic operation of the refrigeration system, changes in the weather, and the physiological response of the stored horticultural produce have influence control of the storage atmosphere. Thus it is necessary to measure O_2 and CO_2 levels at regular time intervals and regulate the concentration if the measured concentrations deviate from the set points.

Automated control systems are usually used in modern and large CA for control of CA conditions, but manual measurements and controls are used in conventional CA to perform just one measurement per day to ensure optimum quality and efficiency (Raghavan et al., 2005).

Different types of controller devices are used to operate equipment such as scrubbers, such as on/off switches, and proportional (P), proportional-integrated (PI), or proportional-integral derivative (PID), and personal computer (PC)-based controllers. PID controllers are more advanced systems, which are more intelligent and most often installed in CA operations that could act as self-learning or self-tuning systems because they can adjust controller parameters automatically.

It is possible to employ online control of O_2 and CO_2 levels in CA storage rooms by PC-based systems. PC systems usually comprise different parts including a computer, a data acquisition system, communication ports, switching devices, and control software. Raghavan et al. (2005) implied that in addition to controlling storage conditions with PC systems, it is possible to program PC systems to compute online parameters to automatically log information for later retrieval and analysis or manage interactions between process variables. Several commercially dedicated systems are interfaced with a PC to allow the operator to enter the required control parameters and to monitor the process, even in a remote mode.

2.3.3.1 Oxygen (O_2) Control

Controlling O_2 is most critical in CA storage, especially in ULO storage. O_2 levels can be determined with chemical analyzers such as the Fyrite analyzer or Orsat analyzer, which are based on the reaction of O_2 with pyrogallol and of CO_2 with alkaline solutions. Concentrations of O_2 and CO_2 are determined by measuring volume changes of a gas sample taken from the storage room. The Fyrite analyzer is an inexpensive and portable system but has insufficient accuracy for O_2 levels lower than 2 kPa. However, the Orsat analyzer is usually installed in the middle of a storage room and a permanent tubing system takes gas samples directly from the room by aspirating with a pump. The Orsat analyzer has lower capital cost and acceptable accuracy at higher O_2 levels, but sampling requires a skilled operator and considerable time. Furthermore, it is not applicable in automated systems. It was proved that paramagnetic sensor-based O_2 analyzers were reliable, accurate, and exhibit longevity. These analyzers measure O_2 via the highly paramagnetic property of O_2. Paramagnetic property is highly specific for O_2 but other common gases lack this property. Electrochemical cells are alternative instruments for O_2 measurement. Electrochemical cells have been greatly improved during recent years and they match the accuracy and resolution of parametric sensors.

2.3.3.2 Carbon Dioxide (CO_2)

As mentioned earlier, the Fyrite or Orsat methods determine CO_2 levels in CA based on CO_2 absorption by alkaline solutions. However, these methods have some drawbacks, such as unsuitability for automatic control, constricted accuracy, and long duration. Consequently, an infrared CO_2 sensor is exclusively used for measurement of CO_2 in CA rooms. The system measures infrared absorbance at specific wavelengths for CO_2 (4260 ± 20 nm or at 15,000 nm) and then attributes it to CO_2 concentration in CA rooms. It was recommended that regularly monitoring O_2 and CO_2 levels using a fixed measuring system is essential for ensuring good storage practice.

2.3.3.3 Ethylene (C_2H_4)

It is not common to measure C_2H_4 in CA storage rooms, since low concentrations of C_2H_4 make measuring difficult. However, C_2H_4 exerts its effects on fruits at low concentrations, and it is necessary to control C_2H_4 levels in CA. A practiced method for indicating C_2H_4 is disposable tubes filled with chemicals that change color, indicating C_2H_4 levels. New C_2H_4 analyzers or C_2H_4 detectors are equipped with electrochemical sensors and could measure concentration ranges of 0–100 ppm with a minimum resolution of 0.2 ppm. Gas chromatography is the most accurate method for C_2H_4 measurement, but it is a costly method and needs well-trained personnel (B3-P40).

2.4 Pretreatment of Fruits and Vegetables for CA Storage

It was proved that good practice CA technology to preserve the fresh fruit and vegetable industry requires combining with other technologies such as special treatments of the crop before it is put into store. Nevertheless, it is advisable to place fruits and vegetables in store as quickly as possible after harvest in most cases, but it has been shown that some pretreatments before CA can be beneficial to maintaining quality and improving stored commodities.

There is a cork layer over the surface of root crops such as potatoes, sweet potatoes, and yams, which protects crops against microorganism infections and excessive water loss. However, the layer may be damaged during harvesting and handling operations. It was shown that exposing the crops to high temperature and humidity for a few days after they have been loaded into the store could induce curing of the damaged tissue and reduce postharvest losses in all types of storage. Curing is also applied to citrus fruits and effectively heals wounds and reduces disease levels. Drying is high-temperature treatment, which is carried out to aid preservation of bulb onions and garlic by drying their outer layers to reduce microorganism infection and water loss. Prestorage treatment with high temperature is less well established for other crops and is still at an experimental stage. Klein and Lurie (1992) kept Granny Smith apples at 46°C for 12 h, 42°C for 24 h, or 38°C for 72 or 96 h before storage at 0°C for 8 months in 2–3% O_2 + 5% CO_2. They found that prestorage heat treatment of apples increased firmness of fruits at the end of storage, decreased incidence of superficial scald on fruits, and increased the soluble solid:acid ratio when compared to untreated fruits.

Prestorage by immersing fruit in hot water or brushing with hot water is also used to control microorganism infection of fruits before storage. Thompson (2003) found that the optimum recommended conditions for disease control vary between crop and disease organism. For example, Kim et al. (2007) found that hot water treatments of mango at 46°C for 75 min combined with storage for 2 weeks at 10°C in either 3% O_2 + 97% N_2 or 3% O_2 + 10% CO_2 effectively inhibited visible appearance of the fungal disease anthracnose (*Colletotrichum gloeosporioides*). Also, Porat et al. (2004) demonstrated that hot water brushing of grapefruit at 56°C for 20 s reduced decay development during storage. It was proved that exposure of fruits to temperatures slightly higher than those used in storage has beneficial effects on retaining their quality characteristics. Van der Merwe et al. (2003) reported that pretreatment of Granny Smith apples with 0.5% O_2 for 10 days at 1°C before CA storage at −0.5°C significantly inhibited the development of superficial scald for fruits picked at preoptimum maturity.

N-Dimethylaminosuccinamic acid is a plant growth regulator which is also known as DPA, daminozide, Alar, B-Nine, or B995. It was shown that DPA retards tissue senescence and cell elongation. In recent years several countries have prohibited its application because of suggestions that it might be carcinogenic. Knee and Looney (1990) compared preharvest and postharvest application of daminozide to Cox's Orange Pippin apples and found that immersion of fruits in a solution containing 4.25 g L^{-1} for 5 min delayed the rise in C_2H_4 production at 15°C by about 2 days, but orchard application of 0.85 g L^{-1} resulted in delays of about 3 days. They also found that preharvest and postharvest application of daminozide reduced the maximum rate of C_2H_4 production by about 30% and it was shown that daminozide-treated apples had less sensitivity to the application of C_2H_4 than untreated fruit. Daminozide (1000 mg L^{-1}) was sprayed on Starking Delicious apple trees in midsummer and after harvesting and stored in two different CA storage facilities: a low-C_2H_4 CA room, equipped with a continuous C_2H_4 removal system, with C_2H_4 concentration ranging from 4 to 15 $\mu L \ L^{-1}$, and a high-C_2H_4 CA room, without any C_2H_4 removing system with C_2H_4 concentration more than 100 $\mu L \ L^{-1}$ (Graell and Recasens, 1992). Graell and Recasens (1992) found that daminozide-sprayed and earlier-harvested fruits were firmer and had more acid production after 8 months' storage at 0–1°C in 3% O_2 + 4% CO_2 with scrubbed C_2H_4 than unsprayed fruits stored in high-C_2H_4 (4–15 μL L^{-1}) CA.

1-MCP is well known as a postharvest C_2H_4 inhibitor. There has been much research dealing with 1-MCP application in the postharvest treatment of various fruits, vegetables, and flowers but mainly 1-MCP is used as a fumigant for a short period directly after harvest of different cultivars of apples to preserve their quality and reduce losses during subsequent storage. 1-MCP was applied in aqueous dip by Warren et al. (2009) and sealed in plastic bags by De Reuck et al. (2009) for treatment of bananas or litchis. SmartFresh[SM] and EthylBloc[TM] are available commercial forms of 1-MCP, which could be used in the store on completion of loading, in gastight tents or in containers prior to loading into the store, and in gastight rooms. 1-MCP is added to gastight curtains that are used temporarily to partition part of a store, with a zippered access door to other parts of the store. Gastight curtains can be used to fumigate a relatively small amount of fruits or vegetables. Also there are gastight pallet covers available for fumigation.

1-MCP treatment was applied by De Wild (2001) as an alternative to short-term CA storage. Controversially, Rizzolo et al. (2005) implied that 1-MCP was not a substitute for CA storage but can reinforce the CA effects. It was observed that a combination of 1-MCP with CA storage had greatest effects on apples (Johnson, 2008). Although 1-MCP is known as a C_2H_4 inhibitor, some research has demonstrated that in certain circumstances 1-MCP can stimulate C_2H_4 production (McCollum and Maul, 2007). Beyond several reported positive effects of 1-MCP treatment, Ella et al. (2003) found that the use of too low concentrations of 1-MCP reduced C_2H_4 autoinhibition and led to a certain degree of senescence acceleration in leafy vegetables. Fabi et al. (2007) also implied that in certain circumstances 1-MCP treatment was related to decreased quality of fruit and increased rotting (Jiang et al., 2010; Baldwin et al., 1995). Jiang et al. (2010) attributed the decreased disease resistance in strawberries treated with 1-MCP to comparatively low levels of phenolics. It was reported that 1-MCP inhibited the activities of aminocyclopropane-1-carboxylic acid (ACC) and delayed the peaks in the ACC concentration, ACC synthase activity, gene expression of these enzymes, and of C_2H_4 receptors at the transcript level (Gang et al., 2009). Also, the beneficial effect of 1-MCP was attributed to its ability to increase the antioxidant potential and delay fruit ripening and senescence (Fu et al., 2007). Fu et al. (2007) found that 1-MCP treatment of pears significantly retarded the activities of pectin methylesterase and polygalacturonase, the activities of the antioxidant enzyme

(a) (b)

Figure 2.7 Effect of controlled atmosphere (CA) on apple decay. (a) Refrigerated storage; (b) CA+ refrigerated storage.

catalase, superoxide dismutase, and peroxidase during ripening of pears.

2.5 Effects of CA on Quality of Fruits and Vegetables

2.5.1 Physiological Disorders and Disease

There are many disorders such as physiological disorders, physiological diseases, or physiological injury in fresh produce during storage, which are not primarily associated with infection by microorganisms. Research has shown that CA storage has positive, negative, and no effect on physiological disorders of stored fresh fruits and vegetables (Fig. 2.7). Not only the concentration of CO_2 and O_2 and duration of exposure have great influence on incidence and extent of storage disorders, but also other factors such as growth condition, cultivar, harvest maturity, storage temperature, and humidity have significant influence on storage disorders. Biochemical and anatomical differences between cultivar and individual fruits, including the size of intercellular spaces and rate of gas diffusion through the skin and other cells, have resulted in variation of their susceptibility to injury. Oxidation of phenolic compounds causes external injuries to the skin or internal disorders, and cavities in the tissue usually become visible as brown spots. This phenomenon is the last step in a reaction chain that starts by impairment of the viability of the cell membrane via shortage of energy, fermentation metabolites, or possibly excess of free radicals (Streif and Saquet, 2003).

2.5.2 Flavor and Off-Flavor

The flavor of fruits and vegetables is affected by CA storage both positively and negatively. Reichel (1974) concluded that CA storage of apples retained flavor longer than those stored in air. Studies showed that in most fruits and vegetables, CA storage maintains better flavor than storage in air (Zhao and Murata, 1988). It was reported that the stage of ripeness of fruit at the beginning of storage has a major effect on its flavor, acidity, sweetness, and texture (Wang, 1990), and consequently it is difficult to exactly separate the effects of CA storage, maturity, and ripening on flavor. Storage of apricots in 1.5% CO_2 + 1.5% O_2 or 5% CO_2 + 2% O_2 after 6 weeks at –0.5°C had an inferior flavor compared with those stored in air (Truter et al., 1994). Urban (1995) studied stored Golden Delicious, Idared, and Gloster apples in 15–16% O_2 + 5–6% CO_2 at 2°C, 95% RH for 100 or 200 days, which were then moved to 5, 10, or 15°C (all at approximately 60% RH) for 16 days to study shelf life and flavor changes. He reported that flavor improvement occurred only in fruits that were removed from CA storage after 100 days; however, in apples that were removed from CA storage after 200 days a decline in flavor was observed during subsequent storage at 5, 10, or 15°C.

Some studies showed that flavor developments in grapes are improved during CA storage. It was reported that grapes exposed to100% CO_2 for 20 h had 114 volatile compounds, but grapes stored in air had 60 volatile compounds. It was proved that early harvesting and CA storage lead to the best flavor maintenance during prolonged storage. It was also reported that the type of storage can interact with cultivars for flavor development (Kluge and Meier, 1979). Bertolini et al. (1991) showed that storage of Abbe Fetel pears at –0.5°C in 0.5% O_2 led to losses in aroma and flavor. They attributed this to raising the O_2 level to 1%. Ortiz et al. (2009) observed that sensory acceptance of peaches stored in air at 2°C was lower than those stored in 3% O_2 + 10% CO_2 for up to 15 days when they were ripened after storage.

Fermentation occurring during storage has considerable effects on the flavor of fruits and vegetables. A rise in ethanol and acetaldehyde production induces off-flavor development. For example, Mateos et al. (1993) attributed off-flavor developing in intact lettuce heads exposed to 20% CO_2 to concentrations of ethanol and acetaldehyde. It was observed that storage of avocados at 2 or 5°C in 5% CO_2 + 5% O_2 or 15% CO_2 + 2% O_2 for 30 days had resulted in lower ethanol and acetaldehyde production in fruits stored in CA than the fruits in air (Corrales-Garcia, 1997). Also, storage of Pajaro strawberries in air or air with 10, 20, or 30% CO_2 for 5 days at 5°C, followed by an additional 4 days in air at the same temperature, led to low ethanol and acetaldehyde accumulation and off-flavor development at transfer from CA, but not after the following storage in air (Colelli and Martelli, 1995). Pariasca et al. (2001) implied that storage of snow pea pods in either 2.5% O_2 + 5% CO_2 or 10%

$CO_2 + 5\%$ O_2 led to the development of slight off-flavors, but after ventilation this effect was partially alleviated.

It was reported that LO levels result in fermentation and the production of off-flavors. Ke et al. (1991) demonstrated that storage of peaches of the cultivar Fairtime in air or in 0.25 or 0.02% O_2 at 0 or 5°C for up to 40 days affected ethanol and acetaldehyde accumulation in 0.02% O_2 at 0°C or 5°C or in 0.25% O_2 at 5°C. They also reported that the fruits stored in air or 0.25% O_2 at 0°C for up to 40 days and those kept in 0.25 or 0.02% O_2 at 5°C, 0.02% O_2 at 0°C or in air for up to 14 days had good to excellent taste, but the flavor of the fruits stored at 5°C for 29 days was unacceptable. Storage of Delicious apples in 0.05% $O_2 + 0.2\%$ CO_2 at 1°C for 30 days led to high concentrations of ethanol, acetaldehyde, and various esters, including ethyl butyrate, ethyl 2-methyl butyrate, ethyl hexanoate, ethyl propanoate, ethyl heptanoate, and ethyl octanoate (Mattheis et al., 1991). Mattheis et al. (1991) reported that emission of these compounds increases simultaneously with a decrease in the amounts of other esters, which required the same carboxylic acid group for synthesis.

2.5.3 Acidity

The flavor and acceptability of fruits and vegetables are obviously affected by their acid levels. Knee and Sharples (1979) reported 50% fall of acidity during storage of apples, which demonstrated a good correlation between fruit acidity and sensory evaluation. It was found that storage of pears in CA led to significantly higher acid levels in comparison with storage in air (Meheriuk, 1989) and that CA storage significantly reduced the loss of acidity in apples (Girard and Lau, 1995). Also it was observed that Valencia oranges lost less acid during storage at 3.5°C in 5% $CO_2 + 3\%$ O_2 than at 0°C in air. Changes in acidity in relation to CA storage and modified atmosphere packaging were confirmed by Batu and Thompson (1995) in tomatoes.

2.5.4 Ethylene Production

Ethylene is a colorless and flammable gas with anaesthetic and asphyxiate properties and has a sweetish odor and taste. As its flammable limits in air are 3.1–32%, it is necessary to take care when the gas is used for fruit ripening to ensure that levels in the atmosphere do not reach 3.1%. All electrical fittings must be of a "spark-free" type and warning notices relating to smoking and fire hazards must be displayed around the rooms.

2.5.5 Respiration Rate

Generally, respiration rate of fruits and vegetables during CA storage is lower than storage in air. It was reported that the enzyme succinate dehydrogenase in the tricarboxylic acid cycle (part of the respiratory pathway) inhibited by CO_2 (Knee, 1973). Also it was suggested by McGlasson and Wills (1972) that LO limited the operation of the Krebs cycle between pyruvate and citrate and 2-oxoglutarate and succinate, but no similar effect of high CO_2 in bananas was found. It was proved that the crop and its stage of development greatly influenced variation of respiration rate when exposed to high CO_2 (Kubo et al., 1989).

The respiration rate of apples and melons fell to about half the initial level when they were stored in 60% CO_2 + 20% O_2 + 20% N_2. Also, Kubo et al. (1989) indicated that ripening tomatoes and bananas showed a reduction in respiration in response to high CO_2, but they showed little response when tested before the climacteric.

It was observed that temperature influenced the effect of reduced O_2 and increased CO_2 on respiration rate. Kubo et al. (1989) indicated that the effects of high CO_2 on respiration rate depended on the crop and its stage of development. Fidler et al. (1973) indicated that the relationship between O_2 and CO_2 levels and respiration was not a simple one. They studied variation of respiration between cultivars, as in the comparison between Golden Delicious and Cox's Orange Pippin apples, where the respiration rate was suppressed more in the former than in the latter in CA storage (Table 2.3).

The respiration rate of nonclimacteric fruits and vegetables is also affected by CA storage. It was reported that exposure of *Citrus natsudaidai*, lemons, potatoes, sweet potatoes, or cabbage to high CO_2 produced little or no effect but it reduced the respiration rate in broccoli. Controversially the respiration rate of lettuce, aubergine, and cucumber was stimulated with high CO_2. Pal and Buescher (1993) found that the respiration rate of ripening bananas, pink tomatoes, and pickling cucumbers reduced when they were exposed to short term 20–30% CO_2, and only at 30% CO_2 did respiration rate increase in potatoes and carrots. Also the treatment with 20–30% CO_2 had no effect on the respiration rate in guavas, oranges, and onions. Izumi et al. (1996) reported that the respiration rate of freshly cut carrots stored in 10% CO_2 + 0.5% O_2 reduced by about 55% at 0°C, by about 65% at 5°C, and 75% at 10°C.

2.5.6 Volatile Compounds

Volatile compounds are produced by fruits and vegetables and give their flavor and aroma character. It was shown that CA storage affects volatile compounds. Willaert et al. (1983) isolated 24 volatile compounds from Golden Delicious apples, but CA storage decreased relative amounts of 18 aroma components. Hatfield and Patterson (1974) implied that the CA storage of

Table 2.3 Rates of Respiration of Some Cultivars of Apples Stored in Different CA Conditions (Fidler et al., 1973)

Cultivar	°C	Storage Conditions CO$_2$ (%)	O$_2$ (%)	Respiration Rate I ton^{-1} day^{-1} O$_2$	CO$_2$
Bramley's Seedling	3.5	8–10	11–13	40	40–45
Cox's Orange Pippin	3.5	5	16	57	62
Cox's Orange Pippin	3.5	5	3	40	42
Cox's Orange Pippin	3.5	<1	2.5	55	80
Golden Delicious	3.5	5	3	20	20
Delicious	0	5	3	—	18
Jonathan	3.5	7	13	38	33
McIntosh	3.5	5	3	—	35

apples in 2% O$_2$ + 98% N$_2$ or 2% O$_2$ + 5% CO$_2$ + 93% N$_2$ decreased production of organic volatile compounds during the storage period, and after removal of fruits from storage, they did not synthesize normal amounts of esters during ripening. Hansen et al. (1992) found that prolonged CA storage in LO reduced volatile ester production in Jonagold apples. Large differences were seen in the production of esters after removing from storage. It was shown that a series of esters with the alcohol 2-methylbut-2-en-1-ol was produced in negative correlation to O$_2$ concentration. Storage of McIntosh and Cortland apples in 100% O$_2$ at 3.3°C for 4 weeks did not enhance production of aroma volatiles compared with those stored in air at the same temperature. Girard and Lau (1995) stored Jonagold apples at 0°C in air or in 1.5% O$_2$ + 1.5% CO$_2$ for 6 months and found that CA storage decreased production of esters, alcohols, and hydrocarbons by 50%. The organic volatile production of the apples was measured over a 10-day period at 20°C after removal from the cold store. Miszczak and Szymczak (2000) stored Gala Must apples in CA storage and

Table 2.4 Effects of CA Storage and Time on the Flavor of Apricots, Which Were Assessed by a Taste Panel Months After Being 3 Canned, Where a Score of 5 or More Was Acceptable (Truter et al., 1994).

Storage Period (weeks)	CO_2 Concentration (%)	O_2 Concentration (%)	Flavor Score	
			Cultivar Peeka	Cultivar Bulida
0	—	—	4.6	7.5
4	1.5	1.5	6.3	6.3
5	1.5	1.5	5.0	5.0
6	1.5	1.5	1.3	1.3
4	5.0	2.0	5.0	6.3
5	5.0	2.0	5.4	5.5
6	5.0	2.0	5.4	2.9
4	0	21	5.8	6.7
5	0	21	5.4	4.2
6	0	21	4.6	2.1

found a slight reduction in volatile production compared with fruit stored in air. They also found similar results from sensory evaluation of aroma intensity after a further 1 week in air. Truter et al. (1994) reported storage of apricots that at −0.5°C in 1.5% CO_2 + 1.5% O_2 or 5% CO_2 + 2% O_2 for 6 weeks resulted in inferior flavor compared with those stored in air (Table 2.4). Harb et al. (2008) stored Golden Delicious apples in 3% CO_2 + 21% O_2, 3% CO_2 + 3% O_2, 3% CO_2 + 1% O_2, 1% CO_2 + 1% O_2, and 1% CO_2 + 21% O_2 and found that the treatment suppressed volatile production, but fruits stored in 1% CO_2 + 3% O_2 had volatile production. Harb et al. (2008) stored apples in ULO storage and found that the biosynthesis of volatiles was greatly reduced, especially after an extended storage period. Biosynthesis of the corresponding volatiles was stimulated by treating fruits with volatile precursors (alcohols and aldehydes), mainly esters; however, this effect was transitory with ULO-stored fruit. Brackmann et al. (1993) found that the largest reduction in aroma production was in ULO at 1% O_2 + 3% CO_2.

Table 2.5 Effects of CA Storage on Ascorbic Acid of Smooth Cayenne Pineapples Stored at 8°C for 3 Weeks and Then 5 Days at 20°C (Haruenkit and Thompson, 1996)

Gas Composition (%)			Ascorbic Acid (mg 100 mL^{-1})
O_2	CO_2	N_2	
1.3	0	98.7	7.14
2.2	0	97.8	8.44
5.4	0	94.6	0.76
1.4	11.2	87.4	9.16
2.3	11.2	86.5	7.94
20.8	0	79.2	0.63
LSD ($P = 0.05$)			5.28

Also, Meheriuk (1989) found that storage of pears in CA did not have a deleterious effect on fruit flavor compared with those stored in air and were generally considered better by a taste panel.

2.5.7 Phytochemical Compounds and Color

It was shown that CA storage has both positive and negative effects on the synthesis and retention of chemicals in fruits and vegetables that are required for human nutrition, other than proteins and carbohydrates, sometimes called phytochemicals.

Loss of ascorbic acid was accelerated in CA storage compared with storage in air. Singh et al. (1993) reported that as the CO_2 concentration in the storage atmosphere increased, ascorbic acid content of the tomato cultivars Punjab Chuhara and Punjab Kesri decreased. In studies of tomatoes by Vidigal et al. (1979), it was observed that the ascorbic acid levels increased during CA storage at 10°C. Haruenkit and Thompson (1996) implied that CA storage of pineapples in O_2 levels below 5.4% maintained ascorbic acid levels but generally had little effect on total soluble solids (Table 2.5).

Agar et al. (1994) stored Elvira strawberry and Thornfree blackberry fruits at 0–1°C in up to 20% CO_2 for strawberries and 30% CO_2 for blackberries, combined with either 1–3% or more than 14% O_2. They found that in the higher CO_2 atmosphere, loss of ascorbic acid was highest and more rapid degradation after 20 days' storage was observed in the low-level O_2 treatments. During simulated shelf life in ambient conditions following storage, degradation of ascorbic acid was even more pronounced.

Ito et al. (1974) stored Satsuma in a low O_2–high CO_2 atmosphere at 1–4°C. They found that the ascorbic acid contents gradually declined in the flesh and peel, but the dehydroascorbic acid content increased. They also indicated that storage at high O_2 reduced changes. Trierweiler et al. (2004) stored Bohnapfel apples in air or 3% CO_2 + 1% O_2 for 7 months and found that the ascorbic acid content was reduced during storage but total antioxidant capacity remained constant. Pariasca et al. (2001) stored peas in film bags at 5°C, giving an equilibrium atmosphere of 5% O_2 + 5% CO_2, and found that ascorbic acid in film bags was maintained better than those stored unwrapped.

The chlorophyll content of Cox's Orange Pippin apples stored in CA remained the same or only reduced slightly over a 6-month storage period (Knee and Sharples, 1979). Pariasca et al. (2001) stored peas at 5°C, giving an equilibrium atmosphere of 5% O_2 + 5% CO_2; they demonstrated that film bags retained chlorophyll better than those stored unwrapped. Bangerth (1977) stored parsley in hypobaric storage at 2–3°C and found an improvement in the retention of chlorophyll.

Four cultivars of *Amelanchier alnifolia* were stored at 0.5°C for 56 days in various CAs (Rogiers and Knowles, 2000) and it was found that 5% CO_2 + 21% O_2 or 5% CO_2 + 10% O_2 were most effective at declining losses in fruit anthocyanins. It was reported that CA storage had little or no effect on phenolic content. Holcroft and Kader (1999) reported that strawberries stored under LO 2 kPa displayed a better color and high anthocyanin concentration and organic acids content than those stored in air. Fruits became darker red and accumulated anthocyanin, although O_2 was not as effective at high CO_2 levels in decreasing decay.

Zheng et al. (2003) stored blueberries at 5°C in 60–100% O_2 for 35 days and found that total phenolics increased higher than those stored in air or 40% O_2. Romero et al. (2008) indicated that anthocyanin levels in grapes were lower after storage at 0°C for those that had been pretreated for 3 days in 20% CO_2 + 20% O_2 compared with those that had not been pretreated.

It was observed that in CA conditions the synthesis of carotenoids, such as lycopene in tomatoes and β-carotene in mangoes, was delayed due to delayed ripening of fruits. However, upon transfer of the fruits to air at ripening temperatures (15–25°C), the synthesis of these pigments resumes. It was also observed by Weichmann (1986) that the retention of carotene in carrots was enhanced in low-oxygen atmospheres and carotene reduced in air at 5 kPa CO_2, while de novo synthesis of carotene started in air at 7.5 kPa CO_2 or higher. Weichmann (1986) found that the carotene content of leeks after storage in 1 kPa O_2, 10 kPa CO_2 was higher than after storage in air. It was observed that peach slices stored in air at 12 kPa CO_2 resulted in lower content of β-carotene and β-cryptoxanthin (retinol equivalent) compared with slices kept in air at 2 kPa O_2 or 2 kPa O_2, 12 kPa CO_2 for 8 days at 5°C. A slightly lower retinol equivalent was also observed in persimmon slices after 8 days' storage at 5°C in 2 kPa O_2 or air at 12 kPa CO_2, while storage of slices under 2 kPa O_2, 12 kPa CO_2 did not have significant effects on loss of these compounds. Jeffery et al. (1984) indicated that storage of tomatoes in 6% CO_2 + 6% O_2 suppressed lycopene synthesis.

2.5.8 Chilling Injury

Some research has proved that development of chilling injury symptoms in stored commodities was affected by CA storage. Sive and Resnizky (1979) observed that storage of plums in air at 0°C for 3–4 weeks led to the development of flesh browning and flesh breakdown, while storage of fruits at 0°C in 2–8% CO_2 + 3% O_2 extended their storage life for 2–3 months, followed by 7 days in air at 0°C and a shelf life of 5 days at 20°C, without showing any symptoms. Also, storage of peach cultivar J.H. Hale at 1°C resulted in flesh discoloration and the development of a soft texture after 37days, while storage of fruits in atmospheres containing 20% CO_2 led to only moderate levels of damage, even after 42 days. Conversely, a higher incidence of chilling injury was reported by Visai et al. (1994) for Passe Crassane pears stored at 2°C in 5% CO_2 + 2% O_2 in the form of internal browning. They attributed this effect to induced production of free radicals in the fruit during storage in CA.

3   Future Trends

CA technology has been undergoing continuous development and refinement during last 50–60 years, leading to continuing construction of CA facilities worldwide. The construction techniques are major refinements that have improved air tightness of the rooms, O_2 and CO_2 scrubbing technology, sensing technology and computerization, and increased knowledge of produce-specific requirements.

Although the large body of laboratory-based research literature demonstrates CA efficacy for storage of a wide array of fruits and vegetables, most commercial CA storage is still used primarily for extending the storage period of apples since slow or nonexistent adoption in the storage of other fruits and vegetables provides insufficient or unreliable financial returns to justify the cost of CA. Commercial experience and empirical research, primarily with apple and pear cultivars, has shown that the timing and degree of CA conditions should be carefully monitored on a cultivar-by-cultivar basis. Thus recommendations for delaying CA or RCA depend on the cultivar. The lack of knowledge about the physiological basis for responses to CA conditions and the determination of the optimum CA condition during the storage period are obvious.

Also, new technologies such as DCA should be studied for dynamic control of both temperature and CA conditions 24 h per day, based entirely on the changing physiology of the produce. Alternatively, development and use of these technologies can reduce the application of chemicals such as 1-MCP or DPA (superficial scald) especially for organic fruits and vegetables. However, other techniques could be incorporated into a CA system, such as control of storage rots by natural antimicrobial compounds delivered as a gas at critical periods during storage or novel gases (NO, N_2O).

Potential benefits and ideal CA for many fruits and vegetables have not been explored and investigated in detail and more research efforts should be directed at CA storage of commercialized fruits. There is a lack of knowledge regarding the tolerance of different crops to CA atmospheres, mortality of different species of insects of quarantine importance, temperature, ideal gas composition, and duration of treatment. The methods of handling CA-treated crop are not well established due to lack of knowledge about the behavior of fruit after CA, therefore more research is needed to investigate the metabolic changes due to CA and select adequate methods of handling. More comprehensive studies are needed to investigate the potential use of other nonconventional gases such as nitrous oxide, nitric oxide, and carbon monoxide in combination with CA, especially during transit.

Also, more comprehensive studies are needed to investigate effects of various factors such as growing environment, season of harvest, and other preharvest factors on the postharvest quality and storage potential of fruits and vegetables, especially under CA. More research is needed to increase the commercial use of the technology for tropical fruits. There is a lack of knowledge regarding protein turnover and gene expression in fruits held in CA, and in-depth molecular studies are needed to identify clones for genes involved in response to LO/high CO_2, to develop molecular markers for monitoring responses of fruits to CA.

The use of intelligent packaging systems has to be evaluated in CA technology. Also the combination of novel methods of food treatment and packaging needs to be examined, for example, irradiation used with modified atmosphere packaging (MAP) and antimicrobial films used in combination with CA. Detailed research is needed to evaluate the antimicrobial effect of super atmospheric O_2 in fresh-cut produce safety. It is necessary to study survival of the enteric pathogens and the behavior of foodborne viruses and protozoan parasites on MAP produce. Another active area of research is edible films for use in MAP systems.

References

Agar, I.T., Streif, J., Bangerth, F., 1994. Effect of high CO_2 and controlled atmosphere (CA) storage on the keepability of blackberry cv, "Thornfree." Commissions C2, D1, D2/3 of the International Institute of Refrigeration International Symposium, June 8–10, Istanbul, Turkey, pp. 271–280.

Allen, D., 1998. Controlled atmosphere storage buildings: construction and operational techniques. Nova Scotia Fruit Growers' Association, Agricultural Center, Kentville, Canada.

Baldwin, E.A., Scott, J.W., Shewfelt, R.L., 1995. Quality of ripened mutant and transgenic tomato cultigens. Tomato Quality Workshop Proceedings, December 11–14, 1995, Davis, CA.

Bangerth, F, 1977. The effect of different partial pressures of CO_2, C_2H_4, and O_2 in the storage atmosphere on the ascorbic acid content of fruits and vegetables. Qual. Plant. 27, 125–133.

Batu, A., Thompson, A.K., 1995. Effects of controlled atmosphere storage on the extension of postharvest qualities and storage life of tomatoes. Workshop of the Belgium Institute for Automatic Control, Ostend, Belgium, June 1995, pp. 263–268.

Bertolini, P., Pratella, G.C., Tonini, G., Gallerani, G., 1991. Physiological disorders of "Abbe Fetel" pears as affected by low-O_2 and regular controlled atmosphere storage. Technical Innovations in Freezing and Refrigeration of Fruits and Vegetables. Paper presented at a conference held in Davis, California, USA, July 9–12, 1989, pp. 61–66.

Bishop, D., 1996. Controlled atmosphere storage: a practical guide. David Bishop Design Consultants, Heathfield, East Sussex, England.

Brackmann, A., Streif, J., Bangerth, F, 1993. Relationship between a reduced aroma production and lipid metabolism of apples after long-term controlled-atmosphere storage. J. Am. Soc. Hortic. Sci. 118, 243–247.

Brecht, J.K., 2006. Controlled atmosphere, modified atmosphere and modified atmosphere packaging for vegetables. Stewart Postharvest Rev. 5 (5), 1–6.

Burdon, J., Lallu, N., Haynes, G., McDermott, K., Billing, D., 2008. The effect of delays in establishment of a static or dynamic controlled atmosphere on the quality of "Hass" avocado fruit. Postharvest Biol. Technol. 49, 61–68.

Burg, S.P., 2004. Postharvest Physiology and Hypobaric Storage of Fresh Produce. CAB International, Wallingford, UK.

Carrier Corporation, 2008. http://www.container.carrier.com/details/0,2806,CLI1-DIV9-ETI653,00. html.

Chapon, J.F., Westercamp, P., 1996. Entreposage frigorifique des pommes et des poires. Tome 2 Conduite de la conservationCtifl, Paris, France.

Colelli, G., Martelli, S., 1995. Beneficial effects on the application of CO_2-enriched atmospheres on fresh strawberries *Fragaria* × ananassa Duch. Adv. Horticult. Sci. 9, 55–60.

Coquinot, J.P., Chapon, J.F., 1992. Entreposage frigorifique des pommes et des poires. Tome 1 EquipementCtifl, Paris, France.

Corrales-Garcia, J., 1997. Physiological and biochemical responses of "Hass" avocado fruits to cold-storage in controlled atmospheres. Seventh International Controlled Atmosphere Research Conference, July 13–18, 1997, University of California, Davis, California 95616, USA [abstract], 50.

Dalrymple, G.D., 1969. The development of an agricultural technology: controlled atmosphere storage of fruits. Technol. Cult. 10 (1), 35–48.

De Reuck, K., Sivakumar, D., Korsten, L., 2009. Integrated application of 1-methylcyclopropene and modified atmosphere packaging to improve quality retention of litchi cultivars during storage. Postharvest Biol. Technol. 52, 71–77.

De Wild, H., 2001. 1-MCP kanvoorgrotedoorbraak in bewaringzorgen [1-MCP can make a big breakthrough for storage]. Fruitteelt Den Haag 91, 12–13.

DeLong, J.M., Prange, R.K., Leyte, J.C., Harrison, P.A., 2004. A new technology that determines low oxygen thresholds in controlled-atmosphere-stored apples. Hort. Technol. 14, 262–266.

Dijkink, B.H., Tomassen, M.M., Willemsen, J.H.A., van Doorn, W.G., 2004. Humidity control during bell pepper storage, using a hollow fiber membrane contactor system. Postharvest Biol. Technol. 32, 311–320.

Dilley, D.R., 2006. Development of controlled atmosphere storage technologies. Stewart Postharvest Rev. 6 (5), 1–8.

Ekman, J.H., Golding, J.B., McGlasson, W.B., 2005. Innovation in cold storage technologies. Stewart Postharvest Rev. 3 (6), 1–14.

Ella, L., Zion, A., Nehemia, A., Amnon, L., 2003. Effect of the ethylene action inhibitor 1 methylcyclopropene on parsley leaf senescence and ethylene biosynthesis. Postharvest Biol. Technol. 30, 67–74.

Fabi, J.P., Cordenunsi, B.R., de MattosBarreto, G.P., Mercadante, A.Z., Lajolo, F.M., Oliveira do Nascimento, J.R., 2007. Papaya fruit ripening: response to ethylene and 1-methylcyclopropene (1-MCP). J. Agric. Food Chem. 55, 6118–6123.

Fidler, J.C., Wilkinson, B.G., Edney, K.L., Sharples, R.O., 1973. The biology of apple and pear storage. Commonwealth Agric. Bureaux Res. Rev. 3, 12–14.

Fu, L., Cao, J., Li, Q., Lin, L., Jiang, W., 2007. Effect of 1-methylcyclopropene on fruit quality and physiological disorders in Yali pear (*Pyrusbretschneideri* Rehd.) during storage. Food Sci. Technol. Int. 13, 49–54.

Gang, M., Wang, R., Cheng-Rong, W., Masaya, K., Kazuki, Y., Fei-Fei, Q., Hui-Lian, X., 2009. Effect of 1-methylcyclopropene on expression of genes for ethylene biosynthesis enzymes and ethylene receptors in post-harvest broccoli. Plant Growth Reg. 57, 223–232.

Gasser, F., Höhn, E., 2004. Lagerung von Kirschen in modifizierter Atmosphäre-ein Überblick. Schweiz. Z. Obst-Weinbau 140 (13), 6–10.

Gasser, F., Dätwyler, D., Schneider, K., Naunheim, W., Hoehn, E., 2005. Effects of decreasing oxygen levels in the storage atmosphere on the respiration and production of volatiles of "Idared" apples. Acta Hort. 682, 1585–1592.

Gasser, F., Eppler, T., Naunheim, W., Gabioud, S., Hoehn, E., 2007. Control of the critical oxygen level during dynamic CA storage of apples by monitoring respiration as well as chlorophyll fluorescence. COST Action 924. International Conference: Ripening Regulation and Postharvest Fruit Quality, November 12–13, Weingarten, Germany.

Gasser, F., Eppler, T., Naunheim, W., Gabioud, S., Höhn, E., 2008. Control of critical oxygen level during dynamic CA storage of apples. Agrarforschung 15, 98–103.

Girard, B., Lau, O.L., 1995. Effect of maturity and storage on quality and volatile production of "Jonagold" apples. Food Res. Int. 28, 465–471.

Graell, J., Recasens, I., 1992. Effects of ethylene removal on "Starking Delicious" apple quality in controlled atmosphere storage. Postharvest Biol. Technol. 2, 101–108.

Hansen, K., Poll, L., Olsen, C.E., Lewis, M.J., 1992. The influence of O_2 concentration in storage atmospheres on the post-storage volatile ester production of "Jonagold" apples. Lebensmittel Wissenschaft and Technologie 25, 457–461.

Harb, J., Streif, J., Bangerth, K.F., 2008. Aroma volatiles of apples as influenced by ripening and storage procedures. Acta Hortic. 796, 93–103.

Haruenkit, R., Thompson, A.K., 1996. Effect of O2 and CO2 levels on internal browning and composition of pineapples Smooth Cayenne. Proceedings of the International Conference on Tropical Fruits, Kuala Lumpur, Malaysia, July 23–26, 1996, pp. 343–350.

Hatfield, S.G.S., Patterson, B.D., 1974. Abnormal volatile production by apples during ripening after controlled atmosphere storage. Facteurset Régulation de la Maturation des Fruits. Colleques Internationaux, CNRS, Paris, pp. 57–64.

Hellickson, M.L., Adre, N., Staples, J., Butte, J., 1995. Computer controlled evaporator operation during fruit cool-down. In Kushwaha, L., Serwatowski, R., Brook, R., Editors. Technologias de Cosecha y Postcosecha de Frutas y Hortalizas. Harvest and Postharvest Technologies for Fresh Fruits and Vegetables. Proceedings of a conference held in Guanajuato, Mexico, pp. 546–553.

Hoehn, E., Prange, R.K., Vigneault, C., 2009. Storage technology and applications. In: Elhadi, M.Y. (Ed.), Modified and Controlled Atmospheres for the Storage, Transportation, and Packaging of Horticultural Commodities. CRC Press, Boca Raton, FL, pp. 16–22.

Holcroft, D.M., Kader, A.A., 1999. Controlled atmosphere-induced changes in pH and organic acid metabolism may affect color of stored strawberry fruit. Postharvest Biol. Technol. 17, 419–432.

Huang, C.C., Huang, H.S., Tsai, C.Y., 2002. A study on controlled atmosphere storage of cabbage with sealed plastic tent. J. Agric. Res. China 51, 33–42.

Hughes, P.A., Thompson, A.K., Plumbley, R.A., Seymour, G.B., 1981. Storage of capsicums Capsicum annum [L.], Sendt. under controlled atmosphere, modified atmosphere and hypobaric conditions. J. Hortic. Sci. 56, 261–265.

Ito, S., Kakiuchi, N., Izumi, Y., Iba, Y., 1974. Studies on the controlled atmosphere storage of Satsuma mandarin. Bull. Fruit Tree Res. Stn., B. Okitsu 1, 39–58.

Izumi, H., Watada, A.E., Nathanee, P.K., Douglas, W., 1996. Controlled atmosphere storage of carrot slices, sticks and shreds. Postharvest Biol. Technol. 9, 165–172.

Jameson, J., 1993. CA storage technology in the 1990s. Postharvest News Inf. 4 (1), 16–17.

Jeffery, D., Smith, C., Goodenough, P.W., Prosser, T., Grierson, D., 1984. Ethylene independent and ethylene dependent biochemical changes in ripening tomatoes. Plant Physiol. 74, 32.

Jiang, C., Driffield, M., Bradley, E.L., Castle, L., Oldring, P.K.T., Guthrie, J.T., 2010. The behavior of MEKO blocked isocyanate compounds in aluminum flake pigmented, polyester–polyurethane can coating systems. J. Coat. Technol. Res. 7, 57–65.

Johnson, D.S., 2008. Factors affecting the efficacy of 1-MCP applied to retard apple ripening. Acta Hortic. 796, 59–67.

Kader, A.A., 2003. A summary of CA requirements and recommendations for fruits other than apples. Acta Hort. 600, 737–740.

Ke, D.Y., Rodriguez Sinobas, L., Kader, A.A., 1991. Physiology and prediction of fruit tolerance to low O_2 atmospheres. J. Am. Soc. Horticult. Sci. 116, 253–260.

Kidd, F., West, C., 1927. Atmosphere control in fruit storage. Great Britain Department Scientific Industrial Research Food Investigation Board Report, 1927, pp. 32–33.

Kim, Y., Brecht, J.K., Talcott, S.T., 2007. Antioxidant phytochemical and fruit quality changes in mango (*Mangifera indica* L) following hot water immersion and controlled atmosphere storage. Food Chem. 105, 1327–1334.

Klein, J.D., Lurie, S., 1992. Prestorage heating of apple fruit for enhanced postharvest quality: interaction of time and temperature. Hort. Sci. 27, 326–328.

Kluge, K., Meier, G., 1979. Flavour development of some apple cultivars during storage. Gartenbau 26, 278–279.

Knee, M., 1973. Effects of controlled atmosphere storage on respiratory metabolism of apple fruit tissue. J. Sci. Food Agric. 24, 289–298.

Knee, M., Looney, N.E., 1990. Effect of orchard and postharvest application of daminozide on ethylene synthesis by apple fruit. J. Plant Growth Reg. 9, 175–179.

Knee, M., Sharples, R.O., 1979. Influence of CA storage on apples. Quality in Stored and Processed Vegetables and Fruit. Proceedings of a Symposium at Long Ashton Research Station, University of Bristol, UK, April 8–12, 1979, pp. 341–352.

Kubo, Y., Inaba, A., Nakamura, R., 1989. Effects of high CO_2 on respiration in various horticultural crops. J. Japanese Soc. Hortic. Sci. 58, 731–736.

Lee, H.D., Yun, H.S., Og Lee, W., Jeong, H., Choe, S.Y., 2009. The effect of pressurized CA (controlled atmosphere) treatment on the storage qualities of peach. 10th International Controlled & Modified Atmosphere Research Conference, April 4–7, 2009, Turkey [abstract], p. 8.

Leyte, J.C., Forney, C.F., 1999. Controlled atmosphere tents for storing fresh commodities in conventional refrigerated rooms. Hort. Technol. 9, 672–674.

Malcolm, G.I., 2005. Advancements in the implementation of CA technology for storage of perishable commodities. Acta Hort. 682, 1593–1597.

Marcellin, P., Leteinturier, J., 1967. Premières applications industrielles des membranes en caoutchouc de silicone à l'entreposage des pommes en atmosphère contrôlée. Inst. Int. Froid. Congr. Intern. Froid. Madrid, Espagne, pp. 1–9.

Markarian, N.R., Vigneault, C., Gariepy, Y., Rennie, T.J., 2003. Computerized monitoring and control for a research controlled-atmosphere storage facility. Comp. Electron. Agric. 39, 23–37.

Mateos, M., Ke, D., Cantwell, M., Kader, A.A., 1993. Phenolic metabolism and ethanolic fermentation of intact and cut lettuce exposed to CO_2-enriched atmospheres. Postharvest Biol. Technol. 3, 225–233.

Matté, P., Buglia, L., Fadanelli, L., Chistè, C., Zeni, F., Boschetti, A., 2005. ILOSULO as a practical technology for apple scald prevention. Acta Hort. 682, 1543–1550.

Mattheis, J.P., Buchanan, D.A., Fellman, J.K., 1991. Change in apple fruit volatiles after storage in atmospheres inducing anaerobic metabolism. J. Agric. Food Chem. 39, 1602–1605.

McCollum, T., Maul, D., 2007. 1-MCP inhibits degreening, but stimulates respiration and ethylene biosynthesis in grapefruit. HortScience 42, 120–124.

McGlasson, W.B., Wills, R.B.H., 1972. Effects of O_2 and CO_2 on respiration, storage life and organic acids of green bananas. Aust. J. Biol. Sci. 25, 35–42.

Meheriuk, M., 1989. CA storage of apples. Proceedings of the Fifth International Controlled Atmosphere Research Conference, Wenatchee, Washington, USA, June 14–16, 1989, vol. 2, pp. 257–284.

Miszczak, A., Szymczak, J.A., 2000. The influence of harvest date and storage conditions on taste and apples aroma. Zeszyty Naukowe Instytutu Sadownictwa i Kwiaciarstwa w Skierniewicach 8, 361–369.

Mitcham, E.J., Lee, T., Martin, A., Zhou, S., Kader, A.A., 2003. Summary of CA for arthropod control on fresh horticultural perishables. Acta Hort. 600, 741–745.

Neale, M.A., Lindsay, R.T., Messer, H.J.M., 1981. An experimental cold store for vegetables. J. Agric. Eng. Res. 26, 529–540.

Ortiz, A., Echeverria, G., Graell, J., Lara, I., 2009. Overall quality of 'Rich Lady' peach fruit after air- or CA storage. The importance of volatile emission. Food Sci. Technol. 42, 1520–1529.

Osterloh, A., 1996. Lagervervahren and Planung, Bau und Ausrüstung von Obstlägern. In: Osterloh, A., Ebert, G., Held, W.-H., Schulz, H., Urban, E. (Eds.), Lagerung von Obst und Südfrüchten. Verlag Eugen Ulmer, Stuttgart, Germany, pp. 113–141.

Pal, R.K., Buescher, R.W., 1993. Respiration and ethylene evolution of certain fruits and vegetables in response to CO_2 in controlled atmosphere storage. J. Food Sci. Technol. Mysore 30, 29–32.

Pariasca, J.A.T., Miyazaki, T., Hisaka, H., Nakagawa, H., Sato, T., 2001. Effect of modified atmosphere packaging (MAP) and controlled atmosphere (CA) storage on the quality of snow pea pods (*Pisumsativum* L. var. *saccharatum*). Postharvest Biol. Technol. 21, 213–223.

Peppelenbos, H., 2003. How to control the atmosphere? Postharvest Biol. Technol. 27, 1–2.

Porat, R., Weiss, B., Cohen, L., Daus, A., Aharoni, N., 2004. Reduction of postharvest rind disorders in citrus fruit by modified atmosphere packaging. Postharvest Biol. Technol. 33, 35–43.

Prange, R.K., DeLong, J.M., 2003. 1-Methylcyclopropene: the "magic bullet" for horticultural products. Chron. Hort. 43 (1), 11–14.

Prange, R.K., DeLong, J.M., Daniels-Lake, B.J., Harrison, P.A., 2005. Innovation in controlled atmosphere technology. Stewart Postharvest Rev. 3 (9), 1–11.

Prange, R.K., DeLong, J.M., Daniels-Lake, B., Harrison, P.A., 2006. Controlled-atmosphere related disorders of fruits and vegetables. Stewart Postharvest Rev. 5 (7), 1–10.

Raghavan, G.S.V., Vigneault, C., Gariépy, Y., Markarian, N.R., Alvo, P., 2005. Refrigerated and controlled/modified atmosphere storage. In: Barett, D.M., Somogy, L., Ramaswamy, H. (Eds.), Processing Fruits. CRC Press, Boca Raton, FL, pp. 23–52.

Reichel, M., 1974. The behavior of Golden Delicious during storage as influenced by different harvest dates. Gartenbau 21, 268–270.

Rizzolo, A., Cambiaghi, P., Grassi, M., Zerbini, P.E., 2005. Influence of 1-methylcyclopropene and storage atmosphere on changes in volatile compounds and fruit quality of Conference pears. J. Agric. Food Chem. 53, 9781–9789.

Robitaille, H.A., Badenhop, A.F., 1981. Mushroom response to postharvest hyperbaric storage. J. Food Sci. 46, 249–253.

Rogiers, S.Y., Knowles, N.R., 2000. Efficacy of low O_2 and high CO_2 atmospheres in maintaining the postharvest quality of saskatoon fruit (*Amelanchieralnifolia* Nutt). Can. J. Plant Sci. 80, 623–630.

Romanazzi, G., Nigro, F., Ippolito, A., 2008. Effectiveness of a short hyperbaric treatment to control postharvest decay of sweet cherries and table grapes. Postharvest Biol. Technol. 49, 440–442.

Romero, I., Sanchez-Ballesta, M.T., Maldonado, R., Escribano, M.I., Merodio, C., 2008. Anthocyanin, antioxidant activity and stress-induced gene expression in high CO_2-treated table grapes stored at low temperature. J. Plant Physiol. 165, 522–530.

Saltveit, M.E., 2003. A summary of CA requirements and recommendations for vegetables. Acta Hort. 600, 723–727.

Salunkhe, D.K., Wu, M.T., 1975. Sub-atmospheric storage of fruits and vegetables. In: Haard, N.F., Salunkhe, D.K. (Eds.), Postharvest Biology and Handling of Fruits and Vegetables. A.V.I. Publishing Company Inc, Westport, Connecticut, USA, pp. 153–171.

Saquet, A.A., Streif, J., Bangerth, F., 2003. Reducing internal browning disorders in "Braeburn" apples by delayed controlled atmosphere storage and some related physiological and biochemical changes. Acta Hort. 682, 453–458.

Schouten, S.P., 1997. Improvement of quality of Elstar apples by dynamic control of ULO conditions. Seventh International Controlled Atmosphere Research Conference, July 13–18, 1997, University of California, Davis, California 95616, USA [abstract], p. 7.

Singh, A.K., Kashyap, M.M., Gupta, A.K., Bhumbla, V.K., 1993. Vitamin-C during controlled atmosphere storage of tomatoes. J. Res. Punjab Agric. Univ. 30, 199–203.

Sive, A., Resnizky, D., 1979. Extension of the storage life of "Red Rosa" plums by controlled atmosphere storage. Bull. de l'Instit. Intern. du Froid 59, 1148.

Streif, J., Saquet, A.A., 2003. Internal flesh browning of "Elstar" apples as influenced by pre- and postharvest factors. Acta Hort. 599, 523–527.

Thompson, A.K., 1996. Postharvest Technology of Fruit and Vegetables. Blackwell Publishing, Oxford, UK.

Thompson, A.K., 2003. Fruit and Vegetables. Blackwell Publishing, Oxford, UK.

Trierweiler, B., Krieg, M., Tauscher, B., 2004. Antioxidative capacity of different apple cultivars after long-time storage. J. Appl. Bot. Food Qual. 78, 117–119.

Truter, A.B., Combrick, J.C., Fourie, P.C., Victor, S.J., 1994. Controlled atmosphere storage of prior to processing of some canning peach and apricot cultivars in South Africa. Commissions C2, D1, D2/3 of the International Institute of Refrigeration International Symposium, June 8–10, Istanbul, Turkey, pp. 243–254.

Urban, E., 1995. Nachlagerungsverhalten von Apfelfruchten [Postharvest storage of apples.]. Erwerbsobstbau 37, 145–151.

Van der Merwe, J.A., Combrink, J.C., Calitz, F.J., 2003. Effect of controlled atmosphere storage after initial low oxygen stress treatment on superficial scald development on South African-grown Granny Smith and Top red apples. Acta Hort. 600, 261–265.

Vidigal, J.C., Sigrist, J.M.M., Figueiredo, I.B., Medina, J.C., 1979. Cold storage and controlled atmosphere storage of tomatoes. Boletim do Instituto de Tecnologia de Alimentos Brasil 16, 421–442.

Vigneault, C., Artés Hernández, F., 2007. Gas treatments for increasing phytochemical content of fruits and vegetables. Stewart Postharvest Rev. 3 (3), 8.1–8.9.

Visai, C., Vanoli, M., Zini, M., Bundini, R., 1994. Cold storage of Passa Crassana pears in normal and controlled atmosphere. Commissions C2, D1, D2/3 of the International Institute of Refrigeration International Symposium, June 8–10, Istanbul, Turkey, pp. 255–262.

Wang, Z., Dilley, D.R., 2000. Initial low oxygen stress controls superficial scald in apples. Postharvest Biol. Technol. 18, 201–213.

Wang, C.Y., 1990. Physiological and biochemical effects of controlled atmosphere on fruit and vegetables. In: Calderon, M., Barkai-Golan, R. (Eds.), Food Preservation by Modified Atmospheres. CRC Press, Boca Raton, Florida and Boston, Massachusetts, pp. 197–223.

Warren, O., Sargent, S.A., Huber, D.J., Brecht, J.K., Plotto, A., Baldwin, E., 2009. Influence of postharvest aqueous 1-methylcyclopropene (1-MCP) on the aroma volatiles and shelf-life of "Arkin" carambola. American Society for Horticultural Science Poster Board # 109. Tuesday July 28, 2009, Millennium Hotel, St. Louis, Illinois. Available from: http://ashs.confex.com/ashs/2009/webprogram/Paper2624.html.

Weichmann, J., 1986. The effect of controlled-atmosphere storage on the sensory and nutritional quality of fruits and vegetables. Hort. Rev. 8, 101–127.

Willaert, G.A., Dirinck, P.J., Pooter, H.L., Schamp, N.N., 1983. Objective measurement of aroma quality of Golden Delicious apples as a function of controlled-atmosphere storage time. J. Agric. Food Chem. 31, 809–813.

Wills, R.B.H., Warton, M.A., Ku, V.V.V., 2000. Ethylene levels associated with fruit and vegetables during marketing. Austr. J. Exp. Agric. 40, 465–470.

Wojciechowski, J., 1989. Ethylene removal from gases by means of catalytic combustion. Acta Hort. 258, 131–141.

Yang, S.F., Hoffmann, N.E., 1984. Ethylene biosynthesis and its regulation in higher plants. Ann. Rev. Plant Physiol. 35, 155–189.

Zhao, H., Murata, T., 1988. A study on the storage of muskmelon "Earl's Favorites". Bull. Faculty Agric. Shizuoka Univ. 38 (713), [abstract].

Zheng, Y.H., Wang, C.Y., Wang, S.Y., Zheng, W., 2003. Effect of high-oxygen atmospheres on blueberry phenolics, anthocyanins, and antioxidant capacity. J. Agric. Food Chem. 51, 7162–7169.

3

RECENT TRENDS IN ACTIVE PACKAGING IN FRUITS AND VEGETABLES

Samad Bodbodak*, Zahra Rafiee**

*University of Tabriz, Department of Food Science and Technology, Faculty of Agriculture, Tabriz, Iran; **Tarbiat Modares University, Department of Food Science and Technology, Faculty of Agriculture, Tehran, Iran

1   Introduction

Consumer demands and market trends are both currently under continuous change in favor of convenience foods, which need mild preservation and should have fresh-like qualities. In addition there is a need for changes in distribution practices intended for foods distributed over increased distances and stored for longer periods (practices such as centralization of activities, market internationalization, and new trends such as Internet shopping). In the last two decades, the concept of active packaging has been introduced as an innovative food-packaging concept taking these demands into consideration. Active packaging defines maintaining food condition in a way that covers various aspects that influence the shelf life of packaged foods, including physiological processes (eg, respiration of fresh fruit and vegetables), chemical processes (eg, lipid oxidation), physical processes (eg, staling of bread, dehydration), microbiological aspects (eg, spoilage by microorganisms), and infestation (eg, by insects). These conditions can be managed in many different ways through the application of appropriate active-packaging systems and in turn food deterioration can be considerably reduced depending on the requirements of the packaged food.

When it comes to fresh commodities, packaging should strictly meet various challenges in order to be able to preserve fruits and vegetables for longer periods during transport and avoid contamination resulting from foodborne pathogens. Packaging has been traditionally assumed to have four basic functions: protection, communication, convenience, and containment. First, the

Eco-Friendly Technology for Postharvest Produce Quality. http://dx.doi.org/10.1016/B978-0-12-804313-4.00003-7
Copyright © 2016 Elsevier Inc. All rights reserved.

package serves to protect the product against the deteriorative effects of the external environment. Second, it communicates with the consumer acting as a marketing tool. Third, it provides greater ease of use and time-saving convenience to the consumer. And finally, it contains products of various shapes and sizes. Although traditional packaging played a huge role in the early development of food distribution systems, it can no longer effectively and sufficiently meet increasingly complex needs. Today, consumers seek innovative packaging with enhanced functions and should have access to minimally processed foods with fewer preservatives, be able to witness an increase in regulatory requirements and market globalization, and be ensured about food safety. Regarding the concept of innovative packaging, distinguishing between active packaging and intelligent packaging is necessary.

Active packaging is defined as packaging aimed at enhancing the performance of the package system by deliberately including subsidiary constituents in either the packaging material or the package headspace. There are two key words in this definition: "deliberately" and "enhancing." There is a positive interaction among the product, the package, and the environment in active packaging toward extending shelf life or reaching other features not achievable otherwise. Alternatively, active packaging has also been defined as a packaging system actively changing the condition of the package to improve food safety, lengthen shelf life, enhance sensory properties, and maintain the quality of the product (Vermeiren et al., 1999). Modifying the environmental or physiological conditions within the food package, active-packaging systems usually involve scavenging or absorption of undesirable compounds such as oxygen, carbon dioxide, ethylene, and excessive water. However, compounds such as carbon dioxide, antioxidants, and preservatives are added or released into the headspace of the package by other active-packaging systems through sachets, labels, or films.

Intelligent packaging has been defined as a packaging system that facilitates decision making on extending shelf life, improves safety, enhances quality, provides information, and warns about possible problems because it is capable of performing intelligent functions such as detecting, sensing, recording, tracing, communicating, and applying scientific logic (Yam et al., 2005). In this type of packaging, a variety of sensors has been developed to be placed in or on the package. These sensors are based on chemical, enzymatic, immunochemical, or mechanical reactions and can detect and communicate such information as time/temperature conditions and history, oxygen and carbon dioxide levels, package leakage or spoilage, commodity ripeness and freshness, and microbial growth, and identify specific foodborne human pathogens (Wilson, 2007). The focus of this chapter is active packaging applied to fruits and vegetables; in this way, modified atmosphere packaging (MAP) is regarded as a basis for active packaging using either films or edible coatings.

2   Active Packaging Technologies

Reducing oxygen levels and increasing that of carbon dioxide, MAP is beneficial in fruit quality maintenance with respect to air storage. However, there are many cases where the modified atmosphere is not low or high enough with respect to oxygen and carbon dioxide levels, respectively. In these situations, active packaging can improve the overall quality by altering the physiology of harvested fruits and vegetables in a desirable manner.

A packaging interacting with the packed food and the environment with a dynamic role in extending shelf life, improving safety, and enhancing sensory properties while maintaining the quality of the food is usually said to be active (Scully, 2009; Vermeiren et al., 1999). Active packaging includes various aspects such as physiological processes (respiration of fresh fruit and vegetables), chemical processes (lipid oxidation), physical processes (dehydration), and microbiological aspects (spoilage by microorganisms) that may be influential in determining the shelf life of packaged fruits.

These conditions can be managed in many different ways through the application of appropriate active-packaging systems and in turn food deterioration can be considerably reduced depending on the requirements of the packaged product.

Techniques for preservation and improving quality and safety of foods in active packaging can be put into three categories: absorbing systems (ie, scavenging), releasing systems, and other systems. Undesired compounds such as oxygen, carbon dioxide, ethylene, excessive water, taints, and other specific compounds are removed through absorbing (scavenging) systems. Releasing systems actively add or release compounds such as carbon dioxide, antioxidants, and preservatives into the headspace of the package or to the packed food. Other systems involve varied tasks, such as self-heating, self-cooling, and preservation. Today, oxygen scavengers, moisture absorbers, and barrier packaging are the technologies dominating more than 80% of the market (Robinson and Morrison, 2010).

The type of absorbers and releasers depends on the physical form of active-packaging systems, and they can be in the form of sachet, label, or film. Sachets are placed freely in the headspace of the package. Labels are attached to the lid of the package. Direct contact with food impairs the function of the packaging system and may cause migration problems; so it should be avoided. Films or materials with antimicrobial properties are of two types: (1) Films or materials that emit an active substance into the headspace of the package or those from which an active substance migrates to the surface of the food. In the first case, the system is not in direct contact with the food, but in the second case it is. (2) Films or materials effective against microbial growth without emitting the active agents into the headspace of the package or migration of those agents to the food. Here the material must be in direct contact with the food.

2.1 Oxygen Scavengers

The presence of oxygen in packaged foods can have significant detrimental effects. It can cause many deteriorative reactions such as nutrient losses, color changes, off-flavor development, and microbial growth. It also has a considerable effect on the respiration rate and ethylene production in fruits and vegetables. Elimination or exclusion of oxygen has been the focus of much of the effort in the preservation of foods and beverages; the presence of oxygen in packaged foods has adverse effects. The following are some of the many adverse end effects of oxygen on foods and beverages:

1. off-flavors and even, in extreme circumstances, toxic end-products due to oxidative rancidity of unsaturated fatty acids;
2. ascorbic acid or vitamin C loss, especially in fruits and vegetable-based foods;
3. darkening and browning of fresh meat pigments;
4. promoting growth of aerobic spoilage microorganisms;
5. staling odors in soft bakery goods;
6. hatching of insect eggs and growth of insects;
7. acceleration of fresh fruit and vegetable respiration;
8. enzymatic and nonenzymatic phenolic browning of fresh fruit flesh;
9. oxidation of aromatic flavor oils of beverages such as coffee and tea;
10. flavor deterioration of beer;
11. discoloration of processed fruit and vegetable pigments.

Indeed the presence of oxygen adversely affects most foods and beverages in one way or another and causes loss in nutritional content, color, flavor, texture, or combinations of these.

Passive barrier packaging materials such as high barrier packaging materials and multilayer structures containing ethylene vinyl alcohol copolymers or aluminum foil are used for packaging oxygen-sensitive food (Lagaron et al., 2004) as well as high barrier nanocomposites (Teixeira et al., 2011). However, complete elimination of oxygen present in the headspace or dissolution of O_2 in the food or O_2 permeated into the package wall is not achieved by passive methods. Therefore, oxygen scavengers can be beneficial as they maintain food product quality through decreasing food metabolism, reducing oxidative rancidity, inhibiting undesirable oxidation of labile pigments and vitamins, inhibiting enzymatic browning, controlling enzymatic discoloration, and inhibiting the growth of aerobic microorganisms (Day, 1989, 2001; Rooney, 1995). Oxygen scavengers are by far considered to be the most commercially important subcategory of active packaging.

O_2 absorbers, also referred to as O_2 scavengers (OS), use either powdered iron or ascorbic acid, the former being more common. Absorption capacity and absorption rate are constant in absorbers reflecting their two typical and main properties. Absorption rate, the parameter of prime importance for food quality, has been evaluated in a few studies in spite of the well-documented absorption capacity of commercial sachets. In general, 1 g of iron can react with 0.0136 mol of O_2 (standard temperature and pressure), which is equal to approximately 300 mL. O_2 sachets are available commercially in various sizes, having the ability to consume 20–2000 mL of O_2 (an air volume of 100–10,000 mL). Selecting the type and size of absorbent required depends on some interrelated factors including:

1. nature of the food (ie, size, shape, weight);
2. water activity (a_w) of the food;
3. amount of dissolved O_2 in the food;
4. desired shelf life of the food;
5. initial O_2 level in the package headspace;
6. O_2 permeability of the packaging material.

Overall performance of the absorbent and the food shelf life is critically affected by the last factor. Films containing polyvinylidene chloride copolymer, ethylene vinyl alcohol (EVOH) copolymer, or a metalized layer as a barrier are necessary if a long shelf life is required. O_2 permeability of such films is less than 0.0004 bar. Provided intact packaging integrity, the headspace O_2 should be reduced to 100 ppm within 1–2 days and remain at that level over the storage period.

Small sachets containing various iron-based powders along with a set of catalysts scavenging O_2 within the food package and irreversibly converting it to a stable oxide are the most widely used OSs. For O_2 absorbents to function, water is necessary. To this aim, either the water is added during manufacture or moisture is absorbed from the food before O_2 can be absorbed. The iron powder is kept in a small sachet (labeled do not eat) so that it can be separated from the food. This that sachet is highly permeable to O_2 and, in some cases, to water vapor. Pereira de Abreu et al. (2012) list commercially available OSs, and the O_2 scavenging capacities of four commercially available iron-based OSs were evaluated at 3°C and 10°C in a study by Brandon et al. (2009). Another critical issue, particularly at low O_2 concentrations, was reproducibility. At low O_2 concentrations, none of the scavengers had a coefficient of variation less than 20%; therefore it was recommended that multiple scavengers be employed to achieve consistent results.

Oxygen scavengers can be used alone or in combination with MAP. If they are used alone, there will be no need for MAP machinery and packaging speeds can increase. In common commercial practice, however, most of the atmospheric oxygen is removed by MAP and then the residual oxygen remaining within the food package is mopped up using a relatively small and inexpensive scavenger (Idol, 1993).

Until recently the effect of chlorine-containing salts [primarily sodium chloride (NaCl)] was not taken into account when describing the mechanism of iron-based O_2 scavenging in scientific/technical literature. However, Polyakov and Miltz (2010) revealed that there is an association between efficiency of O_2 scavenging and the rate of corrosion occurring in the active component, that is, iron powder. This process includes electrochemical and chemical reactions leading to the formation of a porous rust shell around each iron particle core and chloride ions play an important role in this. The electrochemical cathodic reaction of O_2 reduction is the rate-limiting reaction in this process. Having absorbed the water within the rust shell, an electrolyte (water + NaCl) is formed in the rust pores. As the amount of adsorbed water decreases, O_2 diffusion to the iron–rust interface increases. At the same time, as the solubility of the reacting species decreases at low amounts of water, the anodic iron dissolution rate decreases as well. On the other hand a reduction is induced in the "gas–electrolyte" interfacial area due to high amounts of water, which in turn impairs gas transfer within the rust shell.

Polyakov and Miltz (2010) showed that increased rate of O_2 absorption resulted in decreased porosity, increased specific surface area of iron powder's corrosion products, and decreased O_2 diffusivity through the particles. A decrease in the amount of water adsorbed on the corrosion products was attained due to the heat evolved during the exothermic reaction. The results of their study clarified the effect of moisture on O_2 absorption by iron-based OSs. Proper design of packages intended for storage of foods with intermediate and high a_w can be performed with the help of these results. Metal detectors are often installed on packaging lines and iron-based scavengers normally cannot pass them; this is one of the disadvantages of these scavengers. In order to moderate the potential for metallic taints to be imparted to food products, non-metallic oxygen scavengers have been developed as well. Although some modern detectors can now be tuned to gradually cancel the scavenger signal while retaining high sensitivity for ferrous and nonferrous metallic contaminants, inadvertent setting off inline metal detectors is a problem that is also alleviated (Coles et al., 2003). Nonmetallic OSs are those using organic reducing agents and enzymic OS systems using either glucose oxidase or ethanol oxidase. Among organic reducing agents are ascorbic acid, ascorbate salts, and catechol. Enzymic OS systems can be immobilized onto package surfaces or incorporated into sachets and adhesive labels. However, they are not widely used and have had limited commercial success, particularly in North America and Europe. It has been suggested that possible accidental ingestion of the sachet contents by the consumer can be a reason for this limited success. However, as a sachet typically contains 7 g of iron, approximately 160 times less than the LD_{50} for a 70-kg adult, ingestion does not have adverse health impacts. In this regard the development of O_2-absorbing adhesive labels has overcome this perceived problem and helped the commercial acceptance of this technology as they can be attached to the inside of packages. Of course, O_2-absorbing capacity of these adhesive labels is limited to 100 mL. Nanotechnology has offered the potential to solve such problems (Imran et al., 2010). Aegis OX, a blend of active and passive nylon incorporating oxygen scavengers and passive nanocomposite clay particles, is a commercially developed oxygen-scavenging barrier resin. It enhances the barrier properties against O_2, CO_2, and aromas. Direct incorporating of oxygen scavengers into biopolymer films can be useful for packaging applications as it maintains very low O_2 levels. Incorporating ascorbic acid, Janjarasskul et al. (2011) developed edible and biodegradable biopolymer (whey protein) film having an oxygen-scavenging function. Exhibiting improved O_2 barrier properties and acceptable mechanical properties, this biopolymer film revealed potential commercial applications. Xiao et al. (2004) also added titanium dioxide (TiO_2) nanoparticles to different polymers to develop oxygen scavenger films.

As active-packaging materials, nanocomposite films incorporating oxygen scavengers can be employed for a variety of oxygen-sensitive food products.

A wide range of foods can benefit from OSs including sliced, cooked, and cured meat and poultry products, cured fish, coffee, pizzas, specialty bakery goods, fresh cut fruits and vegetables, dried food ingredients, cakes, breads, biscuits, croissants, fresh pastas, tea, powdered milk, dried egg, spices, herbs, confectionery, and snack foods (Day, 2001).

When wet, iron-based label and sachet scavengers rapidly lose their oxygen scavenging capability; they cannot be used for beverages or high a_w foods. Instead, to scavenge oxygen from the bottles' headspace and any ingressing oxygen, nonmetallic reagents and organometallic compounds with an affinity for oxygen have been incorporated into bottle closures, crowns, and caps or blended into polymer materials. It is worth noting that the speed and capacity of oxygen-scavenging plastic films and laminated trays is significantly lower than those of iron-based oxygen scavenger sachets or labels (Hirst, Personal communication, EMCO Packaging Systems Ltd, Worth, Kent, UK, 1998).

2.2 Carbon Dioxide Scavengers/Emitters

Carbon dioxide is mainly produced through respiration of fresh fruits and vegetables and if it is not treated and is allowed to accumulate to excessive levels inside the package it can cause physiological stress in fresh produce. Therefore controlled removal of CO_2 can help maintaining the quality of the product. Calcium hydroxide, activated charcoal, zeolite, and magnesium oxide are the most commonly used CO_2 absorbers. Active charcoal and zeolite have a greater affinity to moisture than to CO_2 and this is why they only work well in low humidity conditions. Since fresh produce needs some level of oxygen for normal respiration metabolism, oxygen removal by absorption is usually not attempted in a fresh produce package.

Kimchi is a general term for fermented vegetables such as oriental cabbage, radish, green onion, and leaf mustard mixed with salt and spices, and it is a CO_2-producing food product. Since the fermentation process continues with the concomitant production of CO_2, kimchi cannot be pasteurized due to its sensory quality. Therefore, scavengers may be useful because the accumulation of CO_2 in the packages causes ballooning or even bursting.

Various commercial sachet and label devices are used to either scavenge or emit carbon dioxide. To scavenge carbon dioxide in polyethylene coffee pouches, a mixture of calcium oxide and activated charcoal can be used. However, dual-action oxygen and carbon dioxide scavenger sachets and labels are commercially used for canned and foil pouched coffees in Japan and the United States and are more common (Day, 1989; Coles et al., 2003; Rooney, 1995). The constituents of these dual-action sachets and labels are typically iron powder and calcium hydroxide. The former scavenges oxygen and the latter scavenges carbon dioxide when converted to calcium carbonate under sufficiently high humidity conditions (Rooney, 1995). Commercially, dual-action oxygen and carbon dioxide scavengers are available from Japanese manufacturers, for example, Mitsubishi Gas Chemical Co. Ltd (Ageless™ type E and Fresh-Lock™) and Toppan Printing Co. Ltd (Freshilizer™ type CV). Carbon dioxide-emitting sachet and label devices can either be used alone or in combination with an oxygen scavenger. The absorption kinetics of two commercial O_2 and CO_2 scavengers were investigated in a study by Charles et al. (2006). Their results emphasized that for a reliable evaluation of the gas kinetics when using O_2 or CO_2 scavengers, it is required to take into consideration the important variation of the absorption rate constant among individual gas scavengers (about 20%), as well as the temperature effect. They also recognized significant "parasite" CO_2 absorption for OSs (ie, a carbonation reaction of the iron hydroxide formed following O_2 absorption). An example of the former is the Verifrais™ package manufactured by SARL Codimer (Paris, France). This innovative package is used for extending the shelf life of fresh meats and fish and consists of a standard MAP tray while a porous sachet containing sodium bicarbonate/ascorbate is positioned under a perforated false bottom. Carbon dioxide is emitted as exudate from modified atmosphere packed meat or fish contacts the sachet's contents, and this antimicrobial gas can replace the carbon dioxide already absorbed by the fresh food; so, pack collapse is avoided (Rooney, 1995). Development of a partial vacuum or pack collapse can also be a problem for foods packed with an oxygen scavenger. Dual-action oxygen scavenger/carbon dioxide emitter sachets and labels have been developed to solve this problem. These sachets and labels absorb oxygen and generate carbon dioxide in an equal volume. Although nonferrous variants of these sachets and labels are available, they usually contain ferrous carbonate and a metal halide catalyst. Mitsubishi Gas Chemical Co. Ltd (Ageless type G) and Multisorb Technologies Inc. (FreshPax™ type M) are commercial manufacturers in this regard. Snack food products, for example, nuts and sponge cakes, have been the main food targets for these dual-action oxygen scavenger/carbon dioxide emitter sachets and labels (Naito et al., 1991; Rooney, 1995).

The use of a lighter-gauge steel can was supposed to be allowed by the use of a carbon dioxide scavenger, but this result was not necessarily achieved. Calcium oxide, or lime, reacts with carbon dioxide and has not been known to be incorporated into package materials. Packets of this compound are widely used in containers for shipment of controlled atmosphere fruit and vegetables. Two truck and shipboard container operators, Transfresh and Transicold, incorporate lime into packets in bunkers through which the internal atmosphere is circulated. Excess carbon dioxide produced from respiration of fruit or vegetables is removed by this operation and in turn the adverse effects of excess carbon dioxide such as reduced pH and color and flavor changes are obviated.

Retarded growth of aerobic microorganisms and reduced respiration and senescence processes result from the high level of carbon dioxide in the headspace of packaged fruits and vegetables (Chakraverty, 2001). When carbon dioxide presents in excess amounts, anaerobic metabolism should not be induced by the use of a carbon dioxide-emitting package. Thus the film permeability and the respiration rate should be taken into account.

Most carbon dioxide emission processes are activated by moisture. This moisture usually comes from packaged foods (Ozdemir and Floros, 2004). This activation process therefore may work well with high moisture foods such as meats, fish, and minimally processed fruits and vegetables and be of limited application with intermediate moisture foods. The reaction of sodium bicarbonate and hydrating agents such as water with acidulates is used in this technology to produce carbon dioxide (Ozdemir and Floros, 2004). The Verifrais package is one application that uses this technology developed by SARL Codimer (Paris, France). This package is a standard MAP tray having a perforated bottom under which a porous sachet is positioned. This sachet contains sodium bicarbonate and ascorbate and the emission process is achieved by the juice leached from the packaged food. This package extends the shelf life of fresh meats and fish (Day, 2008).

2.3 Ethylene Adsorbers

As a plant growth regulator, ethylene accelerates the respiration rate and subsequent senescence of horticultural products such as fruit, vegetables, and flowers. Ethylene has many effects that are necessary, for example, induction of flowering in pineapples, color development in citrus fruits, bananas, and tomatoes, stimulation of root production in baby carrots, and development of bitter flavor in bulk-delivered cucumbers. However, it is desirable to remove ethylene or to suppress its negative effects in most horticultural situations. To this aim incorporating ethylene scavengers into fresh produce packaging and storage areas has been the focus of much research. Some of this research has ended up with commercial success, but much of it has not (Abeles et al., 1992; Rooney, 1995). Research to remove ethylene from storage atmospheres for a wide range of produce has developed packaging that absorbs or actively scavenges ethylene. The active packaging aimed at removing undesirable ethylene from the headspace of a package through absorption, adsorption, or scavenging is the best known and most widely used for fruits. This function is achieved through incorporation of a physical or chemical absorbent or adsorbent in the packaging material, or adding it to the package in the form of a sachet. Although the term "absorption" is used broadly to describe any system that removes a substance from the headspace in most research papers, there is a significant difference between absorption and adsorption. Adsorption involves a substance being taken onto the bulk of a phase and is a two-dimensional phenomenon, while absorption involves a substance being taken into a surface and is a three-dimensional phenomenon. Both absorption and adsorption are physical phenomena while scavenging implies a chemical reaction. In this section, ethylene adsorbers are mainly discussed.

Some phenomena related to adsorption are known from ancient times, although Scheele and Fontana revealed the first scientific evidences. They investigated the efficacy of charcoal and clays on gas adsorption (Dąbrowski, 2001) and their early discoveries are the origin of current applications and possibly of future developments.

In the phenomenon of surface adsorption, particles (gas or solid in solution) are held on the surface of solid material. The particles are commonly called adsorbates and the trapping solid material the adsorbent. In adsorption, the absorbate is accumulated throughout the absorber, not only on its surface. There are two different patterns of adsorption: physicoadsorption, involving binding through van der Waals forces, and chemiadsorption, involving chemical linkages (Martínez-Romero et al., 2007). The amount of adsorbed material depends on temperature, pressure, and adsorbate concentration. Activated carbon and zeolites are the main compounds used as ethylene adsorbers. Activated carbon was commercially applied in the adsorption of gases and vapor in the 1930s, although the specific use for ethylene started in the late 1950s. Any carbonaceous material may be used for making activated carbon, but the raw material should have low inorganic matter content, be easily activated, be easily available, have low cost, and have low degradation during storage (Dąbrowski, 2001). Therefore lignocellulosic material such as wood, fruit shells, fruit stones, apple pulp, wheat, cotton stalks, viscose rayon, and coal, among others, are often used for production of activated carbon. These methods of carbon activation are both physical and chemical. Advantages of chemical procedures over physical ones include greater yield, no previous carbonization being necessary, lower temperatures of activation, and good development of the porous structure (Puziy et al., 2002).

A wide range of properties determine the ability of activated carbon to act as an adsorber (Aygün et al., 2003), such as magnitude and distribution of pore volume (pore structure), surface area, and type and quality of surface-bound functional groups (surface chemistry). The adsorption capacity is proportionally related to both large surface area and pore volume. Although some activated carbons could achieve surface areas as high as 5000 $m^2 g^{-1}$, activated carbons with surface areas ranging between 300 and 2000 $m^2 g^{-1}$ are used for commercial food grade. Specific uses of activated carbon in foods are as decolorizing agents, taste/odor-removing agents, and purification agents. Activated carbon can be in three forms: granular, powdered, or fibered (Ahmedna et al., 2000). The granular type is, however, preferred due to its easier regeneration and versatility. The adsorption process of ethylene on these adsorbers fits a model proposed by Langmuir in 1916. The rate of adsorption is assumed to be directly related to ethylene pressure (temperature and relative humidity [RH]) and surface of the adsorber in this model, achieving a dynamic equilibrium between adsorption and desorption. A study comparing ethylene adsorption capacity of three forms of activated carbon showed that the best results in terms of ethylene adsorption were obtained with granular (over 80%) followed by powered (over 70%) activated carbon and fibered activated carbon had the lower adsorption capacity for this gas (over 40%). In addition, at 2.5, 5.0, or 7.5 $\mu L L^{-1}$ concentrations, the exogenous application of ethylene to a constant mass of activated carbon resulted in the same percentage of adsorbed ethylene independently of the concentration of the applied ethylene. Moreover, temperature in the range of 2–20°C did not affect the adsorption capacity of these activated carbons (Martínez-Romero et al., 2007). This means that ethylene is a very reactive compound due to its double bond and can be altered or degraded in many ways. Compared with activated carbon alone the ethylene adsorption was improved by the use of granular activated carbon (GAC) impregnated with palladium (Pd) as catalyst (Bailèn et al., 2007), and the efficacy was enhanced using Pd at 10% instead of 1% (98 and 85%, respectively). Increased ethylene removal by adding Pd to the activated carbon as a catalyst was attributed to the fact that both an adsorption phenomenon and an oxidation process happened. However, Pd has a high cost, which would limit its practical application. So, GAC-1% Pd could be considered as satisfactory in terms of ethylene adsorption. To create an active packaging, this adsorber/catalyst system was added as sachets to tomatoes under MAP conditions. In tomatoes in MAP packages containing 1% Pd, a reduction happened in color evolution (both internal and external) as well as a delay in the softening process. This indicates a net delay of the tomato ripening process and an increase in shelf life. Also the use of GAC-1% Pd reduced odor intensity, which was attributed to the capacity of the adsorber to trap volatiles and considered as related to lower off-flavor. Other effects of the active packaging were reducing the ethylene accumulation inside the packages, the weight loss, and decay incidence (Bailèn et al., 2006). Moreover, 23 compounds, mainly aldehydes and alcohols, were identified in control tomatoes under MAP conditions, while in those packaged in MAP containing GAC-1% Pd, the predominant compounds were the alcohols while acids, ketones, and hydrocarbons disappeared.

Since panelists judged the treated tomatoes better than controls regarding odor and flavor, this decrease of volatiles was not interestingly correlated to those results obtained from the sensorial panel. Jacobsson et al. (2004) showed in their study that the shelf life of broccoli stored in a plain low-density polyethylene (LDPE) bag was nearly the same as that of broccoli in an ethylene-scavenging LDPE bag stored at 4°C (11 and 12 days, respectively). However, when stored at 10°C the ethylene-scavenging bag presented a longer shelf life of 9 days while the broccoli in a plain bag had a 7-day shelf life. Shelf life was determined based on weight loss, visual inspection, total chlorophyll, and texture. Activated carbon-based scavengers with various metal catalysts are also able to remove ethylene effectively. These scavengers have been used for removing ethylene from produce warehouses or embedded into paper bags or corrugated board boxes for produce storage or incorporated into sachets for inclusion into produce packs. Sekisui Jushi Ltd has marketed a dual-action ethylene scavenger and moisture absorber in Japan. Neupalon™ sachets contain activated carbon, a metal catalyst, and silica gel. These sachets are able to scavenge ethylene and act as a moisture absorber as well (Abeles et al., 1992; Rooney, 1995). Recently, the market has been witness to numerous produce packaging films and bags based on the putative ability of certain finely ground minerals for adsorbing ethylene and emitting antimicrobial far-infrared radiation. However, peer-reviewed scientific journals show little direct evidence for their effects. These activated earth-type minerals are typically clays, pumice, zeolites, coral, ceramics, and even Japanese Oya stone. In packaging, these minerals are embedded or blended into polyethylene film bags used for packaging fresh produce. The claim that manufacturers of such bags make regarding extended shelf life for fresh produce is partly due to the adsorption of ethylene by the minerals dispersed within the bags. To support this claim the evidence is generally based on the extended shelf life of produce and reduced headspace ethylene in mineral-filled bags compared to common polyethylene bags. However, independent research has revealed that mineral-filled polyethylene bags have much greater gas permeability and in turn much faster ethylene diffusion will happen out of these bags, as is the case for commercially available microperforated film bags. Additionally, it is likely that a more favorable equilibrium modified atmosphere will be developed within these bags compared with common polyethylene bags, particularly for a produce with a high respiration rate. Therefore improved produce shelf life and reduced headspace ethylene can be obtained by these effects independently of any ethylene adsorption. Indeed, without relying on expensive Oya stone or other specialty minerals, almost any powdered mineral can present such effects (Abeles et al., 1992; Rooney, 1995).

Other active packaging has used adsorbers and potassium permanganate ($KMnO_4$) as oxidizer. $KMnO_4$ must be adsorbed on a suitable inert carrier with a large surface area (zeolite, vermiculite, silica gel, alumina pellets, or activated carbon) containing about 4–6% $KMnO_4$ to be effective. There are two steps in the process of ethylene oxidation with $KMnO_4$. Ethylene is firstly oxidized to acetaldehyde, which is then oxidized to acetic acid and in turn oxidized to carbon dioxide and water. These reactions are followed by a change in $KMnO_4$ adsorbers from purple to brown as the MnO_4 is reduced to MnO_2, signifying the remaining adsorbing capacity. However, because of their toxicity and purple color, the adsorbent materials containing $KMnO_4$ cannot be integrated into fruit-contact packaging but are supplied only as sachets.

To solve this problem a recent scrubber has been developed to remove ethylene continuously from stored environments (Martínez-Romero et al., 2009a). This scrubber is composed of a cartridge heater tightly joined to the GAC-1% Pd. An increase occurs in ethylene oxidation and autoregeneration of the activated carbon as heat pulses is applied; this fact is very important due to low maintenance cost and the increased adsorbing capacity, which were the limiting factors of the classical ethylene adsorbers. Since ethylene removal efficacy was higher with higher number of heat pulses, several heater core temperatures were tested (100–325°C), and the results showed that 96–99% of ethylene was removed by the temperatures ranging between 150 and 200°C, with low CO_2 accumulation (0.10–0.18 kPa), and consequently less activated carbon was degraded without affecting the storage environment temperature. This hybrid was used with stored tomatoes in cold rooms, and the ripening-related parameters such as respiration rate, ethylene production, ACC (free and conjugated), color changes, softening, decrease in TA (mainly citric and ascorbic acids), and lycopene were significantly lower in tomato fruits stored with the adsorbent-catalyst system in continuous working mode. Since this scrubber device is applied to large storage cold rooms, it could not be considered as an active packaging. However, it can serve as a further step in the concept of a new tool to prevent the detrimental effects of ethylene action and in turn maintain the postharvest quality of fruit and vegetables by eliminating the ethylene surrounding them in the storage areas. Among other additional advantages of this device are the autoregeneration process when applying heat pulses to the adsorbent-catalyst system and the environmentally friendly nature of this technology (Martínez-Romero et al., 2009b).

The use of electron-deficient nitrogen-containing trienes incorporated in ethylene-permeable packaging is one of the latest improvements made in ethylene-removing packaging. The preferred diene or triene is a tetrazine. However, tetrazine must be incorporated in a hydrophobic, ethylene-permeable plastic film not containing hydroxyl groups because it is unstable in the presence of water. Appropriate films would include silicone polycarbonates, polystyrenes, polyethylenes, and polypropylenes. It was demonstrated that approximately 0.01–1.0 M of the dicarboxyoctyl ester derivative of tetrazine incorporated in such a film is able to reduce ethylene in sealed jars by 10-fold within 24 h and by 100-fold within 48 h.

2.4 Ethanol Emitters

Ethyl alcohol or ethanol has been recognized for a century to act as a microbicidal preservative and in very small amounts to be safe for human consumption when ingested (as in beverages). However, there are some difficulties in applying ethanol as a preservative to foodstuffs: off-flavors, rapid volatilization, and consumer resistance.

Using ethanol as an antimicrobial agent is well documented, particularly against mold, but it can also inhibit the growth of yeasts and bacteria. Ethanol can be sprayed directly onto food products just prior to packaging. In this regard, several reports have shown that spraying with 95% ethanol to give concentrations of 0.5–1.5% (w/w) in the products can significantly extend the mold-free shelf life of food products. According to suppliers' commendations, the packaging material should have high barrier characteristics to ethanol, preferably below 2 g m^{-2} day to allow its accumulation in the headspace. The sachet size and product a_w determine the level of ethanol in the packaging headspace [7].

However, using ethanol-emitting films and sachets is considered to be a more practical and safer method for generating ethanol (Rooney, 1995). In some cases legislative problems exist with the ethanol concentration in the product, and the cost of the sachets exerts a limitation on their use to products with low profit margins (Ozdemir and Floros, 2004). Many applications of ethanol emitting films and sachets have been patented, primarily by Japanese manufacturers. These manufacturers include EthiCap™, Anti-mold 102™, and Negamold™ (Freund Industrial Co. Ltd), Oitech™ (Nippon Kayaku Co. Ltd), ET Pack™ (Ueno Seiyaku Co. Ltd), and Ageless™ type SE (Mitsubishi Gas Chemical Co. Ltd). All of these films and sachets contain absorbed or encapsulated ethanol in a carrier material allowing the controlled release of ethanol vapor. As an example, EthiCap™, the most commercially popular ethanol emitter in Japan, consists of food-grade alcohol (55%) and water (10%) adsorbed onto silicon dioxide powder (35%) contained in a sachet made of a paper and ethyl vinyl acetate copolymer laminate. Some sachets contain traces of vanilla or other flavors in order to mask the odor of alcohol. There is a label with the note "Do not eat contents" on sachets and also a diagram illustrating this warning. Other ethanol emitters such as Negamold and Ageless type SE both scavenge oxygen and emit ethanol vapor and thus are dual-action sachets (Rooney, 1995).

The weight of food, a_w of food, and the desired shelf life determine the size and capacity of the ethanol-emitting sachet. In a food package using an ethanol-emitting sachet, moisture is absorbed by the food, and ethanol vapor is released and diffuses into the package headspace. Ethanol emitters are widely popular in Japan where they are used to extend the mold-free shelf life of high moisture bakery products, such as high ratio cakes, by up to 2000% (Rooney, 1995; Hebeda and Zobel, 1996).

It has been demonstrated that ethanol vapors are effective in controlling molds including *Aspergillus* and *Penicillium* species; bacteria including *Staphylococcus*, *Salmonella*, and *Escherichia coli* species, and three species of spoilage yeast. However, a combination of aw and ethanol vapor can control yeast growth and fermentation at higher aw. Studies with apple turnovers with a_w of 0.93 and packaged under various atmospheres reveal that ethanol vapor can effectively extend shelf life and retain the quality of these products. Increased yeast counts in air and gas-packaged apple turnovers were observed from zero after day 1 to approximately 106 after 21 days' storage at 21°C. However, yeast growth was completely inhibited for product packaged under ethanol vapor, alone or in conjunction with MAP. Also, carbon dioxide production was completely inhibited for the product packaged with EthiCap and all packages were normal at the end of the 21-day storage period. The research indicated that it is possible to achieve a longer shelf life of apple turnovers by packaging the product with EthiCap, either alone or in conjunction with MAP. In addition, it appears that ethanol vapor can exert an antistaling effect as well as its antimold properties.

2.5 Flavor/Odor Scavengers

Packaging interaction with food flavors and aromas has long been recognized, especially when undesirable flavor scalping happens with desirable food components. For example, it has been shown that after only 2 weeks' storage in aseptic packs, scalping of a considerable proportion of desirable limonene occurs with orange juice (Rooney, 1995). Commercially, very few attempts have been made to selectively remove undesirable flavors and taints through active-packaging techniques. However, there are many potential opportunities such as debittering of pasteurized orange juices. Some varieties of orange, such as Navel, are particularly prone to bitter flavors caused by limonin, a tetraterpenoid, which is released into the juice after orange pressing and subsequent pasteurization. To debitter such juices, a number of processes have been developed that pass the juices through columns of cellulose triacetate or nylon beads (Rooney, 1995). In this regard, a possible active-packaging solution would incorporate limonin adsorbers (eg, cellulose triacetate or acetylated paper) into orange juice packaging material.

Removing odors from the interior of food packages may be both beneficial and detrimental. However, the benefits of odor/aroma removal are significant in the area of active packaging. Many foods such as cereal products develop confinement odors. Preventing the potentially adverse effects of these confinement odors is one reason for odor removal from the interior of packages. Another reason is obviating the effects of odors developed in the package materials themselves. During plastic processing (ie, extrusion, molding, film and sheet blowing, or casting), some polyolefin components may break down or oxidize into short chain and often odorous hydrocarbon compounds.

Two types of taints are amenable to removal by active packaging: amines and aldehydes. Amines are formed from the breakdown of proteins, and aldehydes from the auto-oxidation of fats and oils. Various acidic compounds can neutralize unpleasant-smelling alkaline volatile amines, such as trimethylamine, which is associated with fish protein breakdown (Franzetti et al., 2001).

Off-flavor or odor formation is an important biochemical process occurring under MAP. Off-flavor serves as a very sensitive indicator for the shelf life of fresh-cut products in packages. The literature increasingly reports that biosynthesis of ethanol and acetaldehyde increases during MAP storage of fresh-cut products, and ethanol and acetaldehyde content is positively related to off-flavor of fresh-cut products and off-odor of sealed fresh-cut packages. Anico Co. Ltd in Japan has marketed Anico™ bags made from film containing a ferrous salt and an organic acid such as citrate or ascorbate. It is claimed that these bags oxidize amines as they are adsorbed by the polymer film (Rooney, 1995) and aldehydes such as hexanal and heptanal are removed from package headspaces by Dupont's Odor and Taste Control (OTC) technology (Bozoğlu et al., 2001). This technology is based on a molecular sieve with pore sizes of around 5 nm, and Dupont claim that their OTC technology removes or neutralizes aldehydes, but no evidence is provided. The food applications claimed to be desired for this technology are snack foods, cereals, dairy products, poultry, and fish (Bozoğlu et al., 2001). Swedish company EKA Noble in cooperation with Dutch company Akzo have also made a similar claim of aldehyde removal (Goddard, 1995). They have developed a range of synthetic alumino silicate zeolites that, according to their claim, are able to adsorb odorous gases within their highly porous structure. Apparently odorous aldehydes are adsorbed in the pore interstices of their BMH™ powder, which can be incorporated into packaging materials, especially paper-based ones (Goddard, 1995).

2.6 Preservative Releasers and Antimicrobial Agents

The primary cause of shelf-life termination of fruits and vegetables is surface microbial spoilage (Jay et al., 2005). The main reasons for this microbial spoilage or contamination are uncontrolled harvesting, transportation, packaging, and processing operations (Erdögrul and Şener, 2005). Freshly harvested fruits and vegetables contain mixed initial flora of coliforms especially *E. coli*, lactic acid bacteria, *Pseudomonas*, and *Erwinia*; however, the primary causes of the contamination of fresh-cut fruits and vegetables are yeasts, molds, and *Pseudomonas*, especially when they are stored aerobically under refrigeration (Ahvenainen, 1996; May and Fickak, 2003). One effective antimicrobial activity is adding antimicrobial agents such as hydrogen peroxide, peroxyacetic acid, ozone, chlorinated water, and plant extracts into the washing water, but total elimination of the microbial spoilage on fruit surfaces will not be successful in this way (Akbas and Ölmez, 2007;

Alegria et al., 2009; Win et al., 2007). As most antimicrobial agents interact quickly with food compounds and in turn lose their effectiveness considerably, this direct application of agents has limited effectiveness (Mehyar et al., 2007).

One of the main applications of active packaging is antimicrobial packaging. Antimicrobial packaging can be defined as a packaging system that adds active ingredients and/or uses actively functional polymers in the packaging system to be able to kill or inhibit spoilage and pathogenic microorganisms involved in contaminating foods (Han, 2003). Antimicrobial active packaging releases antimicrobial agents in a controlled way and maintains the surface concentration of the agents above the minimum inhibitory concentration of the target microorganisms (Han, 2003; Suppakul et al., 2003a,b). Selecting packaging materials and proper antimicrobial substances with structural compatibility is very important to achieve this state. The antimicrobial substances should be selected from materials with intermediate polarity (hydrophilicity/hydrophobicity), which have no strong interaction with the packaging materials when they are binned or are not quickly released from the packaging materials as a result of being repelled (Han and Floros, 2000).

Acquiring antimicrobial activity the packaging system (or material) extends the lag period and reduces the growth rate or decreases live counts of microorganisms in order to limit or prevent microbial growth. Some food products are not sensitive to microbial spoilage and an antimicrobial packaging system is not necessary for them. However, the use of antimicrobial packaging will ensure safety, maintain quality, and increase shelf life of most foods, including fruits and vegetables, because they are perishable and susceptible to contamination.

On the basis of localization of the antimicrobial compound, antimicrobial active-packaging systems can be classified in four groups: (1) the antimicrobial is released to the package headspace to interact with the produce surface, (2) the antimicrobial compound is included in the packaging material and is released to the product through migration, (3) the antimicrobial compound is immobilized in the package surface, and (4) the package material has inherent antimicrobial activity. Antimicrobial substances incorporated in or coated onto film materials encouraged the first developments in antimicrobial packaging (Vermeiren et al., 1999), although they are suitable to be applied mostly to meat, fish, bakery, and cheese products, and fewer results exist for fruits and vegetables. Silver has long been used as an antimicrobial agent with food and beverages and has numerous advantages over other antimicrobial agents. Silver is broad spectrum and toxic (to varying degrees) to numerous strains of bacteria, fungi, algae, and possibly some viruses, compared to molecular antimicrobials (Duncan, 2011). Due to the strong antimicrobial activity of Ag^+ ions, Ag-substituted zeolite was initially incorporated into plastic films, but its commercial use was discharged by the regulatory restriction of addition of Ag to foods.

Several other compounds including organic acids (sorbate, propionate, and benzoate), bacteriocins (nisin), and enzymes (lysozyme) have been proposed or tested for antimicrobial activity in food packaging, but many of the antimicrobials incorporated in packaging are not yet permitted for food use, and incompatibility of the component with the packaging material or heat lability of the component during the extrusion process during film manufacture limits the election of the antimicrobial.

At 0.1–5% w/w of the packaging film, heat-resistant antimicrobials can be incorporated through extrusion and injection molding. Heat-labile compounds can be obtained through solvent compounding. Those antimicrobials that cannot tolerate the temperatures of polymer processing are often added to cast films or coated onto the material after forming. Ionic or covalent linkages can make the antimicrobials immobilized to polymers: here, the presence of functional groups is required in both the antimicrobial and the polymer; slow release of antimicrobials into the food is permitted by ionic bonding of them onto polymers. Some polymers such as chitosan are inherently antimicrobial and have been used in films and coatings. Antimicrobial gas (volatile antimicrobials) releasers were recently developed and commercially employed. Volatile antimicrobials can readily penetrate irregular food surfaces through void spaces or channels. Inspired by this advantage presented by an indirect contact antimicrobial packaging system, many researchers attempted to look for an effective method of incorporating volatile antimicrobials into a polymer matrix. For example, allyl isothiocyanate in a cyclodextrin matrix in the inner liners of plastic films is released to the headspace of the package after triggering by moisture. American Air Liquide and its Japanese partner tested this system against various pathogenic bacteria. Also, chlorine dioxide releasing films for disinfection of packaged fruits and vegetables are commercially available (Scully and Horsham, 2007; Han and Floros, 2007). Han and Floros (2007) provided a list of commercial active-packaging technologies and patents including antimicrobial packaging systems. Quimica Osku (Chile) commercialized sulfur dioxide-releasing pads, and Food Science Australia developed sulfur dioxide-releasing plastic films from a mixture of organic acid and calcium sulfite (Steale and Zhou, 1994).

Systems gradually release SO_2 to control mold growth in some fruits, such as table grapes. However, partial bleaching problems have been observed in grapes due to excessive release of SO_2 from pads of sodium metabisulfite incorporated to microporous material. In addition, toxicological problems can appear because of accumulation or absorption of excess SO_2 by foods and can endanger safety in SO_2-releasing active-packaging systems.

However, research for finding alternatives to these chemical substances is continuing and the results have proposed using a number of natural substances exhibiting antimicrobial and antifungal activities (Tripathi and Dubey, 2004) as part of the active packaging. Essential oils derived from many plant organs are among such natural compounds and have antimicrobial properties, and although they have been empirically recognized for centuries, they have gained scientific attention only recently (Appendini and Hotchkiss, 2002; Burt, 2004). In addition, these volatiles also have antioxidant properties (Ruberto and Baratta, 2000). Essential oils or so-called volatile or ethereal oils (Guenther, 1948) are aromatic oily liquids obtained from plant organs: flower, bud, seed, leave, twig, bark, herb wood fruit, and root. It is thought that the term "essential oil" is derived from the words *quinta essentia* whose medical use is attributed to Paracelsus. Due to their flavor and fragrance, essential oils are used for flavoring foods, but essential oils and their pure components are nowadays gaining increasing interest because of their safe status, wide acceptance by consumers, and their exploitation for multipurpose uses (Cowan, 1999). The most common essential oils and the major components used in the food industry with antioxidant or antimicrobial properties in vitro have been reviewed (Serrano et al., 2008). These natural compounds belong to the genera *Thymus, Origanum, Syzygium, Mentha,* and *Eucalyptus.* The essential oils from citrus species have been very recently assumed as potential antimicrobials. The components of citrus essential oils contain 85–99% volatile and 1–15% nonvolatile components. The volatile components are a mixture of monoterpene (limonene) and sesquiterpene hydrocarbons and their oxygenated derivatives including aldehydes (citral), ketones, acids, alcohols (linalool), and esters (Fisher and Phillips, 2008). Antioxidant activity is observed in the whole essential oils, but their fractionation shows that carvacrol, thymol, eugenol, menthol, and eucalyptol are the main components responsible for the antioxidant effect for oregano, thyme, clove, mint, and eucalyptus, respectively. Fig. 3.1 shows the chemical structures of these natural essential oils. In this figure, eugenol, thymol, and carvacrol are phenols, while eucalyptol and menthol are terpenoids. It has been reported

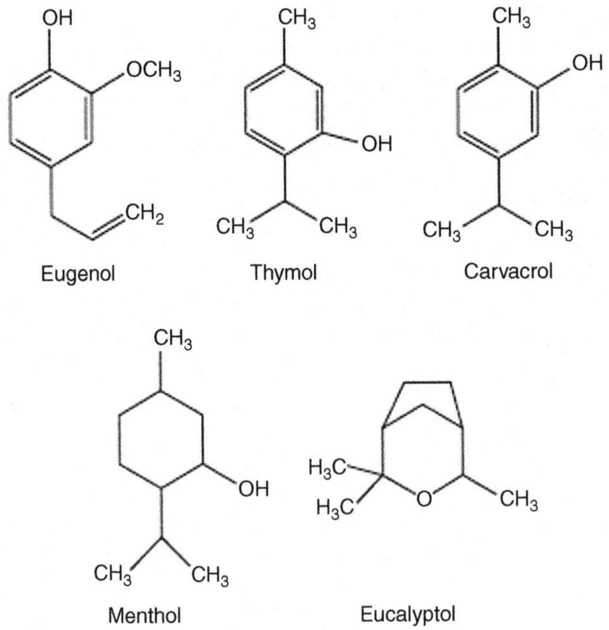

Figure 3.1 Chemical structures of the main essential oils with antioxidant or antimicrobial activities.

that antioxidant activity of these compounds is close to that of α-tocopherol (Ruberto and Baratta, 2000; Sacchetti et al., 2005) or vitamin C (Kim and Lee, 2004), and mainly due to the presence of hydroxyl groups in the benzene ring. However, the capacity of the essential oils to kill microorganisms is the main biological activity and the possible reason for using them in the food industry. The in vitro antimicrobial activity of eugenol, thymol, and carvacrol has been reported against bacteria (Periago et al., 2004), yeasts (Arora and Kaur, 1999), and fungi (Vázquez et al., 2001). Regarding bacteria, essential oils are generally more inhibitory against Gram positive than against Gram negative (Holley and Patel, 2005). However, only a few of the essential oils have been studied in terms of the in vivo efficacy and practical activity, and their exact mechanism of action is not fully clarified. Some authors have attributed their mechanism of action to their hydrophobicity enabling them to partition in the lipids of the cell membrane and to disturb its integrity and the inorganic ions' equilibrium (Bagamboula et al., 2004), but others have assumed that the presence of the phenolic ring is necessary for the antimicrobial activity of eugenol and thymol (Ultee et al., 2002). Moreover, it is thought that the site(s) and number of hydroxyl groups on the phenol ring are related to their relative toxicity to microorganisms. To support this assumption, it is said that increased hydroxylation results in increased toxicity (Cowan, 1999). In addition, it has been assumed that the mechanism of action in essential oils with an absence of phenolic groups such as menthol involves membrane disruption by the lipophilic compounds (Serrano et al., 2008). Specifically, aromatic and phenolic compounds alter the structure of the cytoplasmic membrane and function so as to exert their antimicrobial effects.

An early sign of damage is usually efflux of K^+, which is often followed by efflux of cytoplasmic constituents (Cowan, 1999; Ultee et al., 2002). This in turn leads to loss of the differential permeability character of the cytoplasmic membrane, which is frequently identified as the cause of cell death. Other events such as dissipation of the two components of the proton motive force in cells (ie, the pH gradient and the electrical potential), either by changes in ion transport or by structural changes in the membrane leading to depolarization, interference with the energy (ATP) generation system in the cell; or enzyme inhibition preventing substrate utilization for energy production (Holley and Patel, 2005) could also result in membrane dysfunction and subsequent disruption.

Investigation for identifying the effect of antimicrobial packaging materials and edible coatings on produce shelf life is still continuing. The polysaccharides chitosan, alginate, κ-carrageenan, cellulose ethers, high-amylose product, and starch derivatives dominate the range of matrices for edible films, but protein-based films made with wheat gluten, soy, zein, gelatin, whey, and casein have also been produced. A review by Valencia-Chamorro et al. (2011) provides further details on antimicrobial agents such as benzoic acid, sorbic acid, propionic acid, lactic acid, nisin, and lysozyme, which have been successfully added to edible composite films and coatings.

Rojas-graü et al. (2009) studied the effect of lemongrass, oregano, and vanillin essential oils in alginate coatings on apple cuts and found that the growth of psychrophilic aerobes, yeast, and molds decreased by more than 2 log cfu/g. Natamycin in a bilayer coating of chitosan considerably reduced fresh melon decay caused by two strains of spoilage fungi (Cong et al., 2007). The growth of *Candida albicans*, *Aspergillus flavus*, and *Eurotium repens* was totally inhibited in vitro and strawberry was completely protected from visible fungal growth during storage for 7 days at 4°C by clove, cinnamon, and oregano essential oils as used in paraffin coating of paper packaging materials (Rodriguez et al., 2007). Chitosan, a natural antimicrobial compound, is capable of forming stable coatings on fresh-cut papaya and suppressing microbial growth (González-Aguilar et al., 2004).

According to the European Commission a number of essential oils and their components have been registered to be applied in foodstuffs, including eugenol, menthol, and thymol (Commission Decision, Jan. 23, 2002, CE). These compounds appear also in EAFUS (Everything Added to Food in the US) and GRAS (Generally Recognized as Safe) lists. The potential use of essential oils as natural preservatives in foods has been reported in cheese, bakery products, and meat, among others (Burt, 2004), and the main disadvantages for the use of these natural compounds have been reported as persistence of strong aroma and the fact that they sometimes would change the organoleptic properties of food adversely. The use of natural compounds such as hexanal, 2(E)-hexenal, and hexyl acetate in fruits and vegetables improved shelf life and safety of minimally processed fruits (Lanciotti et al., 2004). In this review, the authors postulated that the focus of future trends in the use of natural compounds should be on the use of specific active packaging having the ability to release the active molecules slowly over time in the headspace. Through these premises the first active packaging in the form of combination of MAP and pure essential oils was reported in sweet cherry (Serrano et al., 2005) and several cultivars of table grapes such as Crimson, Autumn Royal, and Aledo (Valverde et al., 2005; Valero et al., 2006; Guillen et al., 2007). This active packaging can improve overall quality of products in terms of maintenance of organoleptic and functional properties and enhance safety. Table 3.1 shows the efficacy of the essential oils added to MAP in causing a reduction in the total mesophilic aerobic and yeast and mold counts in table grape and sweet cherry regarding the contamination in fruits stored in MAP. It is clear that for both fruit types, the essential oils were much more effective in reducing the yeast and molds than mesophilic aerobics which was due to the lower decay incidence in these fruits as compared to those stored in MAP. Because the concentration of CO_2 was not high enough inside the bags (below 3 kPa) to act as an antimicrobial, the microbial contamination increased during fruit storage under MAP conditions only (control). In these reports the pure volatiles (eugenol, thymol, carvacrol, or menthol) were used instead of the whole essential oils. Although the fungi-toxic properties of the volatile constituents of higher plants have been reported, fungi-toxicity of these substances when combined has gained little attention.

Fungi-toxic potency has been thought to be possibly induced by essential oils, which may be due to synergism between their components. In fact a mixture of essential oils (carvacrol, thymol, and eugenol) was used in Aledo table grapes and a lower concentration was required to control microbial spoilage (Guillen et al., 2007) compared to these essential oils used alone (Valverde et al., 2005;

Table 3.1 Effect of the Essential Oils Addition to MAP Packages on Microbial Spoilage in Table Grape and Sweet Cherry (Serrano et al., 2005; Valverde et al., 2005)

	Total Mesophilic Aerobics (CFU g^{-1})		Yeasts and Molds	
	Table Grape	Sweet Cherry	Table Grape	Sweet Cherry
At harvest	4.77 A	4.20 A	4.61 A	2.10 A
Control	4.90 A	4.77 A	5.04 A	4.89 B
Eugenol	3.33 B	2.93 B	2.10 B	1.11 C
Thymol	3.41 B	2.84 B	2.46 B	0.95 C
Menthol	3.60 B	2.69 B	3.24 C	1.48 D

Each package contains 500 μL of the corresponding essential oil, except in control, in which no essential oils were added. Data obtained after 16 and 35 days of cold storage in MAP packages for sweet cherry and table grape, respectively. For each column, the different letters (A, B, C, D) are significantly different $p < 0.05$.

Valero et al., 2006). Other researchers also reported that fungi-toxic potency of the fungicides and the antimicrobial activity of most microbicides are enhanced when they are used simultaneously (Tripathi and Dubey, 2004) as well as the antimicrobial activity (Burt, 2004). The reason for enhancement of the fungi-toxic potential of mixtures of oils may be the joint action of two or more substances present in the oils. This synergism would be useful in postharvest protection as the pathogen would not easily produce resistance against the components. However, more work is required to study the synergistic action of plant products under in vitro and in vivo conditions. Also, the mode of action of the essential oils as a postharvest antifungal has been scarcely taken into consideration in the literature. Compared to control sweet cherries and table grapes under MAP conditions, this active packaging was able to maintain color and to reduce softening in both fruits (Fig. 3.2). Similarly, the increase in ripening index or ratio TSS/TA was delayed in fruits under active packaging compared to those in MAP alone (Fig. 3.3). Therefore the evolution of these parameters related to postharvest ripening is further delayed by using the combination of MAP and essential oils than by MAP alone, and as gas composition was similar (11–12 O_2 and 2–3 kPa CO_2 for sweet cherry, and 10–14 O_2 and 1.3–2.0 kPa CO_2 for table grapes) in both control bags and active packages, the effects are attributed to the essential oils added.

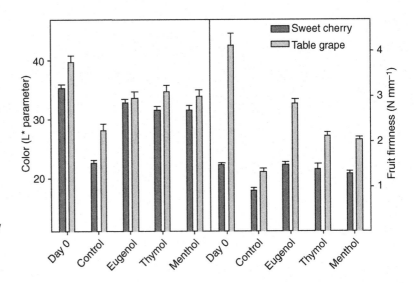

Figure 3.2 Values at harvest (day 0) and after storage at 2°C in color luminosity (L* parameter) and fruit firmness in sweet cherry and table grapes under modified atmosphere packaging (MAP) packages (control) and in active packaging (500 μL of eugenol, thymol, or menthol). Storage times were 16 and 35 days for sweet cherry and table grapes, respectively (Serrano et al., 2005; Valverde et al., 2005).

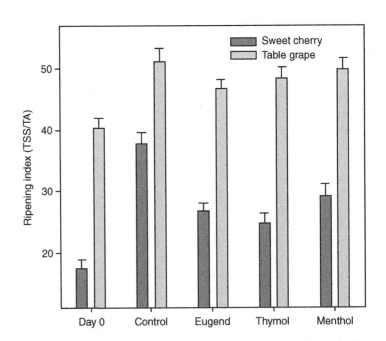

Figure 3.3 Values at harvest (day 0) and after storage at 2°C ripening index in sweet cherry and table grapes under modified atmosphere packaging (MAP) packages (control) and in active packaging (500 μL of eugenol, thymol, or menthol). Storage times were 16 and 35 days for sweet cherry and table grapes, respectively (Serrano et al., 2005; Valverde et al., 2005).

Chitosan as an antimicrobial agent in food packaging has been extensively studied, which is partly due to its intrinsic antimicrobial properties and its ability to perform a dual role as a film matrix and a carrier of antimicrobial additives such as acids and salts, essential oils, lysozyme, and nisin. There is a considerable variability in antimicrobial activity exhibited by chitosan-containing films, which is possibly the result of the variability of different chitosan preparations and the limited availability of active chitosan molecules for interaction with microbes after film formation. Joerger et al. (2009) evaluated the antimicrobial activity of chitosan by covalently attaching it to ethylene copolymer films. Chitosan was most effective when it was used in combination with other treatments such as high pressure or silver ions.

The compounds that have beneficial properties associated with fruit and vegetable intake regarding human health are those with antioxidant activity, including carotenoids, ascorbic acid, flavonoids, anthocyanins, and other phenolic compounds. However, the possible role of active packaging on the behavior of these bioactive compounds has gained little attention. In grapes, diminution of both total phenolics and anthocyanins in the skin (Fig. 3.4) and in the flesh (Fig. 3.5) was also accompanied by previously mentioned loss of quality during storage. Total phenolics and anthocyanins were responsible for the reduction of hydrophilic antioxidant activity (H-TAA) found in both skin and flesh, respectively.

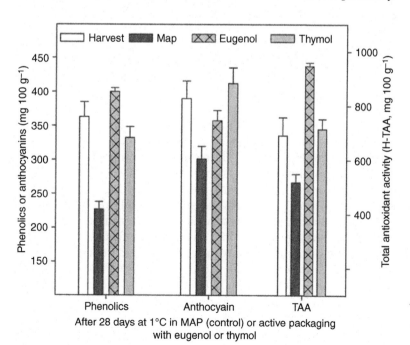

Figure 3.4 Bioactive compounds (total phenolics and anthocyanins) and hydrophilic antioxidant activity (H-TAA) in the table grape skin from control modified atmosphere packaging (MAP) packages and those with active packaging by adding eugenol or thymol after 28 days at 2°C. Each package contains 150 μL of the corresponding essential oil (Serrano et al., 2005; Valverde et al., 2005).

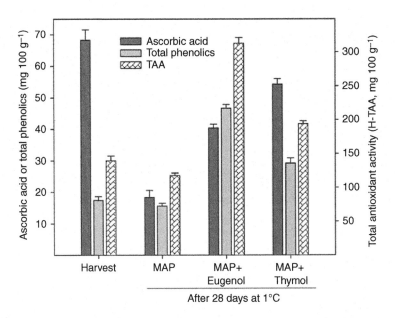

Figure 3.5 Bioactive compounds (total phenolics and ascorbic acid) and hydrophilic antioxidant activity (H-TAA) in table grape flesh from control modified atmosphere packaging (MAP) packages and those with active packaging by adding eugenol or thymol after 28 days at 2°C. Each package contains 150 μL of the corresponding essential oil (Serrano et al., 2005; Valverde et al., 2005).

In contrast, a delay in the loss of total phenolics and total anthocyanins in the skin and ascorbic acid in the flesh resulted from the addition of eugenol or thymol inside the packages. Moreover, use of the active packaging increased total phenolics and total antioxidant activity (TAA). Combined use of both compounds together with MAP storage as an active packaging would help maintain or increase the antioxidant capacity of fruits, for eugenol and thymol exhibit a natural antioxidant activity (Sacchetti et al., 2005) close to that of vitamin C (Kim and Lee, 2004) and are of phenolic nature. Development of this technology for commercial application needs a strong impulse as antimicrobial active packaging is an emerging concept in food technology, which can be highly beneficial in meeting consumers' demands for safe products free of chemicals as a means of preservation. A better understanding of the mechanisms these essential oils exert to affect the fruit physiology and control the ripening process as well as their ability to kill microorganisms needs further studies. Moreover, it should be advisable to use a combination of two or more of these compounds (with different functional groups) for more effectiveness.

Optimization of the packaging system is needed for commercialization of antimicrobial packaging in a way to be able to respond to the specific requirements of the product. Thus this optimization will depend on storage temperature, microbial spoilage behavior, possible safety hazards, shelf life, etc. Regulatory concerns and requirements in the field of food packaging should be incorporated in current intensive research in this area and research should seek compatibility with these regulations.

2.7 Humidity Regulators and Absorbers

One of the major causes of food spoilage is excess moisture; therefore various absorbers or desiccants are used to soak up moisture, maintain food quality, and extend its shelf life by inhibiting microbial growth and moisture-related degradation of texture and flavor.

Control of atmospheric RH during the storage of fresh fruits and vegetables is important for maintaining high quality. Transpiration in fruits and vegetables produces water. Chakraverty (2001) implied that the rate of transpiration depends on temperature and also varies between day and night. Product transpiration and package permeability to water vapor determine the amount of moisture in a food package. Excessive increase of moisture inside a food package leads to induced fungal and bacterial growth. Controversially, Rico et al. (2007) implied that shriveling and loss of quality and sensory properties can occur in packaged fruits and vegetables as a result of excessive water loss.

Moisture absorbers are manufactured in the form of sachets, pads, sheets, or blankets by several companies. Moisture-absorber sachets are usually used for humidity control in packaged dried foods, while moisture-drip absorbent pads, sheets, and blankets are used for liquid water control in high a_w foods such as fruits, vegetables, meats, fish, and poultry. Also, absorber papers and desiccant pads are used to wrap one or more fruits (Ozdemir and Floros, 2004). There are several commercial absorption sheets and blankets in market, such as Toppan Sheet™, Thermarite™, and Luquasorb™ (Day, 2008). The absorbers are basically made of two layers of a microporous nonwoven plastic film, such as polypropylene or polyethylene, and superabsorbent polymer, which is placed between layers and can absorb up to 500 times its own weight with water. Polyacrylate salts, carboxymethyl cellulose, and starch copolymers are typical superabsorbent polymers, which have a very strong affinity for water (Rooney, 1995).

Blocking moisture in the vapor phase is a good approach for the control of excess moisture in high a_w foods. Food packers or even householders use this approach to decrease the a_w on the surface of foods by reducing in-pack RH. In the absorber, one or more humectants are placed between two layers of a water-permeable plastic film such as Pichit™ film, developed by Japanese company Showa Denko Co. Ltd, that consists of a sandwiched layer of humectant propylene glycol and carbohydrate between two layers of polyvinyl alcohol plastic film. Pichit film can be used for wrapping fruits and vegetables, fresh meats, fish, and poultry and is marketed for home use in a roll or single sheet form. It was reported that this film dehydrates the surface of the food after wrapping by osmotic pressure, inhibits microbial growth, and extends shelf life by 3–4 days under chilled storage (Labuza and Breene, 1989; Rooney, 1995). There are various types of moisture scavengers such as silica gel, natural clays (eg, montmorillonite), calcium oxide, calcium chloride, and modified starch, which can modify package humidity (Day, 2008). Also, in the United States microporous sachets of desiccant inorganic salts such as sodium chloride have been used for the distribution of tomatoes (Rooney, 1995). Another approach to control moisture around fruits and vegetables are film perforations with a defined number and size of microholes. High vapor permeabilities composite polymeric films and boxes with large openings on the sides and bottom have been developed as moisture absorbers for fruits and vegetables. It should be mentioned that due to high release of water and uneven distribution of moisture inside the container, these items do not function effectively enough to prevent the deterioration of quality. A novel system was developed by Dijkink et al. (2004) for maintaining RH around $90.5 \pm 0.1\%$ inside a storage room of bell peppers. They reported that after 3 weeks in a controlled atmosphere experiment fungal development reduced without increasing shriveling. Weight loss and shriveling depend on vapor pressure. Fiber board box is an innovative moisture absorber for packaging fruits and vegetables, which functions as a humidity buffer on its own without relying on a desiccant insert. It consists of an unwettable and highly water vapor-permeable that is placed next to the fruits or vegetables, and an integral water vapor barrier on the inner surface of the fiber board, a paper-like material bonded to the barrier that acts as a wick. Patterson and Joyce (1993) implied that when the temperature drops and the RH rises, the multilayered box absorbs water in the vapor state and conversely releases water vapor in response to a lowering of the RH when the temperature rises.

In order to clearly see the product through the packaging films, antifogging films were proposed Antifogging film usually incorporates with humidity absorbers, hydrophilic liners, or microperforations in the film. Ozdemir and Floros (2004) implied that these films are usually used to reduce the internal vapor pressure and prevent water condensation in respiring products such as fresh-cut fruits and vegetables.

2.8 Temperature Control Packaging

It is clearly known that temperature is the most important factor for microbial, respiration, and chemical reactions and has great influence on plant metabolic activity (Erturk and Picha, 2008). Therefore the deterioration process of fruits and vegetables is retarded by precise control of temperature. As a general rule, each increase of 10°C increases the respiration rate of plants nearly twice (Atkin and Tjoelker, 2003). Also, the increase of temperature leads to an exponential increase in microbiological growth and spoilage rate, until the temperature reaches a level at which the microorganisms may be thermally disrupted or destroyed. One suitable approach to prevent temperature changes in the produce is application of temperature control packaging. It is evident that technology developers' demands for temperature-sensitive package materials are gradually in an attempt to develop fresh produce package materials.

Usually, temperature control active packaging is classified as insulating materials and self-heating and self-cooling cans. For example, Thinsulate™ (3M Company, United States) is an insulating material that was developed to guard against undue temperature abuse during storage and distribution of chilled foods. Thinsulate consists of a special nonwoven plastic with many air pore spaces. A self-cooling can is capable of withstanding temperature rises so that it can maintain chilled temperatures by increasing the thermal mass of the food package. For example, Cool Bowl™ (developed by the Adenko Company of Japan) consists of a double-walled polyethylene terephthalate container with an insulating gel deposited between the walls (Labuza and Breene, 1989). Self-heating containers and cans, such as self-heating aluminum and steel cans and containers for coffee, tea, and ready meals, have been commercially produced for decades. They basically use exothermic reactions, for example, lime and water positioned in the base, which when mixed heat the contents. Self-cooling cans use an endothermic reaction, such as dissolution of ammonium nitrate and chloride in water, to cool the product. Chill Can™ (The Joseph Company, United States) is another self-cooling can that relies on a hydrofluorocarbon (HFC) gas refrigerant. HFC gas is released by triggering a button set into the can's base and can cool a drink by 10°C in 2 min. Because of concerns about the environmental impact of HFCs, the commercial success Chill Can will likely be curtailed (Bozoğlu et al., 2001).

Temperature-compensating films are used in temperature control packaging. The films' permeability to gases changes by responding temperature changes. As mentioned earlier, temperature strongly affects the respiration rate of produce, while it slightly affects the permeabilities of traditional films. Thus in traditional film packages a small increase of storage temperature leads to a rapid accumulation of CO_2 and depletion of O_2 in the package. In temperature-compensating films the activation energy of permeability matches more closely the respiration rate activation energy of produce and changes in the film gases' transmission rate by temperature fluctuation-compensated changes in the respiration rate to prevent anoxic conditions. Recent research about temperature compensating films has focused on the application of side-chain crystallizable polymers and temperature-controlled opening pores in polymer films.

In temperature-controlled opening pores in polymer films, pores usually fill with wax and the pore is opened when wax melts as temperature exceeds a certain set value. Intelimer® is produced by Landec Corporation (United States) and is made of an acrylic backbone with fatty acid-based side chains of various lengths. The side chains remain in a crystalline state during cold storage, but as the temperature increases, side chains of different lengths begin to melt at different temperatures, which changes the polymers' physical properties in response to specific, predetermined temperature variation. Also the polymer rapidly becomes amorphous and more permeable to oxygen as the temperature rises above the set temperature, which is a physical reversible change, thus the polymer recrystallizes and if the temperature decreases, permeability to O_2 returns to its originally set level (Fig. 3.6) (Bozoğlu et al., 2001).

2.9 Edible Coatings

Due to environmental and consumer concerns both the food and packaging industries are looking for ways to reduce the amount of food packaging materials. Thus biobased materials

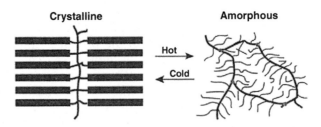

Figure 3.6 State transition in Intelimer™ polymer.

for food packaging were introduced at the end of the last century; however, all of these materials are not necessarily biodegradable (Petersen et al., 1999). Biopolymer-based packages are made of packaging materials that originate from raw agricultural and marine materials extracted directly from natural raw materials such as cellulose, starch, protein, and marine prokaryotes or produced by chemical synthesis from bioderived monomers, and produced by microorganisms such as hydroxybutyrate and hydroxyvalerate (Cha and Chinnan, 2004).

Edible films and edible coatings are main types of biobased packaging materials, which are used along with primary and secondary packaging materials. Edible coatings are defined as a thin layer of biobased material, which covers the surface of the food and can be eaten as part of the whole product. Edible wax coatings have been commonly used on fresh produce surfaces to reduce bruising during handling and shipping, improve appearance, reduce weight loss, and to provide a carrier for active compounds in apples, avocados, grapefruits, lemons, limes, melons, oranges, parsnips, bell peppers, cantaloupes, cucumbers, eggplants, pineapples, pumpkins, passion fruit, peaches, rutabagas, squash, sweet potatoes, tomatoes, turnips, and yucca. European Directive 1998 listed some permissible ingredients that can be incorporated into the formulation of edible coatings as follows: Arabic and karaya gum, pectins, shellac, beeswax, candelilla wax, carnauba wax, lecithin, polysorbates, fatty acids, and fatty acid salts. However, the Food and Drug Administration permitted the use of other additives as components of protective coatings applied to fresh fruits and vegetables, such as morpholine, polydextrose, sorbitan monostearate, sucrose fatty acid esters, cocoa butter, and castor oil. A comprehensive study by Park (1999) reviewed the development of systematic means of selecting edible coatings to maximize quality and shelf life of fresh fruits and vegetables. The study mentioned that edible coatings generally should have the desirable characteristics of being odorless, tasteless, and transparent.

It is also important have knowledge of the physical properties of the coating and its permeability to moisture, oxygen, and carbon dioxide in order to realize its beneficial effects. Edible coatings can be applied to the exterior of horticultural products to improve the safety and quality of fruits and vegetables and protect them from deterioration by slowing gas exchange, moisture and solute migration, reducing or even suppressing physiological disorders, reducing respiration and oxidative reaction rates (Rojas-graü et al., 2009), retaining volatile compounds, improving texture, and preserving nutritional value though limiting gas and water vapor exchanges between fruit and the surrounding atmosphere (Daniel and Zhao, 2007; Olivas et al., 2003; Vargas et al., 2008; Shon and Haque, 2007; Dang et al., 2008). Rojas-graü et al. (2009) reported that edible coatings can be used as carriers of active ingredients such as antibrowning agents, antimicrobial agents, flavors, colorants, spices, and nutrients to delay their senescence, maintain their organoleptic properties, extend their shelf life, and reduce the risk of pathogen growth on produce surfaces. The incorporation of antimicrobials into edible coatings inhibits the surface spoilage of fruits by blocking aerobic microorganisms from the access of oxygen (Park et al., 1998). Treatment of fruits by edible or wax coatings is performed by dipping and brushing, or spraying wax onto the surface of the product.

Treatment of the surface of fruits with edible coatings modifies the internal atmosphere by increasing the carbon dioxide and lowering the oxygen concentrations. Thus it is essential to investigate the effects of edible coatings on internal gas composition and their interactions on quality parameters of coated fresh produce. Selecting suitable films or coatings is a crucial factor for the success of edible coatings of various fruits and developing a desirable internal gas composition for a specific product. Also a thick coating has detrimental effects on the quality of fruit since it can reduce internal O_2 concentration below a desirable level and increase CO_2 concentration above a critical tolerable level. Park (1999) proposed that the O_2 permeability of most edible coatings is lower than that of the conventional plastic films.

Edible films and coatings are typically made of lipids (waxes, acyl glycerols, and fatty acids), hydrocolloids (proteins and polysaccharides, such as starch, cellulose derivatives, alginate, agar, and chitosan), and composites (both hydrocolloid components and lipids).

Selecting film or coating materials is largely dependent on their desired function. The most investigated biopolymer materials are polysaccharide coatings because of their beneficial characteristics such as being less expensive and less allergenic, carrying a larger variety of functional ingredients, and creating various physical properties of produce comparable to those coated with the expensive protein films (Hernández-Muñoz et al., 2006).

Starch is more biodegradable and cost effective than other polysaccharides but is also very hydrophilic; in addition, starch films have moderate gas barrier properties and low mechanical properties compared with synthetic polymer films. The linear fraction of starch "amylose" is responsible for the film-forming capacity of starches that forms a coherent and relatively strong, freestanding film. In contrast, amylopectin films are brittle and noncontinuous (Cha and Chinnan, 2004). Thermoplastic starch films are made from native granular starch in the presence of plasticizers such as water and glycerol. Pea starch coating materials were developed by Mehyar and Han (2004) and had lower O_2 permeability and comparable water vapor permeability similar to protein films.

Chitosan is another polysaccharide of high interest, which is obtained from the deacetylation of chitin of crab and shrimp shells (poly-β-(1→4)-N-acetyl-D-glucosamine). Films and coatings made from chitosan have selective gas permeability (CO_2 and O_2) and good mechanical properties, but their high water vapor permeability limits their applications. Studies showed that chitosan also has antifungal and antibacterial properties, which are attributed to its polycationic nature; however, by now the precise mechanism of its antimicrobial activity is still unknown (Srinivasa and Tharanathan, 2007). Alginates are the salts of alginic acid (a linear copolymer of D-mannuronic and L-glucuronic acid monomers) that are extracted from brown seaweeds of the *Phaephyceae* class. Alginates that react with divalent and trivalent cations are utilized in alginate film formation. Different divalent and trivalent cations such as calcium, magnesium, manganese, and aluminum, ferrous, and ferric ions have been applied as gelling agents but calcium ions are more effective than other ions (Vargas et al., 2008). Proteins derived from animal sources, such as whey protein and casein, or obtained from plant sources such as corn zein, soy protein, wheat gluten, cottonseed protein, and peanut protein are used in the formulation of edible coatings for fruits and vegetables (Gennadios, 2002). Depending on proteins' biological origin and function, they exhibit a wide variety of molecular characteristics that will determine the ability of particular proteins to form coatings and the characteristics of the coatings formed. Casein-based edible coatings have been the subject of intense investigation and are attractive for food applications due to their high nutritional quality, good potential for providing adequate protection for foods against the surrounding environment, and excellent sensory properties. Heat-denatured whey proteins are mixed with plasticizer to produce transparent and flexible water-based edible coatings with excellent oxygen, aroma, and oil barrier properties at low RH. However, whey protein coatings are less effective moisture barriers due to their hydrophilic nature. Lipid-based edible coatings are commonly used on fresh fruits and vegetables to control their desiccation and weight loss due to their low affinity for water and low water vapor permeability (Morillon et al., 2002). Saucedo-Pompa et al. (2007) developed edible coatings containing an oxygen scavenger such as candelilla wax coating incorporating *Aloe vera* and ellagic acid as antioxidants. They indicated that the coating system prevented weight loss and changes in the pH, freshness, and color of fresh-cut fruits stored at 5°C for 6 days.

Edible coatings containing *Aloe vera* gel were first used in table grapes (Valverde et al., 2005) and sweet cherries (Martínez-Romero et al., 2006) and result in satisfactorily reducing weight and lowering the respiration rate during postharvest storage. The authors observed that *A. vera* gel coating had several beneficial effects such as delaying softening, color changes, and TA losses, maintaining fruit quality and reducing both mesophilic aerobics and yeast and mold counts without affecting the sensory properties of the fruits. Vargas et al. (2008) proposed that although edible coatings are primarily used as a barrier to minimize water loss and delay the natural senescence of coated fruits, the new generation of edible coatings is specifically designed to allow the incorporation and/or controlled release of antioxidants, nutraceuticals, vitamins, and natural antimicrobial agents by means of the application of promising technologies such as nanoencapsulation and layer-by-layer assembly.

Zapata et al. (2008) applied alginate or zein-based coating on tomatoes and observed that the tomatoes showed a twofold lower concentration of the ethylene precursor and lower respiration rate and ethylene production than controls. They also reported that softening, color, and weight loss were significantly delayed (4–6 days on average) in coated tomatoes as compared to controls. Also, coated tomatoes had a higher remaining level of sugars, organic acids (and especially ascorbic acid), and scores from sensory analysis at the end of storage than control tomatoes. They also studied edible coatings based on zein (5%) alone or combined with essential oils as antimicrobial (thymol, carvacrol, eugenol, and menthol, 25 μL L^{-1} of each) effects on incidence of decay in tomato fruits. They observed that these treatments reduced incidences of decay along with reducing the color changes and the softening process during postharvest storage at 20°C compared with control fruits (Fig. 3.7).

One of major problems in most stored fresh produce is browning, which strongly influences appearance and consumer acceptance of the product. Enzymatic browning is a result of polyphenol oxidase (PPO) activity in fruits and vegetables. Common dipping treatments with antibrowning compounds such as citric acid, ascorbic acid, and sodium erythorbate are extensively used for inhibition of browning. However, incorporating *N*-acetylcysteine and glutathione to alginate and gellan-based edible coatings can prevent browning in fresh-cut fruits such as apples, pears, and

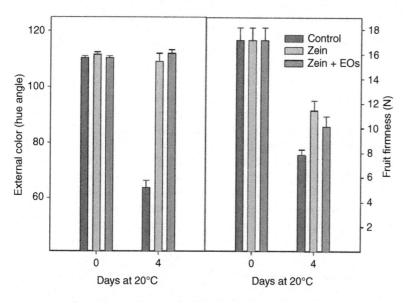

Figure 3.7 Values at harvest 0 and after 4 days of storage at 20°C in external color and fruit firmness in control tomatoes and those coated with zein (5%) alone or with the addition of mixed essential oils. The coating solution contains 25 μL L^{-1} of each essential oil (eugenol, thymol, menthol, and carvacrol) (Zapata et al., 2008).

papayas. Also, Oms-oliu et al. (2010) studied the effects of incorporating acids such as ascorbic acid and sorbic acid into methylcellulose on the browning of fresh-cut pears and observed that the treatments prevented browning. Ponce et al. (2008) investigated effects of chitosan and plant oleoresins from a rosemary and olive mixture on PPO activity and found that the treatments had significant antioxidant activity on PPO in butternut squash. Moreover, these coatings increase the antioxidant potential of the fruits besides preventing browning and extending the shelf life of fresh-cut fruit (Oms-oliu et al., 2010).

One of reasons for fruit softening development is enzymatic degradation of the cell wall of fruit by enzymes such as pectin methylesterase and polygalacturonase during ripening and cutting. In order to maintain the firmness and crispness of the fruit, calcium chloride has been incorporated into edible coatings for fresh-cut fruit to prevent fruit softening. However, due to the bitter taste, calcium chloride is replaced by calcium lactate. Calcium increases the firmness of the fruit through interacting with pectic acids of fruit and forming a cross-linked polymer network. Oms-oliu et al. (2010) incorporated calcium chloride into alginate and gellan coatings and found that the treatments minimized softening of fresh-cut apples and melons by increasing the firmness and preventing loss of moisture and turgor. Also investigated was the possibility of incorporating vitamins, minerals, and fatty acids into edible coating formulations to enhance the nutritional value of some fruits and vegetables that contain low quantities of these micronutrients (Rojas-graü et al., 2009).

2.10   Active Nanocomposites for Fruits and Vegetables Packaging

Nanomaterials are applied for materials with at least one dimension less than 100 nm. There are two approaches to the production of nanomaterials: (1) the "top-down" approach, in which materials are broken down chemically and/or physically into smaller particles, and (2) the "bottom-up" or "self-assembly" approach, which involves arranging molecules one at a time to build up a macrosized complex system (Warad and Dutta, 2005). Reduction of material size dramatically increases the surface-to-volume ratio, decreases cluster size, dramatically increases the number of surface particles, and enhances reactivity of the material with the surrounding medium. Currently, nanostructured materials have limited commercial applications in packaging of horticultural products.

Conventional active plastic technologies or active sachets are being gradually replaced by active nanocomposites for the extension of the quality and safety of packaged food products. Generally active nanocomposites consist of plastic composites (ie, a polymer blend) and an active nanostructured material, which confers an activity on the plastic matrix (Fig. 3.8). Inorganic or organic nanoparticles incorporated into the thermoplastic polymeric materials increase the performance characteristics of plastic packages through high dispersion in the polymeric matrix (Fig. 3.8).

High strength and stiffness fillers combined with polymeric matrix materials through interfacial interactions lead to firm and stiff structures in nanocomposites. In addition to retaining of the original physical and chemical identities in the resulting composite structure, new material properties are superior to those of the pristine polymer, such as improved mechanical and flexural properties, elevated heat distortion temperature, enhanced barrier properties, and improved biodegradation in the case of compostable polymers.

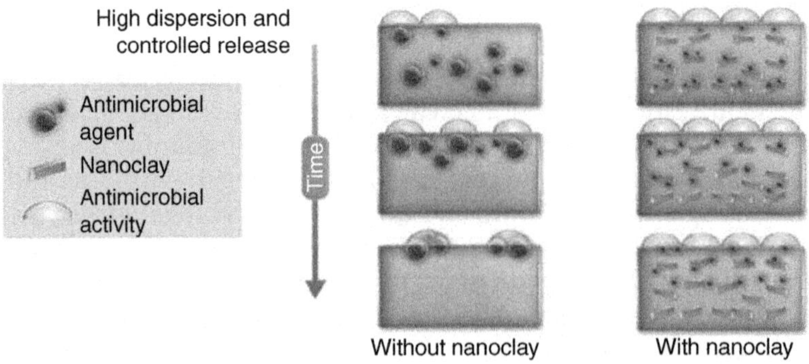

Figure 3.8 Schematics of the expected higher efficiency of active nanoclays containing antimicrobial agents dispersed within packaging plastics and bioplastics.

High dispersion and controlled release

Antimicrobial agent
Nanoclay
Antimicrobial activity

Time

Without nanoclay   With nanoclay

Nanoparticles improve material properties at much lower added quantities (2–8% w/w) due to their larger surface-to-volume ratio compared to micro- and macroscale filler particles (eg, talc, glass fiber, carbon particles). Researchers have utilized various nanomaterials for material enhancement purposes, such as carbon nanotubes, layered silicates, layered titanate, hydroxyapatite, aluminum hydroxide, etc. (Pandey et al., 2005; Ray and Bousmina, 2005; Yu et al., 2006).

Active nanocomposite films incorporating oxygen scavengers could be used for the packaging of a variety of oxygen-sensitive food product materials. Various oxygen-scavenging nanocomposites of active nanoclays consist of iron and food packaging and beverage polymers. Depending on the clay type and the iron-based chemistry used, there are differences in the active performance of various nanocomposites. The physical properties of the polymeric matrices are consolidated by layered nanoclays without serious impact on optics and flexibility.

Study of the DPPH (2,2-diphenyl-1-picrylhydrazyl)-inhibiting properties of EVOH nanocomposites containing O2Block™ RS-R (RS-R) (Nanobio Matters SL, Paterna, Spain) (a proprietary natural bioactive radical scavenging system supported on nanoclays) and other conventional antioxidants such as butylated hydroxytoluene (BHT) and the commercial natural antioxidant extracts CCX45%LS and Cocoanox12% showed that antioxidant capacity of RS-R was higher than that of other nontraditional additives in similar concentrations and similar to that of BHT. It was also found that RS-R could be an alternative to the traditional antioxidant BHT if there are no safety issues. Due to the slow release of the antioxidant from the matrix to the medium under test conditions, the efficiency of the nanoadditive system increased during storage.

Nanocomposites could also be used as antimicrobial packaging to control undesirable microorganisms on foods by incorporating active molecules such as antimicrobial compounds in or coated onto the packaging materials (Appendini and Hotchkiss, 2002; Nigmatullin et al., 2008; Persico et al., 2009). Nanocomposites with an antimicrobial function are particularly effective in minimizing the growth of postpackaging contaminant microorganisms, extending the shelf life of foods, and maintaining product quality and safety due to the high surface-to-volume ratio and enhanced surface reactivity of the nanosized antimicrobial agents. Several investigations have been performed to evaluate the antimicrobial activity of nanoparticles and nanocomposite materials for use as antimicrobial packaging films (Rhim et al., 2006; Wang et al., 2006), antimicrobial agents (Hong and Rhim, 2008), growth inhibitors

(Cioffi et al., 2005), or antimicrobial carriers (Bi et al., 2011). The antimicrobial nanocomposite films could be mainly used in meat, fish, poultry, bread, cheese, fruit, and vegetable packaging (De Oliveira et al., 2007; Kerry et al., 2006; Moreira et al., 2011).

Currently, silver is most common nanoengineered antimicrobial material used in food packaging. It was found that silver nanoparticles (AgNP) have antimicrobial effects on numerous species of bacteria. AgNPs can be engineered to have controlled release in order to retain their antimicrobial properties for long periods of time. Also, incorporating AgNP in polymer nanocomposites (PNCs) is a useful method in food packaging to extend shelf life. Ethylene gas destruction is catalyzed by silver particles; thus storage of fruits in AgNPs/PNC packages lead to slower ripening times and thus extended shelf lives. Duncan (2011) stated that although there were many advances in developing silver nanostructures for food packaging applications, comprehensive studies in various polymer systems are required to elucidate key relationships that influence the antimicrobial strength of various AgNP/PNC materials. Many researchers have investigated the antimicrobial properties of nanoparticles composed of other materials and the results showed that titanium oxide (TiO_2) particles in particular are promising. However, as TiO_2 nanoparticles should be photocatalyzed to show antimicrobial activity, TiO_2-based antimicrobials are only active in the presence of UV light. The probability of using TiO_2-coated packaging film as an ethylene scavenger for horticultural products was studied by several researchers. However, comprehensive studies are needed to address the potential end-use challenges, such as the effect of the available intensity and frequency of UV radiation, the impacts of the shadow effect, and the potential impact of food components that are UV sensitive. Maneerat and Hayata (2006a,b) indicated that the photocatalytic reaction of TiO_2 might be useful during the postharvest-controlled atmosphere storage of fruits and vegetables by reducing the accumulation of ethylene, acetaldehyde, and ethanol.

3 Acceptance, Safety, and Regulatory Issues of Active Packaging

Four food safety and regulatory issues need to be addressed in relation to active packaging of foods:
1. Any required approval for food contact must be established before using active packaging.
2. Any environmental regulations about active-packaging materials must be considered.

3. Labeling must be applied where active packaging may give rise to consumer confusion.
4. Any effects of active packaging on the microbial ecology and safety of foods should be considered (Rooney, 1995).

Food contact approval is often required before using active packaging. Active packaging influences foods in two ways: first, active-packaging substances may migrate into the food or may be removed from it intentionally or unintentionally. Intended migrants (such as antioxidants, ethanol, and antimicrobial preservatives) require regulatory approval for their identity, concentration, and possible toxicology effects, and unintended migrants (such as various metal compounds) should achieve their active purpose inside packaging materials but do not need to or should not enter foods.

Environmental regulations regarding active-packaging materials cover subjects such as reuse, recycling, and identification to assist in recycling or the recovery of energy from active-packaging materials. Food labeling is required in order to reduce the risk of consumers ingesting the contents of oxygen scavenger sachets or other in-pack active-packaging devices.

Food manufacturers should consider the effects of certain types of active packaging on the microbial ecology and safety of foods. For example, using OSs in food packaging may remove all the O_2 from the packs of high a_w chilled perishable food products and stimulate the growth of anaerobic pathogenic bacteria such as *Clostridium botulinum* (Betts, 1996). It is important in antimicrobial films that the spectrum of inhibited microorganisms be determined. For example, antimicrobial films that only inhibit spoilage microorganisms may enhance the growth of pathogenic bacteria and raise food safety concerns.

The main concern regarding the introduction of active packaging to the food industry is that consumers should consider if the components are harmful and whether to accept them. So far, research has mainly concentrated on the development of various methods and their testing in a model system, and more studies are needed to understand the chemical, physiological, and microbiological effects of various active packaging on the packaged food.

Although application of nanomaterials in food packaging may result in enhanced packaging performance, concerns have been raised in terms of their safety since the toxicological properties of many nanomaterials are not well characterized. Taylor (2008) implied that as nanosized particles have greater surface areas, they are more biologically active and therefore interactions of nanomaterials with biological systems are not same as their bulk counterparts. However, it is not always true that all nanoparticles are more toxic than micro- to macrosized particles of similar materials. Tsuji et al. (2006) recommended considering particle size, surface properties, the tendency of particles to aggregate/disaggregate, the method of synthesis, the particle shape, and the surface charge. Acceptability of nanotechnology driven products is dependent on consumers' perceptions and cultural believes. Finally, when assessing nanomaterials the following issues should be considered: chemical risk (characteristics of nanomaterial identity and properties, level of impurities, migration behavior), toxicological risks (appropriateness of current exposure, toxicology data, risk in utilization of macroscale counterpart for the nanomaterial), and environmental risk (adequacy of analytical methodologies, environmental fate, impacts on plant and animal species) (Taylor, 2008).

4 Future Trends

Due to consumer preferences in developing countries for minimally processed, naturally preserved foods and the food industry's interest in investing in product quality and safety, active packaging will probably increase in the near future. More studies are needed regarding the incorporation of absorbing or releasing compounds and adhesive labels to dispense with separate objects in active packaging. Also the studies should focus more attention on the function of preservatives where microbial growth and spoilage mainly occur (on the surface of the food) and develop new antimicrobial packaging materials that are effective against several spoilage and pathogenic microbes. It is understandable that these novel materials should have good appearance, good mechanical properties, proper permeability properties, be reasonable in price, and be suitable both for packaging machines already used in the food industry and for normal sealing procedures (Wilson, 2007). Research into the application of nanocomposites in active packaging should be focused on antioxidant-releasing films, light absorbing/regulating systems, color-containing films, antifogging and antisticking films, susceptors for microwave heating, gas permeable/breathable films, bioactive agents for controlled release, and insect-repellent packaging.

References

Abeles, F.B., Morgan, P.W., Saltveit, M.E., 1992. Ethylene in Plant Biology. Academic Press Ltd, London, UK.

Ahmedna, M., Marshall, W.E., Rao, R.M., 2000. Production of granular activated carbons from select agricultural by-products and evaluation of their physical, chemical and adsorption properties. Bioresource Technol. 71, 113–123.

Ahvenainen, R., 1996. New approaches in improving the shelf life of minimally processed fruits and vegetables. Trends Food Sci. Technol. 7 (6), 179–187.

Akbas, M.Y., Ölmez, H., 2007. Effectiveness of organic acid, ozonated water and chlorine dipping on microbial reduction and storage quality of fresh-cut iceberg lettuce. J. Sci. Food Agric. 87, 2609–2616.

Alegria, C., Pinheiro, J., Gonçalves, E.M., Fernandes, I., Moldão, M., Abreu, M., 2009. Quality attributes of shredded carrot (*Daucuc carota* L. cv Nantes) as affected by alternative decontamination processes to chlorine. Innov. Food Sci. Emerg. Technol. 10, 61–69.

Appendini, P., Hotchkiss, J.H., 2002. Review of antimicrobial food packaging. Innov. Food Sci. Emerg. Technol. 3, 113–126.

Arora, D.S., Kaur, J., 1999. Antimicrobial activity of spices. Int. J. Antimicrob. Agents 12, 257–262.

Atkin, O.K., Tjoelker, M.G., 2003. Thermal acclimation and the dynamic response of plant respiration to temperature. Trends Plant Sci. 8 (7), 343–350.

Aygün, A., Yenisoy-Karakas, S., Duman, I., 2003. Production of granular activated carbon from fruit stones and nutshells and evaluation of their physical, chemical and adsorption properties. Micropor. Mesopor. Mat. 66, 189–195.

Bagamboula, C.F., Uyttendaele, M., Debevere, J., 2004. Inhibitory effect of thyme and basil essential oils, carvacrol, thymol, estragol, linalool and p-cymene towards *Shigella sonnei* and *S. flexneri*. Food Microbiol. 21, 33–42.

Bailèn, G., Guillén, F., Castillo, S., Zapata, P.J., Serrano, M., Valero, D., Martínez-Romero, D., 2006. Use of activated carbon inside modified atmosphere packaging to maintain tomato fruit quality during cold storage. J. Agric. Food Chem. 54, 2229–2235.

Bailèn, G., Guillén, F., Castillo, S., Zapata, P.J., Serrano, M., Valero, D., Martínez-Romero, D., 2007. Use of a palladium catalyst to improve the capacity of activated carbon to absorb ethylene, and its effect on tomato ripening. Spanish J. Agric. Res. 5, 579–586.

Betts, G.D. (Ed.), 1996. Code of practice for the manufacture of vacuum and modified atmosphere packaged chilled foods with particular regards to the risks of botulism. Guideline No. 11, Campden & Chorleywood Food Research Association, Chipping Campden, Glos., UK.

Bi, L., Yang, L., Narsimhan, G., Bhunia, A.K., Yao, Y., 2011. Designing carbohydrate nanoparticles for prolonged efficacy of antimicrobial peptide. J. Contr. Rel. 150, 150–156.

Bozoğlu, T.F., Deak, T., Ray, B. (Eds.), 2001. Novel processes and control technologies in the food industry, vol. 338, IOS press, pp. 204–208.

Brandon, K., Beggan, M., Allen, P., Butler, F., 2009. The performance of several oxygen scavengers in varying oxygen environments at refrigerated temperatures: Implications for low-oxygen modified atmosphere packaging of meat. Int. J. Food Sci. Technol. 44, 188–196.

Burt, S., 2004. Essential oils: their antibacterial properties and potential applications in foods—a review. Int. J. Food Microbiol. 94, 223–253.

Cha, D.S., Chinnan, M.S., 2004. Biopolymer-based antimicrobial packaging: a review. Crit. Rev. Food Sci. Nutr. 44, 223–237.

Chakraverty, A., 2001. Postharvest Technology. Enfield, NH, Scientific Publishers.

Charles, F., Sanchez, J., Gontard, N., 2006. Absorption kinetics of oxygen and carbon dioxide scavengers as part of active modified atmosphere packaging. J. Food Eng. 72, 1–7.

Cioffi, N., Torsi, L., Ditaranto, N., Tantillo, G., Ghibelli, L., Sabbatini, L., 2005. Copper nanoparticle/polymer composites with antifungal and bacteriostatic properties. Chem. Mater. 17, 5255–5262.

Coles, R., McDowell, D., Kirwan, M.J. (Eds.), 2003. Food packaging technology, Vol. 5, CRC Press, pp. 290–300.

Cong, F., Zhang, Y., Dong, W., 2007. Use of surface coatings with natamycin to improve the storability of Hami melon at ambient temperature. Postharvest Biol. Technol. 46, 71–75.

Cowan, M.M., 1999. Plant products as antimicrobial agents. Clin. Microbiol. Rev. 12, 564–582.

Dąbrowski, A., 2001. Adsorption—from theory to practise. Advances Colloid Interface Sci. 93, 135–224.

Dang, K.T.H., Singh, Z., Swinny, E.E., 2008. Edible coatings influence fruit ripening, quality and aroma biosynthesis in mango fruit. J. Agric. Food Chem. 56, 1361–1370.

Daniel, L., Zhao, Y., 2007. Innovations in the development and application of edible coatings for fresh and minimally processed fruits and vegetables. Compr. Rev. Food Sci. Food Saf. 6, 60–75.

Day, B.P.F., 1989. Extension of shelf-life of chilled foods. Eur. Food Drink Rev. 4, 47–56.

Day, B.P.F., 2001. Active packaging – a fresh approach. Brand©—J. Brand Technol 1 (1), 32–41.

Day, B.P.F., 2008. Smart Packaging Technologies for Fast Moving Consumer Goods. Active packaging of food. John Wiley, Hoboken, NJ, pp. 1–18.

De Oliveira, T.M., Soares, N.F.F., Pereira, R.M., Fraga, K.F., 2007. Development and evaluation of antimicrobial natamycin-incorporated film in Gorgonzola cheese conservation. Pack. Technol. Sci. 20, 147–153.

Dijkink, B.H., Tomassen, M.M., Willemsen, J.H., van Doorn, W.G., 2004. Humidity control during bell pepper storage, using a hollow fiber membrane contractor system. Postharvest Biol. Technol. 32, 311–320.

Duncan, T.V., 2011. Applications of nanotechnology in food packaging and food safety: barrier materials, antimicrobials and sensors. J. Colloid Interface Sci. 363, 1–24.

Erdöğrul, Ö., Şener, H., 2005. The contamination of various fruit and vegetables with *Enterobius vermicularis*, *Ascaris* eggs, *Entamoeba histolyca* cysts and *Giardia* cysts. Food Control 16, 559–562.

Erturk, E., Picha, D.H., 2008. The effects of packaging film and storage temperature on the internal package atmosphere and fermentation enzyme activity of sweet potato slices. J. Food Process Preserv. 32, 817–838.

Fisher, K., Phillips, C., 2008. Potential antimicrobial uses of essential oils in food: is citrus the answer? Trends Food Sci. Technol. 19, 156–164.

Franzetti, L., Martinoli, S., Piergiovanni, L., Galli, A., 2001. Influence of active packaging on the shelf-life of minimally processed fish products in a modified atmosphere. Packag. Technol. Sci. 14 (6), 267–274.

Gennadios, A., 2002. Protein-Based Edible Films and Coatings. CRC Press, Boca Raton.

Goddard, R., 1995. Dispersing the scent. Packaging Week 10 (30), 28.

González-Aguilar, G.A., Ayala-Zavala, J.F., Ruiz-Cruz, S., Acedo-Félix, E., Díaz-Cinco, M.E., 2004. Effect of temperature and modified atmosphere packaging on overall quality of fresh-cut bell peppers. LWT—Food Sci. Technol. 37, 817–826.

Guenther, E., 1948. The Essential Oils. Van Nostrand, New York.

Guillen, F., Zapata, P.J., Martinez-Romero, D., Castillo, S., Serrano, M., Valero, D., 2007. Improvement of the overall quality of table grapes stored under modified atmosphere packaging in combination with natural antimicrobial compounds. J. Food Sci. 72, 185–190.

Han, J.H., 2003. Antimicrobial food packaging. Novel Food Packaging Techniques. CRC Press, Washington, DC, pp. 50–70.

Han, J.H., Floros, J.D., 2000. Simulating migration models and determining the release rate of potassium sorbate from antimicrobial plastic film. Food Sci. Biotechnol. 9 (2), 68–72.

Han, J.H., Floros, J.D., 2007. Active packaging. In: Tewari, G., Juneja, V.K. (Eds.), Advances in Thermal and Non-Thermal Food Preservation. Ames, Ia, Blackwell Professional, pp. 167–183.

Hebeda, R.E., Zobel, H.F. (Eds.), 1996. Baked Goods Freshness – Technology Evaluation and Inhibition of Staling. Marcel Dekker, Inc., New York, USA.

Hernández-Muñoz, P., Almenar, E., Ocio, M.J., Gavara, R., 2006. Effect of calcium dips and chitosan coatings on postharvest life of strawberries (*Fragaria × ananassa*). Postharvest Biol. Technol. 39, 247–253.

Holley, R.A., Patel, D., 2005. Improvement in shelf-life and safety of perishable foods by plant essential oils and smoke antimicrobials. Food Microbiol. 22, 273–292.

Hong, S.I., Rhim, J.W., 2008. Antimicrobial activity of organically modified nanoclays. J. Nanosci. Nanotechnol. 8, 5818–5824.

Idol, R., 1993. Oxygen scavenging: top marks. Packag. Week 9 (16), 17–19.

Imran, M., Revol-Junelles, A.M., Martyn, A., Tehrany, E.A., Jacquot, M., Linder, M., 2010. Active food packaging evolution: transformation from micro- to nanotechnology. Crit. Rev. Food Sci. Nutr. 50, 799–821.

Jacobsson, A., Nielsen, T., Sjoholm, I., 2004. Influence of temperature, modified atmosphere packaging, and heat treatment on aroma compounds in broccoli. J. Agric. Food Chem. 52, 1607–1614.

Janjarasskul, I., Tananuwong, K., Krochta, J.M., 2011. Whey protein film with oxygen scavenging function by incorporation of ascorbic acid. J. Food Sci. 76, 561–568.

Jay, J.M., Loessner, M.J., Golden, D.V., 2005. Modern Food Microbiology, third ed. Springer, New York.

Joerger, R.D., Sabesan, S., Visioli, D., Urian, D., Joerger, M.C., 2009. Antimicrobial activity of chitosan attached to ethylene copolymer films. Packag. Technol. Sci. 22, 125–138.

Kerry, J.P., O'Grady, M.N., Hogan, S.A., 2006. Past, current and potential utilization of active and intelligent packaging systems for meat and muscle-based products: a review. Meat Sci. 74, 113–130.

Kim, D.O., Lee, C.Y., 2004. Comprehensive study on vitamin C equivalent antioxidant capacity (VCEAC) of various polyphenolics in scavenging a free radical and its structural relationship. Crit. Rev. Food Sci. Nutr. 44, 153–273.

Labuza, T.P., Breene, W.M., 1989. Applications of active packaging for improvement of shelf-life and nutritional quality of fresh and extended shelf-life foods. J. Food Process. Preserv. 13, 1–69.

Lagaron, J.M., Catala, R., Gavara, R., 2004. Structural characteristics defining high barrier properties in polymeric materials. Mater. Sci. Technol. 20, 1–7.

Lanciotti, R., Gianotti, A., Patrignani, F., Belletti, N., Guerzoni, M.E., Gardini, F., 2004. Use of natural aroma compounds to improve shelf-life and safety of minimally processed fruits. Trends Food Sci. Technol. 15, 201–208.

Maneerat, C., Hayata, Y., 2006a. Antifungal activity of TiO_2 photocatalysis against *Penicillium expansum* in vitro and in fruit tests. Int. J. Microbiol. 107, 99–103.

Maneerat, C., Hayata, Y., 2006b. Efficiency of TiO_2 photocatalytic reaction on delay of fruit ripening and removal of off-flavors from the fruit storage atmosphere. Trans ASABE 49 (3), 833–837.

Martínez-Romero, D., Guillén, F., Castillo, S., Zapata, P.J., Serrano, M., Valero, D., 2009a. Development of a carbon-heat hybrid ethylene scrubber for fresh horticultural produce storage purposes. Postharvest Biol. Technol. 51, 200–205.

Martínez-Romero, D., Guillén, F., Castillo, S., Zapata, P.J., Valero, D., Serrano, M., 2009b. Effect of ethylene concentration on quality parameters of fresh tomatoes stored using a carbon-heat hybrid ethylene scrubber. Postharvest Biol. Technol. 51, 206–211.

Martínez-Romero, D., Bailén, G., Serrano, M., Guillén, F., Valverde, J.M., Zapata, P., Castillo, S., Valero, D., 2007. Tools to maintain postharvest fruit and vegetable quality through the inhibition of ethylene action: a review. Critic. Rev. Food Sci. Nutrit. 47 (6), 543–560.

May, B.K., Fickak, A., 2003. The efficacy of chlorinated water treatments in minimizing yeast and mold growth in fresh and semi-dried tomatoes. Drying Technol. 21 (6), 1127–1135.

Mehyar, G.F., Han, J.H., 2004. Physical and mechanical properties of high-amylose rice and pea starch films as affected by relative humidity and plasticizer. J. Food Sci. 69 (9), 449–454.

Mehyar, G.F., Han, J.H., Holley, R.A., Blank, G., Hydamaka, A., 2007. Suitability of pea starch and calcium alginate as antimicrobial coatings on chicken skin. Poult. Sci. 86, 386–393.

Moreira, M.R., Pereda, M., Marcovich, N.E., Roura, S.I., 2011. Antimicrobial effectiveness of bioactive packaging materials from edible chitosan and casein polymers: assessment on carrot, cheese, and salami. J. Food Sci. 76 (1), 54–63.

Morillon, V., Debeafort, F., Blond, G., Capelle, M., Voilley, A., 2002. Factors affecting the moisture permeability of lipid-based edible films: a review. Crit. Rev. Food Sci. Nutr. 42, 67–89.

Naito, S., Okada, Y., Yamaguchi, N., 1991. Studies on the behaviour of microorganisms in sponge cake during anaerobic storage. Packag. Technol. Sci. 4, 4333–4344.

Nigmatullin, R., Gao, F., Konovalova, V., 2008. Polymer-layered silicate nanocomposites in the design of antimicrobial materials. J. Mater. Sci. 43, 5728–5733.

Olivas, G.I., Rodriguez, J.J., Barbosa-Ćanovas, G.V., 2003. Edible coating composed of methylcellulose stearic acid, and additives to preserve quality of pear wedges. J. Food Process. Preserv. 27, 299–320.

Oms-oliu, G., Rojas-graü, M.A., González, L.A., Varela, P., Soliva-fortuny, R., Hernando, M.I.H., Munuera, I.P., Fiszman, S., Martín-belloso, O., 2010. Recent approaches using chemical treatments to preserve quality of fresh-cut fruit: a review. Postharvest Biol. Technol. 57 (3), 139–148.

Ozdemir, M., Floros, J.D., 2004. Active food packaging technologies. Crit. Rev. Food Nutr. 44, 185–193.

Pandey, J.K., Reddy, K.R., Kumar, A.P., Singh, R.P., 2005. An overview on the degradability of polymer nanocomposites. Polym. Degrad. Stab. 88, 234–250.

Park, H.J., 1999. Development of advanced edible coatings for fruits. Trends Food Sci. Technol. 10, 254–260.

Park, W.P., Cho, S.H., Lee, D.S., 1998. Effect of minimally processing operations on the quality of garlic, green onion, soybean sprouts and watercress. J. Sci. Food Agric. 77, 282–286.

Patterson, B.D., Joyce, D.C., 1993. A package allowing cooling and preservation of horticultural produce without condensation or desiccants. International Patent Application PCT/AU93/00398.

Pereira de Abreu, D.A., Cruz, J.M., Losada, P.P., 2012. Active and intelligent packaging for the food industry. Food Rev. Int. 28, 146–187.

Periago, P.M., Delgado, B., Fernandez, P.S., Palop, A., 2004. Use of carvacrol and cymene to control growth and viability of *Listeria monocytogenes* cells and predictions of survivors using frequency distribution functions. J. Food Protect. 67, 1408–1416.

Persico, P., Ambrogi, V., Carfagna, C., Cerruti, P., Ferrocino, I., Mauriello, G., 2009. Nanocomposite polymer films containing carvacrol for antimicrobial active packaging. Polym. Eng. Sci. 49, 1447–1455.

Petersen, K., Nielsen, P.G., Bertelsen, G., Lawther, M., Olsen, M.B., Nilsson, N.H., Mortensen, G., 1999. Potential of biobased materials for food packaging. Trends Food Sci. Technol. 10, 52-28.

Polyakov, V.A., Miltz, J., 2010. Modeling of the humidity effects on the oxygen absorption by iron-based scavengers. J. Food Sci. 75, 91–99.

Ponce, A.G., Roura, S.I., Del Valle, C.E., Moreira, M.R., 2008. Antimicrobial and antioxidant activities of edible coatings enriched with natural plant extracts. In vitro and in vivo studies'. Postharvest Biol. Technol. 49 (2), 294–300.

Puziy, A.M., Poddubnaya, O.I., Martínez-Alonso, A., Suárez-García, F., Tascón, J.M.D., 2002. Synthetic carbons activated with phosphoric acid. I. Surface chemistry and ion binding properties. Carbon 40, 1493–1505.

Ray, S.S., Bousmina, M., 2005. Biodegradable polymers and their layered silicate nanocomposites: in greening the 21st century materials world. Prog. Mater. Sci. 50, 962–1079.

Rhim, J.W., Hong, S.I., Park, H.M., Ng, P.K.W., 2006. Preparation and characterization of chitosan-based nanocomposite films with antimicrobial activity. J. Agric. Food Chem. 54, 5814–5822.

Rico, D., Martin-Diana, A.B., Barat, J.M., Barry-Ryan, C., 2007. Extending and measuring the quality of fresh-cut fruit and vegetables: a review. Trends Food Sci. Technol. 18, 373–386.

Robinson, D.K.R., Morrison, M.J., 2010. Nanotechnologies for food packaging: reporting the science and technology research trends. Report for ObservatoryNANO. www.observatorynano.eu.

Rodriguez, A., Batlle, R., Nerín, C., 2007. The use of natural essential oils as antimicrobial solutions in paper packaging: Part II. Prog. Org. Coat. 60, 33–38.

Rojas-graü, M.A., Soliva-Fortuny, R., Martín-Belloso, O., 2009. Edible coatings to incorporate active ingredients to fresh-cut fruits: a review. Trends Food Sci. Technol. 20, 438–447.

Rooney, M.L. (Ed.), 1995. Active Food Packaging. Chapman & Hall, London, UK.

Ruberto, G., Baratta, M.T., 2000. Antioxidant activity of selected essential oil components in two lipid model systems. Food Chem. 69, 167–174.

Sacchetti, G., Maietti, S., Muzzoli, M., Scaglianti, M., Manfredini, S., Radice, M., Bruni, R., 2005. Comparative evaluation of 11 essential oils of different origin as functional antioxidants, antiradicals and antimicrobials in foods. Food Chem. 91, 621–632.

Saucedo-Pompa, S., Jasso-Cantu, D., Ventura-Sobrevilla, J., Saenz-GalindoA, A., Rodriguez-Herrera, R., Aguilar, C.N., 2007. Effect of candelilla wax with natural antioxidants on the shelf-life quality of fresh-cut fruits. J. Food Qual. 30, 823–836.

Scully, A., 2009. Active packaging. In: Yam, K.L. (Ed.), The Wiley Encyclopedia of Packaging Technology, third ed. John Wiley & Sons, New York, pp. 2–9.

Scully, A.D., Horsham, M.A., 2007. Active packaging for fruits and vegetables. In: Wilson, C.L. (Ed.), Intelligent and Active Packaging for Fruits and Vegetables. CRC Press, Boca Raton, FL, pp. 57–73.

Serrano, M., Martínez-Romero, D., Castillo, S., Guillen, F., Valero, D., 2005. The use of natural antifungal compounds improves the beneficial effect of MAP in sweet cherry storage. Innov. Food Sci. Emerg. Technol. 6, 115–123.

Serrano, M., Martínez-Romero, D., Guillen, F., Valverde, J.M., Zapata, P.J., Castillo, S., Valero, D., 2008. The addition of essential oils to MAP as a tool to maintain the overall quality of fruits. Trends Food Sci. Technol. 19, 464–471.

Shon, J., Haque, Z.U., 2007. Efficacy of sour whey as a shelf-life enhancer: use in antioxidation edible coatings of cut vegetables and fruit. J. Food Qual. 30, 581–593.

Srinivasa, P.C., Tharanathan, R.N., 2007. Chitin/Chitosan – safe, ecofriendly packaging materials with multiple potential uses. Food Rev. Int. 23, 53–72.

Steale, R.J., Zhou, J.X., 1994. Int. Patent Appl. WO 94/10233.

Suppakul, P., Miltz, J., Sonnenveld, K., Bigger, S.W., 2003a. Active packaging technologies with an emphasis on antimicrobial packaging and its applications. J. Food Sci. 68, 408–420.

Suppakul, P., Miltz, J., Sonneveld, K., Bigger, S.W., 2003b. Active packaging technologies with an emphasis on antimicrobial packaging and its applications. J. Food Sci. 68 (2), 408–420.

Taylor, M.R., 2008. Assuring the Safety of Nanomaterials in Food Packaging – The Regulatory Process and Key Issues. Woodrow Wilson International Center for Scholars, Washington, DC.

Teixeira, V., Carneiro, J., Carvalho, P., Silva, E., Azevedo, S., Batista, C., 2011. High barrier plastics using nanoscale inorganic films. In: Lagarón, J.M. (Ed.), Multifunctional and Nanoreinforced Polymers for Food Packaging. Woodhead Publishing, Cambridge, UK, pp. 285–315.

Tripathi, P., Dubey, N.K., 2004. Exploitation of natural products as alternative strategy to control postharvest fungal rotting of fruit and vegetables. Postharvest Biol. Technol. 32, 235–245.

Tsuji, J.S., Maynard, A.D., Howard, P.C., James, J.T., Lam, C.W., Warheit, D.B., Santamaria, A.B., 2006. Research strategies for safety evaluation of nanomaterials. Part IV: Risk assessment of nanoparticles. Toxicol. Sci. 89 (1), 42–50.

Ultee, A., Bennik, M.H.J., Moezelaar, R., 2002. The phenolic hydroxyl group of carvacrol is essential for action against the food-borne pathogen: *Bacillus cereus*. Appl. Environ. Microbiol. 68, 1561–1568.

Valencia-Chamorro, S.A., Palou, L., del Rio, M.A., Pérez-Gago, M.B., 2011. Antimicrobial edible films and coatings for fresh and minimally processed fruits and vegetables: a review. Crit. Rev. Food Sci. Nutr. 51, 872–900.

Valero, D., Valverde, J.M., Martínez-Romero, D., Guillen, F., Castillo, S., Serrano, M., 2006. The combination of modified atmosphere packaging with eugenol or thymol to maintain quality, safety and functional properties of table grapes. Postharvest Biol. Technol. 41, 317–327.

Valverde, J.M., Guillen, F., Martínez-Romero, D., Castillo, S., Serrano, M., Valero, D., 2005. Improvement of table grapes quality and safety by the combination of modified atmosphere packaging (MAP) and eugenol, menthol or thymol. J. Agric. Food Chem. 53, 7458–7464.

Vargas, M., Pastor, C., Chiralt, A., McClements, J., Gonzalez-Martinez, C., 2008. Recent advances in edible coatings for fresh and minimally processed fruits. Crit. Rev. Food Sci. Nutr. 48, 496–511.

Vázquez, B.I., Gente, C., Franco, C.M., Vazquez, M.J., Cepeda, A., 2001. Inhibitory effects of eugenol and thymol on *Penicillium citrinum* strains in culture media and cheese. Int. J. Food Microbiol. 67, 157–163.

Vermeiren, L., Devlieghere, F., van Beest, M., de Kruijf, N., Debevere, J., 1999. Developments in the active packaging of foods. Trends Food Sci. Technol. 10, 77–86.

Wang, X., Du, Y., Yang, J., Wang, X., Shi, X., Hu, Y., 2006. Preparation, characterization and antimicrobial activity of chitosan/layered silicate nanocomposites. Polymer 47, 6738–6744.

Warad, H.C., Dutta, J., 2005. Nanotechnology for agriculture and food systems—a review. Proceedings of the Second International Conference on Innovations in Food Processing Technology and Engineering, Bangkok, January 11–13, 2005. Pathumthani, Thailand: Asian Institute of Technology.

Wilson, C.L., 2007. Intelligent and Active Packaging for Fruit and Vegetables. CRC Press, Boca Raton.

Win, N.K.K., Jitareerat, P., Kanlayanarat, S., Sangchote, S., 2007. Effect of cinnamon extract, chitosan coating, hot water treatment and their combinations on crown rot disease and quality of banana fruit. Postharvest Biol. Technol. 45, 333–340.

Xiao, E.L., Green, A.N.M., Haque, S.A., Mills, A., Durrant, J.R., 2004. Light driven oxygen scavenging by titania/polymer nanocomposite films. J. Photochem. Photobiol. A: Chem. 162, 253–259.

Yam, K.L., Takhisto, P.T., Miltz, J., 2005. Intelligent packaging: concepts and application. J. Food Sci. 70, 1–10.

Yu, L., Dean, K., Li, L., 2006. Polymer blends and composites from renewable resources. Prog. Polym. Sci. 31, 576–602.

Zapata, P.J., Guillén, F., Martínez-Romero, D., Castillo, S., Valero, D., Serrano, M., 2008. Use of alginate or zein as edible coatings to delay postharvest ripening process and to maintain tomato (*Solanum lycopersicon* Mill) quality. J. Sci. Food Agric. 88, 1287–1293.

4

ADVANCES IN MODIFIED ATMOSPHERE PACKAGING OF FRUITS AND VEGETABLES

Samad Bodbodak*, Mohammad Moshfeghifar**

*University of Tabriz, Department of Food Science and Technology, Faculty of Agriculture, Tabriz, Iran; **Islamic Azad University, Faculty of Food Sciences and Engineering (FFSE), Science & Research Branch Tehran, Tehran, Iran

1   Introduction

There is continuous research into improved methods of transporting food from producers to consumers. It has long been known that the preservative effect of chilling can be greatly enhanced when it is combined with control or modification of the gas atmosphere during storage. Such methods have been used commercially for over 100 years for the bulk storage and transport of fresh meat and fruits and are referred to as controlled atmosphere storage. Since the 1970s and the widespread availability of polymeric packages, this approach has been applied to consumer packs and given the name modified atmosphere packaging (MAP) because the atmosphere surrounding the food is modified but not controlled. MAP is a packaging technology that modifies or alters the gas composition around the products in food packages from normal air (20.95% O_2, 78.09% N_2, 0.93% argon, and 0.038% CO_2) to provide an atmosphere for increasing shelf life and maintaining the quality of food. Much research has been conducted into the positive effects of a modified atmosphere on the quality, texture, and physiology of fresh fruits and vegetables (Robertson, 2006; Zhuang, 2011). Although the commercial application of modified atmospheres began with chilled meat products (Inns, 1987), it is very common for fresh fruits and vegetables, especially fresh-cut (or minimally processed) fruits and vegetables, to be packed with MAP technology in today's marketplace (Toivonen et al., 2009). Compared with MAP for fresh meat products, MAP for fresh fruits and vegetables is much more challenging and complicated. Because fresh fruits and vegetables are still alive after harvesting

Eco-Friendly Technology for Postharvest Produce Quality. http://dx.doi.org/10.1016/B978-0-12-804313-4.00004-9
Copyright © 2016 Elsevier Inc. All rights reserved.

and during marketing, the successful use of MAP will be based not only on the specific O_2 and CO_2 permeation properties of polymer films but also on the respiration activity of packed food (Jayanty et al., 2005; Kader, 1986). MAP can be defined as the enclosure of food in a package in which the atmosphere inside the package is modified or altered to provide an optimum atmosphere for increasing shelf life and maintaining food quality. Modification of the atmosphere may be achieved either actively or passively.

Active modification involves displacing the air with a controlled, desired mixture of gases, a procedure generally referred to as gas flushing. Passive modification occurs as a consequence of the food's respiration and/or the metabolism of microorganisms associated with the food; the package structure normally incorporates a polymeric film, and so the permeation of gases through the film (which varies depending on the nature of the film and the storage temperature) also influences the composition of the atmosphere that develops. Zagory (1990) showed the effects of flushing fresh chilli peppers stored in plastic film with a mixture containing 10% CO_2 + 1% O_2 compared with no gas flushing (Fig. 4.1).

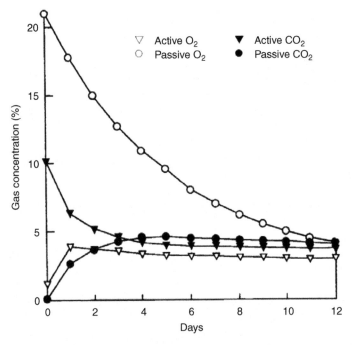

Figure 4.1 A comparison of passive modified atmosphere packaging and active modified atmosphere packaging on the basis of rate of change of CO₂ and O₂ in Anaheim chilli pepper fruit packed in Cryovac SSD-310 film (Zagory, 1990).

Costa et al. (2011) studied the effects of passive and active MAP conditions on the quality of packaged table grapes. They applied three oriented polypropylene (PP) films of different thicknesses (20, 40, and 80 μm, respectively) and various initial head space gas compositions (passive MAP and active MAP) to package the grapes. Their results showed that during a prolonged storage period at refrigerated temperature (5°C) all selected packaging films prevented product decay, thus promoting a substantial shelf-life prolongation (more than 70 days) especially with the thickest polymeric matrix sealed in air. They concluded that the active MAPs had no significant effect on shelf life due to the fast equilibrium of gas reached in the bags and product dehydration prolongation.

Since the late 1980s, many review articles and books on MAP for fresh fruits and vegetables have been published covering different aspects of the technology and mechanisms. For readers who are also interested in the history, mechanisms, and applications of MAP for fresh produce, reviews written by Kader (1986, 2002), Kader et al. (1989), Mir and Beaudry (2003), Jayanty et al. (2005), Toivonen et al. (2009), and Brody et al. (2011) are very valuable references.

Vacuum packaging of respiring foods or foods containing viable microorganisms such as flesh foods is clearly a form of MAP, because after initial modification of the atmosphere by removal of most of the air, biological action continues to alter or modify the atmosphere inside the package. In vacuum packaging, elevated levels of CO_2 can be produced by microorganisms or by respiring fruits and vegetables. Even when no gas is produced inside the package after sealing, vacuum packaging still qualifies as MAP because removing the air has modified the atmosphere inside the package.

As the normal microflora responsible for the spoilage of fruits and vegetables are varied greatly for each product and storage conditions, the elimination or significant reduction of the spoilage organisms could inadvertently enhance the ability for pathogens to grow in MAP. Although different studies showed that MAP is a suitable technology for extending the shelf life of the products, MAP application does not eliminate all of the microorganisms in the package and may only delay the growth of the general spoilage microorganisms. However, MAP could create a condition in which the product seems organoleptically acceptable (ie, look and smell fine) but it actually contains harmful pathogens. This unintended concern requires more comprehensive research to understand, identify, and manage.

2 Modified Atmosphere Packaging

2.1 MAP Gases, Packaging Materials, and Equipment

2.1.1 Gases Used in MAP

MAP usually consists of O_2, CO_2, and N_2. It is the altered ratio of O_2 and CO_2 that makes a difference in the protection of food commodities. Ripening of fruits and vegetables could be delayed, softening could be retarded, respiration and ethylene production rates could be reduced, and various compositional changes associated with ripening could be decelerated by decreasing the O_2 level and increasing the CO_2 level. Oxygen is essential for the respiration of fresh horticultural commodities. The removed O_2 can be replaced with N_2, usually recognized as an inert gas, or CO_2, which is a competitive inhibitor of ethylene action and can lessen the pH or prevent the growth of some bacteria and fungi. When the O_2 level is decreased to below 12 kPa, and levels commonly used for most fresh horticultural commodities are about 3–5 kPa, the respiration rate starts to decrease. The absence of O_2 can produce anaerobic respiration, accelerating deterioration and spoilage. High CO_2 levels effectively prevent bacterial and fungal growth; however, levels more than 10 kPa are needed to suppress fungal and bacterial growth significantly. Atmospheres more than 10 kPa CO_2 can be phytotoxic for many fresh horticultural commodities. N_2 is used as a filler gas since it has no direct biological effects on horticultural commodities. Therefore N_2 is usually used as the inert component of MAP. The diffusivity of O_2, CO_2, and C_2H_4 may be raised by replacing N_2 with argon or helium, but they have no straight effect on plant tissues and are more expensive than N_2 as a modified atmosphere component.

In order to understand the uses of the several gases, it is first necessary to understand the properties of the gases and how they interact with and affect the packaged foods. Second, the chemical and physical properties of the gases will be influenced by their concentrations and particularly by the temperature. Generally, the gases will not react with each other except when exposed to heat or metabolic catalysts. The partial pressures, penetration rates, and diffusion properties of each gas are independent of the other gases present. This simplifies matters immensely since we do not have to be concerned with the gas interactions. O_2 is a reactive gas comprising nearly 21% of the atmosphere. It occurs most usually in its diatomic form (O_2), but can also be present as ozone (O_3). Oxygen is present as an ingredient of nearly all organic molecules, specifically carbohydrates, and can form compounds with virtually any chemical element. Oxygen is slightly soluble in water ($4.89 \text{ cm}^3/100$ mL at $8°C$), but not nearly as soluble as is carbon dioxide. As is the case with all gases, the solubility in water increases as temperature reduces.

Most of the reactions with food constituents including oxygen are degradation reactions involving the oxidative collapse of foods into their fundamental parts. Because of this, many packaging strategies leave out oxygen and thus slow these degradation processes. Many spoilage microorganisms need oxygen and will grow and create off-odors in the presence of enough oxygen. Oxygen acts as the terminal electron acceptor in many metabolic reactions. The rates of some necessary metabolic processes are sensitive to O_2 concentration, therefore it is necessary to maintain normal respiratory metabolism of fresh fruits and vegetables. Normal atmospheric concentrations of oxygen encourage and make easy senescence and degradation of quality; they can also slow the respiration rate of fresh fruits and vegetables and the rates at which they ripen, age, and decay by reducing O_2 concentrations below nearly 10 kPa.

In some cases, reducing the O_2 concentration can reduce oxidative browning reactions, which can be of special concern in precut leafy vegetables. Kader (1986) implied that reduced O_2 level can delay compositional changes such as fruit pigment development, softening, hardening of some vegetables (such as asparagus and broccoli), and development of flavor due to a decrease in the activity of oxidative enzymes such as glycolic acid oxidase, ascorbic acid oxidase, and polyphenol oxidase. Finally, Ke and Kader (1992) reported that there is a great deal of interest in the use of low O_2 as a quarantine treatment to disinfest fresh produce of insects and insect larvae. Suitable combinations of low O_2, low temperature, and time may be effective against some of the most troublesome insect pests in international commerce.

However, O_2 is needed for normal metabolism to proceed. O_2 concentrations less than 1–2 kPa can lead to anaerobic (or fermentative) metabolism and associated production of ethanol and acetaldehyde resulting in off-flavors, off-odors, and loss of quality. Of course the important concern is the potential growth of anaerobic bacteria, some of which are pathogenic to humans under low oxygen conditions. Extreme reduction of O_2 concentration leads to an increase in the potential risk for the growth of pathogenic anaerobic microbes such as *Listeria monocytogenes*, *Clostridium perfringens*, and *Clostridium botulinum*, and excessive reduction of O_2 concentration (<1%) intensifies anaerobic respiration, which leads to production of off-flavors, off-odors, and tissue deterioration (Ares et al., 2007). The proper O_2 concentration will be contingent

Table 4.1 Recommended MAP Conditions of Various Products

Commodity	Temperature Range (°C)	O_2 (%)[a]	CO_2 (%)[a]
Fruits			
Apple (whole)	0–5	2–3	1–5
Apple (sliced)	0–5	10–12	8–11
Avocado	5–13	2–5	3–10
Banana	12–15	2–5	2–5
Kiwifruit	0–5	2	5
Mango	10–15	5	5
Pineapple	10–15	5	10
Strawberry	0–5	10	15–20
Vegetables			
Asparagus	0–5	20	5–10
Broccoli	0–5	1–2	5–10
Cabbage	0–5	3–5	5–7
Lettuce (head)	0–5	2–5	0
Lettuce (shredded)	0–5	1–2	10–12
Mushrooms	0–5	21	10–15
Spinach	0–5	21	10–20
Tomatoes (mature)	12–20	3–5	0

[a]Volume or mole percentage; the remainder is nitrogen.
Adapted from Floros, J.D., Matsos, K.I., 2005. In: Han, J.H. (Ed.), Innovations in Food Packaging. Elsevier Academic Press, New York, Chapter 10.

on the fruit or vegetable and its tolerance to low O_2, the temperature (which will affect the product's tolerance to low O_2), and the time that the product will be exposed to low O_2. Therefore, different fruits and vegetables need different optimal gas formulations (Table 4.1).

Also, in Figs. 4.2 and 4.3 these data are presented with CO_2 concentration as the ordinate and O_2 concentration as the abscissa. Oxygen permeates through plastic polymers at various rates depending upon the polymer, but it generally permeates through more slowly than CO_2. The permeability rate of oxygen (and all gases) in plastics increases when the temperature is highest. Similarly the chemical reactivity of O_2 with food components increases as temperature increases.

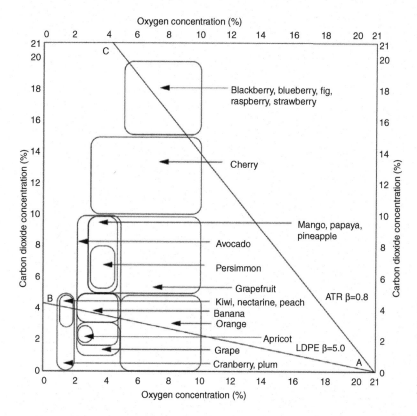

Figure 4.2 Recommended modified atmosphere for storage of fruits. From Mannapperuma, J.D., et al., 1989. In Proceedings of 5th Controlled Atmosphere Research Conference, Wenatchee, WA, p. 225.

Recently, the use of elevated oxygen packaging (more than 50% O_2) has been proposed as a new technique for retaining the quality and firmness of fresh fruits. This approach does not have disadvantages of current gas concentrations (air or low oxygen MAP) in MAP. An elevated O_2 system (more than 50% O_2) has been recently used for cut vegetables as an alternative to elevated CO_2 and effectively prevented microbial spoilage by reducing the proliferation and activity of microorganisms. The studies indicated that elevated O_2 treatment (80% O_2) in comparison to 40% O_2 + 30% CO_2 improved table grapes' vitamin C, °Brix, browning, and visual appearance. Fresh green vegetables treated with elevated O_2 concentrations (60–100% O_2) caused oxygen shock or gas shock. Many researchers reported that elevated O_2 treatments are effectively inhibiting enzymatic discoloration, aerobic and anaerobic microbial growth, and preventing anaerobic fermentation reactions. However, this method is not fully commercialized as yet, and more studies are required for a complete understanding of the basic biological mechanisms involved in inhibiting enzymatic browning and the effect both on respiratory activity and on the quality of packaged fruits and vegetables. Some studies showed that high O_2

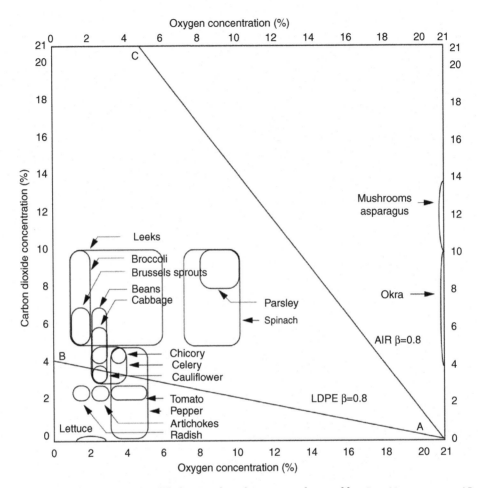

Figure 4.3 Recommended modified atmosphere for storage of vegetables. From Mannapperuma, J.D., et al., 1989. Proceedings of 5th Controlled Atmosphere Research Conference, Wenatchee, WA, p. 225.

levels of 80–90% stimulated the growth of foodborne pathogenic microbes such as *L. monocytogenes* and *Escherichia coli*. Ozone is inhibitory to many microorganisms, specifically bacteria. O_3 has been used to sterilize water, and ozone generators have found some use in cold storage for vegetables and fruits, but ozone is very reactive and collapses to O_2 rapidly, so is not used in MAP of fruits or vegetables.

Carbon dioxide is present in the atmosphere in low levels, typically about 0.03%, but is an important product of ignition and so is easily produced. It is very soluble in water, particularly in cold water ($179.7 \ cm^3/100 \ mL$ at 8°C), and will thus be absorbed by high moisture foods. When CO_2 dissolves in water, it produces carbonic acid, which will cause a fall in pH and an acidifying effect. This acidification can suppress the growth of many spoilage micro-organisms and for this reason, it is necessary in many extended shelf-life packages, as well as in direct antimicrobial effects.

CO_2 also has a minor suppression effect on the respiration of some fresh fruits and vegetables, and so can help extend their shelf life. In addition CO_2 reduces the sensitivity of plant tissues to the ripening hormone ethylene by CO_2 concentrations above 1–2 kPa.

Ethylene has many effects on plant physiology, for example, it is odorless, colorless, and tasteless. Also it is active in such small amounts (ppm) that it is considered a plant hormone. Ethylene has numerous effects on plant tissues. It can enhance ripening and fruit softening, and increase respiration rate, yellowing of leafy vegetables, and senescence of many fruits and vegetables. The prevention of these ethylene effects is important in the main-tenance of quality ascribed to MAP. With some fruits, ethylene is applied in a routine manner as a postharvest treatment to ensure rapid and uniform ripening, such as for bananas and tomatoes. With many other fruits, vegetables, and decorative plants, it is im-portant to prevent exposure to ethylene and its subsequent harm-ful effects.

Many kinds of ripening fruit can produce ethylene normally. Also, ethylene is produced by any aerobic ignition such as fires, automobile exhaust, or from diesel fuel. Such sources should be removed from areas where produce is stored or handled. Herner (1987) and Kader et al. (1988) reported that elevated CO_2 (greater than 2 kPa) can help reduce the damaging effects of ethylene by rendering plant tissues insensitive to ethylene. This may be one of the primary advantages of modified atmospheres for many com-modities. Elevated CO_2 can, like reduced O_2, slow respiratory pro-cesses thereby extending shelf life.

Pretel et al. (1993) investigated the effect of MAP on inhibit-ing ethylene production and observed that ethylene production increased in Larry Ann and Black Amber plums during storage at 2°C, while in those plums stored under MAP conditions ethylene production was significantly lower (Fig. 4.4). Kader et al. (1988) re-ported that although the effects of elevated CO_2 on respiration are not as dramatic as those of low O_2, high CO_2, and low O_2, together they can, mostly, reduce respiration more than either gas alone.

CO_2 at high concentration above 10 kPa has been shown to suppress the growth of a number of decay-causing bacteria and fungi. For example, 15–20 kPa CO_2 is ordinarily applied around strawberries during shipment primarily to suppress growth of the mold *Botrytis cinerea*, which would otherwise greatly lessen the postharvest life of strawberries. Nonetheless these levels of CO_2

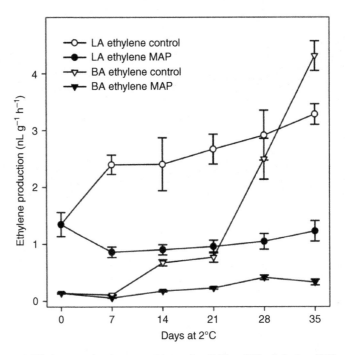

Figure 4.4 Ethylene production rate of Larry Ann (LA) and Black Amber (BA) plum cultivars during storage at 2°C in open air (control) or under modified atmosphere packaging (MAP) conditions using microperforated polyester/ polypropylene (12/60 μm thickness) films. Ethylene production was measured at 2°C and 2 h after plum fruits were taken out of modified atmosphere packages.

do not suppress some human pathogenic bacteria of potential concern on fresh produce. For example, Farber (1991) reported that *C. botulinum* and *L. monocytogenes* are relatively resistant to the effects of CO_2. There is some concern that elevated CO_2 could suppress spoilage microorganisms and would otherwise signal microbial growth and product spoilage while allowing potentially hazardous pathogens to continue their growth. Accordingly, MAP should always work in conjunction with a superior program of sanitation and quality assurance. Also, too much CO_2 can be damaging to plant tissues and individual fruits and vegetables are different in their tolerance to this gas. CO_2 typically penetrates most packaging materials more rapidly than other atmospheric gases.

Nitrogen is the most plentiful constituent in air (~79%) and can be used in either liquid or gaseous form. It is physiologically inert in its gaseous and liquid forms and is used in packaging primarily as a filler and to exclude other more active gases. In its N_2 form, it does not contribute to any physiological reactions inside plant tissues, nor does it affect the growth of microorganisms except to the degree that it considerably replaces O_2. N_2 is frugally soluble in water (2.33 cm^3/100 mL at 8°C). Displacement of O_2 with N_2 leads to retardative oxidative processes as well as the growth of aerobic spoilage microorganisms. Carbon monoxide is an odorless, colorless, tasteless, very toxic gas, which has been shown to be very impressive as a microbial inhibitor. Low levels (<1 kPa) of CO will inhibit many bacteria, molds, and yeasts. When combined with low O_2 (2–5 kPa), it can delay oxidative browning of fruits and vegetables and has found limited use commercially for this goal. However, due to the toxicity of the gas, and its explosive nature at 12.5–74.2 kPa in air, CO must be handled using specific precautions and is used little in MAP of fruits or vegetables.

Sulfur dioxide has been used to control growth of bacteria and mold on soft fruits, particularly grapes and dried fruits. It has also found use in the control of microbial growth in fruit juices, wines, and pickles. Sulfur dioxide is very chemically reactive in aquatic solution and forms sulfite compounds, which are inhibitory to bacteria in acid circumstances (pH <4). However, certain people show hypersensitivity to sulfite compounds in foods and the use of sulfites has come under public and regulatory inspection in recent years. SO_2 is used during storage and shipment of table grapes in order to decelerate fungal spoilage.

The noble gases, which include helium (He), argon (Ar), xenon (Xe), and neon (Ne), are a family of elements characterized by their lack of reactivity. These gases are being used in a number of food applications, for example, potato-based snack products. In the past few decades, it was difficult to see how the use of noble gases would offer any preservation advantages. In comparison with N_2, they are now being used. It has been reported that noble gas applications in MAP reduce microbial growth and maintain the quality of fresh produce, controlled atmosphere, and cold storage conditions. It has been reported that treatment with pressurized argon could reduce the proliferation of spoilage microorganisms such as coliforms, yeast, and molds, inhibit the production of malondialdehyde and the activities of peroxidase and catalase, and maintain the cell integrity of fruits and vegetables. Several studies have shown that application of inert gases in MAP diminishes water activity in fresh and fresh-cut produce, which reduces leaching of organic material from fresh-cuts and disseminates microbes in deeper tissues. It has been reported that inert gases at specific temperatures and pressures form ice-like crystals called clathrate hydrates, in which molecules are trapped within a cage-like structure of water molecules and stabilized by bonding via van der Waals forces, which results in restraining of mobility and activity of intracellular water and maintaining the microbiological quality of modified atmosphere-packed products.

2.1.2 Effect of the Gaseous Environment on the Microbial, Chemical, Biochemical, and Physical Properties of Foods

All foods may include a wide range of microorganisms involving bacteria and their spores, molds, yeasts, protozoa, and viruses. While a technologist will basically be concerned with preventing the growth of microorganisms in foods, one should be aware that certain pathogenic microorganisms, while not growing in the food, may survive during the shelf-life period and cause food poisoning or illness in consumers.

Studies have shown that MAP significantly inhibits spoilage organisms' growth or eradicates desirable produce microflora. There are many variables in the MAP of fresh and fresh-cut produce that affect growth and survival of microorganisms in these products, such as intrinsic factors (pH, water activity [a_w], storage temperature, nutrient composition, and oxidative reduction potential) and extrinsic factors (gas composition, temperature, pretreatment, properties of packaging films, and storage conditions). Among the gases used in MAP just CO_2 has significant nonselective antimicrobial influence on the product. Furthermore, optimal gas composition and competitive effects of natural microflora on food pathogens play a significant role in product safety and inhibit foodborne pathogens. Studies have shown that CO_2 has different inhibitory effects on bacterial and viral pathogen populations, and on the toxin gene expression of some foodborne pathogens. Several theories have been proposed to interpret the antimicrobial influence of CO_2 on MAP products, such as modification of cell membrane function including uptake and absorption of nutrients, decrease of intracellular pH through gas penetration of bacterial membranes, direct inhibition of enzyme systems or decrease in rate of enzyme reactions, and direct changes in the physical and chemical properties of proteins. However, the inhibitory effect of CO_2 is dependent on the microbial flora present and the produce characteristics. Consequently, more research is needed for a complete understanding of the effects of different gas atmospheres on growth, survival of foodborne pathogens, and expression of toxin genes of foodborne pathogens on fresh and fresh-cut fruit and vegetables.

Food spoilage can also be caused by chemical and biochemical reactions in food, including enzyme-catalyzed reactions. The technologist should be aware of these effects and understand the extent to which modified atmospheres can mitigate them. Of the gases involved in MAP, O_2, because of its reactivity, has been studied the most.

2.1.3 Role of Temperature Stability and Generation of the Steady-State Atmosphere

An important factor in maintaining quality and extending the shelf life of fruit and vegetables after harvest is temperature, since most of the physical, microbiological, biochemical, and physiological reactions leading to deterioration of produce quality are mainly dependent on temperature. Beaudry (1999) reported that the creation of an optimal atmosphere inside MAP depends on the respiration rate of the product and the permeability of the films to O_2 and CO_2, both of which are under the influence of temperature. Nevertheless an increase in temperature has various effects on these two parameters: the increment in the respiration rate as a function of temperature, described by Q^R_{10}, is generally significantly greater than the increase in the permeability of packaging material (Q^P_{10}), which may favor the aggregation of CO_2 and discharge of O_2 inside the package.

Indeed, metabolic processes containing respiration, ripening, and transpiration are especially temperature dependent, the rates of biological reactions being generally increased two- to threefold for each 10°C increment in temperature. The storability of postharvest crops is dependent on a number of salient factors such as moisture content, respiration rate (RR), heat production, texture characteristics, and physiological phase of ontogeny (Haard, 1984). Haard (1984) concluded that respiration rate has an inverse relationship with storability. They reported that crops with relatively high respiration rates tend to deteriorate rapidly, whereas crops that respire slowly can be stored for extended periods of time (Fig. 4.5).

On the other hand the O_2 and CO_2 permeability of many packaging films increases markedly as temperature increases, although this depends on film type. Therefore, for example, Beaudry (2000) reported that the permeation of O_2 and other gases through low density polyethylene (LDPE) efficiency produces a 2.5-fold increase in permeability between 0 and 15°C. In contrast, the permeation of the gases through perforations has an extremely low temperature sensitivity factor, with only a 10% increment in the temperature range shown in a situation in which respiratory request for O_2 increments faster than O_2 permeation. This presents problems with maintaining enough O_2 when the package is subject to a temperature increase. Maintenance of the desirable atmosphere combination inside the packages depends on accurate temperature control, since for a given temperature change, wide differences between changes in produce respiration rate and film permeability occur.

So, for example, Tano et al. (2007) reported that the Q^R_{10} values for mushrooms, tomatoes, and broccoli were 3.0, 2.8, and 2.3, respectively, while the Q^P_{10} of the package was lower than 1.2.

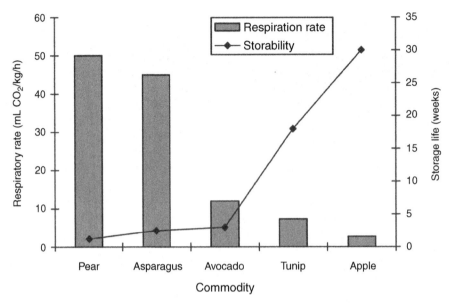

Figure 4.5 Relationship between respiratory rate and storability of selected fruits and vegetables at 5°C (Haard, 1984).

This difference resulted in an aggregation of CO_2 and a decrease in O_2 inside the packages subjected to temperature fluctuations, leading to fermentation (anaerobic respiration) in vegetable tissues. The exact O_2 concentration at which anaerobic respiration (fermentation) begins depends on the kind of produce, on the storage temperature, and on the CO_2 concentration. However, once anaerobic respiration has been initiated the O_2 concentration remains constant during future swing cycles, irrespective of the temperature, likely due to irreversible membrane damage and decreased mitochondrial activity. Therefore, the damage caused by high CO_2 and low O_2 concentrations on fruits and vegetables is irreversible, its intensity being dependent on the duration of storage under these conditions.

De Santana et al. (2009) reported that the lower temperature (1°C) in MAP treatments resulted in lower ethylene synthesis and respiration rate during 6-day storage of peaches, which is an important principle for the successful application of MAP. They also demonstrated that ethylene production in peaches was dependent on respiration rate during ripening at 25°C.

Charles et al. (2006) investigated absorption kinetics of oxygen and carbon dioxide scavengers commonly used in active MAP. They applied scavenger sachets inside polyvinylidene chloride (PVDC) pouches filled with air or modified atmosphere (0% or 100% relative humidity [RH]) and at different temperatures (5, 20, and 35°C). They found that CO_2 absorption had a "parasite" effect on O_2 scavengers. The results of the study indicated that absorption rate constant (about 20%) varied among individual gas scavengers and the temperature rise had a negative effect on absorption rate and time of reaching an anaerobic condition.

The quality of the products stored under the temperature fluctuating regime was intensely affected, compared to products stored at constant temperature, as indicated by loss of firmness, wide browning, weight loss increment, the level of ethanol in the plant tissue, and infection due to physiological damage and excessive condensation. It was clear that temperature oscillation can seriously mitigates the benefits of MAP and safety of the packaged produce, even if it happens just one time. Besides this, adequate control of RH in MAP including fresh produce is a critical design consideration and is also affected by temperature. The majority of polymeric films used in MAP have lower water vapor transmission rate than transpiration rates of fresh produce; thus excessively high RH may occur, leading to moisture condensation, microbial growth, and putrefaction of the produce.

Results of an experiment designed to compare several types of bulk packaging and temperature fluctuating regimes for broccoli heads are shown in Fig. 4.6. Broccoli heads (10 kg) were placed in a plastic-lined carton and packed in commercial microperforated polyethylene (PE), microporous packaging (mineral-impregnated LDPE), and Xtend (XF12), and stored for 19 days at 1°C followed by 1 day at 20°C. After 2 weeks at 1°C the O_2 level was stabilized at around 4%, but CO_2 concentration gradually increased to 14.5% in microporous packaging (Fig. 4.6). At this stage, slight anaerobic respiration began, as determined by ethanol production, and became stronger during the next 5 days. After 1 day at 20°C, concentrations of O_2, CO_2, and ethanol in the sealed packaging were 2.7%, 19.5%, and 190 ppm, respectively.

Tano et al. (2007) reported that the condensation problem is due to temperature conditions, since the atmosphere in MAP preserved at constant temperature is saturated with moisture, while incrementing the temperature reduces the RH inside the packages and increases the water vapor deficit and, consequently, the transpiration rate of fresh produce. This high rate of transpiration causes accelerated produce weight loss and may explain the higher weight losses in packages subjected to temperature oscillations compared to those at constant temperature.

2.1.4 Selection of Packaging Materials for MAP

Yahia et al. (1992, 1998) reported that MAP, a technique used to extend the shelf life of fresh or minimally processed foods,

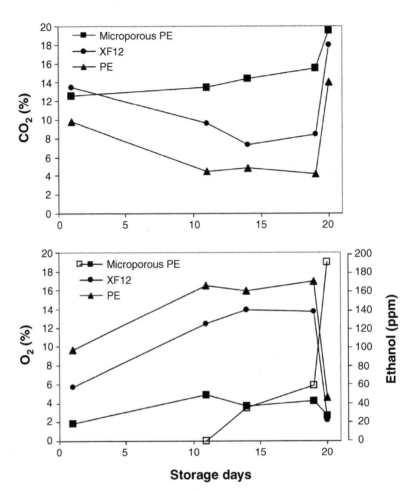

Figure 4.6 Changes in concentrations of CO_2, O_2, and ethanol in bulk packages (10 kg) of broccoli during 19 days at 1°C followed by 1 day at 20°C. Heads (500–600 g each) were packed in liners of microporous polyethylene (PE), microperforated polyethylene (PE), and microperforated Xtend (XF12) (Tano et al., 2007).

refers to the development of a modified atmosphere around the product through the use of permeable polymeric films. Fresh horticultural commodities are respiring products and the interaction of the packaging material with the product is important. If the permeability of the packaging film is adapted to the products' respiration, an equilibrium modified atmosphere will be established in the package and the shelf life of the product can be improved.

Many new developments, for example the design and manufacturing of polymeric films, have come about due to MAP and its profile has been raised due to consumer demand. New techniques have also been established, like the use of an antifogging layer for better product visibility, and equilibrium-modified atmosphere packaging, which is usually used for fresh-cut fruits and vegetables.

The growth in MAP fresh-cut produce is one of the most dynamic techniques of the past decade. Produce packaging includes a delicate balance of the product's respiration rate, the permeability of packaging material, and product temperature. The choice of the correct packaging material is critical to maintain the desired balance of O_2 and CO_2, which in turn slows the product's metabolism, and thus product senescence. Even though gas atmosphere is important, other indices must be considered when contemplating MAP technology, including temperature and RH control, packaging materials, packaging equipment, and food safety issues. High-performance packaging and packaging equipment are continually developing. Technological progress in packaging machinery has focused on higher speeds, washdown sanitation manufacture, and lower remaining oxygen levels. High-performance films can be defined as films that crucially meet the customer's expectations in different roles as both communicator and protector. Packaging is very important as a communicator to reach the consumer via printing and package appearance. Moreover, new packaging technologies are creating developments in obstacle polymers, improved sealant polymers, and abuse properties.

Some of the disadvantages of MAP include added cost, capital cost of packaging, quality control of machinery, added cost of gases and high barrier films, and added transport cost due to incremental pack volume. However, the rapid growth of MAP products in the market shows that the advantages of the system to the retailer, manufacturer, and consumer clearly outweigh the disadvantages.

Choosing the most appropriate packaging materials is essential to maintain the quality and safety of MAP foods. The main factors to be taken into account are the type of package, the physical properties, the barrier properties, strength, durability, transparency, integrity of closure (heat sealing), sealing reliability, resistance to chemical degradation, water vapor transmission rate, nontoxicity and chemical inertia, printability, and commercial appropriateness of packaging material with economic feasibility.

Progress in polymer processing has enabled the development of plastics that are better suited to specific food packaging applications, but no single plastic contains the properties that make it suitable to all food-packaging applications.

Plastic packaging materials mostly include MAP films, which are multilayer structures formed from several layers of various plastics. Using coextrusion, lamination, or coating technologies, it is possible to combine various kinds of plastic to form films, sheets, or rigid packs. Be carefully when choosing each type of plastic, as it is possible to design a material that possesses the key properties of packaging importance to best match the prescriptions of the product package system. Plastics packaging for MAP applications is most usually found in the form of flexible films for bags, pillow packs, pouches, and top webs, or as rigid structures for base trays, cups, dishes, and tubs. The most used plastic flexible laminates are produced from PE, PP, polyethylene terephthalate (PET), polyamide (nylons), polyvinyl chloride (PVC), PVDC, and ethylene vinyl alcohol (EVOH). Rigid and semirigid structures are usually produced from PP, PET, unplasticized PVC, and expanded polystyrene. Table 4.2 gives details of film types and permeability available for packaging of MAP produce (Sandhya, 2010). Alique et al. (2005) investigated the effects of different wrap films and storage conditions (8 days at 4°C plus 4 days at 20°C) on Navalinda

Table 4.2 Polymers, Film Types, and Permeability Available for Packaging of MAP Produce (Sandhya, 2010)

Film	Permeability (cm^3 m^{-2} day^{-1} atm^{-1} for 25 μm film at 25°C)			Water Vapor Transmission (g m^{-2} day^{-1} atm^{-1}; 38°C and 90% RH)
	Oxygen	Nitrogen	Carbon Dioxide	
Ethylene vinyl alcohol (EVOH)	3–5	—	—	16–18
Polyvinylidene chloride coated (PVDC)	9–15	—	20–30	—
Polyethylene, low density	7,800	2,800	42,000	18
Polyethylene, high density	2,600	650	7,600	7–10
Polypropylene, cast	3,700	680	10,000	10–12
Polypropylene, oriented	2,000	400	8,000	6–7
Polypropylene, oriented, PVDC coated	10–20	8–13	35–50	4–5
Rigid PVC	150–350	60–150	450–1,000	30–40
Plasticized PVC	500–30,000	300–10,000	1,500–46,000	15–40
Ethylene vinyl acetate (EVA)	12,500	4,900	50,000	40–60
Polystyrene, oriented	5,000	800	18,000	100–125
Polyurethane (polyester)	800–1,500	600–1,200	7,000–25,000	400–600
PVDC–PVC copolymer (Saran)	8–25	2–2.6	50–150	1.5–5.0
Polyamide (Nylon-6)	40	14	150–190	84–3,100

sweet cherry. They applied punnets and film wrapped one macroperforated film and two microperforated films of 0.30 (MAP.30) and 0.55(MAP.55) μmol cm cm^{-2} atm-day of CO_2 at 0°C for wrapping of Navalinda cherries. They demonstrated that microperforated wrapping effectively retarded loss of acidity and firmness and darkening of color, and generally reduced loss of quality and deterioration of the cherries. They also reported that MAP.55 was the more permeable microperforated film, which was suitable for the packaging of cherries within a maximum of 7 days, where maintenance of the cold chain was not entirely assured.

Polyvinyl alcohol (PVOH) is an excellent gas barrier provided it is dry. In the presence of moisture, PVOH absorbs water, causing the plastic to swell and become plasticized. In this situation, the gas barrier properties of PVOH are greatly reduced. In order to provide greater polymer stability for commercial use, PVOH is copolymerized with ethylene to produce EVOH. The gas barrier properties of EVOH are less than those of PVOH when dry, but EVOH is less sensitive to the presence of moisture, and so it is widely used as a gas barrier layer in MAP applications. This material has good processing properties and is therefore suitable for conversion into plastic films and structures. EVOH is always found laminated as a thin film, commonly in the order of 5 μm thickness, sandwiched between hydrophobic polymers, for example, PP or PE, which protects the polymer from moisture. EVOH also possesses high mechanical stability, high resistance to oils and organic solvents, and high thermal durability.

The polyethylenes are structurally the simplest group of synthetic polymers and the most commonly used plastic materials for packaging applications. There are several types of PE classified on the basis of density. All are composed of a carbon backbone with a degree of branching side chain which influences density. LDPE (density, 0.910–0.925 g cm^{-3}) is generally used in film form, whereas high-density polyethylene (HDPE) (density, 0.940 g cm^{-3}) is commonly used for rigid and semirigid structures. PEs are characterized as poor gas barriers, but their hydrophobic nature makes them very good barriers to water vapor. Therefore, by itself, PE cannot be used as a packaging material in MAP applications that require a high barrier to gases. PE melts at a relatively low temperature ranging from approximately100–120°C (dependent on density and crystallinity). A less branched variant called linear low density polyethylene, which offers good heat sealing properties, is used as a sealant layer to impart heat sealing properties on base trays and lidding films. Modified PE-based materials that contain interchain ionic bonding are called ionomers. These have enhanced heat sealing properties that enable them to seal meat juices, fats, and powders more effectively. Ionomers also form effective heat seals with aluminum. Surlyn is Dupont's trade name for its range of ionomer materials. A copolymer of ethylene and vinyl acetate, ethylene vinylacetate (EVA), offers enhanced heat sealing properties over LDPE and is found as a heat seal layer in some MAP applications.

An et al. (2007) packaged honey peaches in different-thickness LDPE bags stored at 2°C in MAP. They demonstrated that MAP treatments inhibited the climacteric peak, increased flesh color, decreased the development of softness, and retarded the reduction of total soluble solids (TSS), total acidity (TA), and membrane integrity. LDPE25 packages were most effective in keeping the quality of the honey peaches.

PP is a versatile polymer that has applications in flexible, rigid, and semirigid packaging structures. MAP applications are generally for rigid base trays. PP is a good water vapor barrier but a poor gas barrier. Increasing the thickness of the material somewhat compensates for the high gas transmission rate. PP melts at approximately 170°C. It can therefore be used as a container for microwaving low-fat food products. It should not be used for microwaving fatty foods, where temperatures in excess of its melting point could be reached. Foamed PP is used to provide the structural properties in laminates for MAP thermoformed base trays, where it is combined with an EVOH barrier and a PE heat-sealing layer.

PET is the most common polyester used in food packaging applications. PET is a good gas and water vapor barrier, is strong, offers good clarity, and is temperature resistant. Crystalline PET (CPET) has poorer optical properties but improved heat resistance melting at temperatures in excess of 270°C. Flexible PET film is used for barrier pouches and top webs as a lidding material for tray packs. CPET is used for dual ovenable preformed base trays where its high temperature resistance makes it an ideal container for microwave and convection oven cooking of food.

Polyamides comprise the group of plastics usually referred to as nylons, which have widespread application in food packaging. Nylons generally have high tensile stability, good puncture and abrasion resistance, and good gas barrier properties. Nylons are generally moisture sensitive (hydrophilic) and will absorb water from their environment. Moisture in the nylon structure interferes with interchain bonding and adversely affects its properties, including gas barrier. Under conditions of high RH, the gas transmission rate of nylon films generally increases. However, there are commercial nylons that are less affected by moisture. Their relatively high strength and toughness make them ideal as vacuum pouches for fresh meat, where hard bone ends could puncture other plastic materials. In this application, nylon is generally laminated to PE, which provides the heat-sealing properties.

Pure polystyrene is a stiff, brittle material and has limited use in MAP applications. Expanded polystyrene, which is formed from low density blown particles, has been used for many years as a base tray for overwrapped fresh meat, fish, and poultry products. Foamed polystyrene has recently been used as a structural layer for preformed MAP base tray applications. The high gas permeability of foamed polystyrene requires the material to be laminated to a plastic such as EVOH that provides the required gas barrier properties.

PVC has a relatively low softening temperature and good processing properties and is therefore an ideal material for producing thermoformed packaging structures. Although a poor gas barrier in its plasticized form, unplasticized PVC has improved gas and water vapor barrier properties, which can at best be described as moderate. Oil and grease resistance are excellent, but PVC can be softened by certain organic solvents. It is a common structural material in MAP thermoformed base trays, where it is laminated to PE to provide the required heat-sealing properties.

A copolymer of vinyl chloride and vinylidene chloride is PVDC, which possesses excellent gas, water vapor, and odor barrier properties, with good resistance to oil, grease, and organic solvents. Unlike EVOH, the gas barrier properties of PVDC are not significantly affected by the presence of moisture. PVDC effectively heat seals to itself and to other materials. The high temperature resistance enables uses in packs for hot filling and sterilization processes. Homopolymers and copolymers of PVDC are some of the best commercially available barriers for food packaging applications.

The foregoing provides a brief introduction to the main plastic materials used in MAP applications. It should be noted that certain desired properties can be enhanced by further processing the material. For example, coating a plastic with aluminum (metallization) can improve the gas and vapor barrier properties and enhance the visual appearance of the material. PP is usually metalized by passing the film through a mist of vaporized aluminum under vacuum. Similar treatments to improve gas and vapor barrier properties include application of a silicon oxide (SiOx) coating (also referred to as glass coating) to PET film and a diamond-like carbon coating to PET. The former has been used for MAP lidding film, with the advantages of providing excellent and stable barrier properties, which are less influenced by the effects of temperature and humidity. To date the main application of the latter has focused on non-MAP applications including a barrier coating on PET beverage bottles.

It should be mentioned that petroleum- based polymeric materials are not biodegradable, which poses a global ecological challenge and is detrimental to human health. Therefore the tendency is towards packaging films that are biodegradable. Biodegradable films are made from extracts derived from agricultural raw materials (eg, starch, lipids, and protein), byproducts from microorganisms (eg, polyhydroxylalcanoates and poly-3-hydroxybutyrate), a matrix of synthetic and natural polymers (eg, a mixture of wheat starch, ethylene acrylic acid, and low density polyethylene), animal sources, marine food processing industry wastes, and synthesis from bioderived monomers (eg, polylactic acid). One of most common biodegradable polymers is cellophane. Starch-based polymers include amylose, polylactides, polyhydroxylalkanoate, polyhydroxylbutyrate (PHB), a copolymer of PHB and valeric acids, hydroxylpropylated starch, and dextrin. Chitosan, which is derived from the chitin of crustaceans and insect exoskeletons, could be used for the preparation of biodegradable films. Edible films, thin layers of edible materials applied to food as a coating or placed on or between food ingredients, are another form of biodegradable polymer. They serve different goals, involving inhibiting the migration of moisture, antimicrobial activity by lowering the a_w, gases, and aromas, and improving the food's mechanical integrity or handling specifications, with the aim of achieving MAP conditions. Edible films can create a low level of O_2 within MAP (Odriozola-Serrano et al., 2008), which accrete growth of anaerobic pathogens such as *C. botulinum*. However, several antimicrobial compounds such as minerals and vitamins, antioxidants and texture agents, organic acids, bacteriocins, enzymes, proteins and peptides, antibiotics, and fungicides could be added to edible films to inhibit microbial growth on a variety of fresh produce. However, it is necessary to investigate the optimum concentration of these additives and their potential side effects carefully and determine the optimal range of barrier, mechanical, and antimicrobial properties.

At present, substitution would likely result in increased packaging cost because bioplastics are more expensive than petroleum-based polymers.

2.1.5 Equipment Used in MAP

The function of MAP machines is to maintain the product on a thermoformed or preformed base tray or within a flexible bag or pouch, modify the atmosphere, apply a top web, seal the pack, and remove waste to produce the final pack. The necessary factors for the packer filler to consider before selecting a machine for a particular product application are pack format, presentation, machine performance band versatility, and pack costs. The following section provides an overview of the types and operation of MAP machines.

Chamber machines are adequate for low production throughput. These are generally used with preformed pouches, though tray machines are accessible. The filled pack is loaded into the machine, the chamber then closes, and a vacuum is pulled on the pack and backflushed with the modified atmosphere. Heated sealing bars seal the pack, the chamber opens, packs are eliminated, and the cycle continues. Generally, these machines are labor intensive and cheap with a simple operation, but are relatively slow. Some chamber machines can handle large packages and are suitable for bulk packs.

Snorkel machines operate without a chamber and use preformed pouches or bags. The bags or pouches are filled and positioned in the machine. The snorkel is introduced into the pouch or bag, draws a vacuum, and presents the modified atmosphere. The snorkel withdraws and the pouch or bag is heat sealed. Bag-in-box bulk products and retail packs in large MAP master packs can be produced on these machines.

Form-fill-seal (FFS) machines form pouches from a continuous sheet of roll stock (flow wrap), or form flexible or semirigid tray systems containing thermoformed trays with a heat-sealed lid. FFS machines may be oriented in horizontal or vertical planes. Flow-wrapping machines are available in both horizontal and vertical formats. The kind of format is dependent on the nature of the food product being packed. FFS machines using preformed trays or producing thermoformed trays are almost specifically horizontal machines.

Thermoformed FFS tray machines use roll stock film for base web and lidding material. Base film is carried through the machine by claspers that attach to the border of the web and transport it through the forming, filling, evacuation, gas modification, sealing, cutting, and discharge stapes. By applying heat to the base roll stock, base trays are produced that when softened are urgently molded into the desired shape and size. Forming of the heated, softened sheet can be achieved by applying a vacuum, mechanical drawing, air pressure, or an admixture of these processes. The softened heated film is normally drawn into the forming mold under the assistance of vacuum applied through evacuation holes situated along the base borders and corners of the mold. This process produces a more defined and uniform tray mold. Where deep trays are demanded, a more uniform distribution of plastic can be achieved by preextending the film using mechanical devices (plugs) that prevent excessive thinning of the container walls at the base borders and corners.

The tooling for the molds presents a significant initial main cost of the formed FFS tray machines. Molds are usually fabricated from either steel or aluminum, the latter being cheaper but less sturdy than the former. Inserts, called filler plates, can be placed on the base of the die to reduce the forming deepness and so produce shallower depth trays. Roll stock for base tray and lidding is supplied in spools of film wound onto a core of diameter usually 3 or 6″ (standard size), which matches the film unwind system on the thermoforming machine. Spool diameters are usually supplied from 300 mm to 1000 mm, in increments of 50 mm.

2.2 Effect of MAP on Fruit and Vegetable Quality

2.2.1 Nutritional Quality

The shelf life of the packaged products can be extended by 50–200% by using MAP, if the nutritional consequences of MAP on the packaged food products become an issue. This section will discuss the effect of MAP on the nutritional quality of nonrespiring food products and the effect of MAP on the nutritional value of respiring products such as vegetables and fresh fruits. There is little information about the influence of MAP on the nutritional quality of nonrespiring food products. In most cases, packaging for respiring food products is excluded from the atmosphere and so one should expect a deceleration of oxidative reduction reactions. In addition, MAP food products should be stored under refrigeration to allow CO_2 to dissolve and execute its antimicrobial action. Under these chilled conditions, chemical reduction reactions have only a limited importance.

Johnson et al. (1994) have demonstrated that fruit and vegetables are rich sources of micronutrients and dietary fiber. They also contain an immeasurable diversity of biologically active secondary metabolites that provide the plant with color, flavor, and sometimes antinutritional or toxic properties. Among the most important classes of such substances are vitamin C, carotenoids, flavonoids, and more complex phenolics, phytosterols, saponins, glycol alkaloids, and the glucosinolates. The nutrient content of fruits and vegetables can be affected by different factors such as genetic and agronomic factors, maturity and harvesting methods, and postharvest handling procedures. There are some postharvest treatments that certainly improve food quality by inhibiting the action of oxidative enzymes and slowing down harmful processes. Kader (1986) reported that storage of fresh fruits and vegetables within the optimum range of low O_2 and/or elevated CO_2 atmospheres for each commodity reduces their respiration and C_2H_4 production rates.

Nevertheless, little information is available on the impressiveness of MAP on nutrient retention during storage. The influence of MAP on the antioxidant components is also related to nutritional quality of fruits and vegetables. Some nutritional compounds such as vitamin C and carotenoids have an important role in antioxidant properties of fruits and vegetables.

Vitamin C is one of the most important vitamins for human nutrition. In human diets more than 90% of vitamin C is supplied by the intake of fresh fruits and vegetables. It is needed for the prevention of scurvy and maintenance of healthy skin, blood vessels, and gums. Simon (1992) reported that vitamin C as an antioxidant reduces the risk of arteriosclerosis, cardiovascular diseases, and some forms of cancer. Klein and Lurie (1992) reported that ascorbic oxidase has been suggested as the major enzyme responsible for enzymatic reduction of L-ascorbic acid (AA). The oxidation of AA, the active form of vitamin C, to dehydroascorbic acid (DHA) does not result in loss of biological activity since DHA is readily reconverted to L-AA in a living organism (vivo). However, DHA is less stable than AA and may be hydrolyzed to 2,3-diketogulonic acid, which does not have physiological activity, and it has therefore been proposed that measurements of vitamin C in fruits and vegetables in relation to their nutritional value should include both DHA and AA. The vulnerability of diverse fruits and vegetables to oxidative loss of AA varies greatly, as indeed do general quality changes. Citrus fruits (low pH fruits) are comparatively stable, whereas soft fruits (strawberries) undergo more rapid changes. Davey et al. (2000) reported that leaf-like vegetables (eg, spinach) are very vulnerable to spoilage and AA loss, whereas root vegetables (eg, potatoes) retain quality and AA for many months. Fruits and vegetables undergo changes from the moment of harvest and since L-AA is one of the more reactive compounds they are especially vulnerable to treatment and storage situations. Davey et al. (2000) reported that the milder the treatment and the lower the temperature the better the retention of vitamin C, but there are several interacting factors that affect AA retention. Lee and Kader (2002) studied the rate of postharvest oxidation of AA in plant tissues, which depends upon several factors such as temperature, water content, storage atmosphere, and storage time.

However, Haffner et al. (1997) has displayed that AA levels in different apple cultivars, compared to air storage, reduced further under ultralow oxygen. On the other hand, increasing CO_2 concentrations above a certain threshold seems to have an adverse effect on vitamin C content in some fruits and vegetables. Weichmann (1986) reported that elevated CO_2 level, storage temperature, and duration accelerated AA losses in apples and red currants stored in elevated CO_2 atmospheres (Bangerth, 1977). Vitamin C content was decreased by high CO_2 concentrations (10–30% CO_2) in strawberries and blackberries and only a moderate to negligible effect was found for black currants, red currants, and raspberries (Agar et al., 1999). Wang (1977, 1983) reported that storage of sweet pepper for 6 days at 13°C in CO_2-enriched atmospheres resulted in a reduction in AA content; he also noted that 1% O_2 retarded AA degradation in Chinese cabbage stored for 3 months at 0°C. He observed that treatments with 10 or 20% CO_2 for 5 or 10 days produced no effect, and 30% or 40% CO_2 increased AA decomposition. Veltman et al. (1999) observed a 60% loss in AA content of pears after storage in 2% O_2 + 10% CO_2. There were no data available to display whether a parallel reduction in O_2 concentration alleviated the negative CO_2 effect. Agar et al. (1999) suggested that reducing O_2 concentration in the storage atmosphere in the presence of high CO_2 had little effect on vitamin C preservation. The only advantageous effect of low O_2 alleviating the CO_2 effect could be observed when applying CO_2 concentrations lower than 10%. High CO_2 concentration in the storage atmosphere has also been described to cause degradation of vitamin C in fresh-cut products. Therefore Agar et al. (1999) observed that concentrations of 5, 10, or 20% CO_2 caused degradation of vitamin C in fresh-cut kiwifruit slices. They also reported in the same year that enhanced losses of vitamin C in response to CO_2 higher than 10% may be due to the stimulating effects on oxidation of AA and/or inhibition of DHA reduction to AA. In contrast, Howard and Hernandez-Brene (1998) reported that MAP retarded the conversion of AA to DHA, which occurred in air-stored jalapeno pepper rings. Wright and Kader (1997) found no important losses of vitamin C occurring during the postcutting life of fresh-cut strawberries and persimmons for 8 days (2% O_2, air + 12% CO_2, or 2% O_2 + 12% CO_2) at 0°C.

Agar et al. (1999) reported that the reduction of AA and the relative increase in DHA could be an indication that high CO_2 stimulates the oxidation of AA, possibility by ascorbate peroxidase as in the case of strawberries and spinach (Gil et al., 1999). Mehlhorn (1990) demonstrated an increment in ascorbate peroxidase activity in response to ethylene.

Carotenoid is one of the more important kinds of plant pigments and plays a crucial role in defining the quality parameters of fruits and vegetables. Its role in the plant is to act as an accessory pigment for light harvesting and in the prevention of photo-oxidative damage. The best documented and established function of a number of the carotenoids is their provitamin A activity, particularly of β-carotene. Many orange, yellow, or red fruit and root vegetables contain large amounts of carotenoids, which accumulate in the chloroplast during ripening or maturation. In some cases, the carotenoids present are simple, for example, lycopene in tomato or β-carotene in carrot, but in other cases complex compounds of unusual structures are found, for example, in capsicum. Carotenoids are found in membranes, as microcrystals, in association with proteins, or in small oil drops. Britton and Hornero-Mendez (1997) reported that provitamin carotenoids found in significant quantities in fruits may have a role in cancer prevention by acting as free radical scavengers. Lycopene, although it has no provitamin activity, has been identified as a specifically effective quencher of singlet oxygen in an artificial environment (Di Mascio et al., 1989) and as an anticarcinogenic (Giovannucci, 1999). Therefore, Klein and Lurie (1992) reported that carotenoids are unstable when exposed to acidic pH, oxygen, or light.

The effect of modified atmospheres on the carotenoid content of intact fruits has not been well studied. Modified atmospheres including either decreased O_2 or elevated CO_2 are generally considered to reduce the loss of provitamin A, but also to inhibit the biosynthesis of carotenoids (Kader et al., 1989). Weichmann (1986) reported that reducing O_2 to lower concentrations enhanced the retention of carotene in carrots. He also reported that the carotene content of leeks was found to be higher after storage in 1% O_2 + 10% CO_2 than after storage in air.

Tenrio et al. (2004) stored green asparagus spears under refrigeration at 2°C for 14 days, under MAP at 2°C for 26–33 days, and under MAP at 10°C for 20 days. The xanthophylls identified were neoxanthin, violaxanthin, zeaxanthin, and lutein. Therefore only β-carotene was detected in the carotene fraction. In the chlorophyll pigments, three molecules were isolated, chlorophyll b, its epimer chlorophyll b, and chlorophyll a. MAP at 2°C was found to be effective in extending the shelf life for up to 4 weeks and in preserving the color of fresh asparagus.

2.2.2 Weight Loss

Weight loss is one of the main problems during postharvest storage of fruits and vegetables, occurring mostly by transpiration rate, which influences its marketability, incurring important economic losses. In this concept, since films used in MAP have small water vapor diffusion, the internal atmosphere package becomes saturated with water vapor pressure and then transpiration of vegetable tissues decreases limitlessly, leading to low weight losses. Serrano et al. (2006) reported that weight loss of control broccoli stored at 1°C in open air was 46% of its initial weight after 21 days, while broccoli stored in nonperforated and microperforated PP bags lost less than 1.5%. Similar results have been obtained in various fruits, such as table grapes (Martinez-Romero et al., 2003), loquat (Amoros et al., 2008), nectarines (Retamales et al., 2000), cherries (Kappel et al., 2002; Serrano et al., 2005), and peaches (Akbudak and Eris, 2004), among others.

2.2.3 Color

The color of fruits and vegetables is a direct consequence of their natural pigment composition resulting mainly from three families of pigments, carotenoids and chlorophylls, located in the chloroplasts and chromoplasts, and the water soluble phenolic compositions, anthocyanins, flavonols, and proanthocyanins, placed in the vacuole. Betalains (eg, betacyanins and betaxanthins) are a class of plant pigments and are responsible for the red and yellow colors that occur only rarely. Chlorophylls are responsible for green, blue/green, and olive brown colors, while carotenoids are responsible for red/yellow colors. Anthocyanins are responsible for orange, red, purple, blue, and black, and middle colors. It is very important to know the combination of fruit and vegetable pigments until the possible incidence of postharvest treatments for keeping color and quality and extending their shelf life, as well as that of their derived products, can be evaluated (Artés et al., 2002; Kidmos et al., 2002).

During ripening, chloroplasts are slowly replaced by chromoplasts including only carotenoids, although exceptionally in some fruits chlorophyll remains in the pulp of the ripe fruit, for example, avocado. However, in most fruits carotenoids become apparent when chlorophyll disappears upon ripening, and commonly this is accompanied by a marked biosynthesis of carotenoids. Artés et al. (2002) reported that in apple, apricot, artichoke, asparagus, blackberry, blueberry, red carrot, cherry, cranberry, eggplant, peach, pear, plum, pomegranate, fig, grape, red lettuce, nectarine, olive, red onion, "Sanguine" orange, red skinned potato, radish, red and black currant, raspberry, purple sweet potato, strawberry, etc., ripening is associated with an intense anthocyanin biosynthesis. Although all these color and pigment composition changing processes happen at the same time, various biochemical pathways are involved for each class of pigment.

To stay competitive in the fruit and vegetable market, suppliers must offer products with an optimal overall quality. Thus the entire chain from producers and processors to retailers must be increasingly sensitive to consumer requirements, particularly as they relate to color. In fact, perception of sweetness, sourness, and flavor intensity is highly correlated to skin color as has been reported for sweet cherries; full dark red cherries, measured both visually and with a colorimeter, had higher consumer acceptance than full bright red cherries (Crisosto et al., 2002).

Atmospheres with reduced O_2 and/or elevated CO_2 concentrations are known to extend the storage life of fruits and vegetables. Ahvenainen (1996) and Artés (2000) reported that MAP can lower respiratory activity and ethylene production, delay ripening and softening, limit weight losses, and decrease the incidence of physiological disorders and decay-causing pathogens. Artés (1993, 2000) reported that as MAP slows the rate at which energy reserves are used it can be applied in composition with chilling storage for improving the shelf life of fruits and vegetables. At the same time, MAP affects biochemical reactions relevant to pigment synthesis and degradation. Moreover, the effect of respiratory gases on the metabolic behavior of plant materials depends on the temperature of the application due to its effect on the solubility of these gases.

Roy et al. (1996) have observed that the activity of tyrosinase, responsible for mushroom browning, is dependent on O_2 concentration. MAP induced higher L* values and lowered the difference between ideal mushroom target and sample compared to those observed for mushrooms stored in non-MAP (normal packages). The improved color might also be due to lower microbial growth resulting from low O_2.

Fresh processed potato slices stored in MAP with low O_2 showed a better color retention when the O_2 level was lowered from 3.5 to 1.4 kPa, may be due to reduction of oxidase activity such as polyphenol oxidase (PPO), ascorbic acidoxidase, and glycolic acid oxidase. Thompson et al. (1972) reported that fruits stored in moist coir or perforated 100-gauge PE film bags had a longer storage life and higher color score than fruits that were stored nonwrapped (Fig. 4.7). They also reported that an added effect occurred when fruits were stored in nonperforated PE bags, which was presumably due to the effects of the changes in the CO_2 and O_2 levels; thus the positive effects of storage of preclimacteric fruits in sealed plastic films may be, in certain cases, a combination of its effects on the CO_2 and O_2 content within the fruit and the maintenance of high moisture content. Gunes and Lee (1997) observed that storage of minimally processed sliced potato in ambient air resulted in reduction of L* as compared with MAP ones. It was advantageous to have almost no initial O_2 within packages by flushing N_2. This active MAP was very important for the keeping quality of slices, taking into consideration that the remaining O_2 in the packages was enough to prevent anaerobiose. Dipping in chemical agents was necessary to prevent browning of minimally processed potatoes because MAP alone did not avoid this disorder.

The intensity of browning of ready-to-eat apples depends on the atmosphere combination. Apple cubes in MAP were effectively preserved from browning and displayed the lowest color losses

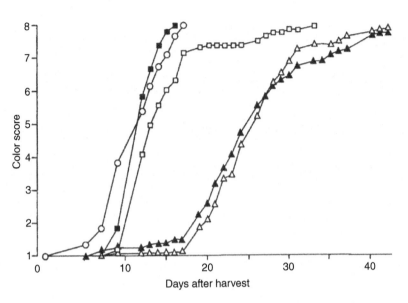

Figure 4.7 Effects of storage in polyethylene film bags on the skin color change of plantain fruits at about 20°C (Thompson et al., 1972). ○, not wrapped; △, sealed in polyethylene film bags; ▲, sealed in evacuated polyethylene film bags; □, individual fruits sealed in perforated polyethylene film bags; ■, six fruits sealed in polyethylene film bags.

when initially displacing O_2 by injecting 100 kPa N_2 and a film with low O_2 permeability was used. This atmosphere was the principal factor affecting lightness, and L* changes happened four times more slowly than when O_2 was about 2 kPa or when medium O_2 permeability films were used (Soliva-Fortuny et al., 2001).

Day (1994) has suggested that O_2 levels greater than 21 kPa may influence the postharvest life of intact and fresh processed fruits and vegetables and PPO is probably substrate inhibited by high O_2 levels. Superatmospheric O_2 could have an effect on respiratory activity and ethylene composition and action, though response depends on the commodity, ripening step, O_2 level, length of storage, and temperature. CO_2 and C_2H_4 levels should also be considered.

Fernandez-Trujillo et al. (1998) reported that tolerance to high CO_2 is usually decreased in fruits and vegetables. MAP-stored peaches kept for 21 days at 2°C, with an equilibrium CO_2 level about 20 kPa, showed a remaining effect of high CO_2 during the subsequent 3 days at 20°C. Color progress was slow and L* and chroma ground values were maintained as at harvest. However, very high CO_2 levels in MAP of about 73 kPa destabilized cyanidin derivatives in the skin of Starkimson apples (Remón et al., 2000).

In contrast to the effect in strawberries, Artes et al. (1996) observed that the juice red color increased in intensity during postharvest storage (8 weeks, 5°C) when 5 kPa CO_2 was combined with 5 kPa O_2, while air-stored fruits showed a small pale red (low a* value) color. Chroma of the skin was better retained when fruits were stored in air plus 10 kPa CO_2, while the L* of the internal skins reduced with time due to browning. Skins were darker after

6 weeks at 10°C and 20 kPa CO_2, as a consequence of CO_2 injury, while chroma and color did not change (Holcroft and Kader, 1999).

Inconsistent results (Remón et al., 2000) have been found in sweet cherries. For red cherries 11 kPa of CO_2 inhibited anthocyanin synthesis and when initially packaged with a high CO_2 level they maintained their anthocyanin content during storage. To avoid the risk of high CO_2 on unpleasant color changes Ambrunés sweet cherries were treated for 26 days at 1–2°C with CO_2 shocks (air plus 20% CO_2) once a week for 24 h every week followed by active aeration, or in a continuous 20% CO_2-enriched air atmosphere.

Anthocyanin accumulation was slow in modified atmosphere (1 kPa O_2 and 5–7 kPa CO_2) during 6 days at 2.5, 10, and 20°C, and tips were still white (a* did not change) at the end of storage. On the contrary, Siomos et al. (2000) found that for spears stored in air, the anthocyanin content increased at all temperatures, resulting in an intense purple color of the tips, the presence of light having little or no effect on any of these treatments.

Barth and Zhuang (1996) reported that MAP with 11 kPa O_2 plus 7.5 kPa CO_2 over 96 h at 5°C resulted in no differences in green color retention of florets evaluated by hue, compared to the level at harvest.

Prepared diced yellow onion did not always expand enzymatic browning during storage. However, discoloration resulting from yellowing has been reported (Blanchard et al., 1996). Keeping O_2 at 2 kPa, while CO_2 increased from 0 to 15 kPa, the b* values were reduced. The CO_2 effect was also observed after cooking. While control diced onion showed an intensification of browning and blackening of the fresh-cut surfaces, browning of cooked onion purée (expressed as b*) was slowed down slightly by reducing O_2, and more strongly by increasing CO_2 (Blanchard et al., 1996).

Color evolution associated with the postharvest ripening process is generally delayed in fruits stored under MAP conditions as has been shown in loquat (Amoros et al., 2008) and table grape (Martinez-Romero et al., 2003). Accordingly, all individual L*, a*, and b* (color parameters) considerably increased in unwrapped control broccoli during storage, which was related to both the yellowing process of broccoli inflorescences and the decrease in chlorophyll (a + b) concentration. However, broccoli under MAP situations retains the green color characteristic of freshly harvested broccoli after 21 days of storage and chlorophyll concentration close to those found at harvest (Serrano et al., 2006). Beaudry (2000) reported that these effects could be attributed to the action of low O_2 on decreasing chlorophyll degradation and browning mediated by the inhibition of pheophorbide oxygenase and

PPO, responsible for chlorophyll loss and browning, respectively. As well as color preservation, MAP storage has been related to the delay in anthocyanin and carotenoid biosynthesis, so preserving alteration of color (Artes-Hernandez et al., 2006).

2.2.4 Phytochemical Compounds

MAP storage has been shown to have an advantageous effect on preserving bioactive compounds of fruits and vegetables, although currently there are only a few reports about this issue.

Amoros et al. (2008) reported that important losses in ascorbic acid occurred in loquat stored at 2°C, while levels at harvest were maintained in loquat stored under MAP conditions. Singh and Rao (2005) studied papaya and concluded that MAP helped in the maintenance of the antioxidant potential of fruit by retaining acceptable levels of antioxidants, such as ascorbic acid and lycopene. Serrano et al. (2006) reported that broccoli heads lost half of their initial hydrophilic total antioxidant activity (H-TAA), phenolics, and ascorbic acid after 21 days of cold storage, while these losses were minimized in broccoli packaged with microperforated and nonperforated PP films (Fig. 4.8). They also concluded that H-TAA was correlated in broccoli with total phenolics and to a lesser degree with ascorbic acid.

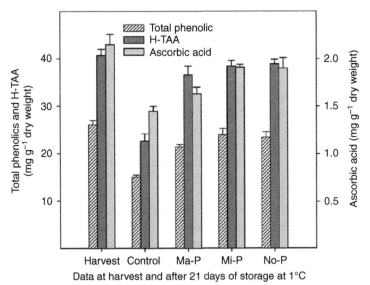

Data at harvest and after 21 days of storage at 1°C

Figure 4.8 Total phenolic and ascorbic acid concentration and total antioxidant activity in the hydrophilic fraction (H-TAA) in broccoli at harvest and after 21 days of storage at 1°C in open air (control) and in modified atmosphere packaging (MAP) conditions, with macroperforated (Ma-P), microperforated (Mi-P), and nonperforated (No-P) polypropylene films.

Anthocyanins tend to increase with ripening during postharvest storage in many fruits, such as apples, strawberries, blueberries, sweet cherries, and raspberries, as well as lycopene in tomato and watermelon. Jones (2007) reported that under MAP conditions, these increases have been reported to be lower than in control fruits stored in open air, due to the effect of MAP on delaying the evolution of the postharvest ripening process.

2.2.5 Chilling Injury

There is strong proof in the literature that MAP can decrease or remove the symptoms of chilling injury under certain conditions. Produce where this effect has been displayed include citrus (Porat et al., 2004), carambola (Zainon et al., 2004), melon (Kang and Park, 2000; Flores et al., 2004), papaya (Singh and Rao, 2005), and okra (Finger et al., 2008). The reasons for this effect and its state of action have not been clearly determined, but Zainon et al. (2004) concluded that suppression of the enzyme activities in fruits in MAP appeared to contribute to increased tolerance to chilling injury. The reduction of ethylene production and water loss in MAP were necessary in preventing chilling injury symptoms in melons (Martinez-Javega et al., 1983).

2.2.6 Decay, Microbial Spoilage, and Sensory Characteristics

Modified atmospheres containing CO_2 are impressive in extending the shelf life of many food products. However, one major concern is the inhibition of normal aerobic spoilage bacteria and the possible growth of psychrotrophic food pathogens, which may result in the food becoming unsafe for utilization before it appears to be organoleptically credible. Most of the pathogenic bacteria can be inhibited by low temperatures of under 7°C. In these situations, only psychrotrophic pathogens can wax. The effect of CO_2 on the different psychrotrophic foodborne pathogens is explained in this section.

A special concern is the possibility that psychrotrophic, nonproteolytic strains of *C. botulinum* types B, E, and F are able to grow and produce toxins under modified atmosphere situations. Little is known about the effects of MAP on toxin production by *C. botulinum*. The possibility of inhibiting *C. botulinum* by incorporating low levels of O_2 in the package does not appear to be possible. Psychrotrophic strains of *C. botulinum* are able to produce toxins in an environment with up to 10% O_2 (Connor et al., 1989).

L. monocytogenes is a psychrotrophic foodborne pathogen. Growth is possible at 1°C (Varnam and Evans, 1991) and has even been reported at temperatures as low as −1.5°C (Hudson et al., 1994). Multiple investigations have shown feasible growth of *L. monocytogenes* on MAP fresh-cut vegetables, although the results depended very much on the kind of vegetables and the storage temperature (Carlin et al., 1996; Thomas et al., 1999; Castillejo-Rodriguez et al., 2000).

Garcia et al. (1995) have proved there is no agreement about the effect of incorporating O_2 in the atmosphere on the antimicrobial activity of CO_2 on *L. monocytogenes*. However, this effect could be very important in practice, as the existence of remaining O_2 levels after packaging, and the diffusion of O_2 through the packaging film, can result in substantial O_2 levels during the storage of industrially "anaerobic" MAP food products. Most publications propose there is a reduction in the inhibitory effect of CO_2 on *L. monocytogenes* when O_2 is incorporated into the atmosphere. Bennik et al. (1995) reported that there was no significant difference in the inhibitory effect of CO_2 between the range of 0% and 50% when 1.5% O_2 or 21% O_2 was present in the atmosphere of gas-packaged brain heart infusion agar plates. When *L. monocytogenes* was cultured in buffered nutrient broth, at 7.5°C in atmospheres containing 30% CO_2, with four various O_2 concentrations (0, 10, 20, and 40%), the results displayed that bacterial growth incremented with the increasing O_2 concentrations (Hendricks and Hotchkiss, 1997).

Manvell and Ackland (1986) reported that lactic acid bacteria have been detected in mixed salads and grated carrots, and may predominate in salads when kept at abnormal (30°C) temperatures. Yeasts usually isolated include *Rhodotorula*, *Cryptococcus*, and *Candida* (Brackett, 1994). Webb and Munds (1978) surveyed 14 different vegetables for molds. The most isolated genera were *Aureobasidium*, *Fusarium*, *Rhizopus*, *Mucor*, *Phoma*, and *Penicillium*.

2.2.7 Ethylene Production

The important advantageous reactions include a decrease in ethylene biosynthesis and perception of the secondary metabolic responses to low O_2. Indeed, low O_2 concentration is known to inhibit 1-aminocyclopropane-1-carboxylate oxidase activity, this effect being dependent of the 1-aminocyclopropane-1-carboxylate (ACC) concentration, since as ACC increase the Km (Michaelis-Menten constant, Km value is defined by the substrate concentration at its half-maximum reaction velocity) of the enzyme for O_2 decreases. O_2 has also been reported to exert an effect on ethylene, which is decreased as O_2 concentration reduces.

Abeles et al. (1992) reported that O_2 concentrations not low enough to decrease respiration rate still decrease the rate of ripening through an effect mediated by ethylene in climacteric fruits. It has been known for many years that CO_2 is an antagonist of ethylene action and prevents its autocatalytic synthesis (Yang and Hoffman, 1984). Artes-Hernandez et al. (2006) reported that CO_2 levels higher than 1% decrease or inhibit ethylene biosynthesis and consequently retard fruit ripening and deterioration, these effects being additive to those of decreased O_2 atmospheres.

2.2.8 Respiration Rate

Advantageous reaction includes a reduction in respiration of the primary metabolic responses to low O_2, manifested as diminution in starch degradation and sugar consumption. The premise has been that decreasing the respiration rate diminishes the rate of deterioration of the tissues, thereby extending storage life. Beaudry (2000) reported that a level of 50% reduction in respiration is suggested to be associated with enough enhancement of shelf life such that the cost of extra handling and materials resulting from MAP will be recovered. However, an important primary negative response to low O_2 is the induction of fermentation that leads to accumulation of acetaldehyde, lactate, and ethanol. Generally, the lower limit of O_2 content in the atmosphere is considered to be the O_2 level at which the fermentation is induced. Moreover, Yahia (2006) and Singh and Rao (2005) reported that in mango and papaya (climacteric fruit), a part from reduction of respiration rate, a delay on climacteric respiration peak occurs.

2.2.9 Ripening Index and Firmness

The ripening index generally increases during postharvest storage in a wide range of fruits, mainly due to a decrease in TA and sometimes also to an increase in TSS. Thus the ripening index at harvest increased after 21 days of storage in four plum cultivars stored at 2°C in open air, while these increases were significantly lower in plum stored under MAP conditions (Fig. 4.9). Accordingly, TSS increased and TA decreased in peaches and nectarines stored in air, while in MAP conditions no changes were observed (Akbudak and Eris, 2004). Moreover, in loquat fruit individual sugars and malic acid decreased over cold storage, these changes being delayed in MAP-stored fruits, showing a clear effect of MAP on decreasing fruit metabolism, especially loss of respiration substrates and in turn on delaying the postharvest ripening process (Amoros et al., 2008). MAP is also effective in delaying the softening process that usually occurs during postharvest storage (Fig. 4.9). In general, MAP with 5–20% CO_2 and 5–10% O_2 are effective on retarding firmness losses during storage in a wide range of fruits, such as strawberries (Garcia et al., 1998), apricot (Pretel et al., 1993), kiwifruit (Agar et al., 1999), loquat (Amoros et al., 2008), peaches, and nectarines (Akbudak and Eris, 2004).

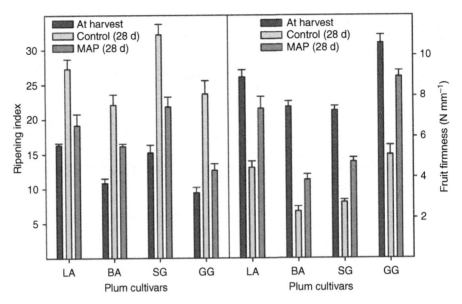

Figure 4.9 Fruit ripening index and firmness of four plum cultivars (LA, Larry Ann; BA, Black Amber; SG, Songold; and GG, Golden Globe) at harvest and after 28 days of storage at 2°C in open air (control) and under modified atmosphere packaging (MAP) conditions with microperforated polyester/polypropylene (12/60 μm thickness) films.

Accordingly, in table grapes packaged in nonperforated PP film, berry and skin firmness were almost double than in control fruits after 14 days of cold storage (Martinez-Romero et al., 2003). This effect has been attributed to the reduction of cellwall-degrading enzymes, such as polygalacturonase (PG), by high CO_2 and low O_2 (Femenia et al., 1998). Nevertheless, the effect of MAP on delaying softening could be also an ethylene-mediated effect, since in apricots decreased film permeability led to increased CO_2 concentration and decreased ethylene production and softening (Pretel et al., 1993). However, it has been also found that low O_2 concentration is more effective at inhibiting fruit softening than high CO_2 (Pretel et al., 1999).

2.3 Combining Map With Other Preservative Techniques (Heat Treatment, Irradiation, Ozone, and Preservatives)

The currently used preservation techniques show their preservative effect by preventing the access of microorganisms to foods, inactivating them through restricted gain access, or preventing or slowing down their growth. Combinations of several factors are used for preservation of almost all foods in industrialized and developing countries to ensure secure microbial safety, stability, and sensory quality. Leistner (2002) implied that the most common food preservation methods are application of low temperature, high temperature (heat treatment), a_w, acidity (pH), redox potential, some preservatives, and a competitive flora. Novel methods are continuously being developed to obtain regulatory approval and are introduced in the marketplace for consumer evaluation and acceptance.

Leistner (2002) proposed the principle of combined preservation, which is often referred to as "hurdle technology" and is widely accepted as a food preservation strategy. Some consideration for intelligent selection of hurdles in MAP is required such as their intensity and the sequence of applications to achieve a specified outcome (McMeekin and Ross, 2002). In modified atmosphere products increase of the intensity or concentration of preservation increases energy depletion and restricts the energy supply to inhibit the repair mechanisms of the microbial cells' factors and leads to growth inhibition or death.

Recently, there has been increasing demand from consumers for minimally processed produce due to its high product quality, convenience, and freshness (Ohlsson, 1994). Using low and stable temperature is a general prerequisite for many modified atmosphere products and has a particular importance in fresh fruit and vegetable storage. Reduction of temperature has a great influence on both enzymatic and microbiological activities. At temperatures below 10°C, growth of many bacteria is inhibited and even psychrotrophic organisms' growth is reduced, and lag phases are extended when temperatures approach 0°C. However, temperature could be used to achieve special effects in modified atmosphere products such as packaging frozen products. By using MAP for ready-to-eat products, they can be distributed frozen, then thawed and sold as chilled products but with an extended shelf life (Morris, 1989).

Combining irradiation with MAP is beneficial as modified atmospheres are not lethal to spoilage organisms and pathogens. Using irradiation below the "threshold" dose (the level at which spoilage organisms and pathogens are killed) and below the level that undesirable organoleptic changes are introduced enhance the attractiveness of MAP. The effects of MAP/irradiation on sensory properties, the depletion of vitamin content during storage, have been examined in comparison to untreated items. The studies showed that deleterious effects of irradiation on vitamins can be removed by modified storage atmospheres (Robins, 1991). The results showed that a radiation dose of 0.25 kGy in an air atmosphere can cause 60% of thiamine content loss over the storage period in comparison to a minimal loss in the nonirradiated control over the same period. Also, Robins (1991) reported that 1 kGy irradiation resulted in 50% loss of α-tocopherol over this period, in comparison to a similar minimal loss in the nonirradiated control sample. It was demonstrated that in both cases, the effects of irradiation on the vitamins were much reduced loss rates in N_2 atmospheres.

In other study the growth rate of surviving microorganisms in the irradiated and nonirradiated food samples was measured as a function of atmospheric composition and the results showed that the optimum lethal atmospheres were in range from CO_2/N_2: 25/75 to CO_2/N_2: 50/50. A similar trend was observed when tests were done at 10°C but the effectiveness of high concentrations of CO_2 was reduced.

The Joint Expert Committee of FAO/WHO/IAEA stated that irradiation up to a dose of 10 kGy has no toxicological effects on any food commodity (WHO, 1999). However, the FDA permitted an irradiation dose up to 1.0 kGy for fresh produce (FDA, 1995).

Irradiation with low-dose gamma is a potential tool for extending the shelf life of many fresh fruits and vegetables by eliminating/inactivating the spoilage-causing and pathogenic microorganisms (Gautam et al., 1998; Kamat et al., 2005). Its use is gradually increasing worldwide (WHO, 1999; Bidawid et al., 2000). Prakash et al. (2000) reported that the combination of MAP with γ-irradiation resulted in reducing the microbial population and maintaining the nutritional quality of fresh-cut lettuce during preservation at low-temperature storage. It was demonstrated that γ-irradiation assures microbial safety without significant loss in quality (Ayun-Joo et al., 2005). A combination of MAP with irradiation (1.0–2.0 kGy) retained the microbiological and physicochemical quality of fresh-cut Chinese cabbage during storage for 3 weeks at 4°C. Studies showed that the dose was effective in reducing the rate of respiration and delaying the browning of *Agaricus bisporus* mushrooms (Benoit et al., 2000), but results showed that 2.0 kGy was required to reduce microbial growth and to extend the shelf life from 2 to 10 days (Gautam et al., 1998). Gautam et al. (1998) also implied that irradiation treatment at 2.0 kGy causes oxidation of phenolic compounds present in vacuoles, which could induce a slight brownish discoloration of mushrooms (Thomas, 1988). The studies showed that γ-irradiation could extend the storage life of *Pleurotus pulmonarius* (Xia et al., 2005) and *Pleurotus sajor-caju* (Roy et al., 2000) without any adverse effects on protein, amino acid, carbohydrate, and vitamin C contents. However, some researchers concluded that application of γ-irradiation (1.0 kGy) induced softening in fruits and vegetables (Prakash et al., 2000; Rastogi and Raghavarao, 2004; Rastogi, 2005). Some reports have implied that use of γ-irradiation reduced ascorbic acid content in some fruits and vegetables such as potatoes (Wang and Dilley, 2000), whereas Lu et al. (2005) demonstrated that γ-irradiation induced accumulation of ascorbic acid in celery. Ayun-Joo et al. (2005) demonstrated that γ-irradiation assures microbial safety without significant loss in quality. Lu et al. (2005) demonstrated that an irradiation dose of 2.0 kGy was effective in maintaining the textural, sensorial, and microbiological quality of minimally processed carrots for 14 days at 5°C. Integrated irradiation and active packaging are effective technologies for pest control and inhibition of growth of aflatoxigenic *Aspergillus* species. Different studies showed that insects were killed at a dose of 1 kGy, and 3 and 5 kGy were suitable for inhibiting mycelium growth and toxin production of several *Aspergillus* species. Jiang et al. (2010) reported that integrated application of γ-irradiation (1.0 kGy) and MAP (in bio-oriented polypropylene [BOPP] bags) on shiitake (*Lentinula edodes*) mushrooms resulted in maintaining a high level of firmness, smaller initial declines in soluble protein, reduction of microbial counts, higher increases in total sugar content, lower levels of malondialdehyde accumulation, higher accumulation of phenolic compounds, and higher antioxidant ability during storage. Their results showed that γ-irradiation in combination with MAP were also effective in retarding mushroom sensory deterioration and extending postharvest life of mushrooms for up to 20 days. They also reported that integrated treatments of γ-irradiation (1.0, 1.5, and 2.0 kGy) + MAP was more effective in reducing microbial counts than stand-alone MAP (Table 4.3). γ-Irradiation (2.0 kGy) + MAP reduced all microbial counts to below detection limits (10 CFU/g) for at least 4 days, with recovery being observed for the γ-irradiation (1.0 and 1.5 kGy) + MAP-treated samples at later time points (Table 4.3).

Mexis et al. (2011) reported that irradiated almonds at doses higher than 3.0 kGy produced free radicals, which interact with both lipid and protein molecules, and made almonds organoleptically unacceptable for consumers. They concluded that a combination of irradiation at lower/medium doses (≤3.0 kGy) with an oxygen absorber, active and MAP were effective in protecting almonds from both lipid oxidation and the growth of *Aspergillus* spp. Their results showed that irradiation decreased polyunsaturated and monounsaturated fatty acids and increased saturated fatty acids during storage. Irradiation had no effect on volatile compounds but they increased during storage indicating enhanced lipid oxidation.

Table 4.3 Microbial Counts (log10 CFU g⁻¹) Changes in Shiitake Mushrooms Packaged in Gamma Irradiation + MAP Stored at 4°C for 20 Days[a,b,c]

Days at 4°C	Control	1.0 kGy	1.5 kGy	2.0 kGy
Mesophilic				
0	4.3 ± 0.03 A	ND	ND	ND
4	4.7 ± 0.08 A	2.2 ± 0.14 B	ND	ND
8	5.3 ± 0.05 A	3.7 ± 0.04 B	2.4 ± 0.04 C	ND
12	5.6 ± 0.23 A	4.5 ± 0.25 B	4.1 ± 0.27 B	2.3 ± 0.03 C
16	6.2 ± 0.06 A	5.1 ± 0.11 B	5.2 ± 0.15 B	4.0 ± 0.07 C
20	7.3 ± 0.13 A	5.8 ± 0.04 B	5.5 ± 0.13 C	4.8 ± 0.26 D
Psychrophilic				
0	1.8 ± 0.12 A	ND	ND	ND
4	2.1 ± 0.17 A	ND	ND	ND
8	2.4 ± 0.06 A	1.6 ± 0.04 B	ND	ND
12	2.6 ± 0.02 A	1.9 ± 0.06 B	1.7 ± 0.14 B	ND
16	3.1 ± 0.24 A	2.3 ± 0.02 B	2.1 ± 0.04 B	1.8 ± 0.09 C
20	3.5 ± 0.11 A	2.6 ± 0.17 B	2.3 ± 0.17 C	2.1 ± 0.04 C
Pseudomonad				
0	6.2 ± 0.22 A	ND	ND	ND
4	6.5 ± 0.17 A	3.2 ± 0.06 B	3.0 ± 0.12 B	ND
8	7.0 ± 0.16 A	4.7 ± 0.12 B	4.3 ± 0.28 C	2.8 ± 0.13 D
12	7.6 ± 0.25 A	5.8 ± 0.19 B	5.5 ± 0.07 C	4.1 ± 0.16 D
16	8.1 ± 0.11 A	6.5 ± 0.07 B	6.1 ± 0.04 C	5.3 ± 0.07 D
20	8.7 ± 0.19 A	6.9 ± 0.13 B	6.4 ± 0.15 C	5.7 ± 0.03 D
Yeasts and molds				
0	4.1 ± 0.04 A	2.5 ± 0.07 B	ND	ND
4	4.6 ± 0.02 A	3.2 ± 0.04 B	1.8 ± 0.09 C	ND
8	5.2 ± 0.16 A	3.8 ± 0.08 B	3.1 ± 0.11 C	2.1 ± 0.15 D
12	5.7 ± 0.21 A	4.5 ± 0.15 B	3.8 ± 0.22 C	2.8 ± 0.08 D
16	6.3 ± 0.25 A	4.9 ± 0.07 B	4.4 ± 0.26 C	3.5 ± 0.04 D
20	6.8 ± 0.17 A	5.4 ± 0.31 B	4.8 ± 0.12 C	4.2 ± 0.24 D

[a]Mean of three replications ± standard deviation.
[b]Means in same row with different letters (A, B, C, D) are significantly different ($P < 0.05$).
[c]ND, not detected, detection limit for mesophilic, psychrophilic, pseudomonad, and yeast and mold counts was 1 log10 CFU g⁻¹.

The other common irradiation method in the food industry is ultraviolet irradiation. UV light has relatively few applications in the food industry such as disinfecting surfaces because of the restricted range of commercially available equipment for disinfecting solids. UV radiation is classified based on wavelength: (1) UV-A, ranges from 315 to 400 nm (near-UV radiation); (2) UV-B, ranges from 280 to 315 nm (mid-range UV); and (3) UV-C, ranges from 100 to 280 nm (far-UV). Most studies in fruits and vegetables were performed with UV-C radiation. Ben-Yehoshua (2003) implied that postharvest treatments with low doses of UV-C radiation (254 nm) induces the resistance of fruits against pathogens and reduces decay of a wide array of fruits and vegetables. Rodov et al. (1992) demonstrated the ability of low doses of UV-C radiation to induce disease resistance in citrus fruits. They reported that fruits inoculated after UV treatment were more resistant to pathogen invasion than those inoculated before the treatment, thus the major effect of UV-C was not germicidal. Moreover, their results showed that UV irradiation inhibited decay of inoculated citrus fruits through eliciting the synthesis of the phytoalexins scoparone and scopoletin, and inducing the production of a new layer of lignin-like compounds on the fruit peel. Recently, UV light has been applied as a sanitation procedure to fresh-cut produce. Nonionizing, germicidal, and artificial UV-C (wavelength ranges of 190–280 nm) has significant effect on surface decontamination of fresh-cut produce. The studies showed that effectiveness of UV-C is independent of the temperature in the range of 5–37°C. However, effectiveness of UV-C depends on the incident irradiation, as determined by the structure and surface of treated produce. Application of UV irradiation in food processes has several advantages, for example, it does not have legal restrictions, it does not leave any residue, it is easy to operate, it is lethal to most types of microorganisms, and it does not require extensive safety equipment to be implemented (Artés et al., 2009).

Although using UV irradiation as postharvest treatment for fruits is permissible in the major fruit-producing countries, supplementary commercial-scale studies of the effects of UV irradiation on each cultivar are still required. The most important problem is determining a safe dose that would greatly impair pathogen growth without damaging the product (Ben-Yehoshua and Mercier, 2005).

Therefore several issues need to be resolved before this method is extensively used in food processes, such as legislative, scientific (food safety), and also consumer attitudes towards irradiated foods (Sivertsvik et al., 2002). Therefore all studies have recommended that the advantages of MAP and irradiation-combined treatment should be determined for specific applications with a fair degree of caution and this requires the ascertainment of exact conditions for every product in terms of microbiological safety.

A broad spectrum of antimicrobial agents is used on foods, especially fresh produce (Moline et al., 1999; Dong et al., 2000; Gorny and Brandenburg, 2002). The studies showed that chlorine dioxide is efficacious against bacteria on a variety of vegetables and fruits, especially fresh produce, including asparagus, tomatoes, lettuce, cabbage, mushrooms, carrots, apples, strawberries, and cherries. Chlorine dioxide increases the shelf lives of these foods by reducing bacterial concentrations on produce. Khanna (2002) found that chlorine dioxide also controls the fungal disease known as late blight and other secondary infections such as soft rot on stored potatoes. Some antimicrobial treatments used include fungicide dipping or spraying on fruits and vegetables, ascorbic acid, citric acid, and antioxidant agents. Valverde et al. (2005) demonstrated that addition of 0.5 mL of eugenol, thymol, or menthol on Crimson Seedless grapes stored at 1°C for 35 days improved the beneficial effect of MAP (1.4–2.0 kPa CO_2 and 10.0–14.5 kPa O_2), delaying rachis deterioration and berry decay, and reducing the total viable counts for both yeast and molds.

Combining methyl jasmonate and modified atmosphere treatments has reduced postharvest decay of papaya caused by fungi such as *Colletotrichum gloeosporioides* and *Alternaria alternata* (Gonzalez-Aguilar et al., 2003). The effects of MAP or waxing before storage on the quality of immature green mangoes were studied by Wickham and Mohammed (1999) during storage at 10°C, 20°C, or 30°C in sealed LDPE or paper bags. They found no evidence of pathological infection on 16% of the fruit stored at 10°C in LDPE bags, whereas they reported that severe chilling injury developed in the waxed and control fruit after 14 days (Wickham and Mohammed, 1999). Yong and Kyung (1998) also reported that dipping peppers in thiabendazol fungicide solution at 50°C and a successive controlled atmosphere (CA) treatment inhibited fungal decay in peppers.

Studies showed that pre- and postharvest treatments of fruits with different calcium salts have beneficial effects on fruit quality at harvest and during postharvest storage, such as preventing fruit decay and enriching the nutritional value of the produce. Several factors have influence on selection of the appropriate source of calcium salts, such as solubility and bioavailability, flavor change, and the interaction with food ingredients. Among different forms of calcium salts, calcium chloride has been extensively used as a firming agent and preservative in fruit and vegetable industries for whole and fresh-cut commodities, and acceptable results were reported in apples, grapefruits, strawberries, and fresh-cut honeydew and cantaloupe melons and peaches. Other forms of calcium salts are used for the treatment of fruits and vegetables, such as calcium carbonate, calcium lactate, calcium propionate, calcium phosphate, calcium citrate, and calcium gluconate (Martin-Diana et al., 2007).

There are two methods for postharvest treatment of calcium in fresh fruits and vegetables: dipping-washing and vacuum infiltration processes. Dipping-washing processes are commonly used for flesh perishable products. In dipping treatment the produce is soaked in salt solution, sometimes applying mechanical agitation, and then excess washing solution is removed. In this method the calcium solution effectively is dispersed on the fruit and vegetable surface and rinsed. The enzymes and substrates on minimally fresh-cut commodities are released from the injured cells during the minimal procedure, which leads to the avoidance of oxidations, browning, and the generation of off-flavors (Lara et al., 2006, 2007; Martin-Diana et al., 2007; Mahmud et al., 2008).

In vacuum infiltration, first the air is extracted from the tissue pores following the application of vacuum and then calcium solution penetrates into the intracellular spaces by capillary and pressure gradients generated by restoration of the atmospheric conditions. Researchers have used different calcium concentrations (1.5–7.5%), pressure applied (2–33 kPa), and time (30 s to 10 min) for the treatment of both whole and sliced fruits (Safizadeh et al., 2007; Mahmud et al., 2008; Eryani-Raqeeb et al., 2009).

Essential oils are natural antimicrobial and antioxidant compounds, which are regarded as alternatives to chemical preservatives. However, essential oils application is limited due to flavor alteration and moderate effectiveness due to their interaction with food ingredients and structures.

A number of essential oils and their components are registered as permissible by the European Commission for applying in foodstuffs, for example, menthol, eugenol, and thymol. These compounds are present in GRAS (Generally Recognized as Safe) and EAFUS (Everything Added to Food in the US) lists. Essential oils as natural preservatives have been used in several food products such as cheese, meat, bakery products, among others (Burt, 2004), but the main disadvantages for the use of these natural compounds is related to persistence of strong aromas and adverse changes in the organoleptic properties of food. Lanciotti et al. (2004) demonstrated that the use of natural compounds such as hexanal, 2-(E)-hexenal, and hexyl acetate in fruits improved safety and shelf life of minimally processed fruits. Serrano et al. (2005) investigated the effects of a combination of MAP and pure essential oils on sweet cherry and several cultivars of table grapes such

Table 4.4 Effect of the Addition of Essential Oils to MAP Packages on Microbial Spoilage in Table Grape and Sweet Cherry[a]

| | Total Mesophilic Aerobics (CFU g^{-1}) | | Yeasts and Molds (CFU g^{-1}) | |
	Table Grape	Sweet Cherry	Table Grape	Sweet Cherry
At harvest	4.77 A	4.20 A	4.61 A	2.10 A
Control	4.90 A	4.77 A	5.04 A	4.89 B
Eugenol	3.33 B	2.93 B	2.10 B	1.11 C
Thymol	3.41 B	2.84 B	2.46 B	0.95 C
Menthol	3.60 B	2.69 B	3.24 C	1.48 D

[a]Each package contains 500 µL of the corresponding essential oil, except in control, in which no essential oils were added. Data obtained after 16 and 35 days of cold storage in MAP packages for sweet cherry and table grape, respectively. For each column, different letters (A, B, C, D) are significantly different at $P < 0.05$ (Guillen et al., 2007).

as Crimson, Autumn Royal, and Aledo (Valverde et al., 2005; Valero et al., 2006; Guillen et al., 2007). They reported that overall quality of the products was improved in terms of maintenance of organoleptic and functional properties together with safety. Guillen et al. (2007) showed that adding essential oils to MAP reduced the total mesophilic aerobic and yeast and mold counts in table grapes and sweet cherries compared to contamination in fruits stored in MAP. As illustrated in Table 4.4, essential oils have higher effectiveness in reducing the yeast and molds than mesophilic aerobics for both fruit types, which was related to the lower decay incidence reported in these fruits as compared to those stored in MAP.

Combination of MAP and essential oils was able to maintain color, reduce softening, and delay the increase in ripening index or TSS/TA ratio in both sweet cherries and table grapes compared to those control fruits under MAP conditions. The effects were attributed to the essential oils added, since gas composition was similar (11–12 O_2 and 2–3 kPa CO_2 for sweet cherries, and 10–14 O_2 and 1.3–2.0 kPa CO_2 for table grapes) in both control bags and treated packages. It should be mentioned that further studies are needed for a comprehensive understanding of the mechanisms by which these essential oils affect the fruit physiology and modulate the ripening process, as well as their ability to kill microorganisms.

Ozone is a gas compound that is composed of three atoms of oxygen to form the molecule O_3. Ozone is a strong natural oxidizing, toxic, and disinfecting agent, and concentrations in excess of

5 ppm produce a significant microbiocidal effect in a short exposure time consistent with modern high-speed production lines. Ozone is an unstable molecule (with half life of 4 to 12 h in air dependent on temperature and humidity) and an oxidization reaction occurs upon any collision between an ozone molecule and microorganisms (bacteria, viruses, and cysts) because of its instability. Ozone inactivates bacteria cells and viruses by oxidization of their DNA chains and cellular membrane disintegration.

There are two commercial methods for generating ozone: corona discharge and UV radiation. In the corona discharge method, ozone is produced by passing air through a high-voltage electric field.

In the UV radiation method, ambient air is irradiated with UV (wavelengths below 200 nm) to split some of the O_2 molecules into two O atoms, which collide with other O_2 molecules to produce ozone (O_3).

It was reported that storage of fruits and vegetables in ozone-rich atmospheres could decontaminate the surface of fruits and vegetables, reduce or eliminate odor, reduce postharvest decay, and control spoilage caused by microbial and fungal pathogens in apples, cherries, carrots, kiwifruits, onions, peaches, plums, potatoes, table grapes, tomatoes, blackberries, and strawberries (Palou et al., 2002; Tzortzakis et al., 2007).

There are different methods for ozone exposure of fruits and vegetables, such as prestorage treatment in air or water, or adding continuously or intermittently to the storage room atmosphere throughout the storage period to prevent or delay fruit decay (Palou et al., 2002; Cayuela et al., 2009). It was reported that ozone significantly reduces postharvest decay of carrots inoculated with *Sclerotinia sclerotiorum* and *B. cinerea* and held in 115–530 nL L^{-1} ozone at 10°C for 20 days. Skog and Chu (2001) found that ozone treatment (0.04 μL L^{-1}) of broccoli and cucumbers at 3°C, extended their storage life. The gaseous ozone exposure of spores of *S. sclerotiorum* and *B. cinerea* and mycelial growth of *B. cinerea* for grapes, apples, carrots, and high bush blueberries resulted in a significant reduction in spore viability of *B. cinerea* of over 99.5% and a reduction in the aerial mycelium from 4.7 mm in the control to less than 1 mm after exposure to 450 or 600 ppb ozone for 48 h at 20°C (Sharpe et al. 2009). Palou et al. (2001) observed a delay of the growth of green and blue mold in ozonated citrus fruit.

However, exposure of fruits and vegetables to high ozone concentrations during storage may cause surface discoloration (blotches). Skog and Chu (2001) demonstrated that ozone has a significant effect on removing ethylene from the atmosphere during pear and apple storage without a significant change in quality attributes. Furthermore, exposure of horticulture crops to ozone can reduce postharvest decay and is effective in reducing application of field-applied fungicides.

Nitric oxide (NO) is a highly reactive free radical gas that has recently been used for resisting vegetative stress and senescence of horticultural products. Several studies showed that short-term treatment with low concentrations of NO gas or its donor compounds resulted in extending postharvest life, inhibited ethylene biosynthesis, inhibited cut-surface browning, delayed ripening, and enhanced resistance to postharvest diseases in different fresh fruits and vegetables. Jiang et al. (2010) studied the effect of a combination of dipping in different concentrations of 2,20(hydroxynitrosohydrazino)-bisethanamine (DETANO) (0.5, 1, and 2 mM), an NO donor, for 10 min and MAP in BOPP bags and storage at 4°C for 16 days on button mushroom (*A. bisporus*) quality retention. They reported that treatment with 1 mM DETANO effectively maintained firmness, delayed browning and cap opening, increased accumulation of ascorbic acid and phenolics, inhibited the activity of PPO, increased the antioxidant enzyme activities of CAT, SOD, and APX, and reduced both O_2 production rate and H_2O_2 content during the storage period. The results indicated that integrated application of NO and MAP could be a useful technique for extending the storage life of button mushrooms by up to 12 days.

Edible coatings can prevent water loss, retain flavor, be carriers of antibrowning or antimicrobial agents, retain less water-soluble volatiles, which affect fruit flavor, prevent surface drying, and perhaps reduce volatile off-gassing in fruits and vegetables. However, Baldwin et al. (1995) showed that a coating barrier can induce anaerobic respiration and the subsequent synthesis of ethanol and acetaldehyde, and then entrap volatiles, including ethanol and acetaldehyde, leading to a fermented off-flavor. Many researchers have studied coating-induced changes in apple (Bai et al., 2003) and citrus (Hagenmaier, 2002).

Shellac and wood rosin have low permeability to water vapor, thus they are moderately effective at reducing water loss; however, they impart the gloss or shine to the fruit, which is highly desired by the fresh fruit industry. Coatings with higher amounts of wood rosin or shellac on citrus cause the development of a more modified atmosphere. However, a severe modified atmosphere created by rosin coatings results in more off-flavors compared to fruit coated with the more permeable PE waxes or carnauba because of the increase in ethanol and a change in the volatile profile (Baldwin et al., 1995; Hagenmaier, 2002).

The waxes are very effective at reducing water loss, are more permeable to gases compared to the rosins, and therefore induce less off-flavor in fruits, while imparting moderate shine (Baldwin, 1994). Coatings have influence on the flavor of grapefruit (*Citrus paradisi* M.) and oranges (Hagenmaier and Baker, 1994), but tangerines (*Citrus reticulata Blanco*) are especially susceptible to anaerobiosis due to coating treatments (Hagenmaier, 2002). Other coating materials have been tested on citrus such as hydroxylpropyl methylcellulose and beeswax. It was observed that the higher solids content in these coatings leads to higher accumulation of internal CO_2, ethanol, and off-flavor. Coatings synthesized from polyvinyl acetate (PVA) (Hagenmaier and Grohman, 2000) and corn zeins (Bai et al., 2003) are shiny and more permeable than the resins. PVA has no problems with discoloration often associated with shellac (Hagenmaier and Grohman, 2000). Apples are another fruit often coated with shellac and carnauba wax, or a mixture of the two with high gloss or shine, which helps to boost sales. Coating choices for apples are restricted in comparison to citrus, and the less permeable wood rosin and the more permeable PE wax are not allowed for use on apples. Saftner (1999) reported that ethanol and ethyl acetate were accumulated in shellac-coated Golden Delicious apples, which were held at 20°C. As is seen with MAP, storage temperature affects the modification of a fruit's internal atmosphere by using a coating, which means that the warmer the storage or holding temperature, the greater the fruit respiration, requirement for O_2, and production of CO_2. Bai et al. (2003) tested other coatings made from corn zein, starch, and PVA on apples in comparison with carnauba wax and shellac. They found that zein, carnauba wax, and PVA coatings resulted in higher internal fruit O_2 concentrations than did shellac or starch coatings especially during a simulated marketing period at 20°C, but they have a similar gloss to shellac. They demonstrated that ethanol and ethyl esters accumulate in apples coated with shellac, starch, or a carnauba-polysaccharide composite coating, but these volatiles decreased after transfer of fruit to 21°C. Bai et al. (2003) found that reaction of apples to coating permeability was dependent on cultivars, in part perhaps due to their anatomical structure (number of stomates and lenticels or pores). They reported that shellac coatings of Braeburn and Granny Smith apples (stored at 20°C) caused excessive modification of internal gases and induced an abrupt rise of the respiratory quotient and accumulation of ethanol, as well as flesh browning at the blossom end of Braeburn fruit. The shellac coating had less effect on Fuji apples and no effect on Delicious fruit. However, coating treatments with both the aqueous antioxidant and the antioxidants led to some volatile retention compared to uncoated fruits (Plotto et al., 2004).

3 Future Trends

It is expected the current trend of using MAP for extending the commercial life of many plant species and varieties, either whole or minimally processed, for transport, commercial distribution, and retail sale, will increase gradually. Recently, certain developments in MAP have been achieved such as fast attainment of the optimal atmosphere by injection of N_2, or by including O_2 and CO_2 scavengers within packages or a preprepared gaseous mixture into the package. Moreover, the introduction of intelligent or dynamic packages into MAPs could significantly increase their permeability to O_2 when the temperature increases. Also, polymers that incorporate in manufacture of antimicrobial substances, or ethylene scrubbers, like MnO_4K could significantly improve MAP efficiency. Also in MAP systems, in-package additives or the use of a biosensor capable of measuring ethanol in the gas phase and indirectly detecting low O_2 levels could improve packaged product aroma.

The potential benefits and ideal modified atmosphere for many fruits and vegetables have not been explored and investigated in detail. In addition, more research efforts should be directed on modified atmosphere storage of commercialized fruits. Also the mode of action of modified atmospheres in alleviating some physiological disorders, especially chilling injury (CI) and mechanisms of modified atmosphere-initiated or -augmented physiological disorders, is still not clearly understood. As variable applied conditions (differences in cultivars used, stages of maturity, types of films, sizes of packages, sealing methods, temperatures, RH, etc.) lead to variable results for MAP, the experiments should distinguish the effects due to atmosphere modification or to other factors. The methods of handling modified atmosphere-treated crop are not very well established due to lack of knowledge regarding the behavior of fruit after MAP, therefore more research is needed to investigate the metabolic changes due to MAP and select adequate methods of handling.

Also, more comprehensive studies are needed to investigate the effects of various factors such as growing environment, season of harvest, and other preharvest factors on the postharvest quality and storage potential of fruits and vegetables, especially under MAP.

The use of intelligent packaging systems has to be evaluated in MAP technology and also the combination of novel methods of food treatment and packaging needs to be examined, for example, irradiation used with MAP and antimicrobial films used in combination with MAP. Detailed research is needed to evaluate the antimicrobial effect of superatmospheric O_2 on fresh-cut produce safety. It is necessary to study survival of enteric pathogens and the behavior of foodborne viruses and protozoan parasites on MAP produce. Another active area of research is edible films for use in MAP systems.

References

Abeles, F.B., Morgan, P.W., Saltveit, M.E., 1992. Ethylene in Plant Biology. San Diego, Academic Press.

Agar, I.T., Massantini, R., Hess-Pierce, B., Kader, A.A., 1999. Postharvest CO_2 and ethylene production and quality maintenance of fresh-cut kiwifruit slices. J. Food Sci. 64, 433–440.

Ahvenainen, R., 1996. New approaches in improving the shelf life of fresh-cut fruits and vegetables. Trends Food Sci. Technol. 7, 179–186.

Akbudak, B., Eris, A., 2004. Physical and chemical changes in peaches and nectarines during the modified atmosphere storage. Food Control 15, 307–313.

Alique, R., Zamorano, J.P., Martinez, A., Alonso, J., 2005. Effect of heat and cold treatments on respiratory metabolism and shelf-life of sweet cherry, type picota cv "Ambrunes". Postharvest Biol. Tech 35, 153–165.

Amoros, A., Pretel, M.T., Zapata, P.J., Botella, M.A., Romojaro, F., Serrano, M., 2008. Use of modified atmosphere packaging with microperforated polypropylene films to maintain postharvest loquat quality. Food Sci. Tech. Int. 14, 95–103.

An, J., Zhang, M., Zhan, Z., 2007. Effect of packaging film on the quality of 'Chaoyang' honey peach fruit in modified atmosphere packages. Packag. Technol. Sci. 20 (1), 71–76.

Ares, G., Lareo, C., Lema, P., 2007. Modified atmosphere packaging for postharvest storage of mushrooms: a review. Fresh Produce 1 (1), 32–40.

Artes-Hernandez, F., Tomas-Barberan, F.A., Artes, F., 2006. Modified atmosphere packaging preserves quality of SO_2-free "Superior seedless" table grapes. Postharvest Biol. Technol. 39, 146–154.

Artés, F., 2000. Conservación de los productos vegetales en atmósfera modificada. Lamúa, M. (Ed.), Aplicación del frío a los alimentos, 4, A. Madrid-Mundi-Prensa, Madrid, Spain, pp. 105–125.

Artés, F., Escriche, A. J., Marin, J. G., 1993. TreatingPrimofiori'Lemons in Cold Storage with Intermittent Warming and Carbon Dioxide. HortScience, 28 (8), 819-821.

Artés, F., Escalona, V.H., Artés-Hernandez, F., 2002. Modified atmosphere packaging of fennel. J. Food Sci. 64, 1550–1554.

Artés, F., Gómez, P.A., Aguayo, E., Escalona, V., Artés-Hernández, F., 2009. Sustainable sanitation techniques for keeping quality and safety of fresh-cut plant commodities. Postharvest Biol. Technol. 51, 287–296.

Artés, F., Marín, J.G., Martínez, J.A., 1996. Controlled atmosphere storage of pomegranate. Zeitschrift für Lebensmittel-Untersuchung und Forschung 203 (1), 33–37.

Ayun-Joo, A., Jae-Hyun, K., Jae Kyung, K., Dong-Ho, K., Hong-Sun, Y., Myung-Woo, B., 2005. Combined effects of irradiation and modified atmosphere packaging on minimally processed Chinese cabbage (Brassica rapa L). Food Chem. 89, 589–597.

Bai, J., Alleyne, V., Hagenmaier, R.D., Mattheis, J.P., Baldwin, E.A., 2003. Formulation of zein coatings for apples (Malus domestica Borkh). Postharvest Biol. Technol. 28, 259–268.

Baldwin, E.A., 1994. Edible coatings for fresh fruits and vegetables: past present and future. In: Krochta, J., Baldwin, E.A., Nisperos-Carriedo, M.O. (Eds.),

Edible Coatings and Films to Improve Food Quality. Technomic Publishing Co., Lancaster, PA, pp. 25–64.

Baldwin, E.A., Scott, J.W., R.L. Shewfelt, R.L., 1995. Quality of ripened mutant and transgenic tomato cultigens. Tomato Quality Workshop Proc. December 11–14, 1995, Davis, CA.

Bangerth, F., 1977. The effect of different partial pressures of CO_2, C_2H_4, and O_2 in the storage atmosphere on the ascorbic acid content of fruits and vegetables. Qual. Plant. 27, 125–133.

Barth, M., Zhuang, H., 1996. Packaging design affects antioxidant vitamin retention and quality of broccoli florets during postharvest storage. Postharvest Biol. Technol. 9, 141–150.

Beaudry, R.M., 1999. Effect of O_2 and CO_2 partial pressure on selected phenomena affecting fruit and vegetable quality. Postharvest Biol. Technol. 15, 293–303.

Beaudry, R.M., 2000. Responses of horticultural commodities to oxygen: limits to the expended use of modified atmosphere packaging. Hort. Technol. 10, 491–500.

Ben-Yehoshua, S., 2003. Effects of postharvest heat and UV applications on decay, chilling injury and resistance against pathogens of citrus and other fruits and vegetables. Acta Hortic. 599, 159–173.

Ben-Yehoshua, S., Mercier, J., 2005. UV irradiation, biological agents, and natural compounds for controlling postharvest decay in fresh fruits and vegetables. In: Ben-Yehoshua, S. (Ed.), Environmentally Friendly Technologies for Agricultural Produce Quality. Boca Raton, Taylor and Francis, pp. 265–299.

Bennik, M.H.J., Smid, E.J., Rombouts, F.M., Gorris, L.G.M., 1995. Growth of psychrotrophic foodborne pathogens in a solid surface model system under the influence of carbon dioxide and oxygen. Food Microbiol. 12, 509–519.

Benoit, M.A., D'Aprano, G., Lacroix, M., 2000. Effects of gamma irradiation onphenylalanine ammonia-lyase activity, total phenolic content and respiration of mushrooms (*Agaricus bisporus*). J. Agric. Food Chem. 48, 6312–6316.

Bidawid, S., Farber, J.M., Sattar, M., 2000. Inactivation of hepatitis A virus (HAV) in fruits and vegetables by gamma-irradiation. Int. J. Food Microbiol. 57, 91–97.

Blanchard, M., Castaigne, F., Willmot, C., Makhlouf, J., 1996. Modified atmosphere preservation of freshly prepared diced yellow onion. Postharvest Biol. Technol. 9, 173–185.

Brackett, R.E., 1994. Microbiological spoilage and pathogens in minimally processed refrigerated fruits and vegetables. In: Wiley, R.C. (Ed.), Minimally Processed Refrigerated Fruits and Vegetables. Chapman & Hall, New York, pp. 269–312.

Britton, G., Hornero-Mendez, D., 1997. Carotenoids and colour in fruit and vegetables. In: Tomás-Barberán, F.A., Robins, R.J. (Eds.), Phytochemistry of Fruit and Vegetables. Oxford, Oxford University Press.

Brody, A.L., Zhuang, H., Han, J.H., 2011. Modified Atmosphere Packaging for Fresh-Cut Fruits and Vegetables. Wiley-Blackwell, Chichester, UK.

Burt, S., 2004. Essential oils: their antibacterial properties and potential applications in foods—a review. Int. J. Food Microbiol. 94, 223–253.

Carlin, F., Nguyen-The, C., Abreu Da Silva, A., Cochet, C., 1996. Effects of carbon dioxide on the fate of *L. monocytogenes*, of aerobic bacteria and on the development of spoilage in minimally processed fresh endive. Int. J. Food Microbiol. 32, 159–172.

Castillejo-Rodriguez, A., Barco-Alcala, E., Garcia-Gimeno, R., Zureracosano, G., 2000. Growth modeling of *Listeria monocytogenes* in packaged fresh green asparagus. Food Microbiol. 17, 421–427.

Cayuela, J.A., Vazquez, A., Perez, A.G., Garcia, J.M., 2009. Control of table grapes postharvest decay by ozone treatment and resveratrol induction. Food Sci. Technol. Int. 15 (5), 495–502.

Charles, F., Sanchez, J., Gontard, N., 2006. Absorption kinetics of oxygen and carbon dioxide scavengers as part of active modified atmosphere packaging. J. Food Eng. 72, 1–7.

Connor, D.E., Scott, V.N., Bernard, D.T., 1989. Potential *Clostridium botulinum* hazards associated with extended shelf-life refrigerated foods: a review. J. Food Safety 10, 131–153.

Costa, C., Mastromatteo, M., Lucera, A., Conte, A., Del Nobile, M.A., 2011. Fresh-cut broccoli florets shelf-life as affected by packaging film mass transport properties. J. Food Eng. 102, 122–129.

Crisosto, C., Crisosto, G., Ritenour, M., 2002. Testing the reliability of skin color as an indicator of quality for early season "Brooks" (*Prunusavium* L) cherry. Postharvest Biol. Technol. 24, 147–154.

Davey, M.W., Van Montagu, M., Inzé, D., Sanmartin, M., Kanellis, A., Smirnoff, N., Benzie, I.J.J., Strain, J.J., Favell, D., Fletcher, J., 2000. Plant L-ascorbic acid: chemistry, function, metabolism, bioavailability and effects of processing. J. Sci. Food Agric. 80, 825–860.

Day B.P.F., 1994. Modified atmosphere packaging and active packaging of fruits and vegetables. Minimal Processing of Foods. VTT-Symposium, vol. 142. 14–15 April 1994, Kirkkonummi, Finland, pp. 173–207.

De Santana, L.R.R., Benedetti, B.C., Sigrist, J.M.M., Sato, H.H., Sarantopoulos, C.I.G.L., 2009. Modified atmosphere packages and cold storage to maintain quality of "Douradao" peaches. 10th International Controlled and Modified Atmosphere Research Conference, Apr. 4–7, 2009, Turkey [abstract], p. 19.

Di Mascio, P., Kaiser, S., Sies, H., 1989. Lycopene as the most efficient biological carotenoid singlet oxygen quencher. Arch Biochem. Biophys. 274, 532–538.

Dong, X., Wrolstad, R.E., Sugar, D., 2000. Extending shelf-life of fresh-cut pears. J. Food Sci. 65, 181–186.

Eryani-Raqeeb, A.A., Mahmud, T.M.M., Omar, S.R.S., Mohamed, A.R., Eryani, A.R.A., 2009. Effects of calcium and chitosan treatments on controlling anthracnose and postharvest quality of papaya (*Carica papaya* L). Int. J. Agric. Res. 4, 53–68.

Farber, J.M., 1991. Microbiological aspects of modified-atmosphere packaging technology—a review. J. Food Protect. 54, 58–70.

FDA, 1995. Section 179.26; Ionizing radiation for the treatment of food. In Code of Federal Regulations: Food and Drugs Title 21. US Government Printing Office, Washington, DC, pp. 389–390.

Femenia, A., Sanchez, E.S., Simal, S., Rosello, C., 1998. Modification of cell wall composition of apricot (*Prunus armeniaca*) during drying and storage under modified atmospheres. J. Agric. Food Chem. 46, 5248–5253.

Fernandez-Trujillo, J.P., Martinez, J.A., Artés, F., 1998. Modified atmosphere packaging affects the incidence of cold storage disorders and keeps "flat" peach quality. Food Res. Int. 31 (8), 571–579.

Finger, F.L., Della-Justina, M.E., Casali, V.W.D., Puiatti, M., 2008. Temperature and modified atmosphere affect the quality of okra. Sci. Agric. 65, 360–364.

Flores, F.B., Martinez-Madrid, M.C., Ben Amor, M., Pech, J.C., Latche, A., Romojaro, F., 2004. Modified atmosphere packaging confers additional chilling tolerance on ethylene-inhibited cantaloupe Charentais melon fruit. Eur. Food Res. Technol. 219, 614–619.

Garcia, D., Fernando, G.D., Nychas, G.J.E., Peck, M.W., Ordonez, J.A., 1995. Growth/survival of psychrotrophic pathogens on meat packaged under modified atmospheres. Int. J. Food Microbiol. 28, 221–231.

Garcia, M.A., Martino, M.N., Zaritzky, N.E., 1998. Plasticized starch-based coatings to improve strawberry (Fragaria × Ananassa) quality and stability. J. Agricult. Food Chem. 46, 3758–3767.

Gautam, S., Sharma, A., Thomas, P., 1998. Gamma irradiation effect on shelf-life, texture, polyphenol oxidase and microflora of mushroom (*Agaricus bisporus*). Int. J. Food Sci. Nutr. 49, 5–10.

Gil, M.I., Ferreres, F., Tomás-Barberán, F.A., 1999. Effect of postharvest storage and processing on the antioxidant constituents (flavonoids and vitamin C) of fresh-cut spinach. J. Agric. Food Chem. 47, 2213–2217.

Giovannucci, E., 1999. Tomatoes, tomato-based products, lycopene and cancer: review of the epidemiologic literature. J. Natl. Cancer Inst. 91, 317–331.

Gonzalez-Aguilar, G.A., Buta, J.G., Wang, C.Y., 2003. Methyl jasmonate and modified atmosphere packaging (MAP) reduce decay and maintain postharvest quality of papaya "Sunrise". Postharverst Biol. Technol. 28, 361–370.

Gorny, J.R., Brandenburg, J., 2002. Packaging Design for Fresh-cut Produce. International Fresh-cut Produce Association, Alexandria, VA.

Guillen, F., Zapata, P.J., Martinez-Romero, D., Castillo, S., Serrano, M., Valero, D., 2007. Improvement of the overall quality of table grapes stored under modified atmosphere packaging in combination with natural antimicrobial compounds. J. Food Sci. 72, 185–190.

Gunes, G., Lee, C., 1997. Color of minimally processed potatoes as affected by modified atmosphere packaging and antibrowning agents. J. Food Sci. 62 (3), 572–575.

Haard, N.F., 1984. Postharvest physiology and biochemistry of fruits and vegetables. J. Chem. Educ. 61 (4), 277–284.

Haffner, K., Jeksrud, W.K., Tengesdal, G., 1997. L-ascorbic acid contents and other quality criteria in apples (*Malus domestica* Borkh) after storage in cold store and controlled atmosphere. In: Micham, E.J. (Ed.), Postharvest Horticultural Series. University of California, 16.

Hagenmaier, R.D., Grohman, K., 2000. Edible food coatings containing polyvinyl acetate. U.S. Patent 6, pp. 162–475.

Hagenmaier, R.D., 2002. The flavor of mandarin hybrids with different coatings. Postharvest Biol. Technol. 24, 79–87.

Hagenmaier, R.D., Baker, R.A., 1994. Internal gases, ethanol content and gloss of citrus fruit coated with polyethylene wax, carnauba wax, shellac or resin at different application levels. Proc. Fla. State Hort. Soc. 107, 261–265.

Hendricks, M.T., Hotchkiss, J.H., 1997. Effect of carbon dioxide on the growth of *Pseudomonas fluorescens* and *Listeria monocytogenes* in aerobic atmospheres. J. Food Prot. 60, 1548–1552.

Herner, R.C., 1987. High CO_2 effects on plant organs. In: Weichmann, J. (Ed.), Postharvest Physiology of Vegetables. Marcel Dekker, New York, p. 239.

Holcroft, D.M., Kader, A.A., 1999. Controlled atmosphere-induced changes in pH and organic acid metabolism may affect color of stored strawberry fruit. Postharvest Biol. Technol. 17, 419–432.

Howard, L.R., Hernandez-Brene, C., 1998. Antioxidant content and market quality of jalapeno pepper rings as affected by minimal processing and modified atmosphere packaging. J. Food Qual. 21, 317–327.

Hudson, J.A., Mott, S.J., Penney, N., 1994. Growth of *Listeria monocytogenes*, *Aeromonas hydrophila*, and *Yersinia enterocolitica* on vacuum and saturated carbon dioxide controlled atmosphere packaged sliced roast beef. J. Food Prot. 57 (3), 204–208.

Inns, R.D., 1987. Modified atmosphere packaging. Paine, F.A. (Ed.), Modern Processing, Packaging and Distribution Systems for Food, 4, Blackie and Son, Glasgow, UK, pp. 36–51.

Jayanty, S., Mir, N., Beaudry, R.M., Fishman, S., Ben-Yehoshua, S., 2005. Modified atmosphere packaging and controlled atmosphere storage. In: Ben-Yehoshua, S. (Ed.), Environmentally Friendly Technologies for Agricultural Produce Quality. CRC Press, Boca Raton, FL, pp. 61–112.

Jiang, C., Driffield, M., Bradley, E.L., Castle, L., Oldring, P.K.T., Guthrie, J.T., 2010. The behavior of MEKO-blocked isocyanate compounds in aluminum flake pigmented, polyester–polyurethane can coating systems. J. Coat. Technol. Res. 7, 57–65.

Johnson, I.T., Williamson, G.M., Musk, S.R.R., 1994. Anti carcinogenic factors in plant foods: a new class of nutrients. Nutr. Res. Rev. 7, 175–204.

Jones, R.B., 2007. The effects of postharvest handling conditions and cooking on anthocyanin, lycopene and glucosinolates content and bioavailability in fruits and vegetables. N.Z. J. Crop Hortic. Sci. 35, 219–227.

Kader, A.A., 1986. Biochemical and physiological basis for effects of controlled and modified atmospheres on fruits and vegetables. Food Technol. 40 (5), 99–100, 102–104.

Kader, A.A., 2002. Modified atmospheres during transportation and storage. In: Kader, A.A. (Ed.), Postharvest Technology of Horticultural Crops. University of California, Division of Agriculture and Natural Resources, Oakland, pp. 135–144.

Kader, A.A., Zagory, D., Kerbel, E.L., 1988. Modified atmosphere packaging of fruits and vegetables. CRC Crit. Rev. Food Sci. Nutr. 28 (1), 1–30.

Kader, A.A., Zagory, D., Kerbel, E.L., 1989. Modified atmosphere packaging of fruits and vegetables. CRC Crit. Rev. Food Sci. Nutr. 28 (1), 1–30.

Kamat, A.S., Ghadge, N., Ramamurthy, M.S., Alur, M.D., 2005. Effect of low-dose irradiation on shelf life and microbiological safety of sliced carrot. J. Sci. Food Agric. 85, 2213–2219.

Kang, H.M., Park, K.W., 2000. Comparison of storability on film sources and storage temperature for oriental melon in modified atmosphere storage. J. Korean Soc. Hortic. Sci. 41, 143–146.

Kappel, E., Toivonen, P., Mckenzie, K.L., Stan, S., 2002. Storage characteristics of new sweet cherry cultivars. Hort. Sci. 37, 139–143.

Ke, D.Y., Kader, A.A., 1992. External and internal factors influence fruit tolerance to low O_2 atmospheres. J. Am. Soc. Hortic. Sci. 117, 913–918.

Khanna, N., 2002. Chlorine dioxide in food applications. In: Proceedings of the 4th International Symposium, Chlorine Dioxide: The State of Science, Regulatory, Environmental Issues, and Case Histories. AWWA Research Foundation and the American Water Works Association, Las Vegas, NV, February 2001, pp. 15–16.

Kidmos, U., Edelenbos, M., Norbake, R., Christensen, L.P., 2002. Color stability in vegetables. In: MacDougall, D.B. (Ed.), Color in Food. Improving Quality. CRC Press and Woodhead Publishing Ltd., Cambridge, England, pp. 179–232.

Klein, J.D., Lurie, S., 1992. Prestorage heating of apple fruit for enhanced postharvest quality: interaction of time and temperature. Hort Sci. 27, 326–328.

Lanciotti, R., Gianotti, A., Patrignani, F., Belletti, N., Guerzoni, M.E., Gardini, F., 2004. Use of natural aroma compounds to improve shelf-life and safety of minimally processed fruits. Trends Food Sci. Technol. 15, 201–208.

Lara, I., Echeverria, G., Graell, J., Lopez, M.L., 2007. Volatile emission after controlled atmosphere storage of Mondial Gala apples (*Malus domestica*): relationship to some involved enzyme activities. J. Agricult. Food Chem. 55, 6087–6095.

Lara, I., Garcia, P., Vendrell, M., 2006. Post-harvest heat treatments modify cell wall composition of strawberry (*Fragaria x ananassa* Duch) fruit. Sci. Hortic. 109, 48–53.

Lee, S.K., Kader, A.A., 2002. Preharvest and postharvest factors influencing vitamin C content of horticultural crops. Postharvest Biol. Technol. 20, 207–220.

Leistner, L., 2002. Hurdle technology. In: Juneja, V.K., Sofos, J.N. (Eds.), Control of Foodborne Microorganisms. Marcel Dekker, Inc, Basel, Switzerland, pp. 493–508.

Lu, Z.X., Yu, Z.F., Gao, X., Lu, F.X., Zhang, L.K., 2005. Preservation effects of gamma irradiation on fresh-cut celery. J. Food Eng. 67, 347–351.

Mahmud, T.M.M., Eryani-Raqeeb, A.A., Omar, S.S.R., Mohamed, Z.A.R., Eryani, A.A.R., 2008. Effects of different concentrations and applications of calcium on storage life and physicochemical characteristics of papaya (*Carica papaya* L). Am. J. Agric. Biol. Sci. 3, 526–533.

Mannapperuma, J.D., Zagory, D., Singh, R.P., Kader, A.A., 1989. Design of polymeric packages for modified atmosphere storage of fresh produce. Proceedings of the 5th International Controlled Atmosphere Research Conference 1, 225–233.

Manvell, P.M., Ackland, M.R., 1986. Rapid detection of microbial growth in vegetable salads at chill and abuse temperatures. Food Microbiol. 3, 59–65.

Martin-Diana, A.B., Rico, D., Frias, J.M., Barat, J.M., Henehan, G.T.M., Barry- Ryan, C., 2007. Calcium for extending the shelf life of fresh whole and minimally processed fruits and vegetables: a review. Trends Food Sci. Technol. 18, 210–218.

Martinez-Javega, J.M., Jimenez Cuesta, M., Cuquerella, J., 1983. Conservacion frigoricdel melon "Tendral". Analesdel Instituto Nacional de Investigaciones Agrarias Agricola 23, 111–124.

Martinez-Romero, D., Guillen, F., Castillo, S., Valero, D., Serrano, M., 2003. Modified atmosphere packaging maintains quality of table grape. J. Food Sci. 68, 1838–1843.

McMeekin, T.A., Ross, T., 2002. Predictive microbiology: providing a knowledge-based framework for change management. Int. J. Food Microbiol. 78, 133–153.

Mehlhorn, H., 1990. Ethylene-promoted ascorbate peroxidase activity protects plants against hydrogen peroxide, ozone and paraquat. Plant Cell Envrion. 13, 971–976.

Mexis, S.F., Chouliara, E., Kontominas, M.G., 2011. Quality evaluation of grated Graviera cheese stored at 4 and 12°C using active and modified atmosphere packaging. Packag. Technol. Sci. 24, 15–29.

Mir, N., Beaudry, R.M., 2003. Modified Atmosphere Packaging U.S. Department of Agriculture. Agricultural Research Service, Beltsville, MD.

Moline, H.E., Buta, J.G., Newman, I.M., 1999. Prevention of browning of banana slices using natural products and their derivatives. J. Food Qual. 22, 499–511.

Morris, C.E., 1989. Convenience for supermarket delis with CAP pizza. Food Eng. 61, 53–54.

Odriozola-Serrano, I., Soliva-Fortuny, R., Martín-Belloso, O., 2008. Effect of minimal processing on bioactive compounds and color attributes of fresh-cut tomatoes. LWT—Food Sci. Technol. 41 (2), 217–226.

Ohlsson, T., 1994. Minimal processing-preservation method and of the future—an overview. Trends Food Sci. Technol. 5, 341–344.

Palou, L., Crisosto, C.H., Smilanick, J.L., Adaskaveg, J.E., Zoffoli, J.P., 2002. Effects of continuous 0.3 ppm ozone exposure on decay development and physiological responses of peaches and table grapes in cold storage. Postharvest Biol. Technol. 24 (1), 39–48.

Palou, L., Smilanick, J.L., Crisosto, C.H., Mansour, M., 2001. Effect of gaseous ozone exposure on the development of green and blue molds on cold stored citrus fruit. Plant Disease 85 (6), 632–638.

Plotto, A., Goodner, K.L., Baldwin, E.A., Bai, J., Rattanapanone, N., 2004. Effect of polysaccharide coatings on quality of fresh cut mangoes (*Mangifera indica*). Proc. Fla. State Hort. Soc. 117, 382–388.

Porat, R., Weiss, B., Cohen, L., Daus, A., Aharoni, N., 2004. Reduction of postharvest rind disorders in citrus fruit by modified atmosphere packaging. Postharvest Biol. Technol. 33, 35–43.

Prakash, A., Inthajak, P., Huibregtse, H., Caporaso, F., Foley, D.M., 2000. Effect of low dose gamma-irradiation and conventional treatments on shelf life and quality characteristics of diced celery. J. Food Sci. 65, 1070–1075.

Pretel, M.T., Serrano, M., Amoros, A., Romojaro, F., 1999. Ripening and ethylene biosynthesis in controlled atmosphere stored apricots. Eur. Food Res. Technol. 209, 130–134.

Pretel, M.T., Serrano, M., Martinez, G., Riquelme, F., Romojaro, F., 1993. Influence of films of different permeability on ethylene synthesis and ripening of MA-packaged apricots. Lebensmittel-Wissenschaft und Technologie 26, 8–13.

Rastogi, N.K., 2005. Impact of gamma irradiation on some mass transfer driven operations in food processing. Radiat. Phys. Chem. 73, 355–361.

Rastogi, N.K., Raghavarao, K.S.M.S., 2004. Increased mass transfer during osmotic dehydration of irradiated potatoes. J. Food Sci. 69 (6), 259–263.

Remón, S., Ferrer, A., Marquina, P., Burgos, J., Oria, R., 2000. Use of modified atmosphere to prolong the postharvest life of Burlat cherries at two different degrees of ripeness. J. Sci. Food Agric. 80, 1545–1552.

Retamales, J., Deffilippi, B., Campos, R., 2000. Alleviation of cold storage disorders in nectarines by modified atmosphere packaging. Fruits 55, 213–219.

Robertson, G.L., 2006. Food Packaging Principles and Practice, second ed. CRC Press, Boca Raton, FL.

Robins, D., 1991. Combination treatments with food irradiation. The Preservation of Food by Irradiation. A Factual Guide to the Process and its Effect on Food Dotesios Limited, Trowbridge, Wiltshire, 53-61.

Rodov, V., Ben-Yehoshua, S., Kim, J.J., Shapiro, B., Ittah, Y., 1992. Ultraviolet illumination induces scoparone production in kumquat and orange fruit and improves decay resistance. J. Am. Soc. Hortic. Sci. 117, 788–792.

Roy, M.K., Chatterjee, S.R., Bakukhandi, D., 2000. Gamma radiation in increasing productivity of *Agaricus bisporus* and *Pleurotus sajor-caju* and enhancing storage life of *P. sajor-caju*. J. Food Sci. Technol. 37, 83–86.

Roy, S., Anantheswaran, C., Beelman, R, 1996. Modified atmosphere and modified humidity packaging of fresh mushrooms. J. Food Sci. 61 (2), 391–397.

Safizadeh, M.R., Rahemi, M., Tafazoli, E., Eman, Y., 2007. Influence of postharvest vacuum infiltration with calcium on chilling injury, firmness and quality of Lisbon lemon fruit. Am. J. Food Technol. 2, 388–396.

Saftner, R.A., 1999. The potential of fruit coating and film treatments for improving the storage and shelf life qualities of "Gala" and "Golden Delicious" apples. J. Amer. Soc. Hort. Sci. 124, 682–689.

Sandhya, 2010. Modified atmosphere packaging of fresh produce: current status and future needs. Review. LWT—Food Science and Technology 43, 381–392.

Serrano, M., Guillen, F., Martinez-Romero, D., Castillo, S., Valero, D., 2005. Chemical constituents and antioxidant activity of sweet cherry at different ripening stages. J. Agric. Food Chem. 53, 2741–2745.

Serrano, M., Martinez-Romero, D., Guillen, F., Castillo, S., Valero, D., 2006. Maintenance of broccoli quality and functional properties during cold storage as affected by modified atmosphere packaging. Postharvest Biol. Technol. 39, 61–68.

Sharpe, D., Fan, L.H., McRae, K., Walker, B., MacKay, R., Doucette, C., 2009. Effects of ozone treatment on *Botrytis cinerea* and *Sclerotinias clerotiorum* in relation to horticultural product quality. J. Food Sci. 74 (6), M250–M257.

Simon, J.A., 1992. Vitamin C and cardiovascular disease: a review. J. Am. Coll. Nutr. 11, 107–125.

Singh, S.P., Rao, D.V.S., 2005. Effect of modified atmosphere packaging (MAP) on the alleviation of chilling injury and dietary antioxidants levels in "Solo" papaya during low temperature storage. Eur. J. Hortic. Sci. 70, 246–252.

Siomos, A.S., Sfakiotakis, E.M., Dogras, C.C., 2000. Modified atmosphere packaging of white asparagus spears: Composition, color and textural quality responses to temperature and light. Sci. Hort. 84, 1–13.

Sivertsvik, M., Rosnes, J.T., Bergslien, H., 2002. Modified atmosphere packaging. In: Ohlsson, T., Bengtsson, N. (Eds.), Minimal Processing Technologies in the Food Industry. Boca Raton, FL, CRC Press, pp. 61–86.

Skog, L.J., Chu, C.L., 2001. Effect of ozone on qualities of fruits and vegetables in cold storage. Can. J. Plant Sci. 81 (4), 773–778.

Soliva-Fortuny, R., Grigelmo-Miguel, N., Odriozola-Serrano, I., Gorinnstein, S., Martin-Belloso, O., 2001. Browning evaluation of ready to eat apples as affected by modified atmosphere packaging. J Agric. Food Chem. 49, 3685–3690.

Tano, K., Oule, K., Doyon, G., Lencki, R.W., Arul, J., 2007. Comparative evaluation of the effect of storage temperature fluctuation on modified atmosphere packages of selected fruit and vegetables. Postharvest Biol. Technol. 46, 212–221.

Tenorio, M.D., Villanueva, M.J., Sagardoy, M., 2004. Changes in carotenoids and chlorophylls in fresh green asparagus (*Asparagus officinalis* L.) stored under modified atmosphere packaging. J. Sci. Food Agric. 84 (4), 357–365.

Thomas, C., Prior, O., O'beirne, D., 1999. Survival and growth of *Listeria* species in a model ready-to-use vegetable product containing raw and cooked ingredients as affected by storage temperature and acidification. Int. J. Food Sci. Technol. 34, 317–324.

Thomas, P., 1988. Radiation preservation of foods of plant origin. Part VI. Mushrooms, tomatoes, minor fruits and vegetables, dried fruits and nuts. CRC Crit. Rev. Food Sci. Nutr. 26, 313–358.

Thompson, A.K., Been, B.O., Perkins, C., 1972. Handling, storage and marketing of plantains. Proc. Trop. Reg. Am. Soc. Horticult. Sci. 16, 205–212.

Toivonen, P.M.A., Brandenburt, J.S., Luo, Y., 2009. Modified atmosphere packaging for fresh-cut produce. In: Yahia, E.M. (Ed.), Modified and Controlled Atmospheres for the Storage, Transportation, and Packaging of Horticultural Commodities. CRC Press, Boca Raton, FL, pp. 456–488.

Tzortzakis, N., Borland, A., Singleton, I., Barnes, J., 2007. Impact of atmospheric ozone-enrichment on quality-related attributes of tomato fruit. Postharvest Biol. Technol. 45 (3), 317–325.

Valero, D., Valverde, J.M., Martinez-Romero, D., Guillen, F., Castillo, S., Serrano, M., 2006. The combination of modified atmosphere packaging with eugenol or thymol to maintain quality, safety and functional properties of table grapes. Postharvest Biol. Technol. 41, 317–327.

Valverde, J.M., Guillen, F., Martinez-Romero, D., Castillo, S., Serrano, M., Valero, D., 2005. Improvement of table grapes quality and safety by the combination of modified atmosphere packaging (MAP) and eugenol, menthol, or thymol. J. Agric. Food Chem. 53, 7458–7464.

Varnam, A.H., Evans, M.G., 1991. Foodborne Pathogens: An Illustrated Text. London, Wolfe Publishing.

Veltman, R.H., Sanders, M.G., Persijn, S.T., Pemppelenbos, H.W., Oosterhaven, J., 1999. Decreased ascorbic acid levels and brown core development in pears (Pyrus communis L. cv. Conference). Physiol. Plant. 107 (1), 39–45.

Wang, C.Y., 1977. Effects of CO_2 treatment on storage and shelf-life of sweet pepper. J. Am. Soc. Horticult. Sci. 102, 808–812.

Wang, C.Y., 1983. Postharvest responses of Chinese cabbage to high CO_2 treatments or low O_2 storage. J. Am. Soc. Hort. Sci. 108, 125–129.

Wang, J., Chao, Y., 2003. Effect of gamma irradiation on quality of dried potato. Radiat. Phys. Chem. 66, 293–297.

Wang, Z., Dilley, D.R., 2000. Initial low oxygen stress controls superficial scald in apples. Postharvest Biol. Technol. 18, 201–213.

Webb, T.A., Mundt, J.O., 1978. Molds on vegetables at the time of harvest. App. Environ. Microb. 35, 655–658.

Weichmann, J., 1986. The effect of controlled-atmosphere storage on the sensory and nutritional quality of fruits and vegetables. Hort. Rev. 8, 101–127.

WHO, 1999. High dose irradiation in wholesomeness of food irradiated with doses above 10 kGy. WHO Technical Report Series 890World Health Organization, Geneva, pp. 9–37.

Wickham, L.D., Mohammed, M., 1999. Storage of immature green mango (*Mangifera indica* L.) fruit for processing. J. Food Qual. 22, 31–40.

Wright, K.P., Kader, A.A., 1997. Effect of controlled-atmosphere storage on the quality and carotenoid content of sliced persimmons and peaches. Postharvest Biol. Technol. 10, 89–97.

Xia, Z.L., Xiong, X.Y., Jiang, X.J., 2005. The studies on *Pleurotus pulmonarius* by 60Co-γ irradiation. Acta Laser Biology Sinica 4, 60–64, (in Chinese).

Yahia, E., 1998. Modified and controlled atmospheres for tropical fruits. Horticult. Rev. 22, 123–183.

Yahia, E.M., Rivera, M., Hernandez, O., 1992. Responses of papaya to short-term insecticidal O_2 atmosphere. J. Am. Soc. Horticult. Sci. 117, 96–99.

Yahia, E.M., 2006. Controlled atmospheres for tropical fruits. In: Yahia, E.M. (Ed.), The current status and future application of modified and controlled atmospheres for horticultural commodities. Stewart Postharvest Rev. 5 (6), 1–10.

Yang, S.F., Hoffman, N.E., 1984. Ethylene biosynthesis and its regulation in higher plants. Ann. Rev. Plant Physiol. 35, 155–189.

Yong, J.W., Kyung, A., 1998. Thiabendazole and CA effects on reduction of chilling injury during cold storage in pepper fruit. J. Korean Soc. Hort. Sci. 39, 680–683.

Zagory, D., 1990. Application of computers in the design of modified atmosphere packaging to fresh produce. International Conference on Modified Atmosphere Packaging, Part 1. Campden Food and Drinks Research Association, Chipping Campden, UK.

Zainon, M.A., Chin, L.H., Muthusamy, M., Hamid, L., 2004. Low temperature storage and modified atmosphere packaging of carambola fruit and their effects on ripening related texture changes, wall modification and chilling injury symptoms. Postharvest Biol. Technol. 33, 181–192.

Zhuang, H., 2011. Introduction. In: Brody, A.L., Zhuang, H., Han, J.H. (Eds.), Modified Atmosphere Packaging for Fresh-Cut Fruits and Vegetables. John Wiley & Sons, Chichester, UK, pp. 3–7.

5

RECENT DEVELOPMENTS OF 1-METHYLCYCLOPROPENE (1-MCP) TREATMENTS ON FRUIT QUALITY ATTRIBUTES

Daniel Valero*, Fabián Guillén*, Juan M. Valverde*, Salvador Castillo*, María Serrano**

*University Miguel Hernández, Department of Food Technology, Orihuela, Alicante, Spain; **University Miguel Hernández, Department of Applied Biology, Orihuela, Alicante, Spain

1 Introduction

The plant hormone ethylene is involved in a wide range of physiological processes in horticultural crops, including abscission, senescence and ripening, chlorophyll loss, softening, physiological disorders, sprouting, isocoumarin synthesis, lignification, discoloration (browning), decay, and stimulation of defense systems (Saltveit, 1999). These effects can be positive or negative depending on the desired use of the horticultural product (Martínez-Romero et al., 2007). However, most postharvest handling is focused on controlling ethylene production or its action. Among the available methods, chemical control of ethylene biosynthesis by aminoethoxyvinylglycine, polyamine treatments (Serrano et al., 2016, chapter: Polyamines as an Ecofriendly Postharvest Tool to Maintain Fruit Quality (of this book); Valero et al., 2002), and inhibition of its action by 1-methylcyclopropene (1-MCP) have become useful tools for the horticulture industry as it seeks to maintain quality of produce after harvest (Watkins, 2006; Martínez-Romero et al., 2007; Valero and Serrano, 2010).

The US Environmental Protection Agency approved use of 1-MCP on floriculture and ornamental products in 1999 and on edible food products in 2002, and registered as a GRAS (Generally Recognized As Safe) chemical by the Food and Drug Administration in 2004 (FDA, 2004). By 2011, more than 40 countries had approved the use of 1-MCP for horticultural produce. It is registered

Eco-Friendly Technology for Postharvest Produce Quality. http://dx.doi.org/10.1016/B978-0-12-804313-4.00005-0
Copyright © 2016 Elsevier Inc. All rights reserved.

for use on a wide variety of fruits and vegetables including apple, apricot, Asian pear, avocado, banana, broccoli, calabrese, cauliflower, Brussels sprouts, cabbage, carrot, cherimoya, cucumber, date, guava, kiwifruit, lime, mango, melon, nectarine, papaya, paprika, peach, pear, pepper, persimmon, pineapple, plantain, plum, squash, tomato, and many ornamentals. The specific products for which 1-MCP is registered in each country vary greatly according to the importance of the crop in that country (Watkins, 2008). In the European Union, the active substance 1-MCP has been included in Annex I of the Directive 91/414/EEC (2005), and its use approved in a wide range of fruit including apple, pear, plum, tomato, banana, persimmon, among others. Under normal environmental conditions, the active ingredient 1-MCP is a gas. End-use products EthylBloc®, SamartFresh™, SmartTabs™, and EthylBloc™ Sachet contain, respectively, 0.14, 3.3, 0.63%, and 0.014% of 1-MCP, and when the product is mixed with water or a buffer solution, it releases the gas 1-MCP. 1-MCP is to be used in confined areas to extend the life of harvested fruits and vegetable by inhibiting the negative effects of ethylene, and thus the use is classified as an indoor food and nonfood crop application as postharvest treatment. Recently, EFSA (European Food Safety Authority) has reviewed the Maximum Residue Levels currently established at European level for the pesticide active substance 1-MCP. In order to assess the occurrence of 1-MCP residues in plants, processed commodities, rotational crops and livestock, they concluded that the toxicological profile of 1-MCP evaluated in the framework of Directive 91/414/EEC (2005) resulted in an admissible daily ingestion established at 0.0009 mg/kg body weight per day (EFSA, 2014).

Our aim in this chapter is to provide the latest knowledge about the use of 1-MCP, either applied as preharvest or postharvest treatment, on fruit ripening and quality extension by interacting the ethylene receptor and action. Special attention will be devoted on the content of bioactive compounds with antioxidant activity, as well as the reduction of physiological disorders and decay.

2   1-MCP and Ethylene Receptors

1-MCP belongs to a class of compounds known as cyclopropenes. The discovery that cyclopropenes inhibit ethylene perception by competitively binding to ethylene receptors represented a major breakthrough in controlling ethylene responses of horticultural products (Blankenship and Dole, 2003). The process of discovery of the effects of cyclopropenes and their proposed method of action has been described (Sisler and Serek, 2003; Sisler, 2006).

The plant hormone ethylene is the simplest plant hormone, which plays numerous roles in the development and environmental responses of the plant, since seed germination, seedling growth, organ development and senescence, leaf and petal abscission, fruit ripening, stress and pathogen responses, among other many processes, are controlled at least in part by ethylene (Bleecker and Kende, 2000). In a paper, the current model of ethylene signaling is proposed (Merchante et al., 2013). The ethylene-signaling cascade starts with ethylene binding to its receptors. In all plants examined to date, the ethylene receptors exist as a multimember family that in *Arabidopsis* is composed of ETR1, ERS1, ETR2, ERS2, and EIN4. These receptors work as negative regulators of the pathway, actively repressing the ethylene response in the absence of the hormone. The current thinking on ethylene action is based on a negative regulator model of ethylene receptor function. In the absence of ethylene, ethylene receptors (ETR1, ETR2, EIN4, ERS1, and ERS2) are in the active (inhibitory) state. Some of these receptors, for example, ETR1 and ERS1, act directly on the CTR1 protein, whereas other receptors, for example, ETR2, EIN4, and ERS2, act more indirectly. In this active state, they allow CTR1 protein to inactivate the EIN2 protein, which is essential in promoting known ethylene responses. When ethylene is present it binds to their receptors and inactivates them and CTR1 as well. With CTR1 inactivated the EIN2 protein can revert to its active form and produce known ethylene responses in the plant. When there are only ETR1 and ERS1 receptors or only ETR2, EIN4, and ERS2 receptors there is insufficient activation of CTR1 and ethylene responses proceed without any ethylene binding to these receptors. Using this model of ethylene action, it is proposed that 1-MCP suppresses the ethylene response pathway by permanently binding to a sufficient number of ethylene receptors (ETR1, ETR2, EIN4, ERS1, and/or ERS2), which keeps CTR1 in its active (inhibiting) state (Binder et al., 2012).

1-MCP binds to ethylene receptors irreversibly so that ethylene cannot bind and exert its action. It has been proposed that 1-MCP has affinity to the receptors 10-fold greater than that of ethylene, although many studies have found that the effect of 1-MCP disappeared with time, which has been attributed to the synthesis of new receptors (Lurie, 2005). Thus, how 1-MCP binds to the ethylene receptors and why it can bind to such sites but not deactivate them as ethylene does is not well known. However, the scientific research on this compound has demonstrated that 1-MCP is a potent inhibitor of ethylene action and capable of maintaining postharvest quality in many fresh horticultural products. In addition an exciting new strategy for controlling ethylene production and thus ripening of climacteric fruits as well as senescence of vegetative tissues has emerged with the discovery and commercialization of the inhibitor of ethylene perception, 1-MCP. Most of the scientific evidence was performed as postharvest treatments but only recently has useful information arisen for preharvest treatments.

3 Preharvest 1-MCP Application

The gaseous compound 1-MCP is becoming an invaluable tool to counteract the undesirable ethylene effects in horticultural produce, especially in climacteric fruits, since the postharvest physiological effects are mediated by ethylene. Although most of the work on 1-MCP has been performed as postharvest treatments with a large number of benefits on many fruit and vegetables, the potential of 1-MCP applied as a preharvest application is much limited, mainly due to the difficulty in successfully applying gaseous 1-MCP to plants in the field. However, Harvista™ technology (AgroFresh Co.) is a preharvest tool that brings ethylene management to the orchard and positively impacts the size and firmness of the fruit by selectively delaying harvest. With this system, 1-MCP can be sprayed due to improvement of the formulation, which can be dissolved in water and applied as fumigation. Table 5.1 shows some examples in which 1-MCP has been used as preharvest treatment on several fruit commodities. Most of the aims of these reports have been focused on the ability of 1-MCP to delay the on-tree ripening process. Mango fruits sprayed before harvesting showed significantly slower peel color development and deterioration in visual quality with a net extension of shelf life due to a delay of ethylene climacteric peak (Sun et al., 2014). In apple, preharvest 1-MCP treatment at 60, 125, or 250 mg L^{-1} maintained higher firmness during storage in air or under controlled atmosphere by reducing ethylene production, while other quality traits such as total soluble solids (TSS) and total acidity (TA) contents remained unaffected (Elfving et al., 2007; Varanasi et al., 2013). In pear, 50 mg L^{-1} 1-MCP reduced the incidence of premature fruit drop at time of harvest and retarded color, softening, and ethylene production during ripening (Villalobos-Acuña et al., 2010). Similarly, 5 mM 1-MCP was effective in reducing fruit abscission on orange trees, which was accompanied by lower leaves abscission (Burns, 2008). The preharvest treatment with 1-MCP of persimmon allowed the fruit to be stored for 40 days with reduced symptoms of chilling injury (CI), while the combination of GA_3 and 1-MCP delayed also the symptoms of CI, extending the storability

Table 5.1 A Summary of Several Fruits in Which Preharvest 1-MCP Application was Performed Based on 1-MCP Concentration, Main Observed Effect and Additional Effects During Postharvest Storage

Fruit	1-MCP Dose	Main Effect	Other Effects	References
Apple	125/250 mg L^{-1} 60 mg L^{-1}	High firmness	Low ethylene	Elfving et al. (2007) Varanasi et al. (2013)
Mango	10 mg L^{-1}	Color delay	Reduced decay	Sun et al. (2014)
Pear	10/100 mg L^{-1}	Low fruit drop	Low ethylene, reduced color and firmness	Villalobos-Acuña et al. (2010)
Persimmon	5 mg L^{-1}	Desastringency	Low chilling injury symptom	Besada et al. (2008)
Fig	5 mg L^{-1}	Delayed ripening	High firmness, reduced decay	Freiman et al. (2012)
Mangosteen	5 mg L^{-1}	Delayed ripening	High firmness	Lerslerwong et al. (2013)
Orange	5 mM	Low fruit abscission	Low leaf abscission	Burns (2008)

at 1°C for up to nearly 3 months (Besada et al., 2008). In addition, this treatment is useful as a desastringency tool in persimmon, one of the main problems in some persimmon cultivars with a negative impact on consumer acceptability. In figs, immediately after treatment, the ethylene production rate of 1-MCP-exposed fruit was six times higher than the nontreated figs, but development of the treated fruit was delayed. At harvest most of the figs in the 1-MCP-treated group were at commercial harvest maturity, while many of the control fruits had reached full ripening. During storage, senescence, and spoilage of the 1-MCP-treated figs were slower and lower than in controls, as manifested by fruit color, firmness, internal texture, weight, size, shriveling, and decay. Thus 1-MCP applied on fig trees at the figs' preclimacteric stage can delay the senescence of Brown Turkey figs and improve their storage and transportation potential (Freiman et al., 2012). The ripening of mangosteen fruit was significantly affected by preharvest 1-MCP treatment, so that harvest date was delayed in 1-MCP-treated fruit based on external color (Lerslerwong et al., 2013).

4 Postharvest 1-MCP Application

1-MCP is a successful technology for controlling postharvest fruit ripening with a continuous exploitation in many countries for commercial purposes. 1-MCP is used in combination with proper temperature and relative humidity management, and can replace or be utilized in combination with controlled atmospheres. Commercial application of 1-MCP to fruit commodities and other edible crops was assumed by AgroFresh Inc., a subsidiary of Rohm and Haas (Springhouse, PA, United States), under the trade name Smart-Fresh™ (Sozzy and Beaudry, 2005).

4.1 Ethylene Production and Respiration Rate

In the last few years some review reports have described the effects of 1-MCP on fruit commodities based on the interaction between 1-MCP and ethylene receptors and the prevention of ethylene-dependent responses (Blankenship and Dole, 2003; Sozzy and Beaudry, 2005; Watkins, 2006, 2008; Valero and Serrano, 2010). The most studied fruit species are tomato, apple, banana, pear, and plum. Table 5.2 shows the different fruit types, 1-MCP concentration, duration for treatment with positive effects in retarding the ripening process, as well as the main observed adverse effects. It is clear that the appropriate 1-MCP concentration and duration of treatment need to be studied to obtain beneficial effects on enhancing shelf life by delaying the postharvest ripening process through the inhibition of ethylene production.

In apple, 1-MCP was assayed in several cultivars (Gala, Fuji, Golden Delicious, McIntosh, Granny Smith, Red Chief Delicious, Law Rome, Jonagold, and Empire) and the main effect was a retard of fruit ripening by drastically reducing the internal ethylene production (Watkins, 2006, 2008). Overall, a dose–response of internal ethylene production to 1-MCP-applied concentrations existed. Respiration rates in 1-MCP-treated apple have been less commonly reported, although some reports have found reduction in respiration rate to levels close to that found at preclimacteric stages after 1-MCP treatments (Watkins, 2006).

1-MCP has been proven to have enormous benefit for controlling ripening and senescence of bananas. Good results have been obtained in terms of ethylene inhibition during postharvest storage, especially in the "Cavendish subgroup," with the cultivar Williams being the most studied. The earliest report of banana and 1-MCP established that the increased "green life" after 1-MCP was a function of concentration × exposure time (Golding et al., 1998), in which 1-MCP dose (0.45 µL L^{-1}) was applied

Table 5.2 A Summary of Fruit Species, 1-MCP Applied Dose and Duration Time of Treatment for Which Beneficial Effects in Retarding the Postharvest Ripening Process by Reducing Ethylene Production was Obtained, as well as the Main Adverse Effects

Fruit	1-MCP (μL L^{-1})	Time (h)	Adverse Effects
Apple	0.5–10	12	Reduced volatiles
Banana	0.01–1	6–24	
Pear	0.1–4	12–24	
Tomato	0.1–100	1–24	
Peach	0.02–0.5	18–24	Internal browning
Apricot	0-05–0.75	6–48	
Nectarine	0.2–1	12–24	Flesh woolliness
Plum	0.1–40	6–24	
Mango	1–100	6–14	Decay
Avocado	0.1–25	6–48	
Kiwifruit	0.5–5	16–20	
Papaya	0.5–10	4–24	

Data obtained from Blankenship and Dole (2003), Watkins (2006), Guillén (2009), Valero and Serrano (2010).

at several intervals. Both ethylene production and respiration rates were lower in 1-MCP-treated fruit than in nontreated fruit, even in those fruits treated with propylene to stimulate the ripening process, and thus 1-MCP can disrupt the normal sequence of biochemical changes associated with or dependent on ethylene. On a general basis, concentration over 0.30 μL L^{-1} is necessary to inhibit the ethylene production, since lower concentrations just show a delay on the onset of the ethylene climacteric peak. Very recently, as an alternative to the fumigation technique inside cold store rooms, a new system named microbubble (MB) technology has been used in banana (Pongpraserta and Srilaonga, 2014). 1-MCP-MBs were more effective in delaying postharvest ripening than conventional 1-MCP fumigation. 1-MCP-MBs reduced the respiration rate and ethylene production compared to the control and 1-MCP-fumigated fruit. Moreover, 1-MCP-MBs delayed yellowing and maintained firmness of banana fruit during storage.

The effects of 1-MCP have been investigated in pears from summer, fall, and winter cultivars. High-quality pear fruit have a buttery texture, with color change appropriate to the cultivar, and development of characteristic taste and aroma associated with sugar and acid contents and volatile production. Unlike most fruits, pear requires exposure to chilling temperatures to ripen properly, with winter pears requiring as long as 8 weeks. In addition, postharvest cold treatment is required to induce endogenous ethylene production and subsequent ripening of green pears. Among pear cultivars, Conference, d'Anjou, Blanquilla, and Barlett have been the most studied. d'Anjou pears treated with 1-MCP ($0.1–1$ μL L^{-1}) extended the preclimacteric period with low ethylene production and respiration rates, although total inhibition was not observed (Argenta et al., 2003). A dose–response of 1-MCP for delaying ethylene production was also evident. Fruit treated with 0.1 or 1 μL L^{-1} 1-MCP began to produce ethylene 2 and 4 months later than controls, respectively, and fruit treated with 1 μL L^{-1} had ethylene production lower than controls at 2 and 4 months after treatment. In Barlett pears the degree and duration of the effects of 1-MCP on CO_2 and ethylene production at 20°C were related to the treatment concentration (Ekman et al., 2004). Ethylene production during ripening was inhibited by exposure to 0.1 μL L^{-1} 1-MCP compared with untreated fruit when fruit was stored for 6 weeks at -1°C, but not when the fruit was stored for longer periods. Both positive and negative aspects of 1-MCP that may be commercially important for pear fruit have been identified. 1-MCP reduces susceptibility of fruit to skin browning, and vibration and impact bruising, and therefore its use may permit greater flexibility during grading, packaging, and transport operations (Calvo and Sozzi, 2004; Ekman et al., 2004).

An early report on plum and 1-MCP (Abdi et al., 1998) revealed that application of 1-MCP to the climacteric cultivars (Gulfruby and Beauty) slightly delayed the onset of the climacteric ethylene and was dose dependent, and contrarily in suppressed-climacteric varieties absence of ethylene production or a clear respiratory climacteric was observed after 1-MCP treatment, although fruits became overripe and rotted. In Golden Japan and Santa Rosa plums, 1-MCP prevented or delayed the climacteric increase in ethylene production of plums (Martínez-Romero et al., 2003; Salvador et al., 2003; Valero et al., 2003, 2004), even when fruit were harvested close to the climacteric peak. Respiration rates were also decreased or the climacteric increase delayed. It is interesting to point out that the percentage of ethylene inhibition by 1-MCP was correlated inversely to the maximum value of ethylene production at the climacteric peak (Martínez-Romero et al., 2003, 2007).

The influence of ripening stage at harvest on the 1-MCP effect was also studied in plums (Valero et al., 2003), in which 1-MCP was equally effective on inhibiting the ethylene production in plums harvested at the commercial ripening stage or in those picked 10 days later, although in the more mature ones a slight increase in ethylene was detected after 5 weeks of storage, which could be associated with some kind of ethylene receptor generation. Moreover, for commercial purposes, the effect of 1-MCP applied to plum packaged in small cardboard boxes or in bulk revealed that when 1-MCP was applied to fruit handled and packaged in perforated cardboard boxes, ethylene production was totally inhibited during all storage periods, while in those plums treated with 1-MCP in bulk (before handling and packaging), ethylene production increased after 3 and 4 weeks of cold storage plus 7 days at 20°C, the differences being attributed to the higher gas diffusion around the fruit when they are packaged in small-perforated boxes (Valero et al., 2004). As stated earlier, the applications were achieved by mixing the product with water to release the 1-MCP gas in enclosed areas. However, the availability of the proper facilities to treat the fruit could be a limitation under certain commercial situations. For this reason, alternatives are being developed, such as sprays or dips, and in the case of plums a novel 1-MCP immersion formulation both delayed and reduced ethylene production in a dose-dependent manner, reaching the saturation points at 1000 ng kg^{-1} (Manganaris et al., 2008).

Ripening of green tomatoes held at 20°C in air containing 0.1 μL L^{-1} ethylene was substantially delayed by exposure to 1-MCP in the concentration range 0.1–100 μL L^{-1} with the extent of the delay being directly related to the concentration of 1-MCP and exposure time, while ripe tomatoes needed over 20 μL L^{-1} to extend the shelf life (Wills and Ku, 2002). For commercial purposes, different combinations of 1-MCP doses (0.5 or 1 μL L^{-1}) and duration (3, 6, 12, or 24 h) were used on tomatoes harvested at the mature-green stage, with the main conclusion being that 0.5 μL L^{-1} for 24 h induced the maximum benefit in terms of ethylene inhibition and retarding the ripening process (Guillén et al., 2007). Based on this result these authors studied the effect of tomato cultivar and ripening stage at harvest and concluded that for both stages, 1-MCP treatment blocked the tomato receptors, and absence of a sharp increase in ethylene production or respiration rate was obtained, indicating that typical autocatalytic ethylene biosynthesis was also inhibited in tomatoes at both ripening stages (Guillén et al., 2006). The inhibition of both ethylene production and respiration rate by 1-MCP was negatively correlated with the maximum ethylene value reached for each of the cultivars and ripening stage assayed.

4.2 Fruit Quality Parameters

In climacteric fruits, those parameters dependent on ethylene are delayed after 1-MCP treatments, including firmness, color, soluble solids concentration (TSS), and loss of TA and weight.

Fruit softening is prevented or delayed by 1-MCP, the effects of treatment often being closely associated with ethylene production. This effect has been observed for most of the studied fruits (apple, pear, tomato, plum, banana, avocado, etc.), although the components of texture that are affected by 1-MCP have not been adequately investigated. In this sense, studies of 1-MCP on cell wall changes of treated fruit are limited, but a number of investigations on cell wall enzymes are available (Watkins, 2006; Valero and Serrano, 2010).

In most vegetable produce, loss of greenness or yellowing is inhibited by 1-MCP. For many products, especially leafy vegetables and certain fruits such as apple, maintenance of green color is desirable in the marketplace as yellowness is regarded as a sign of senescence. 1-MCP application delayed, but not irreversible inhibited, the processes involved in pigment metabolism, as has been observed in plums (Valero et al., 2003), apple (Watkins, 2008), and banana (Golding et al., 1998).

Another fruit quality parameter such as TA is clearly maintained during postharvest storage after 1-MCP treatment, as has been observed in apricot, plum avocado, pear, tomato, etc. (Watkins, 2006; Valero and Serrano, 2010). TA was maintained at levels to those close at harvest after prolonged storage (21–28 days) in plum (Martínez-Romero et al., 2003; Valero et al., 2003) or tomatoes (Guillén et al., 2006). However, soluble solid concentration in treated 1-MCP apple can be higher, lower, or the same as those in untreated fruit. These contrasting results with apples are notable and may be due to different cultivars or other experimental conditions used. Watkins (2000) found differences in responses of apple cultivars to 1-MCP treatment, with McIntosh and Law Rome-treated fruit having lower soluble solids than controls, and Delicious and Empire having higher soluble solids than untreated fruit. In peaches and nectarines, 1-MCP treatment either did not affect or resulted in lower TSS (Bregoli et al., 2005).

With respect to weight loss, few reports have described the effect of 1-MCP on this parameter, which has importance from the point of view of both fruit quality and economic issue. Thus, 1-MCP-treated avocado had lower weight loss than untreated fruit, but the contrary occurred in pear with an increase in weight loss followed by 1-MCP application (Watkins, 2006); a potential risk of 1-MCP treatment is that weight loss may be greater because of the extension of the ripening period. In the case of plums (Valero et al., 2003) or tomatoes (Guillén et al., 2006), significant reductions in weight loss have been reported independently of the ripening stage at harvest or the climacteric-suppressed climacteric pattern (Martínez-Romero et al., 2003). The mechanism by which 1-MCP is delaying the transpiration process is not well known and could be related to the lower respiration rate found in 1-MCP fruits, since weight loss is not ethylene dependent (Valero et al., 2003; Guillén et al., 2007). It is well known that relative humidity control is more important at warm than at cold storage temperatures. Even if the relative humidity is maintained, the vapor-pressure deficit is greater at higher storage temperatures. Some products are more susceptible to moisture loss than others (Sozzi and Beaudry, 2005), for example, apples and kiwifruit have a low moisture loss rate, while postharvest water loss can cause rapid deterioration and reduction in the marketable quality of a range of other tree fruit crops that respond to 1-MCP and have a high moisture loss rate, such as persimmons, plums, mangoes, and guavas. To reduce moisture loss, products must be effectively precooled, and relative humidity during transit and storage must be kept high as long as possible.

4.3 Bioactive Constituents and Antioxidant Activity

Storage at low temperatures is the main postharvest treatment used to reduce produce metabolism, maintain quality, and prolong storability in those perishable fruits and vegetables considered as nonchilling sensitive. Some evidence exists for the changes in bioactive compounds and antioxidant activity during cold storage although no general tendency has been found. Thus loss of health-beneficial compounds (phenolics and ascorbic acid) has been found in table grapes, broccoli, pomegranate, and apple, in which the loss of phenolics was highly dependent on the cultivar, although increases in phytochemicals were reported for sweet cherry and plum cultivars during cold storage (Serrano et al., 2011; Valero and Serrano, 2013), which were related to the advancement of the ripening process. On the other hand, fruit ripening and senescence may be regarded as an oxidative process involving marked alterations in fruit metabolism and the activity of a number of enzymatic systems, including those related to the regulation of reactive oxidative species (ROS) (Masia, 1998). The involvement of plant hormones in stress-induced antioxidant systems has been reported (Arora et al., 2002). For example, stimulation of ethylene synthesis is known to involve the generation of ROS (Steinite et al., 2004). Thus the deleterious effects of ethylene have been linked with ROS detoxifying enzymes. Catalase (CAT, EC 1.11.1.6) and superoxide dismutase (SOD, EC 1.15.11) activities have been closely related to the onset of apple ripening, signaled by an ethylene burst (Masia, 1998).

Table 5.3 shows the effect of 1-MCP application on the content of phenolic compounds, antioxidant activity, and antioxidant enzymes during postharvest storage on certain climacteric fruit. Generally, 1-MCP slowed the decrease of ascorbic acid (vitamin C) in peach, pineapple, quince, and tomato, but ascorbic acid in apple showed lower content in 1-MCP-treated than in control fruits (Valero and Serrano, 2010; Vilaplana et al., 2006). With respect to total antioxidant activity (TAA), both hydrophilic (H-TAA) and lipophilic (L-TAA), 1-MCP treatment increased the antioxidant capacity in sweet cherry by increasing the content of total phenolics or flavonoids, although hydroxycinnamic acids and anthocyanins were unaffected (Mozetiĉ et al., 2006). Conversely, 1-MCP delayed the increase in total phenolics and anthocyanins occurring during ripening of strawberry, which was associated with lower phenylalanine ammonia lyase (PAL, EC 4.3.1.5) activity (Jiang et al., 2001).

In mango, 1-MCP inhibited the production of H_2O_2 during storage and ascorbic acid was maintained at a high concentration in 1-MCP-treated fruit accompanied by inhibition on the activities of antioxidant enzymes including CAT, SOD, and ascorbate peroxidase (APX), suggesting that 1-MCP could play a positive role in regulating the activated oxygen metabolism balance (Wang et al., 2009). Contrarily, in avocado (Zhang et al., 2013), in bitter melon (Han et al., 2015), and in green pepper (Cao et al., 2012), increases in these antioxidant enzymes were reported. In apples, total phenolic concentrations were higher in the peel of 1-MCP-treated fruit than in the control fruit, but slightly lower in the flesh of 1-MCP-treated fruit (Fawbush et al., 2009). 1-MCP-treated apricots improved the antioxidant defense systems, both enzymatic (SOD) and nonenzymatic (ascorbic acid, carotenoids, and TAA), responsible for the removal of ROS such as $O^{\bullet-2}$, $OH^{\bullet}$, and H_2O_2, suggesting that apricots treated with 1-MCP were better protected against oxidation than untreated fruits, which could have delayed senescence and improved their functional nutritional value (Egea et al., 2009).

Table 5.3 A Summary of Fruit Species, 1-MCP Application on Increasing (↑), Decreasing (↓), or Unaffected (↔) Content of Phenolic Compounds, Antioxidant Activity, and Antioxidant Enzymes During Postharvest Storage

Fruit	Phenolics	Antioxidant Activity	Antioxidant Enzymes	References
Goldenberry	↑	↑		Valdenegro et al. (2012)
Medlar	↑	↑		Selcuk and Erkan (2015)
Gac fruit	↔	↔		Win et al. (2015)
Barberry	↑	↑		Rodoni et al. (2014)
Kiwifruit	↑	↑		Park et al. (2015)
Apple	↑	↑		Kolniak-Ostek et al. (2014)
	↔	↔		Fawbush et al. (2009)
Avocado			↑ SOD, CAT, POD, APX	Zhang et al. (2013)
Bitter melon			↑ SOD, CAT, POD	Han et al. (2015)
Green pepper			↑ SOD, CAT, POD, APX	Cao et al. (2012)
Mango			↓ SOD, CAT, APX	Wang et al. (2009)
Apricot		↑	↑ SOD	Egea et al. (2009)

SOD, Superoxide dismutase; CAT, catalase; POD, peroxidase; APX, ascorbate peroxidase.

5 Concluding Remarks and Future Trends

The 1-MCP technology has shown a dramatic impact on the understanding of the involvement of ethylene in plant metabolism as well as the storage and handling of horticultural products. At receptor level, 1-MCP has been found as a potent ethylene antagonist with satisfactory results on extending shelf life and maintaining fruit and vegetable quality. Due to the importance of bioactive compounds and antioxidant activity of fruit consumption for human health, further research is warranted on the effects of 1-MCP on various nonenzymatic and enzymatic antioxidant systems to better understand how 1-MCP can enhance TAA.

References

Abdi, N., McGlasson, W.B., Holford, P., Williams, M., Mizrahi, Y., 1998. Responses of climacteric and suppressed-climacteric plums to treatment with propylene and 1-methylcyclopropene. Postharvest Biol. Technol. 12, 21–34.

Argenta, L.C., Krammes, J.G., Megguer, C.A., Amarante, C.V.T., Mattheis, J., 2003. Ripening and quality of "Laetitia" plums following harvest and cold storage as affected by inhibition of ethylene action. Pesq. Agropec. Bras. 38, 1139–1148.

Arora, A., Sairam, R.K., Srivastava, G.C., 2002. Oxidative stress and antioxidative system in plants. Curr. Sci. 82, 1227–1238.

Besada, C., Arnal, L., Salvador, A., 2008. Improving storability of persimmon cv. Rojo Brillante by combined use of preharvest and postharvest treatments. Postharvest Biol. Technol. 50, 169–175.

Binder, B.M., Chang, C., Schaller, G.E., 2012. Perception of ethylene by plants—ethylene receptors. Ann. Plant Rev. 44, 117–145.

Blankenship, S.M., Dole, J.M., 2003. 1-Methylcyclopropene: a review. Postharvest Biol. Technol. 28, 1–25.

Bleecker, A.B., Kende, H., 2000. Ethylene: a gaseous signal molecule in plants. Annu. Rev. Cell. Dev. Biol. 16, 1–18.

Bregoli, A.M., Ziosi, V., Biondi, S., Costa, G., Torrigiani, P., 2005. Postharvest 1-methylcyclopropene application in ripening control of "Stark Red Gold" nectarines: temperature-dependent effects on ethylene production and biosynthetic gene expression, fruit quality, and polyamine levels. Postharvest Biol. Technol. 37, 111–121.

Burns, J.K., 2008. 1-Methylcyclopropene applications in preharvest systems: focus on Citrus. HortScience 43, 112–114.

Calvo, G., Sozzi, G.O., 2004. Improvement of postharvest storage quality of "Red Clapp's" pears by treatment with 1-methylcyclopropene at low temperature. J. Hortic. Sci. Biotechnol. 79, 930–934.

Cao, S., Yang, Z., Zheng, Y., 2012. Effect of 1-methylcyclopene on senescence and quality maintenance of green bell pepper fruit during storage at 20°C. Postharvest Biol. Technol. 70, 1–6.

Directive 91/414/EEC, 2005. Review report for the active substance 1-methylcyclopropene.

EFSA, 2014. Reasoned opinion on the review of the existing maximum residue levels (MRLs) for 1-methylcyclopropene according to Article 12 of Regulation (EC) No. 396/2005 . EFSA J. 123746, 23 pp.

Egea, I., Flores, F.B., Martínez-Madrid, M.C., Romojaro, F., Sánchez-Bel, P., 2009. 1-Methylcyclopropene affects the antioxidant system of apricots (*Prunus armeniaca* L. cv. Búlida) during storage at low temperature. J. Sci. Food Agric. 90, 549–555.

Ekman, J.H., Clayton, M., Biasi, W.V., Mitcham, E.J., 2004. Interactions between 1-MCP concentration, treatment interval and storage time for "Bartlett" pears. Postharvest Biol. Technol. 31, 127–136.

Elfving, D.C., Drake, S.R., Reed, A.N., Visser, D.B., 2007. Preharvest applications of sprayable 1-methylcyclopropene in the orchard for management of apple harvest and postharvest condition. HortScience 42, 1192–1199.

Fawbush, F., Nock, J.F., Watkins, C.B., 2009. Antioxidant contents and activity of 1-methylcyclopropene (1-MCP)-treated "Empire" apples in air and controlled atmosphere storage. Postharvest Biol. Technol. 52, 30–37.

FDA, 2004. 1-Methylcyclopropene (PC Code 224459).

Freiman, Z.E., Rodov, V., Yablovitz, Z., Horev, B., Flaishman, M.A., 2012. Preharvest application of 1-methylcyclopropene inhibits ripening and improves keeping quality of "Brown Turkey" figs (*Ficus carica* L.). Sci. Hortic. 138, 266–272.

Golding, J.B., Shearer, D., Wyllie, S.G., McGlasson, W.B., 1998. Application of 1-MCP and propylene to identify ethylene-dependent ripening processes in mature banana fruit. Postharvest Biol. Technol. 14, 87–98.

Guillén, F., 2009. 1-MCP como estrategia de conservación. Horticultura Extra 2009 Poscosecha 69, 18–24.

Guillén, F., Castillo, S., Zapata, P.J., Martínez-Romero, D., Valero, D., Serrano, M., 2006. Efficacy of 1-MCP treatment in tomato fruit. 2. Effect of cultivar and ripening stage at harvest. Postharvest Biol. Technol. 42, 235–242.

Guillén, F., Castillo, S., Zapata, P.J., Martínez-Romero, D., Serrano, M., Valero, D., 2007. Efficacy of 1-MCP treatment in tomato fruit. 1. Duration and concentration of 1-MCP treatment to gain an effective delay of postharvest ripening. Postharvest Biol. Technol. 43, 23–27.

Han, C., Zuo, J., Wang, Q., Xu, L., Wang, Z., Dong, H., Gao, L., 2015. Effects of 1-MCP on postharvest physiology and quality of bitter melon (*Momordica charantia* L.). Sci. Hort. 182, 86–91.

Jiang, Y., Joyce, D.C., Terry, L.A., 2001. 1-Methylcyclopropene treatment affects strawberry fruit decay. Postharvest Biol. Technol. 23, 227–232.

Kolniak-Ostek, J., Wojdyło, A., Markowski, J., Siucińska, K., 2014. 1-Methylcyclopropene postharvest treatment and their effect on apple quality during long-term storage time. Eur. Food Res. Technol. 239, 603–612.

Lerslerwong, L., Rugkong, A., Imsabai, W., Ketsa, S., 2013. The harvest period of mangosteen fruit can be extended by chemical control of ripening—a proof of concept study. Sci. Hort. 157, 13–18.

Lurie, S., 2005. Regulation of ethylene biosynthesis in fruits by aminoethoxyvinylglycine and 1-methylcyclopropene. Stewart Postharvest Rev. 2005 3, 4.

Manganaris, G.A., Crisosto, C.H., Bremer, V., Holcroft, D., 2008. Novel 1-methylcyclopropene immersion formulation extends shelf life of advanced maturity "Joanna Red" plums (*Prunus salicina* Lindell). Postharvest Biol. Technol. 47, 429–433.

Martínez-Romero, D., Dupille, E., Guillen, F., Valverde, J.M., Serrano, M., Valero, D., 2003. 1-Methylcyclopropene increases storability and shelf life in climacteric and nonclimacteric plums. J. Agric. Food Chem. 51, 4680–4686.

Martínez-Romero, D., Bailén, G., Serrano, M., Guillén, F., Valverde, J.M., Zapata, P., Castillo, S., Valero, D., 2007. Tools to maintain postharvest fruit and vegetable quality thorough the inhibition of the ethylene action. Crit. Rev. Food Sci. Nutr. 47, 543–560.

Masia, A., 1998. Superoxide dismutase and catalase activities in apple fruit during ripening and post-harvest and with special reference to ethylene. Physiol. Plant. 104, 668–672.

Merchante, C., Alonso, J.M., Stepanova, A.N., 2013. Ethylene signaling and response: where different regulatory modules meet. Curr. Opin. Plant Biol. 12, 548–555.

Mozetič, B., Simčič, M., Trebše, P., 2006. Anthocyanins and hydroxycinnamic acids of Lambert Compact cherries (*Prunus avium* L.) after cold storage and 1-methylcyclopropene treatment. Food Chem. 97, 302–309.

Park, Y.S., Im, M.H., Gorinstein, S., 2015. Shelf life extension and antioxidant activity of "Hayward" kiwi fruit as a result of prestorage conditioning and 1-methylcyclopropene treatment. J. Food Sci. Technol. 52 (5), 2711–2720.

Pongpraserta, N., Srilaonga, V., 2014. A novel technique using 1-MCP microbubbles for delaying postharvest ripening of banana fruit. Postharvest Biol. Technol. 95, 42–45.

Rodoni, L.M., Feuring, V., Zaro, M.J., Sozzi, G.O., Vicente, A.R., Arena, M.E., 2014. Ethylene responses and quality of antioxidant-rich stored barberry fruit (*Berberis microphylla*). Sci. Hort. 179, 233–238.

Saltveit, M.E., 1999. Effect of ethylene on quality of fresh fruits and vegetables. Postharvest Biol. Technol. 15, 279–292.

Salvador, A., Cuquerella, J., Martínez-Jávega, J.M., 2003. 1-MCP treatment prolongs postharvest life of "Santa Rosa" plums. J. Food Sci. 68, 1504–1510.

Selcuk, N., Erkan, M., 2015. The effects of 1-MCP treatment on fruit quality of medlar fruit (*Mespilus germanica* L. cv. Istanbul) during long term storage in the palliflex storage system. Postharvest Biol. Technol. 100, 81–90.

Serrano, M., Díaz-Mula, H.M., Valero, D., 2011. Antioxidant compounds in fruits and vegetables and changes during postharvest storage and processing. Stewart Postharvest Rev. 2011 1, 1.

Serrano, M., Zapata, P.J., Martínez-Romero, D., Díaz-Mula, H.M., Valero, D., 2016. Polyamines as an eco-friendly postharvest tool to maintain fruit quality In: Eco-Friendly Technology for Postharvest produce Quality. Elsevier (Chapter 7) .

Sisler, E.C., 2006. The discovery and development of compounds counteracting ethylene at the receptor level. Biotechnol. Adv. 24, 357–367.

Sisler, E.C., Serek, M., 2003. Compounds interacting with the ethylene receptor in plants. Plant Biol. 5, 473–480.

Sozzy, G., Beaudry, R.M., 2005. Current perspectives on the use of 1-methylcyclopropene in tree fruit crops: an international survey. Stewart Postharvest Rev. 207 2, 8.

Steinite, I., Gailite, A., Levinsh, G., 2004. Reactive oxygen and ethylene are involved in the regulation of regurgitant-induce responses in bean plants. J. Plant Physiol. 161, 191–196.

Sun, B., Sun, H., He, X., Zhao, J., Feng, X., 2014. Effect of treatment with 1-pentyl-cyclopropene and 1-MCP on storage quality of mango fruits in cold storage. J. Chinese Inst. Food Sci. Technol. 14, 171–179.

Valdenegro, M., Fuentes, L., Herrera, R., Moya-León, M.A., 2012. Changes in antioxidant capacity during development and ripening of goldenberry (*Physalis peruviana* L.) fruit and in response to 1-methylcyclopropene treatment. Postharvest Biol. Technol. 67, 110–117.

Valero, D., Serrano, M., 2010. Postharvest Biology and Technology for Preserving Fruit Quality. CRC-Taylor & Francis, Boca Raton, Florida, USA.

Valero, D., Serrano, M., 2013. Growth and ripening stage at harvest modulates postharvest quality and bioactive compounds with antioxidant activity. Stewart Postharvest Rev. 2013 3, 7.

Valero, D., Martínez-Romero, D., Serrano, M., 2002. The role of polyamines in the improvement of the shelf life of fruit. Trends Food Sci. Technol. 13, 228–234.

Valero, D., Martínez-Romero, D., Valverde, J.M., Guillén, F., Serrano, M., 2003. Quality improvement and extension of shelf life by 1-methylcyclopropene in plum as affected by ripening stage at harvest. Innov. Food Sci. Emerg. Technol. 4, 339–348.

Valero, D., Martínez-Romero, D., Valverde, J.M., Guillén, F., Castillo, S., Serrano, M., 2004. Could the 1-MCP treatment effectiveness on plum be affected by packaging? Postharvest Biol. Technol. 34, 295–303.

Varanasi, V., Shin, S., Johnson, F., Mattheis, J.P., Zhu, Y., 2013. Differential suppression of ethylene biosynthesis and receptor genes in "Golden Delicious" apple by preharvest and postharvest 1-MCP treatments. J. Plant Growth Regul. 32, 585–595.

Vilaplana, R., Valentines, M.C., Toivonen, P., Larrigaudiére, C., 2006. Antioxidant potential and peroxidative state of "Golden Smoothee" apples treated with 1-methylcyclopropene. J. Am. Soc. Hort. Sci. 131, 104–109.

Villalobos-Acuña, M.G., Biasi, W.V., Flores, S., Elkins, R.B., Willits, N.H., 2010. Preharvest application of 1-methylcyclopropene influences fruit drop and storage potential of "Bartlett" pears. HortScience 45, 610–616.

Wang, B., Wang, J., Feng, X., Lin, L., Zhao, Y., Jiang, W., 2009. Effects of 1-MCP and exogenous ethylene on fruit ripening and antioxidants in stored mango. Plant Growth Regul. 57, 185–192.

Watkins, C.B., 2000. Responses to horticultural commodities to high carbon dioxide as related to modified atmosphere packaging. Hort. Technol. 10, 501–506.

Watkins, C.B., 2006. The use of 1-methylcyclopropene (1-MCP) on fruits and vegetables. Biotechnol. Adv. 24, 389–409.

Watkins, C.B., 2008. Overview of 1-methylcyclopropene trials and uses for edible horticultural crops. HortScience 43, 86–94.

Wills, R.B.H., Ku, V.V.V., 2002. Use of 1-MCP to extend the time to ripen of green tomatoes and postharvest life of ripe tomatoes. Postharvest Biol. Technol. 26, 85–90.

Win, S., Buanong, M., Kanlayanarat, S., Wongs-Aree, C., 2015. Response of gac fruit (*Momordica cochinchinensis* Spreng) to postharvest treatments with storage temperature and 1-MCP. Int. Food Res. J. 22, 178–189.

Zhang, Z., Huber, D.J., Rao, J., 2013. Antioxidant systems of ripening avocado (*Persea americana* Mill.) fruit following treatment at the preclimacteric stage with aqueous 1-methylcyclopropene. Postharvest Biol. Technol. 76, 58–64.

6

IMPACT OF BRASSINOSTEROIDS ON POSTHARVEST PHYSIOLOGY OF FRUITS AND VEGETABLES

Morteza Soleimani Aghdam, Mesbah Babalar, Mohammad Ali Askari Sarcheshmeh
University of Tehran, Department of Horticultural Science, College of Agriculture and Natural Resource, Karaj, Iran

1 Introduction

Brassinosteroids (BRs) as natural steroid hormones play crucial roles in plant development and response to biotic and abiotic stresses (Bajguz and Hayat, 2009), such as cold stress (Fariduddin et al., 2011), salt (Özdemir et al., 2004), pathogen infection (Nakashita et al., 2003), oxidative damage (Cao et al., 2005), and heat stress (Ogweno et al., 2008).

The increasing demand for consumption of fresh fruits and vegetables, along with restriction on the use of synthetic chemicals on postharvest operations for alleviating postharvest chilling injury (CI) along with minimizing decay, has encouraged scientific research to develop new technologies based on natural product such as BRs. The potential of BRs for enhancing chilling resistance as well as decay reducing in fruits and vegetables has been evaluated. Membrane damage and reactive oxygen species (ROS) production are multifarious adverse effects of chilling with oxidative facet in fruits and vegetables. Alleviating chilling in fruits and vegetables treated with BRs could be attributed to (1) enhancing membrane integrity by reducing phospholipase D (PLD) and lipoxygenase (LOX) enzyme activities and increasing the unsaturated fatty acid/saturated fatty acid (unSFA/SFA) ratio, (2) enhancing antioxidant system activity, and (3) alteration in phenylalanine ammonia-lyase (PAL) and polyphenol oxidase (PPO) enzyme activities (Aghdam et al., 2013; Aghdam and Mohammadkhani, 2014; Li et al., 2012; Wang et al., 2012).

With regard to postharvest decay, it has been accepted that postharvest natural disease resistance in fruits and vegetables

Eco-Friendly Technology for Postharvest Produce Quality. http://dx.doi.org/10.1016/B978-0-12-804313-4.00006-2
Copyright © 2016 Elsevier Inc. All rights reserved.

declines with ripening and senescence, which have an oxidative nature and are associated with ROS accumulation (Prusky, 1996). Zhu et al. (2015a) reported that the BRs treatment reduced disease incidence, which was associated with H_2O_2 accumulation. Also, Zhu et al. (2015a) showed that the mandarin fruits treated with BRs exhibited higher expression of PR genes such as chitinase and PAL, which led to the suggestion that BRs generate pathogen resistance by activating systemic acquired resistance (SAR).

It can be presumed that the innovative postharvest BRs treatments not only alleviates postharvest CI along with minimizing decay but also enhances nutritional quality of fruits and vegetables (Wang et al., 2012). Zhu et al. (2015b) reported that tomato fruit treated with BRs during postharvest ripening exhibited lower chlorophyll content and higher lycopene content, which results from decreasing Golden 2-like (GLK2) gene expression along with increasing phytoene synthase 1 (PSY1) gene expression in tomato fruits in response to BRs treatment. Also, Zhu et al. (2015b) showed that the tomato fruit treated with BRs during postharvest ripening exhibited higher climacteric ethylene biosynthesis genes expressing 1-aminocyclopropane-1-carboxylic acid (ACC) synthase 2, 4 (ACS2, ACS4) and ACC oxidase 1, 4 (ACO1, ACO4), which coincide with increasing ethylene biosynthesis. Zhu et al. (2015b) suggested that the enhanced lycopene biosynthesis along with suppressed chlorophyll biosynthesis can result from directly upregulating of PSY1 and downregulating GLK2 gene expression or indirectly from ethylene biosynthesis.

BRs as an environmentally friendly safe regulator can be used not only for minimizing postharvest losses by alleviation CI along with reducing decay but also for maintaining nutritional quality of fruits and vegetables (Table 6.1).

2 Brassinosteroids Regulate Fruit Ripening and Its Nutritional Quality

Ethylene, a simple gaseous plant hormone, plays a crucial role in plant growth and development such as fruit ripening. In plants, methionine is converted to S-adenosyl-L-methionine (SAM) by SAM synthetase, which is associated with ATP consumption. Then, SAM is converted to ACC by ACC synthase (ACS), which is encoded by ACS gene families, which are under developmental, environmental, and hormonal regulation. ACC is oxidized to ethylene by ACC oxidase (ACO), which requires iron and ascorbate as cofactor (Shi and Zhang, 2014). The potential of BRs for regulation of fruit ripening has also been investigated. Zhu et al. (2015b)

Table 6.1 Postharvest Brassinosteroids Treatment for Alleviation of Chilling Injury and Decay in Fruits and Vegetables and Also for Maintaining Their Nutritional Quality

References	Commodity	Biochemical and Molecular Effects	Effective Concentration
Aghdam and Mohammadkhani (2014)	Tomato	Alleviating chilling injury Decreasing electrolyte leakage and MDA content Increasing proline content Decreasing PLD and LOX enzyme activity	6 μM
Aghdam et al. (2012)	Tomato	Alleviating chilling injury Decreasing electrolyte leakage and MDA content Increasing proline content Enhancing PAL enzyme activity Enhancing total phenol accumulation	6 μM
Li et al. (2012)	Mango	Alleviating chilling injury Reducing electrolyte leakage Increasing linoleic and linolenic acids Increasing remorin, ASR, TIL, and TSD gene expression Maintaining membrane integrity	10 μM
Wang et al. (2012)	Green bell pepper	Alleviating chilling injury Decreasing electrolyte leakage and MDA content Enhancing CAT, APX, and GR enzyme activity Maintaining chlorophyll and ascorbic acid content	15 μM
Gao et al. (2015)	Eggplant	Maintaining membrane integrity Maintaining moisture content Declining total phenolic accumulation Decreasing PAL, PPO, and peroxidase (POD) activities Reducing tissue browning	10 μM

(Continue)

Table 6.1 Postharvest Brassinosteroids Treatment for Alleviation of Chilling Injury and Decay in Fruits and Vegetables and Also for Maintaining Their Nutritional Quality (*cont.*)

References	Commodity	Biochemical and Molecular Effects	Effective Concentration
Zhu et al. (2010)	Jujube	Minimizing postharvest decay Enhancing of PAL, PPO, CAT, and SOD activities Delaying fruit senescence Inhibiting ethylene production Declining fruit respiration	5 μM
Zhu et al. (2015)	Mandarin	Decreasing fruit decay Enhancing H_2O_2 accumulation Enhancing CAT, APX, and SOD enzyme activity Enhancing PR genes such as chitinase and PAL expression Enhancing WRKY6 gene expression Increasing ornithine, proline, GABA, D-xylose, and D-galactose accumulation	10 μM
Zhu et al. (2015b)	Tomato	Enhancing ethylene biosynthesis Increasing ACS2, ACS4, ACO1, and ACO4 gene expression Increasing PSY1 gene expression Decreasing GLK2 gene expression Increasing lycopene content Decreasing chlorophyll content	10 μM
Xi et al. (2013a)	Grapevine	Enhancing total soluble solids and reduced sugar Decreasing titratable acids Increasing PAL and UFGT activities Enhancing total phenols, tannins, flavonoids, and anthocyanins accumulation Enhancing total antioxidant capacity assayed by HRSA, ABTS, and DPPH	8 μM

reported that the ethylene biosynthesis in tomato fruit during ripening increased by BRs treatment, which was associated with increasing climacteric ethylene biosynthesis gene expression ACS2, ACS4, ACO1, and ACO4. Chai et al. (2013) reported that the BRs status increased during strawberry fruit development and exogenous use of BRs led to acceleration of strawberry fruit ripening. Chai et al. (2013) reported the expression of the BR receptor, BRI1, upsurge during strawberry fruit ripening, and downregulation of BRI1 expression delayed strawberry fruit pigmentation.

The transition of chloroplast to chromoplast during fruit ripening is associated with chlorophyll degradation and carotenoid biosynthesis. PSY is responsible for carotenoid biosynthesis, which catalyzes condensation of two geranylgeranyl diphosphate (GGDP) molecules to phytoene. In tomato fruit, PSY1, the expression of which increased during fruit ripening, is responsible for the biosynthesis of chromoplastic carotenoids, but PSY2 is responsible for the biosynthesis of chloroplastic carotenoids, and has no participation in carotenoid biosynthesis during fruit ripening (Nguyen et al., 2014).

Powell et al. (2012) reported that the GLK2 transcription factors, belonging to the GARP subfamily of the myb transcription factor superfamily, affects plastid development and determines chlorophyll accumulation and distribution in developing tomato fruits. U encodes the GLK2 transcription factor, which determines chlorophyll accumulation and distribution in developing fruits, and the U phenotype of tomato fruits exhibits dark green shoulders on the stem end. GLK2 expands the photosynthetic structures within green fruit chloroplasts, which lead to accumulation of photosynthesis and carbon fixation yields such as antioxidants, carotenoids, starch, and soluble sugars in ripe fruit. Also a single base insertion in GLK2 generates a U phenotype, which exhibits light green tomato fruit during development (Powell et al., 2012; Nguyen et al., 2014). Zhu et al. (2015b) reported that BRs treatment increased PSY1 gene expression and decreased GLK2 gene expression in tomato during fruit ripening, which led to increasing lycopene content and decreasing chlorophyll content, respectively. Zhu et al. (2015b) suggested that the enhanced lycopene biosynthesis along with suppressed chlorophyll biosynthesis can result from directly upregulating PSY1 and downregulating GLK2 gene expression or indirectly from ethylene biosynthesis. Liu et al. (2014) reported that the tomato ethylene-insensitive mutant, Nr, treated with BRs has higher carotenoid accumulation during ripening. Liu et al. (2014) suggested that BRs enhanced carotenoid accumulation independent of ethylene signal transduction. These results suggested that the promotion of carotenoid accumulation in tomato fruits under BRs treatment may result from ethylene dependence or ethylene independence. Liu et al. (2014) overexpressed BZR1 transcription factors in tomato and showed that ripening of transgenic fruits accelerated. Also, transgenic fruits showed U phenotype with dark green shoulders on the stem end, which have higher chlorophyll content associated with higher GLK2 expression, higher soluble sugar and ascorbic acid content, more and larger chloroplasts, higher grana thylakoid accumulation, and higher plastoglobules per chloroplast, but nontransgenic fruits showed U phenotype with light green fruit (Liu et al., 2014). Liu et al. (2014) reported that the BZR1 promotes HSP21 accumulation; HSP21 not only enhances tomato fruit carotenoid accumulation during the transition of chloroplasts to chromoplasts but also protects tomato photosystem II from temperature-dependent oxidative stress (Neta-Sharir et al., 2005).

Xi et al. (2013a) reported that spraying grapevine with BRs during veraison led to the enhancement of total soluble solids and reduced sugar, and decreased titratable acids content. Also, BRs-treated grapes exhibited higher PAL and uridine diphosphate glucose: flavonoid 3-O-glucosyltransferase (UFGT) activities, which led to accumulation of total phenolics, tannins, flavonoids, and anthocyanins associated with antioxidant capacity (hydroxyl radical scavenging activity, 2,2′-azino-*bis*-3-ethylbenzthiazoline-6-sulfonic acid, and 2,2-diphenyl-1-picrylhydrazyl). Xi et al. (2013a) suggested that accumulation of total phenolics, tannin, flavonoids, and anthocyanins contributed to the enhanced antioxidant capacity of the grape. Serna et al. (2013) reported that the total antioxidant activity and total phenols increased significantly in endive treated with BRs.

Mazorra et al. (2013) reported that BRs and ethylene regulating antagonistically alternative oxidase (AOX) capacity during papaya fruit ripening. The exogenous application of BRs could enhance AOX capacity. The effects of lower ethylene sensitivity due to use of 1-methylcyclopropene (1-MCP) treatment as an ethylene action inhibitor or BRs content due to use of brassinazole (BRZ) as a BRs biosynthesis inhibitor could increase AOX capacity. But the enhanced AOX capacity in response to externally applied BRs is inhibited when the proper BRs/ethylene ratio is disrupted by use of 1-MCP or BRZ. Since it has been accepted that the shelf life of fruits and vegetables is strongly dependent on respiratory activity, manipulation of fruits and vegetables respiration by regulation of BRs/ethylene can be used for extending shelf life of economically important fruits and vegetables such as papaya.

Glucosinolates as nitrogen- and sulfur-containing secondary metabolites are health promoting molecules in broccoli plants due to the anticarcinogenic activity of their hydrolysis products, iso-thiocyanates (Guo et al., 2014). Guo et al. (2013) reported that the BRs treatment decreased glucosinolate accumulation in *Arabidopsis*. Guo et al. (2013) suggested that binding of BRs to the receptor BRI1 activates BZR1 and BES1, transcriptional factors downstream of BRI1, and BZR1 and BES1 inhibited glucosinolate biosynthesis directly by binding to glucosinolate biosynthetic genes or indirectly by MYB transcription factors. Guo et al. (2014) reported that the broccoli sprouts treated with 20 nM BRs exhibited lower glucosinolate accumulation. Addition of 2 nM BRs plus 40 mM NaCl enhanced the accumulation of glucosinolates in broccoli sprouts, suggesting that BRs could provoke glucosinolate biosynthesis under salt stress. In addition, to impact BRs on glucosinolate biosynthesis, BRs regulate glucosinolate accumulation by impacting myrosinase activity, which is responsible for glucosinolate hydrolysis. Guo et al. (2014) suggested that the decreased glucosinolate accumulation in broccoli sprouts treated with 20 nM BRs plus 40 mM NaCl could be due to increased myrosinase activity.

Guo et al. (2014) reported that ascorbic acid content increased in broccoli sprouts after treatment with 20 nM 24-epibrassinolide. Mazorra Morales et al. (2014) suggested that the BRs control L-galactono-1,4-lactone dehydrogenase activity influencing leaf amino acid biosynthesis, which suggested that BRs control amino acid accumulation at the final biosynthetic step, and BRs promote amino acid accumulation in tomato leaves. Also, Mazorra Morales et al. (2014) suggested that BRs and ethylene have opposite impacts on amino acid biosynthesis; ethylene suppresses and BRs promote amino acid biosynthesis and accumulation. Ramakrishna and Seeta Ram Rao (2013) reported that BRs treatment enhanced ascorbate peroxidase (APOD), monodehydroascorbate reductase, dehydroascorbate reductase, glutathione reductase (GR), as well as glutathione-S-transferase, and γ-glutamylcysteine synthetase activities and ascorbate/dehydroascorbate and glutathione/glutathione disulfide ratios in Zn^{2+}-stressed radish seedlings, which led to mitigation of oxidative stress generated by Zn^{2+} stress. Taken together, treatments with BRs could be a promising strategy for enhancement of the nutritional quality of fruits and vegetables.

3 Brassinosteroids and Chilling Injury in Fruits and Vegetables

In line with consumers' concerns about residues of chemicals in fruits and vegetables, applications of safe and environmentally friendly technologies to prevent or alleviate CI are of great importance, and considerable efforts have been invested in this postharvest research field. The increasing demand for consumption of fruits and vegetables, along with restriction on the use of synthetic chemicals, has encouraged scientific research to develop new technologies based on natural products (Aghdam et al., 2013; Aghdam and Bodbodak, 2013).

Li et al. (2012) observed that treatment of mango fruit with BRs mitigated CI impact, a phenomenon associated with reduction of electrolyte leakage. This BR treatment of mango fruit induced an increase of unSFAs content such as linoleic and linolenic acids. The double bond index, which is an assessment criterion of the unsaturation degree of membrane fatty acids, was significantly higher in mango fruit treated with BRs. Thus, fluidity of cell membrane in BRs-treated mangoes was enhanced due to an increase in the proportion of unSFAs within the membrane, so it had a lower tendency to phase transitions from the flexible liquid-crystalline stage to rigid solid-gel (Li et al., 2012). In addition, mango fruits treated with BRs exhibited higher expression of genes encoding membrane proteins, such as remorin, abscisic stress ripening-like protein (ASR), temperature-induced lipocalin protein (TIL), and type II Sk2 dehydrin (TSD), all of which result in an increase of membrane integrity because of their important roles in membrane biogenesis and repair, scavenging harmful molecules, stabilizing the membrane, and participating in the transduction of the cold signal to activate expression of cold acclimation-dependent genes (Li et al., 2012).

Aghdam and Mohammadkhani (2014) reported that the treatment with BRs, especially at 6 μM, significantly alleviated CI, which was manifested by reduced electrolyte leakage and malonyldialdehyde (MDA) content and increased proline content. Treatment with BRs resulted in a decrease in MDA content and inhibited lipid peroxidation under chilling stress, which clearly indicated that BRs could strongly protect tomato fruit from oxidative damage and thus enhance chilling tolerance (Li et al., 2012; Wang et al., 2012). It was reported that treatment with BRs could decrease the lipid peroxidation and MDA content induced by heat (Ogweno et al., 2008) and drought stress (Robinson and Bunce, 2000). Yuan et al. (2010) reported that drought stress increased the H_2O_2 and MDA content of tomato seedlings, but this effect was significantly alleviated by application of BRs. Proline, as a multifunctional amino acid, plays crucial roles in the osmotic regulation between cytoplasm and vacuole, the redox regulation of the $NAD^+/NADH$ ratio, membrane stabilizer, and finally in promoting ROS scavenging systems (Sharp et al., 1990; Bohnert and Jensen, 1996). Aghdam and Mohammadkhani

(2014) showed that the proline content in control tomato fruit decreased with storage but increased in BRs-treated fruit during storage duration.

Aghdam et al. (2014) reported that PLD and LOX activities in tomato fruit increased during development of CI symptoms, a fact indicating aggravation of membrane integrity loss. Activation of membranous lipolytic enzymes such as PLD and LOX under chilling temperature might cause irreversible membrane damage and finally the occurrence of CI (Mao et al., 2007). Aghdam and Mohammadkhani (2014) showed that the tomato fruit treated with BRs exhibited significantly lower PLD and LOX activities. These results suggested that PLD and LOX are associated with the induction of CI in tomato fruit. BRs might reduce CI by inhibiting PLD and LOX activities and by enhancing membrane integrity.

Wang et al. (2012) reported that BRs treatment mitigated CI in green bell pepper, which is accompanied by reducing electrolyte leakage and MDA content. In addition, BRs treatment enhanced the activity of antioxidant enzymes such as catalase (CAT), APX, and GR, and thus mitigated chilling stress in green bell pepper by maintaining membrane integrity. Also, BRs maintained chlorophyll and ascorbic acid content leading to enhanced pepper nutritional quality. Meng et al. (2009) reported that phenolics have a dual function; first, phenolics can be oxidized by PPO, which leads to flesh browning, the main CI symptom in fruits and vegetables, second, phenolics, which accumulate in fruits and vegetables in response to chilling stress, have antioxidant capacity. Aghdam et al. (2012) reported that the BRs treatment mitigated CI in tomato fruit, which was accompanied by a reduction of electrolyte leakage and MDA content and an increase of proline content. Aghdam et al. (2012) showed that BRs treatment significantly enhanced PAL enzyme activity, which led to total phenol accumulation. Gao et al. (2015) reported eggplant fruits stored at 1°C for 15 days showed CI, which manifested in higher weight loss, electrolyte leakage, and MDA content along with higher PAL, PPO, and POD activities, which led to total phenolics accumulation and ultimately fruit pulp browning. Alleviation of CI in eggplant fruits by BRs treatment may be attributed to maintaining membrane integrity along with moisture content, declining total phenolic accumulation, and decreasing PAL, PPO, and POD activities, which lead to reducing browning. H_2O_2 as second messenger can activate PAL enzyme activity and ultimately higher total phenols and flavonoids accumulation (Wang et al., 2015). Gao et al. (2015) suggested that decreasing the impact of BRs on PAL activity in eggplant fruits might be due to reducing H_2O_2 accumulation during chilling storage.

Serna et al. (2015) reported that BRs treatment at 0.1 and 1 μM ameliorated the weight loss of lettuce plants under salinity stress. Serna et al. (2015) showed that BRs treatment slowed down the increase in ethylene production in shoots and roots under salinity. These results suggested that BRs treatment enhanced tolerance to salinity in lettuce plants by decreasing ethylene production and minimizing weight loss. Serna et al. (2015) reported that the shoots and roots of lettuce plants under salinity stress exhibited higher endogenous ACC accumulation, which may result from enhancing ACS and ACO activity by NaCl. Also, BRs treatment decreased endogenous ACC accumulation by decreasing ACS and ACO activity, which led to minimizing stress ethylene production. Serna et al. (2015) reported that BRs treatment reversed the effect of salinity on decreasing putrescine content in the shoots of lettuce plants. Also, BRs treatment reversed the effect of salinity on increasing spermidine and spermine contents in both shoots and roots of lettuce plants.

Serna et al. (2015) suggested that the increased total polyamine in lettuce plants under salinity stress may be a physiological response of plants to protect the root against NaCl. Since polyamines and BRs have antioxidant activity (Groppa and Benavides, 2008), it can be suggested that BRs treatment may enhance the antioxidant capacity of lettuce plants under salinity stress, and polyamine accumulation would not be so necessary to protect the roots against salinity stress. Liu et al. (2009) reported that BRs treatment alleviated chilling injury in *Chorispora bungeana* suspension cells by enhancing antioxidant enzymes APX, CAT, POD, and superoxide dismutase (SOD) activity, which was associated with higher ascorbic acid and glutathione (AsA and GSH) content leading to decreased H_2O_2 and OH^- contents and O_2^- production rate and ultimately minimizing electrolyte leakage and MDA accumulation, which clearly indicated that BRs could strongly protect membranes from oxidative damage.

Xi et al. (2013b) reported that BRs treatment enhanced the activities of antioxidant enzymes CAT, SOD, and APX in the young grapevine leaves under chilling stress. The AsA and GSH contents increased, while ROS accumulation and lipid peroxidation decreased by BRs treatment. In addition, BRs treatment also enhanced proline, soluble protein, and soluble sugar accumulation. Xi et al. (2013b) suggested that exogenous BRs treatment could enhance the antioxidant system activity and minimize oxidative damage caused by ROS and lipid peroxidation in the young grapevine leaves under chilling stress with oxidative facet. Alleviating chilling in fruits and vegetables treated with BRs could be attributed to (1) enhancing membrane integrity by reducing PLD and LOX

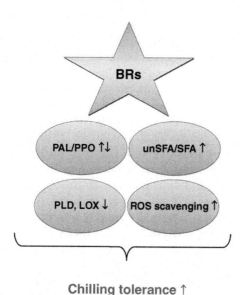

Figure 6.1 Enhancement of chilling tolerance in fruits and vegetables by brassinosteroids.

enzyme activities and increasing unSFA/SFA ratio, (2) enhancing antioxidant system activity, and (3) regulating PAL/PPO enzyme activities (Fig. 6.1).

4   Brassinosteroids and Their Function in Postharvest Immunity of Fruits and Vegetables

Fresh fruits and vegetables are perishable commodities that have living cells, which, during postharvest life, gain energy from respiration, which leads to ripening, fruit suitable for consumption, and increasing susceptibility to decay. Postharvest decay is associated with quality and quantity losses and results from fungi and bacteria, but fungi are crucial for decay (Hussain et al., 2015).

Fruit and vegetable postharvest decay results from latent infection in the field or via wounding during harvesting and handling systems (Hussain et al., 2015). In developed countries, 20–25% of fruits and vegetables are decayed during postharvest handling by pathogens, but in developing countries due to insufficient storage and transport operations, postharvest losses result from disease and can be as much as 30–50%. The use of synthetic fungicides for controlling postharvest disease in fruits and vegetables not only has an adverse effect on users, consumers, and the environment, but is also due to intense application leading to the build-up of resistance in pathogens (Asghari and Aghdam, 2010; Hussain et al., 2015). This has encouraged researchers to develop new eco-friendly and safe strategies to reduce postharvest diseases along with a declining application of synthetic fungicides (Hussain et al., 2015).

Zhu et al. (2010) reported that BRs treatment minimized post-harvest decay in jujube fruit caused by *Penicillium expansum* by enhancing activities of PAL, PPO, CAT, and SOD and delayed fruit senescence by inhibiting ethylene production and declining respiration rate. But, in vitro, direct antimicrobial activity of BRs against *P. expansum* was not shown by Zhu et al. (2010).

Zhu et al. (2015a) reported that BRs treatment reduced decay without decreasing the commercial qualities of the mandarin fruit; reduced disease incidence was associated with H_2O_2 accumulation in mandarin fruit under BRs treatment, which may result from enhancing SOD, peroxidase (POD), and NADPH oxidase activities. According to Zhou et al. (2014), perception of BRs by membrane receptor NADPH oxidase located at the plasma membrane activated and led to accumulation of apoplastic H_2O_2, which in turn enhanced abscisic acid biosynthesis, leading to a higher apoplastic and chloroplastic H_2O_2 accumulation, which ultimately led to stress tolerance. The increased H_2O_2 associated with the oxidative burst induced by infection with the virulent pathogens may contribute to resistance via directly killing the invading pathogen and/or activating cell wall crosslinking and lignification, thereby strengthening the cell wall and helping confine the pathogen to the infection site (Asghari and Aghdam, 2010). Also, Zhu et al. (2015a) showed that the mandarin fruits treated with BRs exhibited higher expression of PR genes such as chitinase and PAL, which led to the suggestion that BRs generate pathogen resistance by activating SAR. Xia et al. (2011) reported that the treatment of *Cucumis sativus* leaves with BRs led to systemic tolerance to photooxidative stress in leaves without BRs treatment, which was accompanied by the systemic accumulation of H_2O_2. Xia et al. (2011) suggested that local BRs treatment led to H_2O_2 accumulation, and H_2O_2 signaling results in the generation of systemic tolerance. It has been reported that the WRKY transcription factors can regulate PR gene expression via binding to PR gene promoters (Rushton et al., 2012). Zhu et al. (2015a) reported that the mandarin fruits treated with BRs exhibited higher expression of the WRKY6 gene, and suggested that the activation of mandarin PR and WRKY genes by BRs treatment, and WRKY6 transcription factor binding to PR promoters, may be attributed to BRs enhanced pathogen resistance.

5 Conclusions

Fresh fruits and vegetables, as very important suppliers of essential nutrients for human health, are perishable and their quality is impacted by both abiotic and biotic stresses. During postharvest life, due to internal and external factors, chemical and physical changes occur in fresh fruits and vegetables, which may result in serious losses in nutritional and sensory quality. In order to enhance the natural resistance of fruits and vegetables against postharvest stresses and also maintain fresh products sensory and nutritional quality, which in turn will extend postharvest life, use of environmentally friendly technologies such as BRs has been recommended. BRs as an environmentally friendly safe regulator can be used not only for minimizing postharvest losses by alleviation CI along with reducing decay but also for maintaining nutritional quality of fruits and vegetables. Membrane damage and ROS production are multifarious adverse effects of chilling with oxidative facet in fruits and vegetables. Alleviating chilling in fruits and vegetables treated with BRs could be attributed to (1) enhancing membrane integrity by reducing PLD and LOX enzyme activities and increasing unSFA/SFA ratio, (2) enhancing antioxidant system activity, and (3) regulating PAL/PPO enzyme activities.

Postharvest decay is associated with quality and quantity losses. The use of synthetic fungicides for controlling postharvest disease in fruits and vegetables not only has an adverse effect on users, consumers, and the environment, but is also due to intense application and leads to the development of resistance in pathogens. These facts have encouraged researchers to find new ecofriendly and safe strategies to reduce postharvest diseases along with declined application of synthetic fungicides. BRs treatment reduced disease incidence in fruits and vegetables, which was associated with H_2O_2 accumulation. Also, fruits and vegetables treated with BRs exhibited higher expression of PR genes such as chitinase and PAL, which led to the suggestion that BRs generate pathogen resistance by activating SAR.

References

Aghdam, M.S., Bodbodak, S., 2013. Physiological and biochemical mechanisms regulating chilling tolerance in fruit and vegetables under postharvest salicylates and jasmonates treatments. Sci. Hortic. 156, 73–85.

Aghdam, M.S., Mohammadkhani, N., 2014. Enhancement of chilling stress tolerance of tomato fruit by postharvest brassinolide treatment. Food Biol. Technol. 7, 909–914.

Aghdam, M.S., Asghari, M., Farmani, B., Mohayeji, M., Moradbeygi, H., 2012. Impact of postharvest brassinosteroids treatment on PAL activity in tomato fruit in response to chilling stress. Sci. Hortic. 144, 116–120.

Aghdam, M.S., Sevillano, L., Flores, F.B., Bodbodak, S., 2013. Heat shock proteins as biochemical markers for postharvest chilling stress in fruit and vegetables. Sci. Hortic. 160, 54–64.

Aghdam, M.S., Asghari, M., Khorsandi, O., Mohayeji, M., 2014. Alleviation of postharvest chilling injury of tomato fruit by salicylic acid treatment. J. Food Sci. Technol. 51, 2815–2820.

Asghari, M., Aghdam, M.S., 2010. Impact of salicylic acid on post-harvest physiology of horticultural crops. Trend Food Sci. Technol. 21, 502–509.

Bajguz, A., Hayat, S., 2009. Effects of brassinosteroids on the plant responses to environmental stresses. Plant Physiol. Biochem. 47, 1–8.

Bohnert, H.J., Jensen, R.G., 1996. Strategies for engineering water-stress tolerance in plants. Trends Biotech. 14, 89–97.

Cao, S., Xu, Q., Cao, Y., Qian, K., An, K., Zhu, Y., Binzeng, H., Zhao, H., Kuai, B., 2005. Loss-of-function mutations in DET2 gene lead to an enhanced resistance to oxidative stress in *Arabidopsis*. Physiol. Plant. 123, 57–66.

Chai, Y.M., Zhang, Q., Tian, L., Li, C.L., Xing, Y., Qin, L., Shen, Y.Y., 2013. Brassinosteroid is involved in strawberry fruit ripening. Plant. Grow Reg. 69, 63–69.

Fariduddin, Q., Yusuf, M., Chalkoo, S., Hayat, S., Ahmad, A., 2011. 28-homobrassinolide improves growth and photosynthesis in *Cucumis sativus* L. through an enhanced antioxidant system in the presence of chilling stress. Photosynthetica 49, 55–64.

Gao, H., Kang, L., Liu, Q., Cheng, N., Wang, B., Cao, W., 2015. Effect of 24-epibrassinolide treatment on the metabolism of eggplant fruits in relation to development of pulp browning under chilling stress. J. Food Sci. Technol. 52 (6), 3394–3401.

Groppa, M.D., Benavides, P., 2008. Polyamines and abiotic stress: recent advances. Amino Acids 34, 35–45.

Guo, R., Qian, H., Shen, W., Liu, L., Zhang, M., Cai, C., Zhao, Y., Qiao, J., Wang, Q., 2013. BZR1 and BES1 participate in regulation of glucosinolate biosynthesis by brassinosteroids in *Arabidopsis*. J. Exp. Bot. 64, 2401–2412.

Guo, R., Hou, Q., Yuan, G., Zhao, Y., Wang, Q., 2014. Effect of 2,4-epibrassinolide on main health-promoting compounds in broccoli sprouts. LWT—Food Sci. Technol. 58, 287–292.

Hussain, M., Hamid, M.I., Ghazanfar, M.U., 2015. Salicylic acid induced resistance in fruits to combat against postharvest pathogens: a review. Arch. Phytopathol. Plant Protec. 48, 34–42.

Li, B., Zhang, C., Cao, B., Qin, G., Wang, W., Tian, S., 2012. Brassinolide enhances cold stress tolerance of fruit by regulating plasma membrane proteins and lipids. Amino Acids 43, 2469–2480.

Liu, L., Jia, C., Zhang, M., Chen, D., Chen, S., Guo, R., Guo, D., Wang, Q., 2014. Ectopic expression of a BZR1-1D transcription factor in brassinosteroid signalling enhances carotenoid accumulation and fruit quality attributes in tomato. Plant. Biotech. J. 12, 105–115.

Liu, Y., Zhao, Z., Si, J., Di, C., Han, J., An, L., 2009. Brassinosteroids alleviate chilling-induced oxidative damage by enhancing antioxidant defense system in suspension cultured cells of *Chorispora bungeana*. Plant Growth Regul. 59, 207–214.

Mao, L., Pang, H., Wang, G., Zhu, C., 2007. Phospholipase D and lipoxygenase activity of cucumber fruit in response to chilling stress. Postharvest Biol. Technol. 44, 42–47.

Mazorra, L.M., Oliveira, M.G., Souza, A.F., da Silva, W.B., dos Santos, G.M., da Silva, L.R.A., da Silva, M.G., Bartoli, C.G., de Oliveira, J.G., 2013. Involvement of brassinosteroids and ethylene in the control of mitochondrial electron transport chain in postharvest papaya fruit. Theoretic. Exper. Plant Physiol. 25, 223–230.

Mazorra Morales, L.M., Senn, M.E., Gergoff Grozeff, G.E., Fanello, D.D., Carrion, C.A., Nunez, M., Bishop, G.J., Bartoli, C.G., 2014. Impact of brassinosteroids and ethylene on ascorbic acid accumulation in tomato leaves. Plant. Physiol. Biochem. 74, 315–322.

Meng, X., Han, J., Wang, Q., Tian, S., 2009. Changes in physiology and quality of peach fruits treated by methyl jasmonate under low temperature stress. Food Chem. 114, 1028–1035.

Nakashita, H., Yasuda, M., Nitta, T., Asami, T., Fujioka, S., Arai, Y., Sekimata, K., Takatsuto, S., Yamaguchi, I., Yoshida, S., 2003. Brassinosteroid functions in a broad range of disease resistance in tobacco and rice. Plant J. 33, 887–898.

Neta-Sharir, I., Isaacson, T., Lurie, S., Weiss, D., 2005. Dual role for tomato heat shock protein 21: protecting photosystem II from oxidative stress and promoting color changes during fruit maturation. Plant Cell 17, 1829–1838.

Nguyen, C.V., Vrebalov, J.T., Gapper, N.E., Zheng, Y., Zhong, S., Fei, Z., Giovannoni, J.J., 2014. Tomato GOLDEN2-LIKE transcription factors reveal molecular gradients that function during fruit development and ripening. Plant Cell 26, 585–601.

Ogweno, J., Song, X., Shi, K., Hu, W., Mao, W., Zhou, Y., Yu, J., Nogués, S., 2008. Brassinosteroids alleviate heat-induced inhibition of photosynthesis by increasing carboxylation efficiency and enhancing antioxidant systems in *Lycopersicon esculentum*. J. Plant Growth Reg. 27, 49–57.

Özdemir, F., Bor, M., Demiral, T., Türkan, İ., 2004. Effects of 24-epibrassinolide on seed germination, seedling growth, lipid peroxidation, proline content and antioxidative system of rice (*Oryza sativa* L.) under salinity stress. J. Plant Growth Reg. 42, 203–211.

Powell, A.L., Nguyen, C.V., Hill, T., Cheng, K.L., Figueroa-Balderas, R., Aktas, H., Ashrafi, H., Pons, C., Fernandez-Munoz, R., Vicente, A., Lopez-Baltazar, J., Barry, C.S., Liu, Y., Chetelat, R., Granell, A., Van Deynze, A., Giovannoni, J.J., Bennett, A.B., 2012. Uniform ripening encodes a Golden 2-like transcription factor regulating tomato fruit chloroplast development. Science 336, 1711–1715.

Prusky, D., 1996. Pathogen quiescence in postharvest diseases. Ann. Rev. Phytopathol. 34, 413–434.

Ramakrishna, B., Seeta Ram Rao, S., 2013. 24-Epibrassinolide maintains elevated redox state of AsA and GSH in radish (*Raphanus sativus* L.) seedlings under zinc stress. Acta Physiol. Plant. 35, 1291–1302.

Robinson, J.M., Bunce, J.A., 2000. Influence of drought-induced water stress on soybean and spinach leaf ascorbate-dehydroascorbate level and redox status. Int. J. Plant Sci. 161, 271–279.

Rushton, D.L., Tripathi, P., Rabara, R.C., Lin, J., Ringler, P., Boken, A.K., Langum, T.J., Smidt, L., Boomsma, D.D., Emme, N.J., Chen, X., Finer, J.J., Shen, Q.J., Rushton, P.J., 2012. WRKY transcription factors: key components in abscisic acid signalling. Plant Biotech. J. 10, 2–11.

Serna, M., Hernandez, F., Coll, F., Coll, Y., Amoros, A., 2013. Effects of brassinosteroid analogues on total phenols, antioxidant activity, sugars, organic acids and yield of field grown endive (*Cichorium endivia* L.). J. Sci. Food Agric. 93, 1765–1771.

Serna, M., Coll, Y., Zapata, P.J., Botella, M.A., Pretel, M.T., Amorós, A., 2015. A brassinosteroid analogue prevented the effect of salt stress on ethylene synthesis and polyamines in lettuce plants. Sci. Hortic. 185, 105–112.

Sharp, R.E., Hsiao, T.C., Silk, W.K., 1990. Growth of the maize primary root at low water potentials: II. Role of growth and deposition of hexose and potassium in osmotic adjustment. Plant Physiol. 93, 1337–1346.

Shi, H.Y., Zhang, Y.X., 2014. Expression and regulation of pear 1-aminocyclopropane-1-carboxylic acid synthase gene (*PpACS1a*) during fruit ripening, under salicylic acid and indole-3-acetic acid treatment, and in diseased fruit. Mol. Biol. Rep. 41, 4147–4154.

Wang, Q., Ding, T., Gao, L., Pang, J., Yang, N., 2012. Effect of brassinolide on chilling injury of green bell pepper in storage. Sci. Hortic. 144, 195–200.

Wang, Z., Ma, L., Zhang, X., Xu, L., Cao, J., Jiang, W., 2015. The effect of exogenous salicylic acid on antioxidant activity, bioactive compounds and antioxidant system in apricot fruit. Sci. Hortic. 181, 113–120.

Xi, Z.M., Zhang, Z.W., Huo, S.S., Luan, L.Y., Gao, X., Ma, L.N., Fang, Y.L., 2013a. Regulating the secondary metabolism in grape berry using exogenous 24-epibrassinolide for enhanced phenolics content and antioxidant capacity. Food Chem. 141, 3056–3065.

Xi, Z., Wang, Z., Fang, Y., Hu, Z., Hu, Y., Deng, M., Zhang, Z., 2013b. Effects of 24-epibrassinolide on antioxidation defense and osmoregulation systems of young grapevines (*V. vinifera* L.) under chilling stress. Plant Growth Regul. 71, 57–65.

Xia, X.J., Zhou, Y.H., Ding, J., Shi, K., Asami, T., Chen, Z., Yu, J.Q., 2011. Induction of systemic stress tolerance by brassinosteroid in *Cucumis sativus*. New Phytol. 191, 706–720.

Yuan, G.F., Jia, C.G., Li, Z., Sun, B., Zhang, L.P., Liu, N., Wang, Q.M., 2010. Effect of brassinosteroids on drought resistance and abscisic acid concentration in tomato under water stress. Sci. Hortic. 126, 103–108.

Zhou, J., Wang, J., Li, X., Xia, X.J., Zhou, Y.H., Shi, K., Chen, Z., Yu, J.Q., 2014. H$_2$O$_2$ mediates the crosstalk of brassinosteroid and abscisic acid in tomato responses to heat and oxidative stresses. J. Exp. Bot. 65, 4371–4383.

Zhu, F., Yun, Z., Ma, Q., Gong, Q., Zeng, Y., Xu, J., Cheng, Y., Deng, X., 2015a. Effects of exogenous 24-epibrassinolide treatment on postharvest quality and resistance of Satsuma mandarin (*Citrus unshiu*). Postharvest Biol. Technol. 100, 8–15.

Zhu, T., Tan, W.R., Deng, X.G., Zheng, T., Zhang, D.W., Lin, H.H., 2015b. Effects of brassinosteroids on quality attributes and ethylene synthesis in postharvest tomato fruit. Postharvest Biol. Technol. 100, 196–204.

Zhu, Z., Zhang, Z., Qin, G., Tian, S., 2010. Effects of brassinosteroids on postharvest disease and senescence of jujube fruit in storage. Postharvest Biol. Technol. 56, 50–55.

7

POLYAMINES AS AN ECOFRIENDLY POSTHARVEST TOOL TO MAINTAIN FRUIT QUALITY

María Serrano*, Pedro J. Zapata**, Domingo Martínez-Romero**, Huertas M. Díaz-Mula**, Daniel Valero**
*University Miguel Hernández, Department of Applied Biology, Orihuela, Alicante, Spain; **University Miguel Hernández, Department of Food Technology, Orihuela, Alicante, Spain

1 Introduction

Polyamines (PAs) are present in all eukaryotic cells (both animal and plant) and have important roles in several biological functions related with cell growth and differentiation. In plant organs, the main PAs are putrescine (Put, 1,4-diaminobutane), spermidine (Spd, N-3-aminopropyl-1,4-diaminobutane), and spermine [Spm, bis(N-3-aminopropyl)-1,4-diaminobutane]. These PAs are involved in a wide range of growth and developmental process, such as cell division, dormancy breaking, germination, development of flower buds, fruit set, growth and ripening, as well as in plant responses to environmental stresses including chilling injury (CI) (Groppa and Benavides, 2008; Valero and Serrano, 2010; Tiburcio et al., 2014). This chapter will focus on the role of PAs in fruit growth and ripening, with special emphasis on the effects of pre- and postharvest PA treatment on fruit quality attributes, bioactive constituents with antioxidant activity, and tolerance of fruit to CI damages.

2 Polyamine Biosynthesis and Regulation in Plant Tissues

The PA biosynthetic pathway in plants is shown in Fig. 7.1, in which the connection with ethylene biosynthesis is also provided. The biosynthesis pathway starts with Put, which is produced by

Eco-Friendly Technology for Postharvest Produce Quality. http://dx.doi.org/10.1016/B978-0-12-804313-4.00007-4
Copyright © 2016 Elsevier Inc. All rights reserved.

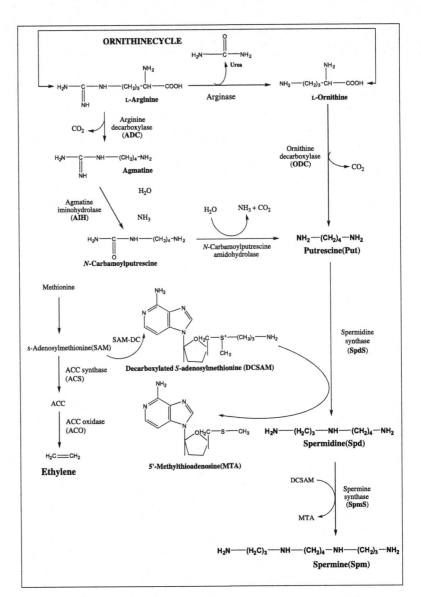

Figure 7.1 Polyamine biosynthesis pathway and interconnection with ethylene biosynthesis in plant tissues.

two alternative pathways, from ornithine in a reaction catalyzed by ornithine decarboxylase (ODC, EC 4.1.1.17) and from arginine as a result of the action of arginine decarboxylase (ADC, EC 4.1.1.19) via agmatine. These two enzymes involved in Put synthesis are differentially compartmentalized, since ADC is located at the chloroplast and ODC at the cytoplasm. In addition, arginase hydrolyzes arginine to urea and ornithine, the latter being converted into Put by ODC. Put is subsequently converted into Spd and Spm by the addition of two aminopropyl residues from decarboxylated S-adenosylmethionine (DCSAM), which is derived from S-adenosylmethionine (SAM) by SAM decarboxylase (SAMDC, EC 4.1.1.50). These reactions are sequentially catalyzed by two closely related enzymes, Spd synthase (SpdS, EC 2.5.1.16) and Spm synthase (SpmS, EC 2.5.1.22). There is evidence supporting that the two pathways for Put biosynthesis play different roles in plant development and growth, ADC being related to maturation and response to environmental stresses, and ODC having the main role in cell division. On the other hand, SAM is also a precursor of ethylene via the synthesis of 1-aminocyclopropane-1-caboxylic acid (ACC) by ACC synthase (ACS), which is further converted to ethylene by ACC oxidase (ACO). Furthermore, in some plants, the methyl moiety of SAM can be transferred to Put via Put-N-methyltransferase, to form N-methyl-Put, which serves as a precursor of nicotine and other alkaloids. Thus the multiple essential roles of SAM require regulation of its synthesis, recycling, and distribution to sustain these different pathways, this SAM metabolism being highly compartmentalized and regulated by various feedback loops that also control synthesis of methionine precursors in plastids (Kusano et al., 2007; Groppa and Benavides, 2008; Valero and Serrano, 2010; Sauter et al., 2013).

The intracellular free PA pool depends on its synthesis and also on several metabolic pathways including degradation, conjugation, and transport. Thus, copper containing diamine oxidases catalyze the oxidation of Put, and flavine-containing PA oxidases (PAO) oxidize Spd and Spm, producing 4-aminobutanal, and N-(3-aminopropyl)-4-aminobutanal, respectively. Finally, PAs can be conjugated either with small molecules, especially hydroxycinnamic acids to form soluble Pas, or with high molecular mass substances, such as hemicelluloses, lignin, or protein of the cell wall to form cell wall-bound PAs and could serve as a pool of free PAs (Valero et al., 2002; Bianchi et al., 2006; Tiburcio et al., 2014).

In spite of ethylene and PA (Spd and Spm) biosynthesis sharing a common precursor (SAM), they exert opposite effects in fruit ripening and senescence, and the balance between these two opposite growth regulators is crucial to retard or to accelerate both processes. Thus, reduced levels of PAs have been correlated with increased ethylene production, fruit ripening, and senescence, while high endogenous concentrations of PAs are associated with a delay in these processes (Valero et al., 2002; Valero and Serrano, 2010; Tiburcio et al., 2014).

3 Role of Endogenous Polyamines in Fruit Development and Ripening

PAs are involved in the overall physiological process from floral development to fruit growth and ripening. Thus, increase in total PAs or in a single PA type accompanies floral development, while inhibition of PA biosynthesis causes a strong decrease in flowering, this inhibitory effect being abolished by applying exogenous Spd. Moreover, PAs are also related to flower genders or fertility as well as to the pollen germination and pollen tube growth and promote flowering of some plants under noninductive conditions. Some mutant plants deficient in PA metabolism demonstrated aberrant morphology in anthers and ovules (Liu et al., 2006a). In addition, a clear relationship has been reported between the concentration of free PAs (mainly Spd and Spm) in the apricot ovary and the ovule development, its viability, and fruit set (Alburquerque et al., 2006). Accordingly, a large accumulation of free PAs occurs concomitantly with flower development in damson plum, being closely related to the onset of ovarian development (De Dios et al., 2006). In addition, fruit set in grape vine was positively influenced by the increase in free and soluble-conjugated Spd in the floral organs (Aziz et al., 2001) and Put directly applied to the flower 2 days before pollination increased fruit set in Japanese pears, due to stimulation of pollen germination and initial pollen tube growth (Franco-Mora et al., 2005b). Similarly, spray treatments of date palm tree at bloom phase with 0.45 mM Put, alone or in combination with 2% potassium citrate, increased fruit set and fruit retention percentages (Abd El-Migeed et al., 2013). In a similar way, fruit retention was increased in mango tree by Put, Spd, and Spm treatments, especially with Spm when applied at full blossom stage (Malik and Singh, 2006). This effect has been ascribed to the increased levels of endogenous PAs in the fruitlets and pedicels making them less prone to abscise, especially during the initial 4–6 weeks of heavy fruitlet abscission, by inhibiting endogenous ethylene biosynthesis, which is the known trigger in abscission. Moreover, PA treatments have also led to improved fruit volume and weight in date (Abd El-Migeed et al., 2013) and apricot (Ali et al., 2010) fruits, due to the PA effects on increasing fruit sink strength and favoring phloem sugar translocation towards them.

In a wide range of fruit species, it has been found that the concentration of PAs is high at the early phase of fruit growth, while a decline occurred as the growth rate decreased, reaching the lowest concentrations at the ripening phase, these PA changes occurring in climacteric fruits such as tomato (Martínez-Madrid et al., 1996; Yahia et al., 2001; Pandey et al., 2015), plum (Zuzunaga et al., 2001), peach (Liu et al., 2006b), and apricot (Paksasorn et al., 1995) as well as in nonclimacteric ones, such as pepper (Pretel et al., 1995), strawberry (Ponappa and Miller, 1996), and grapevine (Agudelo-Romero et al., 2013). In grapevine the decrease in free and conjugated PA content during grape ripening was due to their catabolism, since it was accompanied by upregulation of genes coding for diamine oxidase (CuAO) and PAO, together with a significant increase in their enzymatic activity and in the hydrogen peroxide content, in spite of an increase in ADC expression (Agudelo-Romero et al., 2013). The high PA concentration soon after full bloom has been related to the high growth rate and active cell division. However, in avocado mesocarp cells continue to divide as long as the fruit remains attached to the tree and nevertheless PAs also decreased during fruit growth (Kushad et al., 1988).

The decrease in PAs at late stages of fruit growth has been regarded as a signal for fruit ripening, although a few exceptions exist. Thus Put increased during ripening in long-keeping tomato (Martínez-Madrid et al., 1996; Yahia et al., 2001) and both Put and Spd levels raised in Golden Japan plum (Zuzunaga et al., 2001), a suppressed climacteric plum phenotype. The high levels of PAs in these mature fruits may be responsible for the long-keeping quality and low ethylene production of these tomato and plum cultivars. Moreover, since ethylene and PAs share their common precursor, it is normally accepted that they compete each other during fruit development and ripening and then diminution in Spd and Spm during fruit ripening may be a consequence of SAM diversion to ACC for ethylene biosynthesis, concomitantly with the increase of Put (Valero et al., 2002). In agreement with this proposal an inverse relationship has been found between PA content and ethylene production and ACC concentration during ripening of seven pear cultivars, ranging from low to moderate and high ethylene production rates at ripening (Franco-Mora et al., 2005a). In addition the genetic modification of tomato fruit by overexpressing human-*SAMDC* led to fruit with elevated PA levels and reduced levels of ethylene in comparison to wild type, due to lower accumulation of *ACS* and *ACO* gene transcript, these transgenic fruits exhibiting delay in on-vine ripening and extended postharvest storage (Madhulatha et al., 2014). Accordingly, transgenic tomato plants overexpressing the mouse *ODC* gene produced fruit with enhanced levels of Put, Spd, and Spm and reduced ethylene production and respiration rate, the on-vine ripening process being delayed with respect to fruits from untransformed plants (Pandey et al., 2015).

However, increase in Put concentration during ripening has been also found in some climacteric fruits, such as paraguayo

(Martínez-Madrid et al., 2000), peach (Liu et al., 2006b), and cherimolla (Escribano and Merodio, 1994) as well as increases in Put, Spd, and Spm in the climacteric damson plum (De Dios et al., 2006). Moreover, the introduction of the yeast *SAMDC* gene into a commercial variety of tomato led to increased levels of Spd and Spm, although these transgenic tomatoes produced more ethylene than did the parental line (Mehta et al., 2002). On the other hand, 1-methylcyclopropene (1-MCP) treatment of apple fruit inhibited the autocatalytic production of ethylene but no evidence for elevated levels of total PAs, Put, Spd, or Spm during apple storage were observed (Deyman et al., 2014), while in 1-MCP-treated tomatoes ethylene production was inhibited and PA content increased (Van de Poel et al., 2013). Thus it seems that the level of the precursor SAM is not generally the limiting factor for ethylene and PA biosynthesis pathways and that both metabolic pathways can operate simultaneously in vivo, at least in some fruit species.

4 Effects of Pre- and Postharvest Polyamine Application on Fruit Ripening and Quality Attributes

According to consumers the term "quality" can be defined as a fruit with a perfect shape, size, color, firmness, aroma, and absence of defects such as cuts, bruises, or decay. However, fruits are appreciated not only because of their attractive sensorial properties, but also because of their nutritional and health benefits, due to their antioxidant compound content with the beneficial role in the prevention of degenerative diseases (Serrano et al., 2011; Villa-Rodriguez et al., 2015). The highest quality attributes are reached at the appropriate ripening stage, but fruits deteriorate rapidly after harvest with significant losses in their quality properties (Valero and Serrano, 2013).

Given the opposite effects of PAs and ethylene on retarding or accelerating fruit ripening and senescence, respectively, as commented in the previous section, a great deal of research has been focused on the effect of pre- or postharvest PA treatments on fruit quality parameters related to the ripening process. In this sense several experiments have shown that preharvest treatments with PAs during the fruit growing season can decrease ethylene production and delay the ripening process in a wide range of fruit species. However, most of the research about the effect of PAs on fruit ripening has been performed with postharvest treatments and their effects are similar to those of preharvest treatments, thus there is a delay in the postharvest ripening process leading to maintenance of fruit quality attributes.

4.1 Ethylene Production

Foliar spray treatments of peach trees 19 days before fruit harvest with Put (10 mM), Spd (0.1, 1, and 5 mM), or Spm (2 mM) strongly reduced or even nullified ethylene production during peach on-tree ripening, with Spd being more efficient than Put or Spm (Bregoli et al., 2002). In addition, field applications of 1 mM Spd on peach trees at 41 days after full bloom led to a lower accumulation of *ACO* and *ACS* transcripts at harvest, in accordance with their effect on inhibiting ethylene biosynthesis (Torrigiani et al., 2012). Moreover, it has been reported that *SAMDC* and *ADC* transcript levels were initially depressed in peach fruit by preharvest Spd treatment, as well as *ACO* and *ACS* transcripts, and later, at harvest time, recovered up to control levels, while the effect of Put treatments on ACO and ACS were still evident at harvest, in which an increase of ethylene receptor mRNA was also found (Ziosi et al., 2006). Similar results regarding the efficacy of PAs on decreasing ethylene production were obtained in nectarine during on-tree fruit ripening (Torrigiani et al., 2004). Moreover, preharvest treatments with PAs have been shown to be also effective in delaying ethylene production during postharvest storage. Thus preharvest treatments of apricot trees with 0.1 mM of Put, Spd, or Spm 20 days before harvest decreased postharvest ethylene production (Paksasorn et al., 1995). Accordingly, preharvest foliar spray treatment of plum trees with Put delayed and inhibited both ethylene production and respiration rate during postharvest storage, these effects being higher as Put concentration increased from 0.1 to 2 mM, and also evident after a 6-week period of cold storage (Khan et al., 2008).

On the other hand, postharvest application of PAs, by immersion or vacuum infiltration, has been reported to inhibit ethylene production in some climacteric fruits, including Kesington Pride mango (Malik and Singh, 2005), Babygold-6 peach (Martínez-Romero et al., 2000), Mauricio apricot (Martínez-Romero et al., 2002), and Black Diamond, Black Star, Santa Rosa, and Angeleno plums (Pérez-Vicente et al., 2002; Serrano et al., 2003; Khan et al., 2008) delaying fruit ripening and extending shelf life. The inhibitory effects of exogenous PAs in ethylene production have been ascribed to both the competitive biosynthesis mechanism between ethylene and PAs and to the inhibition of ACC synthase and ACC oxidase. However, in apples Put treatment did not decrease ethylene production through the normal course of ripening during storage (Wang et al., 1993). Since ethylene inhibition by Put treatment has been shown to be inversely correlated to the maximum level at the climacteric peak (Valero et al., 2002; Serrano et al., 2003), the failures of PA treatments on inhibiting synthesis of ethylene in some fruits may be due to their high levels of ethylene production. The effect of PA treatments on inhibiting ethylene production in climacteric fruits led to a delay in the evolution of the postharvest ripening process, since in these fruits ethylene is the main responsible hormone regulating this process (Cherian et al., 2014). Nevertheless, the delayed postharvest ripening process as a consequence of PA treatments has been also observed in nonclimacteric fruits, such as Mollar de Elche pomegranate (Mirdehghan et al., 2007a), blueberry (Basiouny, 1996), and table grape (Harindra Champa et al., 2015).

4.2 Fruit Quality Parameters

Pre- and postharvest PA treatments have shown to have beneficial effects on fruit quality attributes. Thus foliar spray with Put and Spm to apricot Canino trees increased yield, fruit weight, and fruit volume compared with fruits from control trees. In addition, at harvest time, fruits of treated trees with both Put and Spm had a significantly higher total soluble solids (TSSs) concentration and they were firmer than fruits of control trees, whereas fruit total acidity (TA) was lower in fruits from PA treated trees, showing that PAs could be recommended in cultural practices to enhance the production of apricot tree orchards and improve fruit quality (Ali et al., 2010). Accordingly, Put treatment of date palm tree at bloom stage increased fruit weight, length, diameter, and volume, as well as the content of reducing and nonreducing sugars, and reduced TA and tannin concentration, leading to date fruits with improved quality attributes at harvest (Abd El-Migeed et al., 2013). Moreover, the activation of the Put biosynthetic pathway in tomato fruits from transgenic tomato plants overexpressing the mouse *ODC* gene led to fruit with higher Put, Spd, and Spm content, which also had improved quality traits, such as TSS, TA, and sugar content (Pandey et al., 2015) as well as in transgenic tomatoes overexpressing human-*SAMDC* (Madhulatha et al., 2014). On the other hand, treatments of mango trees with Put (0.5, 1, or 2 mM) 7 days prior to harvest led to higher levels of firmness and TSS and lower fruit rot index after 20 days of storage at 20°C as compared to fruit from nontreated trees (Malik and Singh, 2005), although sugar content was at a lower concentration, probably due to a slower conversion of starch to sugars and delay in the evolution of color development (Malik and Singh, 2006). Accordingly, Put treatments of plum trees also decreased fruit softening, maintained TA at higher levels, diminished the increase in TSS, and delayed the color evolution during postharvest storage as compared to control fruits, showing a delay in ripening evolution and leading to a net extension of plum shelf life (Khan et al., 2008). Moreover, foliar spray treatments of peach trees 19 days before fruit harvest with Put (10 mM), Spd (0.1, 1, and 5 mM), or Spm (2 mM) markedly slowed down the softening process, while only Spd affected the accumulation of TSS, leading to lower levels at harvest as compared with control fruits (Bregoli et al., 2002). Similar results were obtained in nectarine during on-tree fruit ripening, in which PA treatments decreased flesh softening and acidity losses and increased TSS (Torrigiani et al., 2004).

Accordingly, postharvest Put application markedly slowed softening during ripening at ambient temperature in Angelino plum, this effect being higher as Put concentration increased from 0.1 to 2 mM (Khan et al., 2008) as well as in Black Star, Black Diamond, Golden Japan, and Santa Rosa cultivars (Serrano et al., 2003). Put treatment at 10 mM was also effective in delaying softening in blueberry, while no effect was observed with 1 mM Spd treatment (Basiouny, 1996). However, in apricot, both Put and Spd were effective in reducing fruit softening during cold storage (Koushesh-saba et al., 2012). Several mechanisms have been postulated to explain the increased fruit firmness after Put treatment. One is supported by decreased activity of cell wall hydrolytic enzymes involved in softening, such as endo- and exo-polygalacturonase (PG), pectin esterase (PE), and pectin methyl esterase (PME). Thus Spm at the dose of 1.0 mM effectively maintained grape berry firmness during long-term cold storage, because the enzymatic activity of PME was effectively repressed (Harindra Champa et al., 2015). Accordingly in peach fruit it has been shown that the effect of PA treatment on reducing fruit softening is due to a strong downregulation of genes responsible for fruit softening, such as those codifying for PG and PME (Torrigiani et al., 2012). Other mechanisms involve the PA capacity to cross-link pectic substances in the cell wall, producing rigidification and also blocking the access of such degrading enzymes reducing the rate of softening during storage (Valero and Serrano, 2010 and references cited therein). However, it is also true that exogenous 10 mM Put or 1mM Spd treatments of Redhaven peaches harvested at two different ripening stages failed in maintaining fruit firmness, while positive effects of these treatments were found in nectarines, because Put was taken to a higher extent in nectarines than in peaches (Bregoli et al., 2006).

On the other hand, postharvest Put treatments decreased the weight loss throughout storage in plum cultivars with respect to those observed in control fruits (Serrano et al., 2003), as well as

Put or Spm treatment of table grape, which was attributed to the improved biophysical properties of the berries by means of stabilization and consolidation of both cell integrity and permeability as a consequence of Spm treatment manifested as lower electrolyte leakage during storage (Shiri et al., 2013; Harindra Champa et al., 2015). In table grape, Put treatments were also effective in reducing decay incidence, rachis browning, and berry shattering and cracking during prolonged cold storage (Shiri et al., 2013). Another effect of PA treatments is amelioration of chlorophyll breakdown in several fruits, such as lemon and apricot, which is an indicator of reduced senescence rate (Martínez-Romero et al., 2002; Valero et al., 2002). Also, exogenous PAs retarded chlorophyll loss in muskmelon by reducing the hydrolytic activities acting on chloroplast thylakoid membranes (Lester, 2000). Similarly, Put treatments reduced color change during low-temperature storage in a wide range of plum cultivars, the effect being also attributed to lower chlorophyll degradation and delay in the senescence process (Serrano et al., 2003; Khan et al., 2008). The effects of PAs on retarding color evolution were in the order: $SPM^{4+} > SPD^{3+} > PUT^{2+}$, following the order of their available number of cations, which has been argued as the reason for their difference in effectiveness (Valero et al., 2002). In addition, 1-MCP treatments of pepper fruits delayed senescence manifested as lower chlorophyll degradation and weight loss in treated pepper with respect to controls, throughout maintenance of higher Put, Spd, and Spm concentrations (Cao et al., 2012). Finally, most of the reports about PA postharvest treatments have shown to have little or no effect on TSS evolution during fruit postharvest storage, while they significantly delayed the diminution in TA that normally occurs during storage in a wide range of fruits, such as plum, pomegranate, and blueberry (Basiouny, 1996; Mirdehghan et al., 2007a; Khan et al., 2008; Valero and Serrano, 2010).

Taking into account data of the observed parameters relating to fruit quality (firmness, color, TSS, and TA), as well as the visual appearance of the fruits, it could be concluded that PA treatment, either at pre- or postharvest time, delayed the postharvest ripening process, with a net effect on maintaining fruit quality attributes and increasing the fruit shelf life. These effects could be because PA treatments led to increases in endogenous Put and Spd concentrations, as have been shown in lemon (Valero et al., 1997), peach (Martínez-Romero et al., 2000), apricot (Martínez-Romero et al., 2002), plum (Pérez-Vicente et al., 2002; Serrano et al., 2003), and pomegranate (Mirdehghan et al., 2007a), the increased PA concentration being evident after treatment and remaining during postharvest storage.

4.3 Bioactive Constituents With Antioxidant Activity

Fruits and vegetables contain a wide range of phytochemical compounds that exhibit antioxidant activity, the most common being phenolics, including anthocyanins, carotenoids, vitamins (C and E), and glucosinolates (Valero and Serrano, 2013), which are related with the protective effects of fruit consumption against several chronic diseases associated with aging including atherosclerosis, cardiovascular diseases, several types of cancer, cataracts, blood pressure increase, ulcers, neurodegenerative diseases, brain and immune dysfunction, and even against bacterial and viral diseases (Martin et al., 2013; Nile and Park, 2014). There is little information about the effect of PA treatment on the concentration of bioactive compounds in fruits. The first evidence of the in vivo role of PAs in the fruit content of bioactive compounds was obtained with transgenic tomatoes having the yeast *SAMDC* gene, in which Spd and Spm concentrations in ripe fruits were higher than in controls and these red ripe transgenic tomatoes accumulated threefold more lycopene than did the red fruits from the parental lines (Mehta et al., 2002). Accordingly, tomato plants overexpressing the mouse *ODC* gene produced fruits with higher PA concentration as compared with fruits from untransformed plants, these transgenic fruits having also higher concentration of lycopene and ascorbic acid (Pandey et al., 2015). Similarly, higher levels of PAs as well as ascorbic acid and lycopene were found in transgenic tomatoes overexpressing the human *SAMDC* gene, the higher lycopene accumulation being attributed to elevated levels of lycopene gene transcripts in transgenic tomatoes, while the higher ascorbic acid content could be due to the lower ethylene production of these tomatoes, since it is used as a cofactor for the ACO enzyme (Madhulatha et al., 2014). Moreover, treatments with Put, Spd, or Spm at concentrations of 0.01, 0.1, and 1 mM of mango trees by foliar spraying at final fruit set stage led to fruits with significantly higher total carotenoids in the pulp at harvest time as compared with fruits from control trees, the maximum increase being observed with Put treatments (95%) followed by Spd (33%) (Malik and Singh, 2006). This is of special significance as carotenoids including lycopene as well as ascorbic acid are bioactive compounds with high antioxidant activity and beneficial effects for human health (Friedman, 2013; Martin et al., 2013; Nile and Park, 2014).

On the other hand, it has been reported that in Mollar de Elche pomegranate arils, the application of 1 mM of Put or Spd, either by pressure infiltration or immersion, was effective in maintaining the concentration of total anthocyanins at higher levels than in control fruits during storage, these effects being similar in Put- and Spd-treated fruits, independently of the method of application (Mirdehghan et al., 2007c). Accordingly, Mridula pomegranate treated with 2 mM Put by the immersion method retained higher anthocyanin, ascorbic acid, and tannin concentrations and antioxidant activity than control fruits, the effects being increased when Put was applied in combination with carnauba wax (Barman et al., 2014). In grape berries, total anthocyanin content showed an increasing trend up to 45 days and then declined rapidly during next 30 days of storage, while in Spm-treated berries at 0.5, 1, and 1.5 mM anthocyanin concentration was increased in a dose-dependent manner (Harindra Champa et al., 2015). Delaying of fruit skin color degradation when treated with Spm has been also reported in mangos by Malik and Singh (2005, 2006). The mechanism by which Put and Spd induce these effects is still unknown, although they may be related to their antisenescent effects, which are allied to the suppression of membrane lipid peroxidation and maintenance of the integrity of membranes (Lester, 2000; Valero and Serrano, 2010). However, pre- or postharvest treatments of plums with Put led to reduced levels of total antioxidants after postharvest storage and were lower in treated plum than in controls (Khan et al., 2008), which could be due to the effect of Put on delaying the ripening process, since the bioactive compounds with antioxidant activity have been reported to increase during plum fruit ripening on trees and during postharvest storage (Díaz-Mula et al., 2009).

With respect to the effect of PA treatment on phenolic compounds, different results have been obtained, depending of the applied PA, concentration, and fruit species. Thus table grape Spm treatment at 0.5 and 1 mM retained higher total phenol content (TPC) over the control, while Spm at 1.5 mM resulted in significantly lower TPC (Harindra Champa et al., 2015). On the other hand, higher TPC as a consequence of Put and Spd treatments has been reported in pomegranate (Mirdehghan et al., 2007c). Accordingly, Put at concentrations of 1 and 2 mM applied as dipping treatment to table grape led to increased TPC, catechin, total quercetin, and antioxidant activity as compared with control berries (Shiri et al., 2013). On the contrary, Koushesh-saba et al. (2012) observed lower TPC in Put- and Spd-treated apricots than in controls. Thus the effects of PAs on TPC remain elusive.

On the other hand, the enhancement of hydrophilic total antioxidant activity found in pomegranate arils after PA treatments could be attributed to the PA capacity acting as effective scavengers of free radicals, and even to their role on the superoxide dismutase (SOD)/ascorbate–glutathione cycle (Mirdehghan et al., 2007c). On the contrary, pre- and postharvest Put application to Angelino plum led to a linear reduction in the levels of ascorbic acid, carotenoids, and TAA during postharvest storage, which were more pronounced with increased concentrations of Put and storage periods, these effects being ascribed to increased ascorbate oxidase activity (Khan et al., 2008), according to a previous report on pepper and tomato (Yahia et al., 2001). Thus more research is needed to clarify the effects of PA treatments on fruit functional compounds.

5 Polyamines and Chilling Injury

Storage at low temperature is widely used as a postharvest tool to delay fruit ripening and senescence processes and to maintain quality attributes. However, many tropical and subtropical fruits suffer physiological alterations know as chilling injury (CI) when stored at low but nonchilling temperatures, usually below 10–12°C depending on commodities. Chilling symptoms mainly develop during shelf life after removing fruits from low-temperature storage and are manifested as surface pitting and higher susceptibility to decay in pepper, zucchini, or pomegranate (Serrano et al., 1997, 1998; Mirdehghan et al., 2007b), flesh browning and mealiness in apricot, peach, and nectarines (Valero et al., 1997; Lurie and Crisosto, 2005), flesh browning and translucency in plums (Luo et al., 2011), or flesh browning and water-soaked appearance in bamboo shoots (Luo et al., 2012). Other reported CI symptoms are failure of fruit to ripen, or uneven or slow ripening, accelerated senescence and ethylene production, shortened storage or shelf life, compositional changes affecting flavor and texture, loss of growth or sprouting capability, wilting, and increased decay due to leakage of plant metabolites, which encourage growth of microorganisms, especially fungi (Valero and Serrano, 2010). Development of these chilling disorders reduces fruit quality and consumer acceptance, and then the onset of CI symptoms becomes an economically important postharvest problem that determines the postharvest storage potential of the fruit. In this sense, scientific researchers are focused on developing new technologies based on natural, safe, and environmentally friendly compounds to prevent or alleviate CI symptoms, satisfying the consumer's concerns about chemical residues in fruits and vegetables along with legal restriction on the use of synthetic chemicals.

Cell membranes are the first cell structures affected by CI, which change from a flexible liquid-crystalline phase to a solid-gel structure at chilling temperatures, leading to losses of the cell membrane semipermeability and functionality (Rui et al., 2010).

In addition, disorganization of mitochondria and chloroplast occurs, which sets off a cascade of secondary reactions, including ethylene production, increased respiration, reduced photosynthesis, and interference with energy production, accumulation of toxic compounds, such as ethanol and acetaldehyde, and altered cellular structure (Kratsch and Wise, 2000). In pomegranate skin it has been found that membrane lipid composition changes during storage, with losses of saturated and unsaturated fatty acids and reduction in the ratio of unsaturated/saturated fatty acids, affecting membrane permeability and causing leakage of intracellular water, ions, and metabolites, which can be monitored by determining electrolyte leakage (EL) (Mirdehghan et al., 2007b). Thus EL is a measurement of loss of semipermeability of cell membranes, which increases as a consequence of membrane damage, and has been widely used as an indicator of CI (Mirdehghan et al., 2007b; Rui et al., 2010; Sayyari et al., 2009). Another indicator of the structural integrity of the plant membranes is malondialdehyde (MDA), which is a secondary end product of the oxidation of the membrane polyunsaturated fatty acid, and increases in chilling injured fruit and vegetable tissues (Luo et al., 2011, 2012; Palma et al., 2015). In addition, increases in phospholipase-D and lipoxigenase activities, responsible for the degradation of unsaturated fatty acids, reduced cell membrane integrity and therefore increased CI impact (Aghdam et al., 2015). Membrane lipid peroxidation can be also stimulated by radical oxygen species (ROS) generated as a consequence of chilling stress (Sevillano et al., 2009).

PAs, as polycationic molecules at physiological pH, can bind strongly to anionic components of the cell membranes, such as phospholipids, leading to stabilization of the bilayer surface. Then, as the maintenance of membrane stability at low temperature is an important factor for plant resistance to cold stress and given the relationship between PAs and membrane protection, the possible role of PAs on protecting fruit tissues against CI is of great interest (Mirdehghan et al., 2007a, 2007b; Groppa and Benavides, 2008; Zhang et al., 2010). In addition, PAs exhibit antioxidant activity by scavenging ROS, leading to enhanced membrane stability and integrity under CI stress (Hussain et al., 2011). In this sense, increases in Put concentration have been found in several fruits suffering CI, such as lemon, orange, lime, grapefruit, pepper, tomato, peach, pepino, and zucchini, among others (Serrano et al., 1997, 1998; Martínez-Romero et al., 2003; González-Aguilar et al., 2000; Shang et al., 2011; Zhang et al., 2013a). In addition, in peach fruit it was shown that wooliness was associated with an increase in Spd concentration (Valero et al., 1997). Moreover, increases in Spd concentration have been also reported in pomegranate skin in storage, being associated with enhanced CI symptoms (Mirdehghan et al., 2007b). Accordingly, Put and Spd concentrations increased in bamboo shoots in storage at 1°C and they were correlated with CI incidence (Luo et al., 2012). Such results support the proposal that accumulation of Put and/or Spd or Spm in tissues seems to be a general response of fruit to chilling temperatures, although they do not indicate whether the increase in Put or Spd is a protective response to CI or whether Put or Spd themselves are the result of the stress-induced injury.

In this sense, it has been shown that prestorage treatments that reduce CI are related with increased PA concentration in fruit tissues. Thus CO_2 treatments of zucchini before storage reduced CI throughout increases in PA levels (Serrano et al., 1998). Accordingly, pretreatment at 25°C for 2 days before cold storage reduced CI in peach by elevating all the three PA levels (Xu et al., 2005). In Fortune mandarins, temperature pretreatments for 3 days above 20°C increased progressively both Put and Spd levels in flavedo, as did temperature treatment, and reduced CI (González-Aguilar et al., 2000). Heat treatments have been also effective on decreasing CI by increasing PA concentration in a wide range of fruits (Aghdam and Bodbodak, 2014). Likewise, in plum fruits, CI symptoms were reduced by prestorage treatment at 45 and 50°C for 35 and 30 min, respectively, which also maintained increased PA levels (Abu-Kpawoh et al., 2002). Accordingly, heat treatment of pomegranate fruit led to a decrease in CI and an increase in Put and Spd concentrations in the skin during cold storage (Mirdehghan et al., 2007b). Additionally, the levels of sugars (glucose and fructose), organic acids (malic, citric, and oxalic acids), total phenolics, ascorbic acid, and anthocyanin remained also at higher concentrations in arils from treated fruits, showing that with this simple and noncontaminant technology, the functional and nutritive properties, after long periods of storage, could then be even greater than in recently harvested fruits (Mirdehghan et al., 2006). The induction of resistance to CI by heat treatment associated with increased Put concentration has also been reported in peach (Cao et al., 2010). On the other hand, tomato hot air treatment at 38°C for 12 h before storage at 2°C reduced CI symptoms and enhanced the accumulation of endogenous Put, due to the activation of arginine catabolism, by enhancing transcript levels of ADC, ODC, OAT, and arginase (Zhang et al., 2013a). Similarly, arginine treatment of tomato fruit reduced CI and enhanced accumulation of PAs, especially Put, as well as proline and nitric oxide concentrations, which resulted from the increased activities of these arginine catabolic enzymes (Zhang et al., 2013b). As stated in earlier, previous studies showed that ODC plays a main role in cell division and ADC in plant responses to stress, although these results provide evidence that both ADC and ODC pathways may account for PA accumulation under chilling conditions.

On the other hand, UV-C irradiation (for 3, 5, or 10 min) of peach fruits before storage at 5°C significantly reduced CI after 14 and 21 days of cold storage + 7 days at 20°C, this effect being related with higher accumulation of Spd and Spm and with the additional benefit of reducing fruit decay and softening (Gonzalez-Aguilar et al., 2004). Other natural compounds, such as salicylic acid (SA), acetyl salicylic acid (ASA), methyl salicylate (MeSa), and methyl jasmonate (MeJa), have been reported as easy to apply treatments for alleviating CI in fruits, vegetables, and even in cut flowers (Asghari and Aghdam, 2010; Aghdam and Bodbodak, 2013). For instance, Zhang et al. (2011) observed that tomato postharvest treatment with 0.05 mM MeSa for 12 h alleviated CI by increasing gene expression and enzymatic activity of arginase, ODC, and ADC, leading to higher Put, Spd, and Spm concentration in MeSa-treated fruit than in controls. Similar results have been found in cherry tomato after treatment with 0.05 mM MeJa for 12 h before storage at chilling temperature (Zhang et al., 2012). Accordingly, SA treatment (at 1.5 mM for 10 min) significantly reduced CI in plums and this event was associated with enhanced endogenous Put and Spd concentrations and led to reduction of MDA, indicating an improvement of cell membrane integrity, due to protection of cell membrane lipids from peroxidation (Luo et al., 2011). SA treatment led also to reduction in both respiration rate and ethylene production, with the additional benefit of delaying the postharvest ripening process of this climacteric fruit. SA (applied at 1 mM for 5 min) was also effective in reducing CI in peaches by increasing endogenous PA content (Put, Spd, and Spm), this effect being higher when SA treatment was combined with hot air (38°C for 12 h) treatment (Cao et al., 2010). In bamboo shoots, SA treatments (by dipping in 1 mM SA for 15 min) reduced CI symptoms, EL, MDA content, and disease incidence, while Put, Spd, and Spm increased in storage, these increases being higher than in control shoots (Luo et al., 2012). SA (at 0.7, 1.4, or 2 mM) treatments applied by dipping for 10 min in pomegranate fruit were highly effective on reducing CI on the husk, although the role of PAs on these effects has not yet been elucidated (Sayyari et al., 2009).

Since most of these treatments, which showed beneficial effects in alleviating chilling injury, were accompanied by increases in PAs, a particular role for endogenous PAs in increasing fruit tolerance to cold stress could be proposed. Thus PAs could work as free radical scavengers, stabilizing membranes by means of ionic interactions to provide protection against chilling stress, this effect being greater as the number of positive charges per molecules is increased, that is, Spm > Spd > Put.

This hypothesis is supported by the fact that exogenous PA treatments after harvest but before cold storage decreased CI in chilling sensitive fruits, such as apple (Kramer et al., 1991), mango (Kondo et al., 2003; Nair and Singh, 2004), and zucchini (Martínez-Téllez et al., 2002). In zucchini fruits, Put treatment was more effective than those of Spd or Spm and its effects on improving fruit chilling tolerance have been attributed to enhancement of betaine and proline concentrations, which can act not only as osmoprotectants but also as a membrane stabilizer contributing to the stabilization and integrity of cellular membranes under chilling stress (Palma et al., 2015). Accordingly, CI was reduced in apricot fruits by Put and Spd treatments before storage at chilling temperatures, by increasing the activity of antioxidant enzymes, such as SOD, CAT, and peroxidase, which are involved in protecting plants from damage caused by ROS at low temperature (Koushesh-saba et al., 2012). Moreover, prestorage treatments of pomegranate with Put or Spd (1 mM), by immersion or pressure infiltration, decreased significantly the occurrence of CI after cold storage at chilling temperatures, which was related to increases in Put and Spd concentrations in the skin, these concentrations being three- and twofold higher, respectively, in treated than in control fruits (Mirdehghan et al., 2007a). This evidence suggests an activation of the PA biosynthesis pathway, with part of the exogenous Put being used to transform to Spd using DCSAM, while the increased concentration of Put after Spd treatment could be attributed to an upregulation of ADC, a key enzyme of one of the routes for Put biosynthesis. These treatments were also effective at maintaining the concentration of ascorbic acid, total phenolics, and total anthocyanins in the arils at higher levels than in control fruits, as well as the TAA, leading to increases in the health beneficial effects of fruit consumption (Mirdehghan et al., 2007c). In addition, 20 mM Spm spray treatment of whole branches of apple tree decreased low-temperature injuries of apple fruitlets, such as splitting and spotting, which are related to an increase in Put and Spd concentrations (Yoshikawa et al., 2007).

Thus the results presented here support the hypothesis that the PA treatments could induce acclimation of fruits to low temperature, and in turn protect them from CI. In this sense, PAs may be involved in reducing CI due to their ability to preserve membrane integrity, both by lowering the membrane phase transition temperature fluidity and by retarding lipid peroxidation, resulting in increased cell viability, due to their membrane-binding capacity and/or antioxidant properties. Thus the increases of PAs occurring in chilling injured fruits could be a natural defense mechanism of fruit tissues against this stress, although this effect itself may not be totally accurate if the increase in PAs is not high enough.

6   Concluding Remarks and Future Trends

The results of this chapter provide evidence for the numerous beneficial effects of the exogenous PA treatments, both at pre- and postharvest time in fruit quality attributes including their concentration in antioxidant compounds. However, commercial application is nowadays limited, since no specific regulations exist regarding the use of exogenous PAs in Europe. Nevertheless, in the United States a patent was filed many years ago (Law et al., 1988) for the use of PAs as a method of extending shelf life and enhancing the quality of fruits. Taking into account that PAs are naturally occurring molecules their application as pre- or postharvest treatment could be considered as an environmentally compatible tool as they can be metabolized by fruit cells. In addition, it should be pointed out that although exogenous application of PAs enhances their endogenous levels, the concentrations remain far lower than the toxic ones. Finally, more extensive metabolic profiling is needed in order to gain deeper insight into the nutritional attributes of PA-enriched/-treated fruit. We are only now beginning to understand their role in growth, development, and senescence through molecular genetics and modern biochemical approaches, and the elucidation of PA roles in modulating pre- and postharvest biology will contribute to the development of functional foods using modern biotechnology. Then, modern agriculture, which is searching for effective biological molecules with well-known metabolic effects but without toxicological effects, may have the answer in PAs.

References

Abd El-Migeed, M.M.M., Mostafa, E.A.M., Ashour, N.E., Hassan, H.S.A., Mohamed, D.M., Saleh, M.M.S., 2013. Effect of potassium and polyamine sprays on fruit set, fruit retention, yield and fruit quality of Amhat date palm. Int. Jo. Agric. Res. 8, 77–86.

Abu-Kpawoh, J.C., Xi, Y.E., Zhang, Y.Z., Jin, Y.F., 2002. Polyamine accumulation following hot-water dips influences chilling injury and decay in "Friar" plum fruit. J. Food Sci. 67, 2649–2653.

Aghdam, M., Asghari, M., Khorsandi, O., Mohayeji, M., 2015. Alleviation of postharvest chilling injury of tomato fruit by salicylic acid treatment. J. Food Sci. Technol. 51 (10), 2815–2820.

Aghdam, M.S., Bodbodak, S., 2013. Physiological and biochemical mechanisms regulating chilling tolerance in fruits and vegetables under postharvest salicylates and jasmonates treatments. Sci. Hortic. 156, 73–85.

Aghdam, M.S., Bodbodak, S., 2014. Postharvest heat treatment for mitigation of chilling injury in fruits and vegetables. Food Bioprocess Technol. 7, 37–53.

Agudelo-Romero, P., Bortolloti, C., Pais, M.S., Tiburcio, A.F., Fortes, A.M., 2013. Study of polyamines during grape ripening indicate an important role of polyamine catabolism. Plant Physiol. Biochem. 67, 105–119.

Alburquerque, N., Egea, J., Burgos, L., Martínez-Romero, D., Valero, D., Serrano, M., 2006. The influence of polyamines on apricot ovary development and fruit set. Ann. Appl. Biol. 149, 27–33.

Ali, E.A., Sarrwy, S.M.A., Hassan, H.S.A., 2010. Improving Canino apricot trees productivity by foliar spraying with polyamines. J. Appl. Sci. Res. 6, 1359–1365.

Asghari, M., Aghdam, M.S., 2010. Impact of salicylic acid on post-harvest physiology of horticultural crops. Trend Food Sci. Technol. 21, 502–509.

Aziz, A., Brun, O., Audran, J.C., 2001. Involvement of polyamines in the control of fruitlet physiological abscission in grapevine (*Vitis vinifera*). Physiol. Plant. 113, 50–58.

Barman, K., Asrey, R., Pal, R.K., Kaur, C., Jha, S.K., 2014. Influence of putrescine and carnauba wax on functional and sensory quality of pomegranate (*Punica granatum* L.) fruits during storage. J. Food Sci. Technol. 51, 111–117.

Basiouny, F.M., 1996. Blueberry fruit quality and storability influenced by postharvest application of polyamines and heat treatments. Proc. Florida State Hortic. Soc. 109, 269–272.

Bianchi, M., Polticelli, F., Ascenzi, P., Botta, M., Federico, R., Mariottini, P., Cona, A., 2006. Inhibition of polyamine and spermine oxidases by polyamine analogues. FEBS J. 273, 1115–1123.

Bregoli, A.M., Scaramagli, S., Costa, G., Sabatini, E., Ziosi, V., Biondi, S., Torrigiani, P., 2002. Peach (*Prunus persica*) fruit ripening: aminoetoxyvinil-glycine (AVG) and exogenous polyamines affect ethylene emission and flesh firmness. Physiol. Plant. 114, 472–481.

Bregoli, A.M., Ziosi, V., Biondi, S., Claudio, B., Costa, G., Torrigiani, P., 2006. A comparison between intact fruit and fruit explants to study the effect of polyamines and aminoethoxyvinylglycine (AVG) on fruit ripening in peach and nectarine (*Prunus persica* L. Batch). Postharvest Biol. Technol. 42, 31–40.

Cao, S., Hu, Z., Zheng, Y., Lu, B., 2010. Synergistic effect of heat treatment and salicylic acid on alleviating internal browning in cold-stored peach fruit. Postharvest Biol. Technol. 58, 93–97.

Cao, S., Yang, Z., Zheng, Y., 2012. Effect of 1-methylcyclopene on senescence and quality maintenance of green bell pepper fruit during storage at 20°C. Postharvest Biol. Technol. 70, 1–6.

Cherian, S., Figueroa, C.R., Nair, H., 2014. "Movers and shakers" in the regulation of fruit ripening: a cross-dissection of climacteric versus non-climacteric fruit. J. Exp. Bot. 65, 4705–4722.

De Dios, P., Matilla, A.J., Gallardo, M., 2006. Flower fertilization and fruit development prompt changes in free polyamines and ethylene in damson plum (*Prunus insititia* L.). J. Plant Physiol. 163, 86–97.

Deyman, K.L., Brikis, C.J., Bozzo, G.G., Shelp, B.J., 2014. Impact of 1-methylcyclopropene and controlled atmosphere storage on polyamine and 4-aminobutyrate levels in "Empire" apple fruit. Front. Plant Sci. 5, 144.

Díaz-Mula, H.M., Zapata, P.J., Guillén, F., Martínez-Romero, D., Castillo, S., Serrano, M., Valero, D., 2009. Changes in hydrophilic and lipophilic antioxidant activity and related bioactive compounds during postharvest storage of yellow and purple plum cultivars. Postharvest Biol. Technol. 51, 354–363.

Escribano, M.I., Merodio, C., 1994. The relevance of polyamine levels in cherimoya (*Annona cherimola* Mill.) fruit ripening. J. Plant Physiol. 143, 207–212.

Franco-Mora, O., Tanabe, K., Itai, A., Tamura, F., Itamura, H., 2005a. Relationship between endogenous free polyamine content and ethylene evolution during fruit growth and ripening of Japanese pear (*Pyrus pyrifolia* Nakai). J. Japan. Soc. Hortic. Sci. 74, 221–227.

Franco-Mora, O., Tanabe, K., Tamura, F., Itai, A., 2005b. Effects of putrescine application on fruit set in "Housui" Japanese pear (*Pyrus pyrifolia* Nakai). Sci. Hortic. 104, 265–273.

Friedman, M., 2013. Anticarcinogenic, cardioprotective, and other health benefits of tomato compounds lycopene, α-tomatine, and tomatidine in pure form and in fresh and processed tomatoes. J. Agric. Food Chem. 61, 9534–9550.

Gonzalez-Aguilar, G., Wang, C.Y., Buta, G.J., 2004. UV-C irradiation reduces breakdown and chilling injury of peaches during cold storage. J. Sci. Food Agric. 84, 415–422.

González-Aguilar, G.A., Zacarías, L., Perez-Amador, M.A., Carbonell, J., Lafuente, M.T., 2000. Polyamine content and chilling susceptibility are affected by seasonal changes in temperature and by conditioning temperature in cold-stored "Fortune" mandarin fruit. Physiol. Plant. 108, 140–146.

Groppa, M.D., Benavides, M.P., 2008. Polyamines and abiotic stress: recent advances. Amino Acids 34, 35–45.

Harindra Champa, W.A., Gill, M.I.S., Mahajan, B.V.C., Bedi, S., 2015. Exogenous treatment of spermine to maintain quality and extend postharvest life of table grapes (*Vitis vinifera* L.) cv. Flame Seedless under low temperature storage. LWT—Food Sci. Technol. 60, 412–419.

Hussain, S.S., Ali, M., Ahmad, M., Siddique, K.H.M., 2011. Polyamines: natural and engineered abiotic and biotic stress tolerance in plants. Biotechnol. Adv. 29, 300–311.

Khan, A.S., Singh, Z., Abbasi, N.A., Swinny, E.E., 2008. Pre- or post-harvest applications of putrescine at low temperature storage affect fruit ripening and quality of "Angelino" plum. J. Sci. Food Agric. 88, 1686–1695.

Kondo, S., Ponrod, W., Sutthiwal, S., 2003. Polyamines in developing mangosteens and their relationship to postharvest chilling injury. J. Japan. Soc. Hortic. Sci. 72, 318–320.

Koushesh-saba, M., Arzani, K., Barzegar, M., 2012. Postharvest polyamine application alleviates chilling injury and affects apricot storage ability. J. Agric. Food Chem. 60, 8947–8953.

Kramer, G.F., Wang, C.Y., Conway, W.S., 1991. Inhibition of softening by polyamine application in "Golden Delicious" and "McIntosh" apples. J. Am. Soc. Hortic. Sci. 116, 813–817.

Kratsch, H.A., Wise, R.R., 2000. The ultrastructure of chilling stress. Plant Cell Environ. 23, 337–350.

Kusano, T., Yamaguchi, K., Berberich, T., Takahashi, Y., 2007. Advances in polyamine research in 2007. J. Plant Res. 120, 345–350.

Kushad, M.M., Yelenosky, G., Knight, R., 1988. Interrelationship of polyamine and ethylene biosynthesis during avocado fruit development and ripening. Plant Physiol. 87, 463–467.

Law, D.M., Davies, P.J., Mutschler, M.A., 1988. Method of extending shelf life and enhancing keeping quality of fruits. US patent 4,957,757.

Lester, G.E., 2000. Polyamines and their cellular anti-senescence properties in "Honey Dew" muskmelon fruit. Plant Sci. 160, 105–112.

Liu, J., Nada, K., Pang, X., Honda, C., Kitashiba, H., Moriguchi, T., 2006b. Role of polyamines in peach fruit development and storage. Tree Physiol. 26, 791–798.

Liu, J.H., Honda, C., Moriguchi, T., 2006a. Review: Involvement of polyamines in floral and fruit development. Japan Agric. Res. Q. 40, 51–58.

Luo, Z., Wu, X., Xie, Y., Chen, C., 2012. Alleviation of chilling injury and browning of postharvest bamboo shoot by salicylic acid treatment. Food Chem. 131, 456–461.

Luo, Z., Chen, C., Xie, J., 2011. Effect of salicylic acid treatment on alleviating postharvest chilling injury of "Qingnai" plum fruit. Postharvest Biol. Technol. 62, 115–120.

Lurie, S., Crisosto, C.H., 2005. Chilling injury in peach and nectarine. Postharvest Biol. Technol. 37, 195–208.

Madhulatha, P., Gupta, A., Gupta, S., Kumar, A., Pal, R.K., Rajam, M.V., 2014. Fruit-specific over-expression of human S-adenosylmethionine decarboxylase gene results in polyamine accumulation and affects diverse aspects of tomato fruit development and quality. J. Plant Biochem. Biotechnol. 23, 151–160.

Malik, A.U., Singh, Z., 2005. Pre-storage application of polyamines improves shelf-life and fruit quality of mango. J. Hortic. Sci. Biotechnol. 80, 363–369.

Malik, A.U., Singh, Z., 2006. Improved fruit retention, yield and fruit quality in mango with exogenous application of polyamines. Sci. Hortic. 110, 167–174.

Martin, C., Zhang, Y., Tonelli, C., Petroni, K., 2013. Plants, Diet, and Health. Annu. Rev. Plant Biol. 64, 19–46.

Martínez-Madrid, M.C., Serrano, M., Pretel, M.T., Martiínez-Reina, G., Romojaro, F., 2000. Note. The ripening of *Prunus persica* fruits with a dominant flat allele. Food Sci. Technol. Int. 6, 399–405.

Martínez-Madrid, M.C., Serrano, M., Riquelme, F., Romojaro, F., 1996. Polyamines, abscisic acid and ethylene production in tomato fruit. Phytochemistry 43, 323–326.

Martínez-Romero, D., Serrano, M., Valero, D., 2003. Physiological changes in pepino (*Solanum muricatum* Ait.) fruit stored at chilling and non-chilling temperatures. Postharvest Biol. Technol. 30, 177–186.

Martínez-Romero, D., Serrano, M., Carbonell, A., Burgos, L., Riquelme, F., Valero, D., 2002. Effects of postharvest putrescine treatment on extending shelf life and reducing mechanical damage in apricot. J. Sci. Food Agric. 67, 1706–1712.

Martínez-Romero, D., Valero, D., Serrano, M., Burló, F., Carbonell, A., Burgos, L., Riquelme, F., 2000. Exogenous polyamines and gibberellic acid effects on peach (*Prunus persica* L.) storability improvement. J. Food Sci. 65, 288–294.

Martínez-Téllez, M.A., Ramos-Clamont, M.G., Gardena, A.A., Vargas-Arispuro, I., 2002. Effect of infiltrated polyamines on polygalacturonase activity and chilling injury responses in zucchini squash (*Cucurbita pepo* L). Biochem. Biophys. Res. Commun. 295, 98–101.

Mehta, R.A., Cassol, T., Li, N., Ali, N., Handa, A.K., Mattoo, A.K., 2002. Engineered polyamine accumulation in tomato enhances phytonutrient content, juice quality, and vine life. Nat. Biotechnol. 20, 613–618.

Mirdehghan, S.H., Rahemi, M., Castillo, S., Martínez-Romero, D., Serrano, M., Valero, D., 2007a. Pre-storage application of polyamines by pressure or immersion improves shelf-life of pomegranate stored at chilling temperature by increasing endogenous polyamine levels. Postharvest Biol. Technol. 44, 26–33.

Mirdehghan, S.H., Rahemi, M., Martínez-Romero, D., Guillén, F., Valverde, J.M., Zapata, P.J., Serrano, M., Valero, D., 2007b. Reduction of pomegranate chilling injury during storage after heat treatment: role of polyamines. Postharvest Biol. Technol. 44, 19–25.

Mirdehghan, S.H., Rahemi, M., Serrano, M., Guillén, F., Martínez-Romero, D., Valero, D., 2007c. The application of polyamines by pressure or immersion as a tool to maintain functional properties in stored pomegranates arils. J. Agric. Food Chem. 55, 755–760.

Mirdehghan, S.H., Rahemi, M., Serrano, M., Guillén, F., Martínez-Romero, D., Valero, D., 2006. Prestorage heat treatment to maintain nutritive and functional properties during postharvest cold storage of pomegranate. J. Agric. Food Chem. 54, 8495–8500.

Nair, S., Singh, Z., 2004. Chilling injury in mango fruit in relation to biosynthesis of free polyamines. J. Hortic. Sci. Biotechnol. 79, 515–522.

Nile, S.H., Park, S.W., 2014. Edible berries: bioactive components and their effect on human health. Nutrition 30, 134–144.

Palma, F., Carvajal, F., Ramos, J.M., Jamilena, M., Garrido, D., 2015. Effect of putrescine application on maintenance of zucchini fruit quality during cold storage: contribution of GABA shunt and other related nitrogen metabolites. Postharvest Biol. Technol. 99, 131–140.

Paksasorn, A., Hayasaka, T., Matsui, H., Ohara, H., Hirata, N., 1995. Relationship of polyamine content to ACC content and ethylene evolution in Japanese apricot fruit. J. Japan. Soc. Hortic. Sci. 63, 761–766.

Pandey, R., Gupta, A., Chowdhary, A., Pal, R.K., Rajam, M.V., 2015. Over-expression of mouse ornithine decarboxylase gene under the control of fruit-specific promoter enhances fruit quality in tomato. Plant Mol. Biol. 87, 249–260.

Pérez-Vicente, A., Martínez-Romero, D., Carbonell, A., Serrano, M., Riquelme, F., Guillén, F., Valero, D., 2002. Role of polyamines in extending shelf life and the reduction of mechanical damage during plum (*Prunus salicina* Lindl) storage. Postharvest Biol. Technol. 25, 25–32.

Ponappa, T., Miller, A.R., 1996. Polyamines in normal and auxin-induced strawberry fruit development. Physiol. Plant. 98, 447–454.

Pretel, M.T., Serrano, M., Amorós, A., Riquelme, F., Romojaro, F., 1995. Non-involvement of ACC and ACC oxidase activity in pepper fruit ripening. Postharvest Biol. Technol. 5, 295–302.

Rui, H., Cao, S., Shang, H., Jin, P., Wang, K., Zheng, Y., 2010. Effects of heat treatment on internal browning and membrane fatty acid in loquat fruit in response to chilling stress. J. Sci. Food Agric. 90, 1557–1561.

Sauter, M., Moffatt, B., Saechao, M.C., Hell, R., Wirtz, M., 2013. Methionine salvage and S-adenosylmethionine: essential links between sulfur, ethylene and polyamine biosynthesis. Biochem. J. 451, 145–154.

Sayyari, M., Babalar, M., Kalantari, S., Serrano, M., Valero, D., 2009. Effect of salicylic acid treatment on reducing chilling injury in stored pomegranates. Postharvest Biol. Technol. 53, 152–154.

Serrano, M., Martínez-Romero, D., Guillén, F., Valero, D., 2003. Effects of exogenous putrescine on improving shelf life of four plum cultivars. Postharvest Biol. Technol. 30, 259–271.

Serrano, M., Díaz-Mula, H.M., Valero, D., 2011. Antioxidant compounds in fruits and vegetables and changes during postharvest storage and processing. Stewart Postharvest Rev. 2011 1, 1.

Serrano, M., Martínez-Madrid, M.C., Pretel, M.T., Riquelme, F., Romojaro, F., 1997. Modified atmosphere packaging minimizes increases in putrescine and abscisic acid levels caused by chilling injury in pepper fruit. J. Agric. Food Chem. 45, 1668–1672.

Serrano, M., Pretel, M.T., Martínez-Madrid, M.C., Romojaro, F., Riquelme, F., 1998. CO_2 treatment of zucchini squash reduces chilling-induced physiological changes. J. Agric. Food Chem. 46, 2465–2468.

Sevillano, L., Sanchez-Ballesta, M.T., Romojaro, F., Flores, F.B., 2009. Physiological, hormonal and molecular mechanisms regulating chilling injury in horticultural species. Postharvest technologies applied to reduce its impact. J. Sci. Food Agric. 89, 555–573.

Shang, H., Cao, S., Yang, Z., Cai, Y., Zheng, Y., 2011. Effect of exogenous gamma-aminobutyric acid treatment on proline accumulation and chilling injury in peach fruit after long-term cold storage. J. Agric. Food Chem. 59, 1264–1268.

Shiri, M.A., Ghasemnezhad, M., Bakhshi, D., Sarikhani, H., 2013. Effect of postharvest putrescine application and chitosan coating on maintaining quality of table grape cv. "shahroudi" during long-term storage. J. Food Process. Preserv. 37, 999–1007.

Tiburcio, A.F., Altabella, T., Bitrián, M., Alcázar, R., 2014. The roles of polyamines during the lifespan of plants: from development to stress. Planta 240, 1–18.

Torrigiani, P., Bregoli, A.M., Ziosi, V., Scaramagli, S., Ciriaci, T., Rasori, A., Biondi, S., Costa, G., 2004. Pre-harvest polyamine and aminoethoxyvinylglycine (AVG) applications modulate fruit ripening in Stark Red Gold nectarines (*Prunus persica* L. Batsch). Postharvest Biol. Technol. 33, 293–308.

Torrigiani, P., Bressanin, D., Beatriz Ruiz, K., Tadiello, A., Trainotti, L., Bonghi, C., Ziosi, V., Costa, G., 2012. Spermidine application to young developing peach fruits leads to a slowing down of ripening by impairing ripening-related ethylene and auxin metabolism and signaling. Physiol. Plant. 146, 86–98.

Valero, D., Serrano, M., 2010. Postharvest Biology and Technology for Preserving Fruit Quality. CRC/Taylor & Francis, Boca Raton.

Valero, D., Serrano, M., 2013. Growth and ripening stage at harvest modulates postharvest quality and bioactive compounds with antioxidant activity. Stewart Postharvest Rev. 2013 3, 5.

Valero, D., Martínez-Romero, D., Serrano, M., 2002. The role of polyamines in the improvement of the shelf life of fruit. Trends Food Sci. Technol. 13, 228–234.

Valero, D., Serrano, M., Martínez-Madrid, M.C., Riquelme, F., 1997. Polyamines, ethylene, and physicochemical changes in low-temperature-stored peach (*Prunus persica* L. Cv. Maycrest). J. Agric. Food Chem. 45, 3406–3410.

Van de Poel, B., Bulens, I., Oppermann, Y., Hertog, M.L.A.T.M., Nicolai, B.M., Sauter, M., Geeraer, A.H., 2013. S-Adenosyl-ʟ-methionine usage during climacteric ripening of tomato in relation to ethylene and polyamine biosynthesis and transmethylation capacity. Physiol. Plant. 148, 176–188.

Villa-Rodriguez, J.A., Palafox-Carlos, H., Yahia, E.M., Ayala-Zavala, J.F., Gonzalez-Aguilar, G.A., 2015. Maintaining antioxidant potential of fresh fruits and vegetables after harvest. Crit. Rev. Food Sci. Nutr. 55, 806–822.

Wang, C.Y., Conway, W.S., Abbott, J.A., Kramer, G.F., Sams, C.E., 1993. Postharvest infiltration of polyamines and calcium influences ethylene production and texture changes in "Golden Delicious" apples. J. Am. Soc. Hortic. Sci. 118, 801–806.

Xu, C., Jin, Z., Yang, S., 2005. Polyamines induced by heat treatment before cold-storage reduce mealiness and decay in peach fruit. J. Hortic. Sci. Biotechnol. 80, 557–560.

Yahia, E.M., Contreras-Padilla, M., González-Aguilar, G., 2001. Ascorbic acid content in relation to ascorbic acid oxidase and polyamine content in tomato and bell pepper fruits during development, maturation and senescence. Lebensmmittel Wissenschaft und Technologie 34, 452–457.

Yoshikawa, H., Honda, C., Kondo, S., 2007. Effect of low-temperature stress on abscisic acid, jasmonates, and polyamines in apples. Plant Growth Reg. 52, 199–206.

Zhang, X., Shen, L., Li, F., Meng, D., Sheng, J., 2013a. Hot air treatment-induced arginine catabolism is associated with elevated polyamines and proline levels and alleviates chilling injury in postharvest tomato fruit. J. Sci. Food Agric. 93, 3245–3251.

Zhang, X., Shen, L., Li, F., Meng, D., Sheng, J., 2013b. Amelioration of chilling stress by arginine in tomato fruit: changes in endogenous arginine catabolism. Postharvest Biol. Technol. 76, 106–111.

Zhang, X., Shen, L., Li, F., Meng, D., Sheng, J., 2011. Methyl salicylate-induced arginine catabolism is associated with up-regulation of polyamine and nitric oxide levels and improves chilling tolerance in cherry tomato fruit. J. Agric. Food Chem. 59, 9351–9357.

Zhang, X., Shen, L., Li, F., Zhang, Y., Meng, D., Sheng, J., 2010. Up-regulating arginase contributes to amelioration of chilling stress and the antioxidant system in cherry tomato fruits. J. Sci. Food Agric. 90, 2195–2202.

Zhang, X., Sheng, J., Li, F., Meng, D., Shen, L., 2012. Methyl jasmonate alters arginine catabolism and improves postharvest chilling tolerance in cherry tomato fruit. Postharvest Biol. Technol. 64, 160–167.

Ziosi, V., Bregoli, A.M., Bonghi, C., Fossati, T., Biondi, S., Costa, G., Torrigiani, P., 2006. Transcription of ethylene perception and biosynthesis genes is altered by putrescine, spermidine and aminoethoxyvinylglycine (AVG) during ripening in peach fruit (*Prunus persica*). New Phytol. 172, 229–238.

Zuzunaga, M., Serrano, M., Martínez-Romero, D., Valero, D., Riquelme, F., 2001. Comparative study of two plum (*Prunus salicina* Lindl.) cultivars during growth and ripening. Food Sci. Technol. Int. 7, 123–130.

8

IMPACT OF SALICYLIC ACID ON POSTHARVEST PHYSIOLOGY OF FRUITS AND VEGETABLES

Morteza Soleimani Aghdam*, Mohammadreza Asghari**, Mesbah Babalar*, Mohammad Ali Askari Sarcheshmeh*

*University of Tehran, Department of Horticultural Science, College of Agriculture and Natural Resource, Karaj, Iran; **Urmia University, Department of Horticulture, Faculty of Agriculture, Urmia, Iran

1   Introduction

Fresh fruits and vegetables, as very important suppliers of human health essential nutrients, are perishable and their quality is impacted by both abiotic and biotic stresses. During postharvest life, due to internal and external factors, chemical and physical changes occur in fresh fruits and vegetables, which may result in serious losses in nutritional and sensory quality. Chilling injury (CI) as an abiotic stress during storage of fruits and vegetables, which also greatly increases susceptibility to decay, leads to economic losses (Yang et al., 2013).

In order to enhance the natural resistance of fruits and vegetables against postharvest stresses and also maintain fresh products' sensory and nutritional quality, which in turn will extend postharvest life, use of environmentally friendly technologies such as salicylic acid (SA) as a natural and safe signaling molecule has been recommended. SA and its natural analog acetyl salicylic acid (ASA) have been shown to exhibit a high potential in delaying ripening, enhancing quality, and controlling postharvest losses of fruits and vegetables (Asghari and Aghdam, 2010). Moreover, dietary salicylates from fruits and vegetables are described as bioactive molecules with health care potentials and are considered as generally recognized as safe (GRAS) (Hooper and Cassidy, 2006). Both pre- and postharvest treatment with SA and ASA in extending shelf life and maintaining quality of harvested fruits and vegetables has been investigated and developed for commercial uses. The common dipping technique is used for postharvest treatment

Eco-Friendly Technology for Postharvest Produce Quality. http://dx.doi.org/10.1016/B978-0-12-804313-4.00008-6
Copyright © 2016 Elsevier Inc. All rights reserved.

of fruits and vegetables. Dokhanieh et al. (2013) reported that the cornelian cherry fruit treated with SA exhibited significantly higher total phenolics, flavonoids, anthocyanins, and ascorbic acid (AA) contents and phenylalanine ammonia-lyase (PAL) enzyme activity. Also, DPPH• scavenging activity of the cornelian cherry fruit was significantly increased by SA treatment. Sayyari et al. (2011a) reported that the treatment of pomegranate fruit with ASA was effective in maintaining higher contents of sugars and organic acids, bioactive compounds (total phenolics and anthocyanins) and total antioxidant activity (TAA) in both hydrophilic (H-TAA) and lipophilic (L-TAA) fractions. Sayyari et al. (2011b) reported that the methyl salicylate (MeSA) and methyl jasmonate (MeJA) treatments not only alleviate CI in pomegranate fruit but also maintain fruit nutritional quality during cold storage. MeSA and MeJA treatments enhanced total phenolics and anthocyanins content in pomegranate fruit, which both contribute to higher total antioxidant activity. Innovative postharvest MeSA and MeJA vapor treatments not only alleviate CI but also enhance the nutritional quality of fruits and vegetables (Valero et al., 2015).

In addition to postharvest dipping, SA can be used by spraying onto and adding to growth medium as approaches used for preharvest treatments. Babalar et al. (2007) suggested that the use of preharvest treatment in combination with postharvest application of SA was the effective strategy for reducing fungal decay and maintaining overall quality of strawberry fruit. Giménez et al. (2014) reported that preharvest treatment of sweet cherries with SA at 0.5 mM and ASA at 1 mM has been significantly effective in enhancing total phenolics and total anthocyanins, as well as hydrophilic and lipophilic antioxidant activity of cherries at commercial harvest.

2 Salicylates: Potential Regulators of Fruit Ripening

Ethylene, a simple gaseous plant hormone, plays crucial roles in plant growth and development processes such as fruit ripening. In plants, methionine is converted to S-adenosyl-L-methionine (SAM) by SAM synthetase, which is associated with ATP consumption. Then, SAM is converted to 1-aminocyclopropane-1-carboxylic acid (ACC) by ACC synthase (ACS), which is encoded by the ACS gene family, whose genes are under developmental, environmental, and hormonal regulation. ACC is oxidized to ethylene by ACC oxidase (ACO), which requires iron and ascorbate as cofactors (Shi and Zhang, 2014). Srivastava and Dwivedi (2000) reported that SA treatment delayed banana fruit ripening by inhibition of ethylene biosynthesis or action. SA decreases ethylene biosynthesis by decreasing both ACS and ACO gene expression and also enzyme activity. Zhang et al. (2003) reported that ASA treatment led to decreasing ACO and ACS activity, which led to decrease in ethylene biosynthesis during kiwifruit ripening. According to the findings of Zhang et al. (2003), with progress in softening of kiwifruit stored at 20°C, the SA status declined, which was associated with increased lipoxygenase (LOX) activity and climacteric ethylene production. Superoxide free radical production by LOX not only directly leads to peroxidation of cell membrane lipids and malonyl dialdehyde (MDA) accumulation, but also plays a regulatory role in biosynthesis of ethylene by contributing in the conversion of ACC to ethylene (Xu et al., 2000). Xu et al. (2000) reported that treatment with SA reduced LOX activity in kiwifruit, which was associated with declined free radical generation as well as ethylene biosynthesis. LOX activity via production of superoxide radical positively regulates ethylene biosynthesis in apple and tomato fruits (Todd et al., 1990). Kiwifruit treated with ASA exhibited higher SA accumulation associated with lower LOX activity and superoxide free radical production, as well as lower ACS and ACO activities and ultimately delayed climacteric ethylene biosynthesis. Zhang et al. (2003) suggested that the higher endogenous fruit SA levels was associated with higher fruit firmness.

Yin et al. (2013) reported that ASA treatment decreased ethylene biosynthesis by decreasing ACC accumulation and ACS and ACO enzyme activity. In addition to ethylene biosynthesis, SA also interferes with ethylene signaling. Yin et al. (2013) reported that combination treatments of ASA and ethylene inhibited kiwifruit ripening and softening, suggesting that ASA not only decreases ethylene biosynthesis but also inhibits the perception of exogenous ethylene. They demonstrated that ASA suppresses ethylene-induced expression of *AdETR1*, *AdETR2*, *AdETR3*, *AdERF6*, *AdERF10*, *AdERF11*, *AdERF13*, and *AdERF14*, supporting inhibitory effects of ASA on ethylene perception and signaling. According to the findings of Hong et al. (2014), both pre- and postharvest SA and nitric oxide (NO) treatments have been shown to inhibit the expression of ethylene biosynthesis and signaling genes (ACO and ERS1), and increase the expression of *ETR1* and *EIN2* genes in mango fruit during storage, which lead to decline in ethylene biosynthesis and delay in fruit ripening. Also, SA- and NO-treated fruit exhibited higher firmness as well as total soluble solids (TSS), TA, and AA. They suggested that SA and NO combined treatment could be a promising technology for delaying fruit ripening and maintaining the postharvest quality of mango fruit.

Fruit softening results from cell wall degradation by cell wall hydrolases such as polygalactosidases (PG), pectin methylesterases

(PME), β-galactosidase (β-Gal), and xylanase along with cell membrane deterioration (Srivastava and Dwivedi, 2000). As an ethylene inhibitor, SA delays fruit ripening and prevents fruit softening by reducing the activity of cell wall-degrading enzymes. Srivastava and Dwivedi (2000) reported that SA reduced PG, xylanase, and cellulase enzyme activity in harvested banana fruits, in which cellulase and PG were most sensitive to SA treatment. It has been suggested that SA maintains cell membrane integrity by reducing phospholipase D (PLD) and LOX activity and also enhancing antioxidant systems in harvested fruits and vegetables, which lead to reduced electrolyte leakage and MDA accumulation (Aghdam et al., 2013; Zhang et al., 2003; Mo et al., 2008; Aghdam and Bodbodak, 2013; Imran et al., 2007; Huang et al., 2008; Wei et al., 2011). It can be suggested that SA treatment maintains fruit firmness during postharvest life by reducing the activity of cell wall hydrolases and maintaining cell membrane integrity.

Accumulation of sucrose in fruit during development results from increasing sucrose phosphate synthase and sucrose phosphatase activity (Hubbard et al., 1991; Asghari and Aghdam, 2010). Sucrose is the common form of carbohydrate produced during photosynthesis and transferred from source to sink, leading to an increase in TSS in the fruit. During fruit ripening the decrease in nonreducing sugar content, mainly sucrose, is associated with an increase in reducing sugars fructose and glucose, which results from increasing invertase activity. Both sucrose phosphate synthase and invertase are activated by the action of ethylene during the ripening process (Langenkämper et al., 1998; Srivastava and Dwivedi, 2000; Asghari and Aghdam, 2010). As a potential inhibitor for ethylene biosynthesis and action, SA could delay the increase in reducing sugar content during storage, preventing the dramatic increase in respiration (Asghari and Aghdam, 2010). According to Aghdam et al. (2011), a lower TSS in kiwifruit treated with MeSA was concomitant with reduced ethylene production. Srivastava and Dwivedi (2000) reported that SA treatment leads to a decrease in invertase activity, which in turn decreases the reducing sugar content in banana fruit during ripening.

3 Salicylates Enhance the Nutritional Quality of Fruits and Vegetables

Fresh fruits and vegetables, as very important sources of human health essential nutrients, are perishable and their quality is impacted by both abiotic and biotic stresses. During postharvest life, due to internal and external factors, chemical and physical changes occur in fresh fruits and vegetables, which may result in serious losses in nutritional and sensory quality. To prevent these adverse effects caused by postharvest factors, use of environmentally friendly technologies such as SA and ASA, as natural and safe signaling molecules, has been recommended (Asghari and Aghdam, 2010). SA exhibits a high potential in delaying ripening, enhancing quality, and controlling postharvest losses of fruits and vegetables (Asghari and Aghdam, 2010). Phenolics have been associated with a lowered risk of heart disease via their action toward low-density lipoproteins (LDL) (Vinson et al., 2001). Also, phenolics are important because of their contribution to the nutritional quality attributes of fruits and vegetables, such as color, astringency, bitterness, and flavor. Phenolics and flavonoids are beneficial antioxidants and exhibit scavenging activity against reactive oxygen species (ROS) (Hassanpour et al., 2011). It has been reported that application of SA on *Thymus membranaceus* shoot culture has led to enhanced rosmarinic acid content and phenolic levels as well as DPPH•, FRAP, and ABTS+ scavenging activity, which in turn improved the antioxidant capacity (Pérez-Tortosa et al., 2012). Tareen et al. (2012) reported that SA enhanced DPPH• scavenging activity in peach fruit. They also demonstrated that the ROS scavenging activity increased by increasing SA concentrations. It has been reported that SA treatment selectively reduced the cytosine DNA methylation of the stilbene synthase (STS) gene and enhanced resveratrol accumulation in cell cultures of *Vitis amurensis* (Kiselev et al., 2015). T-resveratrol as a bioactive molecule is synthesized via the phenylpropanoid pathway, in which STS genes are the key enzymes. According to the findings of Sun et al. (2012), preharvest treatment of Chinese kale with SA enhanced the beneficial glucosinolates, total phenolics, and antioxidant capacity of this leafy vegetable. They suggested that the total antioxidant capacity in Chinese kale might be contributed to total phenolics and glucosinolates contents.

Dokhanieh et al. (2013) showed that the total phenolics and flavonoids contents in SA-treated cornelian cherry fruit were significantly higher than that of control fruit during storage. They suggested that the effect of SA on enhancing the total phenolics and flavonoids contents of cherry fruit was increased in a concentration-dependent manner by increase SA concentration from 1 to 2 mM. Pérez-Balibrea et al. (2011) reported that the total phenolics and flavonoids contents in broccoli sprouts were significantly increased by SA treatment. Also, Dokhanieh et al. (2013) showed that treatment with SA at 1 mM significantly maintained total anthocyanins content in cornelian cherry fruit. ROS damage contributes to chronic diseases and thus antioxidants may have beneficial effects on human health. Anthocyanins have shown to be potent antioxidant and ROS scavengers (Hassanpour et al., 2011). Kumar et al. (2013) reported that treatment of litchi fruit with SA enhanced the total anthocyanin content.

Sayyari et al. (2011a) reported that treatment of pomegranate fruit with ASA was effective in maintaining higher contents of nutritive and bioactive compounds such as total phenolics, anthocyanins, and TAA, in both H-TAA and L-TAA fractions. Innovative postharvest MeSA and MeJA vapor treatments not only alleviate CI in pomegranate fruit but also maintain fruit nutritional quality during low-temperature storage (Valero et al., 2015). Both treatments enhanced total phenolics and anthocyanins content in pomegranate, which may contribute to higher H-TAA antioxidant capacity. Valero et al. (2011) reported that treatment of sweet cherry fruit with SA and ASA at 1 mM enhanced total anthocyanin, total phenolics, and H-TAA during cold storage. Giménez et al. (2014) reported that the sweet cherry fruit treated at preharvest with SA at 0.5 mM and ASA at 1 mM has higher total phenolics and total anthocyanins, as well as higher H-TAA and L-TAA antioxidant activity at commercial harvest. Champa et al. (2015) reported that the table grapes treated with 2 mM SA at preharvest stage exhibited higher total phenolics and anthocyanin contents as well as lower weight loss, rachis browning, and decay during postharvest storage at 4°C. Also, table grapes treated with SA at preharvest stage have higher firmness due to lower PME enzyme activity and lower electrolyte leakage. Since SA treatment increased the PAL activity in sweet cherry fruit during storage (Qin et al., 2003), it can be revealed that the higher total phenolics, flavonoids, and anthocyanins contents in SA-treated fruit may attributed to higher PAL activity.

Oxidative damage plays an important role in disease initiation and progress in humans (Yamaguchi et al., 1998). Damage is generally reduced by endogenous antioxidants, but additional protection is necessary, and therefore fruits and vegetable phytochemicals are critical for disease prevention. AA as an important vitamin in fruits and vegetables is a water-soluble antioxidant (Kinsella et al., 1993). The role of AA is to reduce H_2O_2, which preserves cells against ROS (Davey et al., 2000). Humans are not able to synthesize AA, and fruits and vegetables, especially citrus fruit, strawberries, cornelian cherry, peppers, tomatoes, cabbage, and spinach, are main sources of AA (Davey et al., 2000; Hassanpour et al., 2011). AA content in cornelian cherry fruit treated with SA was significantly maintained during storage at 4°C (Dokhanieh et al., 2013). Kumar et al. (2013) reported that treatment of litchi fruit with SA enhanced AA content. Dokhanieh et al. (2013)'s results with regard to enhanced AA content in SA-treated cornelian cherry fruit are in agreement with Pérez-Balibrea et al. (2011), who reported that treatment of broccoli sprouts with SA enhances AA content. Increase in AA content of broccoli sprouts treated with SA has been reported to be due to indirect activation of AA biosynthesis from carbohydrates such as sucrose and glucose, key factors in the biosynthetic pathway of L-ascorbate that involves enzymatic steps from D-glucose to L-ascorbate (Jahangir et al., 2009; Pérez-Balibrea et al., 2011). Huang et al. (2008) reported that AA content in the pulp of SA-treated Cara cara navel orange fruit was higher than that in the controls. They suggested that SA treatment causes transition of Ca^{2+} from the vacuole and intercellular spaces to cytosol and increases cytosolic Ca^{2+} concentrations. Increase in cytosolic Ca^{2+} through enhancement of glutathione reductase (GR) enzyme activity could increase GR/APX system activity and lead to increase in ascorbate/dehydroascorbate (AA/DHA) and glutathione/glutathione disulfide (GSH/GSSG) ratios in Cara cara navel orange. Wang and Li (2006) reported that postharvest SA treatment significantly enhanced AA/DHA and GSH/GSSG ratios in peach. Sayyari et al. (2009) mentioned that SA treatments were highly effective in reducing AA loss compared with control fruit. Also, Rao et al. (2011) reported that treatment of sweet pepper with SA and $CaCl_2$ inhibited the ascorbic acid oxidase (AAO) enzyme activity, which is responsible for AA oxidation and enhanced AA content. High contents of AA in treated pineapple could improve the fruit nutritional quality, and inhibition of AAO enzyme activity is necessary for maintaining AA content and for antibrowning. It has been demonstrated that SA significantly reduces internal browning (IB) incidence and intensity and delays the decline of AA content in pineapple. Since AA content could be negatively related to IB symptoms, alleviated IB in winter pineapple fruit treated with SA is attributed to high AA content (Lu et al., 2011). SA maintained higher AA and chlorophyll contents, delayed membrane lipid peroxidation, and mitigated CI in cucumber fruit during cold storage (Cao et al., 2009).

DPPH$^{\bullet}$ scavenging activity is mainly attributed to the phenolics, flavonoids, anthocyanins, as well as AA contents in cornelian cherry fruit (Hassanpour et al., 2011). Dokhanieh et al. (2013) showed that the DPPH$^{\bullet}$ scavenging capacity of the cornelian cherry fruit treated with SA was significantly enhanced. Moreover, the results showed that the cornelian cherry fruit treated with 1 mM SA had higher DPPH$^{\bullet}$ scavenging capacity than fruit treated with 2 mM SA, suggesting that 1 mM might be optimal for enhancing the DPPH$^{\bullet}$ scavenging capacity of the cornelian cherry fruit. Considering total phenolics, flavonoids, anthocyanins, and AA contents as main components of fruit antioxidant activity, they concluded that SA may stimulate the antioxidant activity of fruit by enhancing total phenolics, flavonoids, anthocyanins, and AA contents. Biosynthesis of phenolics and flavonoids in plants is carried out via the shikimate–phenylpropanoid–flavonoids pathways (Tsai et al., 2006). PAL, as a key enzyme in the phenylpropanoid pathway, catalyzes conversion of phenylalanine to *trans*-cinnamic acid. PAL connects primary metabolism (shikimic acid pathway) to secondary metabolism (phenylpropanoid pathway) (Dixon and Paiva, 1995). Dokhanieh et al. (2013) reported that the activity of PAL in cornelian cherry fruit treated with SA increases compared with control, showing that SA treatment triggers the key enzymes of the secondary metabolite's biosynthetic pathways. Plant secondary metabolites are generally associated with plant defense responses against herbivores and pathogens and involved in a broad array of ecological functions (Tsai et al., 2006). SA could favor the phenolics biosynthesis by triggering gene expression, leading to accumulation of these secondary metabolites in broccoli sprouts (Jahangir et al., 2009). Total phenolics content in broccoli sprouts was significantly increased by SA treatment. Also, activity of PAL, a key regulatory responsible enzyme for phenylpropanoid metabolism, was induced by SA treatment (Kim et al., 2006; Pérez-Balibrea et al., 2011). Dokhanieh et al. (2013) demonstrated that SA might be a potential molecule for activating phenylpropanoid–flavonoids pathways in the cornelian cherry fruit. They also suggested that SA may stimulate the accumulation of phenolics, flavonoids, and anthocyanins in cornelian cherry fruit by activating their biosynthetic pathways. SA, as a natural signaling molecule, is present in fruits and vegetables, and has an important role in delaying the ripening process and enhancing nutritional quality when applied as a pre- or postharvest treatment. Thus, use of SA and ASA as a pre- or postharvest treatment could be a promising technology for enhancing nutritional quality of fruits and vegetables.

4 Salicylates and Chilling Injury in Fruits and Vegetables

Low-temperature storage (LTS) has been the main strategy applied in postharvest technology to prolong the shelf life of fruits and vegetables and maintain their quality. Storage at low temperature reduces all metabolic activities including the respiratory rate and minimizes fungal disease extension. However, tropical and subtropical fruits and vegetables are susceptible to low-temperature treatment, and they suffer from CI. CI leads to undesirable effects on quality of fruits and vegetables, such as abnormal ripening, pitting, or browning. In cases where its impact is very severe, it brings significant deterioration of the produce and therefore has a great negative effect on its final market value and leads to substantial economic losses (Aghdam et al., 2013, 2015; Aghdam and Bodbodak, 2013). It can be suggested that a high ratio of unsaturated fatty acids/saturated fatty acid (unSFA/SFA) due to higher FAD gene expression and activity, high levels of cell metabolic energy (ATP and AEC), and a lower level of PLD and LOX prooxidant enzyme activities accompanied by boosted activities of enzymes from the antioxidant system (AOX and SOD, CAT, GPX, GST, APX, DHAR, and MDHAR) result in reduction of cell membrane damage because of membrane lipid peroxidation, and, ultimately, to the avoidance of ROS accumulation, all of which has a positive effect on CI tolerance, which is reflected in an improved membrane integrity (Figs. 8.1 and 8.2).

SA, as a natural and safe phenolic molecule, at nontoxic concentrations may be commercially used in alleviating CI in fruits, vegetables, and flowers. SA treatment at nontoxic concentrations alleviates postharvest CI in fruits, vegetables, and flowers such as tomato (Ding et al., 2001, 2002; Fung et al., 2006; Zhang et al., 2011; Aghdam et al., 2012, 2014), loquat (Cai et al., 2006), peach (Wang and Li, 2006; Cao et al., 2010; Yang et al., 2012), pomegranate (Sayyari et al., 2009, 2011a,b), pineapple (Lu et al., 2010, 2011), sweet pepper (Fung et al., 2004), anthurium (Promyou et al., 2012),

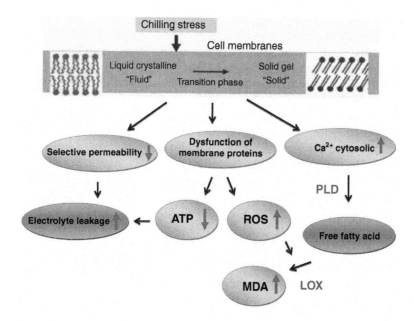

Figure 8.1 Chilling injury and its impacts on membrane integrity (Aghdam et al., 2013).

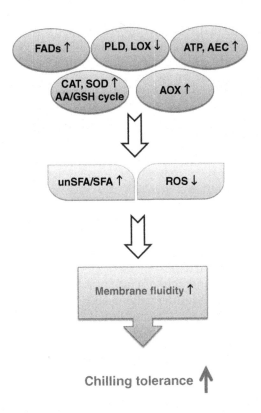

Figure 8.2 Factors affecting chilling tolerance in fruits and vegetables (Aghdam and Bodbodak, 2014).

bamboo shoot (Luo et al., 2012), and plum (Luo et al., 2011). Thus, SA has, at low concentrations, a high commercial potential to be used in alleviating CI in fruits, vegetables, and cut flowers. CI alleviating in fruits and vegetables due to salicylates could be attributed to (1) enhancing membrane integrity by reducing PLD, PLC, and LOX enzyme activity, enhancing the unSFA/SFA ratio probably through increasing FAD gene expression, and maintaining energy status, ATP, and AEC, (2) enhancing heat shock protein (HSP) gene expression and protein accumulation, (3) enhancing antioxidant system activity, (4) enhancing the arginine pathway, which results in accumulation of signaling molecules with pivotal roles in chilling tolerance such as polyamines, NO, and proline, and (5) alteration in PAL and polyphenol oxidase (PPO) enzyme activity.

5 Enhancing Membrane Integrity

Membrane fluidity, which greatly depends on the dynamics of alkyl chains from the cellular membrane phospholipids, plays a critical role in CI tolerance in fruits and vegetables (Zhang and

Tian, 2009). Membrane fluidity has the ability to regulate membrane function through its effects on the integral membrane protein arrangement, the membrane semipermeability, and the transmembrane transport activity (Los and Murata, 2004). Increase in the membrane unsaturation degree, due to an increase in unsaturated fatty acids such as linolenic acid, entails the enhancement of membrane fluidity, so its cellular function can be boosted by improved membrane integrity. The rise in membrane fluidity diminishes the tendency to phase transition from flexible liquid-crystalline to rigid sol-gel stages resulting in improved resistance against CI (Los and Murata, 2004). Resistance toward CI in chilling-tolerant Qingzhong loquat fruit in comparison with chilling-sensitive Fuyang has been attributed to higher contents of linolenic and linoleic acids, characteristic unsaturated fatty acids, lower levels of palmitic and stearic acid, and characteristic SFA, with both events yielding a higher unSFA/SFA ratio (Cao et al., 2011). According to the findings of Aghdam et al. (2014), PLD and LOX activities in tomato fruit increased during development of CI symptoms, a fact indicating aggravation of membrane integrity loss. SA treatment significantly reduced these enzymatic activities during storage at chilling temperature and resulted in maintenance of membrane integrity (Aghdam et al., 2014). The authors suggested that SA induces CI tolerance in tomato fruit by rising membrane integrity maintenance by means of reducing the prooxidant PLD and LOX enzymatic activities, decreasing lipid peroxidation rate, and maintaining cell membrane semipermeability.

6 Enhancing Antioxidant System Activity

Yang et al. (2012) reported that postharvest treatment of peach fruit with 1.0 mM SA for 10 min, alone or in combination with ultrasound treatment (40 kHz, 10 min), alleviated CI impact, but SA in combination with ultrasounds was more effective than SA treatment alone. They reported that SA also enhanced antioxidant enzyme activity (SOD, GST, CAT, APX, MDHAR, DHAR, and GR) resulting in alleviating CI. Postharvest treatment of sweet pepper with SA and $CaCl_2$ has been reported to maintain high levels of AA via reduction of AAO activity, the enzyme responsible for AA oxidation (Rao et al., 2011). Reduction of AAO enzyme activity by this postharvest treatment was useful for the upholding of nutritional and organoleptic quality due to maintenance of AA content, which crucially contributes to the antioxidant capacity and is also critical for its antibrowning property (Rao et al., 2011). Cao et al. (2010) reported that hot air (38°C for 12 h) treatment and SA application (1 mM for 5 min), individually or in combination, alleviated

CI in peach fruit. In peach fruit treated with a combination of both treatments, antioxidant enzyme activities (SOD, CAT, APX, and GR) increased and LOX activity decreased. LOX is responsible for superoxide radical production that after intervention of the SOD enzyme could be converted into H_2O_2. H_2O_2 can be scavenged as a result of CAT, APX, and GR enzyme activity (Mittler, 2002). Peaches treated with hot air in combination with SA increase SOD enzyme activity and decrease LOX activity, meaning a rise in SOD/LOX ratio, which led to a substantial reduction in superoxide radical level and increase in CAT, APX, and GR enzyme activity leading to a decrease in H_2O_2 levels (Cao et al., 2010). Promyou et al. (2012) noted that postharvest treatment with SA (2 mM for 15 min) alleviated CI in anthurium flower, an effect associated with decreasing electrolyte leakage, MDA content, and LOX activity, and increasing CAT and SOD activities, which led to a diminution of spathe browning and fresh weight loss, two detrimental effects of CI on this ornamental. Huang et al. (2008) reported that postharvest SA treatment (2 mM for 30 min) increased H_2O_2 accumulation and SOD activity and decreased MDA content and CAT activity of Cara cara navel orange fruit at 6 and 20°C. This postharvest treatment stimulated GR and DHAR activities and GSH and AA contents that led to enhanced AA/DHA and GSH/GSSG ratios. Ding et al. (2002) reported that MeSA and MeJA treatments (0.01 mM for 16 h at 23°C) significantly alleviated CI, manifested as surface pitting, and decay in tomato fruit and this beneficial effect took place by induction of PRs gene expression, such as chitinase and β-1,3-glucanase. Ding et al. (2002) found that CAT gene expression in MeJA-treated tomato fruit has increased but in MeSA-treated tomato fruit it decreased. The authors concluded that MeSA increases H_2O_2 accumulation through reduction of CAT gene expression. H_2O_2 as a signal molecule has the ability to activate PRs genes expression. In fruit treated with MeSA, CAT gene expression was reduced in the early period of cold storage, leading to H_2O_2 accumulation up to a level that was sufficiently high to activate PRs gene expression, but CAT gene expression rose in longer periods of cold storage in order to prevent excessive H_2O_2 accumulation. Higher concentrations of MeSA had a negative impact on CI resistance in tomato fruit that could be attributed to the excessive accumulation of H_2O_2 as a consequence of the extreme reduction of CAT activity (Ding et al., 2002). Wang and Li (2006) reported that postharvest SA treatment (1 mM for 5 min) significantly alleviated CI and decay in peach fruit. This CI alleviating was associated with decrease in MDA content and fruit firmness maintenance. AA/DHA and GSH/GSSG ratios and GSH content were increased in peach fruit treated with SA (Wang and Li, 2006). Treatment of peach fruit with SA enhanced APX and GR enzyme activity. In SA-treated peach fruit, the highest APX and GR enzyme activity coincided with the highest AA/DHA and GSH/GSSG ratios and GSH content (Wang and Li, 2006). Fung et al. (2004) reported that sweet peppers treated with 10^{-4} mM MeSA and MeJA conferred CI tolerance by means of increasing AOX gene expression. AOX as an enzymatic mechanism to avoid ROS production has a potential role in preventing ROS overproduction and thus inhibiting oxidative stress (Moller, 2001). Fung et al. (2004) observed that MeSA and MeJA-treated sweet pepper fruit stored at 0°C had higher AOX gene expression and lower CI degree than untreated fruit stored at 0°C. The authors suggested that these postharvest treatments and the so low-temperature storage acted synergistically and caused further increase in AOX gene expression, which may ultimately be responsible for increased resistance toward CI since AOX expression induction is faster and broader in comparison with gene expression of ROS scavengers such as SOD, CAT, and APX. MeSA treatment had the ability to alleviate CI via increasing AOX gene expression in tomato fruit harvested at pink maturation stage (Fung et al., 2006).

7 Enhancing HSP Accumulation

HSPs constitute a stress-responsive family of proteins whose molecular weights range between 15 and 115 kDa. Five families of HSPs have been identified: HSP70s, chaperonins (HSP60s), HSP90s, HSP100s, and HSPs with low molecular weight, so-called small HSPs (sHSPs). HSPs are found to be widely spread within the cytoplasm and nucleus but also in cell compartments such as mitochondria, chloroplast, and endoplasmic reticulum (Timperio et al., 2008; Wang et al., 2004). Small HSPs (sHSPs), of low molecular weight ranging between 15 and 42 kDa, have chaperone activity, which, in contrast to HSPs of higher molecular weight, is independent of ATP (Gusev et al., 2002). Ding et al. (2001) reported that heat (38°C for 2 days), MeSA, and MeJA (0.01 mM for 16 h at 23°C) treatments significantly alleviated CI and decay in tomato fruit. These treatments increased sHSP gene expression during low-temperature storage, especially that of HSP17.6. There is much evidence that HSPs exert their protective role against stress by means of their chaperone activity, which consists of (1) recognizing and binding to unfolded proteins in order to correctly complete their folding, (2) preventing protein aggregation, and (3) facilitating renaturation of aggregated proteins. This chaperone activity of HSPs has been observed both in vivo and in vitro (Sun et al., 2010).

It is accepted that environmental stresses lead to a reduction of cell membrane integrity due to increasing ROS levels occurring in this situation, which provokes membrane lipid peroxidation. sHSPs contribute to abiotic stress tolerance due to their role in stabilizing cell membranes (Horváth et al., 2008). Therefore membrane attributes such as fluidity and semipermeability are at least partially under the control of sHSPs and thus sHSPs may assist in maintaining fluidity and integrity of cell membranes in fruits and vegetables subjected to postharvest chilling stress (Torok et al., 2001; Tsvetkova et al., 2002; Horváth et al., 2008). Zou et al. (2012) showed that electrolyte leakage is significantly reduced in transgenic rice plants overexpressing *OsHSP23.7* and *OsHSP17.0* genes encoding for sHSPs and these transgenic lines displayed a higher tolerance to drought and salt stress. Zou et al. (2012) observed that MDA levels were significantly lower in the transgenic rice plants overexpressing *OsHSP23.7* and *OsHSP17.0* subjected to salinity and drought stresses than in nontransformed plants. Regarding this last aspect, it has been suggested that sHSPs may even be involved in ROS scavenging (Härndahl et al., 1999; Fedoroff, 2006). Hamilton and Heckathorn (2001) showed that in maize plants subjected to salt stress, complex I of mitochondrial electron transport chain is protected by antioxidant systems and sHSPs, but complex II is protected by osmoprotectants such as proline and betaine. These results indicate that NaCl stress damage to complex I is caused through oxidative stress and that HSPs may protect this complex by inducing some form of antioxidant activity. Taking into account these results, it can be envisaged that sHSPs not only have a role in prevention of protein misfolding under oxidative stress, but they also have the capability of inducing antioxidant activity. Zou et al. (2012), Lee et al. (2012), and Härndahl et al. (1999) suggested that the sHSPs have ROS scavenging activity and the beneficial effect of this activity is enhancing resistance against chilling stress. Neta-Sharir et al. (2005) reported that HSP21 protects tomato photosystem II from temperature-dependent oxidative stress.

Plants are protected against secondary oxidative stress by a complex antioxidant system including antioxidant enzymes and antioxidant metabolites. HSPs cooperate with this system at both levels. HSTFs, like molecular sensors, are able to sense ROS such as H_2O_2 and accordingly regulate expression of oxidative stress response genes. The gene encoding for a pea ascorbate peroxidase (*APX1*), an enzyme responsible for scavenging H_2O_2, contains in its promoter region a functional HSTF-binding motif (Mittler and Zilinskas, 1992). HSTF-dependent *APX1* gene expression in *Arabidopsis* suggests that HSTFs are not only involved in regulating HSP gene expression but also in the expression of genes involved in antioxidant system functioning in order to enhance resistance to oxidative stress (Panchuk et al., 2002).

In addition to this action of HSTFs regulating the expression of genes encoding for antioxidant enzymes, HSPs are able to induce the activity of antioxidant enzymes. Zhang et al. (2005) reported that hot air treatment (38°C for 10 h) alleviated CI in grape berry, with this rise of CI resistance being accompanied by a reduction of electrolyte leakage, MDA content, and, finally, an increase in SOD and CAT activities. The authors observed that the hot air treatment led to an increase of *HSP70* gene expression and that the accumulation of the HSP70 in grape directed an increase of gene expression and activity of antioxidant enzymes, and, finally, the synergistic action between HSP70 and antioxidant system, resulting in maintenance of membrane integrity and induction of CI resistance (Zhang et al., 2005). As well as increasing the activity of antioxidant enzymes, HSPs are able to improve the cell defense systems against oxidative stresses by inducing the accumulation of powerful antioxidant molecules such as GSH. Postharvest SA treatment significantly alleviated peach fruit CI, apparently by induction of HSP101 and HSP73 protein expression, which in turn seems to influence the rise of AA/DHA and GSH/GSSG ratios (Wang and Li, 2006). Indeed, the authors suggested that the stimulation of HSP101 and HSP73 biosynthesis is correlated with GSH levels in SA-treated peaches, and the surge in CI tolerance in this fruit may be due to the synergic action of both HSPs and the antioxidant system. By positively influencing the GSH/GSSG balance, HSP action allows the maintenance of GSH supply to DHAR, which is responsible for conversion of DHA to AA (Sala, 1998). Thus in fruits and vegetables, HSPs may play a pivotal role in regulating the antioxidant system such as enhancing GSH level and increasing antioxidant enzyme gene expression and/or activity, with both effects leading to a rise of resistance against postharvest CI in its oxidative stress facet.

8 Enhancing Arginine Pathways

Arginine as a metabolically multifunctional amino acid plays crucial roles not only as a building block of proteins, but also as a precursor for the biosynthesis of signaling molecules with potential roles in enhancing tolerance to CI such as polyamines (putrescine, spermidine, spermine), proline, and NO (Jubault et al., 2008). Arginine can be catabolized through the action of three crucial enzymes: arginase, arginine decarboxylase (ADC), and nitric oxide synthase (NOS) (Morris, 2009). Arginase catalyzes the conversion of arginine to ornithine, which in turn can serve as a precursor for biosynthesis of proline and polyamines. It has been suggested that the production of polyamines or proline can serve as a tolerance mechanism to chilling stress, an economically important postharvest problem in sensitive fruits and vegetables (Zhang et al., 2011; Shang et al., 2011).

Arginine could be converted to ornithine by arginase. Ornithine is one of the two main precursors of polyamines and is converted to putrescine by ornithine decarboxylase (ODC). The second pathway for polyamine biosynthesis is possible via the ADC enzyme, which is responsible for converting arginine to putrescine. The antisenescence biogenic polyamines putrescine (Put), spermidine (Spd), and spermine (Spm) are able to bind to negatively charged molecules such as phospholipids, proteins, and nucleic acids because of their polycationic nature at physiological pH. Because of the interaction between polyamines and the anionic groups of membrane phospholipids, binding of these molecules to this group of lipids could stabilize cell membranes under CI stress and therefore delay their disintegration (Groppa and Benavides, 2008). Also, polyamines exhibit antioxidant activity scavenging ROS and enhancing membrane stability and integrity under CI stress (Hussain et al., 2011).

Also, arginine can also be converted to NO, a hydrophobic diffusible gaseous molecule, via NOS activity (Zhang et al., 2011). Polyamines and NO as signaling molecules play crucial roles in enhancing resistance to CI in fruits and vegetables. Zhang et al. (2011) reported that postharvest treatment with 0.05 mM MeSA for 12 h at 20°C alleviated CI in tomato fruit during storage at 2°C for up to 28 days. Fruit treated with MeSA exhibited an increased gene expression and enzymatic activity for arginase, ODC, and ADC, all involved in polyamine biosynthesis. These authors determined higher polyamine content (Put, Spd, and Spm) in MeSA-treated fruit. Augmented endogenous polyamine contents along with increasing endogenous NO, due to higher activity of the enzyme responsible for its biosynthesis, NOS activity, have led to increased CI resistance in tomato fruit under postharvest MeSA treatment (Zhang et al., 2011).

Luo et al. (2011) significantly reduced CI in plum fruit with postharvest SA treatment (at 1.5 mM for 10 min) and this event was associated with enhanced endogenous polyamine accumulation leading to reduction in MDA, demonstrating improved cell membrane integrity (Luo et al., 2011). Postharvest treatment of bamboo shoot with 1.0 mM SA for 15 min effectively alleviated CI, and this effect was associated with reducing electrolyte leakage, MDA and total phenolics contents, and shoot tissue browning

(Luo et al., 2012). It was suggested that SA alleviated CI in bamboo shoot via enhancement of endogenous polyamine contents (Put, Spd, and Spm). Hot air treatment (38°C for 12 h) and SA (1 mM for 5 min) treatment, individually or in combination, alleviated CI in peach fruit. Both treatments enhanced endogenous polyamine content (Put, Spd, and Spm), which was associated with lower CI (Cao et al., 2010).

9 Regulation of PAL/PPO Enzyme Activity

It is well known that when fruits and vegetables are stored under chilling temperature: (1) PAL activity increases due to CI effect inducing increase in total phenolics, as a resistance mechanism, that accumulates in vacuoles; (2) a membrane selective permeability loss occurs; (3) PPO activity increases in cytoplasm that is responsible for flesh or IB; and (4) phenolic compounds accumulated in vacuoles leak to cytoplasm due to loss of vacuole membrane selective permeability and contribute to IB incidence, an effect influenced by PAL activity (Sevillano et al., 2009). PAL is a key enzyme in the phenylpropanoids pathway catalyzing the conversion of phenylalanine to *trans*-cinnamic acid. PAL connects the primary metabolism (shikimic acid pathway) with secondary metabolism (phenylpropanoids pathway) (Dixon and Paiva, 1995). In general terms it has been accepted by the scientific community that an increase in PAL activity in fruit stored at chilling temperatures is a part of the response of the fruits and vegetables in order to exert resistance to CI (Rinaldo et al., 2010). Luo et al. (2011) observed that SA (1.5 mM for 10 min) significantly reduced CI effect in plum fruit and this event was associated with decreased electrolyte leakage and MDA content, and diminished peroxidase (POD) and PPO activity, which are responsible for fruit flesh browning, a major CI detrimental effect on peach quality. But even SA can be applied during preharvest to exert its beneficial effect during postharvest. Lu et al. (2011) applied preharvest SA spray (at 2 mM for 15 min) and postharvest SA immersion (5 mM for 15 min) treatments in pineapple and observed that both treatments alleviated CI. They reported that the observed IB reduction in pineapple fruit treated at pre- and postharvest stages could be attributed to diminution of PPO and PAL activities. Also AA is known as an antibrowning molecule and the high levels of this antioxidant found in pineapple fruit treated with pre- and postharvest SA could contribute to IB reduction, so maintenance of AA levels is also a beneficial effect of pre- and postharvest SA treatments (Lu et al., 2011).

10 Salicylates and Postharvest Decay in Fruits and Vegetables

Plants protect themselves against the pathogen infection by activating defense mechanisms such as local acquired resistance (LAR) and systemic acquired resistance (SAR) (Vlot et al., 2009). Once plant defense responses are activated at the site of infection (LAR), a systemic defense response is often triggered in distal plant parts to protect these uninfected tissues against subsequent invasion by the pathogen (SAR), which is characterized by the coordinate activation of PR genes such as chitinase (CHT), β-1,3-glucanase (GLU), PAL, and POD, which encode proteins with antimicrobial activity (Yao and Tian, 2005). The onset of SAR is associated with increased levels of SA, locally at the site of infection and often also systemically in distant tissues (Tsuda et al., 2008). PR proteins have antimicrobial activities in vitro via hydrolytic activities on cell walls and contact toxicity (Van Loon et al., 2006).

Two SA binding proteins have been identified. The first is CAT, which when SA is bound to CAT leads to inhibition of its H_2O_2 decomposition activity. The second is APX, which when SA is bound to APX inhibits the H_2O_2 scavenging activity of cytosolic APX. Inhibition of CAT and APX by SA results in upholding H_2O_2 levels. Thus SA could facilitate H_2O_2 accumulation during the oxidative burst (OB) induced by infection with avirulent pathogens (Vlot et al., 2009). According to the reports of Cao et al. (2013), SA inhibited disease in jujube fruit infected with *Alternaria alternata*. SA has been shown to increase defense enzymes of PAL, POX, CHT, and GLU activities in jujube fruit during storage. Also, SA treatment declined CAT activity and increased SOD activity and AA content in jujube fruit. SA increases H_2O_2 accumulation in jujube fruit via binding to CAT, and accumulation of H_2O_2 contributes to signal transduction pathway leading to SAR activation. Also, SA could increase H_2O_2 accumulation via increasing SOD activity, which is responsible for formation of H_2O_2 from O_2^- generated during infection. Excessive H_2O_2 accumulation in the jujube fruit under SA treatment may have a damaging impact on fruit. Increment of AA in jujube fruit under SA treatment can be used for mitigation of excessive H_2O_2 damaging impacts. It has been shown that MeSA vapor treatment is effective in reducing fungal decay in kiwifruit by reducing CAT and APX activities, leading to increased H_2O_2 level (Aghdam et al., 2011). Zeng et al. (2006) in a study on mangoes reported that after 4 days of treatment the activity of GLU in SA-treated fruit was higher than in controls. They found that the level of H_2O_2 and the rate of O_2^- generation in SA-treated fruit were higher than in controls after 8 days of treatment. According to the findings of Tian et al. (2007), the balance between SOD, POD, and CAT activities in cells is crucial for determining the steady-state level of O_2^- and H_2O_2. Thus SA may also facilitate H_2O_2 accumulation during the OB induced by infection with the virulent pathogens. The increased ROS associated with the OB may contribute to resistance via directly killing the invading pathogen and/or activating cell wall cross-linking and lignification, thereby strengthening the cell wall and helping confine the pathogen to the infection site (Dempsey et al., 1999). SA also exhibits direct antifungal effects against pathogens. Lu and Chen (2005) have demonstrated the inhibitory action of SA on botrytis rot in lily leaves. Foliar application of acibenzolar-S-methyl (a synthetic analog of SA) has led to protection of postharvest Rock melons and Hami melons from diseases (Huang et al., 2000). SA at 2 mM has shown to directly inhibit the fungal toxicity on *Monilinia fructicola* and significantly inhibit the mycelial growth and spore germination of the pathogen in vitro (Yao and Tian, 2005).

SA has shown to enhance the effects of biological controls in postharvest systems. Since SA effectively enhances the biocontrol efficacy of antagonist yeasts, as an integrated strategy, combination of antagonist yeasts with signaling molecule SA can be used as an authentic technology at the industrial scale for minimizing postharvest decays in fruits and vegetables (Droby et al., 2009). It has been reported that SA can enhance the efficacy of biocontrol antagonist yeasts for reducing blue mold decay in apple and pear fruit (Yu and Zheng, 2006; Yu et al., 2007), brown rot and gray mold in peach fruit (Xu et al., 2008; Zhang et al., 2008), and Rhizopus rot in strawberry fruit (Zhang et al., 2010). Chitosan coating in combination with ASA has reduced the severity of carrot rot caused by *Sclerotinia sclerotiorum* by enhancing PAL, POD, and PPO enzyme activity (Ojaghian et al., 2013). The study of Qin et al. (2015) has demonstrated that treatment of yeast *Hanseniaspora uvarum* in combination with SA or sodium bicarbonate (SBC) may enhance the control efficiency against *Botrytis cinerea* infections in grapes. Treatment of table grapes with *H. uvarum* alone or combined with SA or SBC reduced disease incidence and lesion diameter. Also, *H. uvarum* combined with SA or SBC reduced the browning index, the decay incidence, weight loss while maintaining the fruit appearance, firmness, TSS, and titratable acidity of the grapes. Also the combination of *H. uvarum* and SA or SBC has been shown to increase POD, SOD, CAT, PAL, APX, and PPO enzyme activity. Application of *H. uvarum* in integration with SA or SBC delayed the postharvest ripening of grapes, manifested by reducing the browning index and weight loss and retaining fruit firmness.

11 Conclusions

Fresh fruits and vegetables, as very important suppliers of human health essential nutrients, are perishable and their quality is impacted by both abiotic and biotic stresses. During postharvest life, due to internal and external factors, chemical and physical changes occur in fresh fruits and vegetables, which may result in serious losses in nutritional and sensory quality. The use of SA as pre- or postharvest treatment could be a promising technology for enhancing nutritional quality of fruits and vegetables. In order to enhance the natural resistance of fruits and vegetables against postharvest stresses and also maintain fresh products' sensory and nutritional quality, which in turn will extend postharvest life, use of environmentally friendly technologies such as SA, as a natural and safe signaling molecule, has been recommended. SA has been shown to exhibit a high potential in delaying ripening, enhancing quality, and controlling postharvest losses of fruits and vegetables. CI is an abiotic stress during the storage of fruits and vegetables, which also greatly increases susceptibility to decay and leads to economic losses. Alleviating CI in fruits and vegetables due to salicylates could be attributed to (1) enhancing membrane integrity by reducing PLD, PLC, and LOX enzyme activity, by enhancing the unSFA/SFA ratio probably through increasing FAD gene expression, and maintaining energy status, ATP, and AEC, by enhancing HSP gene expression and protein accumulation, and (2) enhancing antioxidant system activity, by enhancing the arginine pathway, which results in accumulation of signaling molecules with pivotal roles in chilling tolerance, such as polyamines, NO, and proline and by regulation of PAL/PPO enzyme activity. Postharvest decay is associated with quality and quantity losses. The use of synthetic fungicides for controlling postharvest disease in fruits and vegetables not only has an adverse effect on users, consumers, and the environment, but is also due to intense application, which leads to the development of resistance in pathogens. These facts have encouraged researchers to find new ecofriendly and safe strategies to reduce postharvest diseases along with the declining application of synthetic fungicides. Exogenous application of SA at nontoxic concentrations to susceptible fruits and vegetables could enhance resistance to pathogens and control postharvest decay.

References

Aghdam, M.S., Bodbodak, S., 2013. Physiological and biochemical mechanisms regulating chilling tolerance in fruit and vegetables under postharvest salicylates and jasmonates treatments. Sci. Hortic. 156, 73–85.

Aghdam, M.S., Bodbodak, S., 2014. Postharvest heat treatment for mitigation of chilling injury in fruit and vegetables. Food Bioprocess. Tech. 7, 37–53.

Aghdam, M.S., Motallebiazar, A., Mostofi, Y., Moghaddam, J.F., Ghasemnezhad, M., 2011. Methyl salicylate affects the quality of Hayward kiwifruit during storage at low temperature. J. Agric. Sci. 3, 149–156.

Aghdam, M.S., Asghari, M., Moradbeygi, H., Mohammadkhani, N., Mohayeji, M., Rezapour-Fard, J., 2012. Effect of postharvest salicylic acid treatment on reducing chilling injury in tomato fruit. Rom. Biotechnol. Lett. 17, 7466–7473.

Aghdam, M.S., Sevillano, L., Flores, F.B., Bodbodak, S., 2013. Heat shock proteins as biochemical markers for postharvest chilling stress in fruit and vegetables. Sci. Hortic. 160, 54–64.

Aghdam, M.S., Asghari, M., Khorsandi, O., Mohayeji, M., 2014. Alleviation of postharvest chilling injury of tomato fruit by salicylic acid treatment. J. Food Sci. Technol. 51, 2815–2820.

Aghdam, M.S., Sevillano, L., Flores, F.B., Bodbodak, S., 2015. The contribution of biotechnology to improving post-harvest chilling tolerance in fruit and vegetables using heat-shock proteins. J. Agric. Sci. Cambridge 153, 7–24.

Asghari, M., Aghdam, M.S., 2010. Impact of salicylic acid on post-harvest physiology of horticultural crops. Trend Food Sci. Technol. 21, 502–509.

Babalar, M., Asghari, M., Talaei, A., Khosroshahi, A., 2007. Effect of pre- and postharvest salicylic acid treatment on ethylene production, fungal decay and overall quality of Selva strawberry fruit. Food Chem. 105, 449–453.

Cai, C., Li, X., Chen, K., 2006. Acetylsalicylic acid alleviates chilling injury of postharvest loquat (*Eriobotrya japonica* Lindl.) fruit. Eur. Food. Res. Technol. 223, 533–539.

Cao, S.F., Hu, Z.C., Wang, H.O., 2009. Effect of salicylic acid on the activities of anti-oxidant enzymes and phenylalanine ammonia-lyase in cucumber fruit in relation to chilling injury. J. Hortic. Sci. Biotechnol. 84, 125–130.

Cao, S., Hu, Z., Zheng, Y., Lu, B., 2010. Synergistic effect of heat treatment and salicylic acid on alleviating internal browning in cold-stored peach fruit. Postharvest Biol. Technol. 58, 93–97.

Cao, S., Yang, Z., Cai, Y., Zheng, Y., 2011. Fatty acid composition and antioxidant system in relation to susceptibility of loquat fruit to chilling injury. Food Chem. 127, 1777–1783.

Cao, J., Yan, J., Zhao, Y., Jiang, W., 2013. Effects of postharvest salicylic acid dipping on *Alternaria* rot and disease resistance of jujube fruit during storage. J. Sci. Food Agric. 93, 3252–3258.

Champa, W.A.H., Gill, M.I.S., Mahajan, B.V.C., Arora, N.K., 2015. Preharvest salicylic acid treatments to improve quality and postharvest life of table grapes (*Vitis vinifera* L.) cv. Flame Seedless. J. Food Sci. Technol. 52 (6), 3607–3616.

Davey, M.W., van Montagu, M., Inzé, D., Sanmartin, M., Kanellis, A., Smirnoff, N., Benzie, I.J.J., Strain, J.J., Favell, D., Fletcher, J., 2000. Plant l-ascorbic acid: chemistry, function, metabolism, bioavailability and effects of processing. J. Sci. Food Agric. 80, 825–860.

Dempsey, D.M.A., Shah, J., Klessig, D.F., 1999. Salicylic acid and disease resistance in plants. Crit. Rev. Plant Sci. 18, 547–575.

Ding, C.-K., Wang, C.Y., Gross, K.C., Smith, D.L., 2001. Reduction of chilling injury and transcript accumulation of heat shock proteins in tomato fruit by methyl jasmonate and methyl salicylate. Plant Sci. 161, 1153–1159.

Ding, C.K., Wang, C.Y., Gross, K.C., Smith, D.L., 2002. Jasmonate and salicylate induce the expression of pathogenesis-related-protein genes and increase resistance to chilling injury in tomato fruit. Planta 214, 895–901.

Dixon, R.A., Paiva, N.L., 1995. Stress-induced phenylpropanoid metabolism. Plant Cell 7, 1085–1097.

Dokhanieh, A.Y., Aghdam, M.S., Rezapour Fard, J., Hassanpour, H., 2013. Postharvest salicylic acid treatment enhances antioxidant potential of cornelian cherry fruit. Sci. Hortic. 154, 31–36.

Droby, S., Wisniewski, M., Macarisin, D., Wilson, C., 2009. Twenty years of postharvest biocontrol research: is it time for a new paradigm? Postharvest Biol. Technol. 52, 137–145.

Fedoroff, N., 2006. Redox regulatory mechanisms in cellular stress responses. Ann. Bot. 98, 289–300.

Fung, R.W.M., Wang, C.Y., Smith, D.L., Gross, K.C., Tian, M., 2004. MeSA and MeJA increase steady-state transcript levels of alternative oxidase and resistance against chilling injury in sweet peppers (*Capsicum annuum* L.). Plant Sci. 166, 711–719.

Fung, R.W.M., Wang, C.Y., Smith, D.L., Gross, K.C., Tao, Y., Tian, M., 2006. Characterization of alternative oxidase (AOX) gene expression in response to methyl salicylate and methyl jasmonate pre-treatment and low temperature in tomatoes. J. Plant Physiol. 163, 1049–1060.

Giménez, M.J., Valverde, J.M., Valero, D., Guillen, F., Martinez-Romero, D., Serrano, M., Castillo, S., 2014. Quality and antioxidant properties on sweet cherries as affected by preharvest salicylic and acetylsalicylic acids treatments. Food Chem. 160, 226–232.

Groppa, M.D., Benavides, M.P., 2008. Polyamines and abiotic stress: recent advances. Amino Acids 34, 35–45.

Gusev, N.B., Bogatcheva, N.V., Marston, S.B., 2002. Structure and properties of small heat shock proteins (sHsp) and their interaction with cytoskeleton proteins. Biochemistry 67, 511–516.

Hamilton, 3rd, E.W., Heckathorn, S.A., 2001. Mitochondrial adaptations to NaCl. Complex I is protected by anti-oxidants and small heat shock proteins, whereas complex II is protected by proline and betaine. Plant Physiol. 126, 1266–1274.

Härndahl, U., Hall, R.B., Osteryoung, K.W., Vierling, E., Bornman, J.F., Sundby, C., 1999. The chloroplast small heat shock protein undergoes oxidation-dependent conformational changes and may protect plants from oxidative stress. Cell Stress Chap. 4, 129–138.

Hassanpour, H., Hamidoghli, Y., Hajilo, J., Adlipour, M., 2011. Antioxidant capacity and phytochemical properties of cornelian cherry (*Cornus mas* L.) genotypes in Iran. Sci. Hortic. 129, 459–463.

Hong, K., Gong, D., Xu, H., Wang, S., Jia, Z., Chen, J., Zhang, L., 2014. Effects of salicylic acid and nitric oxide pretreatment on the expression of genes involved in the ethylene signalling pathway and the quality of postharvest mango fruit. N.Z. J. Crop. Hortic. Sci. 42, 205–216.

Hooper, L., Cassidy, A., 2006. A review of the health care potential of bioactive compounds. J. Sci. Food Agric. 86, 1805–1813.

Horváth, I., Multhoff, G., Sonnleitner, A., Vígh, L., 2008. Membrane-associated stress proteins: more than simply chaperones. Biochim. Biophys. Acta 1778, 1653–1664.

Huang, R.H., Liu, J.H., Lu, Y.M., Xia, R.X., 2008. Effect of salicylic acid on the antioxidant system in the pulp of "Cara cara" navel orange (*Citrus sinensis* L. Osbeck) at different storage temperatures. Postharvest Biol. Technol. 47, 168–175.

Huang, Y., Deverall, B.J., Tang, W.H., Wang, W., Wu, F.W., 2000. Foliar application of asilbenzolar-S-methyl and protection of postharvest rock melons and Hami melons from disease. Eur. J. Plant Path. 106, 651–656.

Hubbard, N.L., Pharr, D.M., Huber, S.C., 1991. Sucrose phosphate synthase and other sucrose metabolizing enzymes in fruit of various species. Physiol. Plant 82, 191–196.

Hussain, S.S., Ali, M., Ahmad, M., Siddique, K.H.M., 2011. Polyamines: natural and engineered abiotic and biotic stress tolerance in plants. Biotechnol. Adv. 29, 300–311.

Imran, H., Zhang, Y., Du, G., Wang, G., Zhang, J., 2007. Effect of salicylic acid (SA) on delaying fruit senescence of Huang Kum pear. Front. Agric. China 1, 456–459.

Jahangir, M., Abdel-Farid, I.B., Kim, H.K., Choi, Y.H., Verpoorte, R., 2009. Healthy and unhealthy plants: the effect of stress on the metabolism of Brassicaceae. Environ. Exp. Bot. 67, 23–33.

Jubault, M., Hamon, C., Gravot, A., Lariagon, C., Delourme, R., Bouchereau, A., Manzanares-Dauleux, M.J., 2008. Differential regulation of root arginine catabolism and polyamine metabolism in clubroot-susceptible and partially resistant *Arabidopsis* genotypes. Plant Physiol. 146, 2008–2019.

Kim, H.J., Chen, F., Wang, X., Choi, J.H., 2006. Effect of methyl jasmonate on phenolics, isothiocyanate, and metabolic enzymes in radish sprout (*Raphanus sativus* L.). J. Agric. Food Chem. 54, 7263–7269.

Kinsella, J.E., Frankel, E., German, B., Kanner, J., 1993. Possible mechanism for the protective role of antioxidants in wine and plants foods. Food Technol. 47, 85–89.

Kiselev, K.V., Tyunin, A.P., Karetin, Y.A., 2015. Salicylic acid induces alterations in the methylation pattern of the VaSTS1, VaSTS2, and VaSTS10 genes in *Vitis amurensis* Rupr. cell cultures. Plant Cell Rep. 34, 311–320.

Kumar, D., Mishra, D., Chakraborty, B., Kumar, P., 2013. Pericarp browning and quality management of litchi fruit by antioxidants and salicylic acid during ambient storage. J. Food Sci. Technol. 50, 797–802.

Langenkämper, G., McHale, R., Gardner, R.C., MacRae, E., 1998. Sucrose-phosphate synthase steady-state mRNA increases in ripening kiwifruit. Plant Mol. Biol. 36, 857–869.

Lee, K.W., Cha, J.Y., Kim, K.H., Kim, Y.G., Lee, B.H., Lee, S.H., 2012. Overexpression of alfalfa mitochondrial HSP23 in prokaryotic and eukaryotic model systems confers enhanced tolerance to salinity and arsenic stress. Biotechnol. Lett. 34, 167–174.

Los, D.A., Murata, N., 2004. Membrane fluidity and its roles in the perception of environmental signals. Biochim. Biophys. Acta 1666, 142–157.

Lu, Y.-Y., Chen, C.-Y., 2005. Molecular analysis of lily leaves in response to salicylic acid effective towards protection against *Botrytis elliptica*. Plant Sci. 169, 1–9.

Lu, X.H., Sun, D.Q., Mo, Y.W., Xi, J.G., Sun, G.M., 2010. Effects of post-harvest salicylic acid treatment on fruit quality and anti-oxidant metabolism in pineapple during cold storage. J. Hort. Sci. Biotechnol. 85, 454–458.

Lu, X., Sun, D., Li, Y., Shi, W., Sun, G., 2011. Pre- and post-harvest salicylic acid treatments alleviate internal browning and maintain quality of winter pineapple fruit. Sci. Hortic. 130, 97–101.

Luo, Z., Chen, C., Xie, J., 2011. Effect of salicylic acid treatment on alleviating postharvest chilling injury of "Qingnai" plum fruit. Postharvest Biol. Technol. 62, 115–120.

Luo, Z., Wu, X., Xie, Y., Chen, C., 2012. Alleviation of chilling injury and browning of postharvest bamboo shoot by salicylic acid treatment. Food Chem. 131, 456–461.

Mittler, R., 2002. Oxidative stress, antioxidants and stress tolerance. Trends Plant Sci. 7, 405–410.

Mittler, R., Zilinskas, B.A., 1992. Molecular cloning and characterization of a gene encoding pea cytosolic ascorbate peroxidase. J. Biol. Chem. 267, 21802–21807.

Mo, Y., Gong, D., Liang, G., Han, R., Xie, J., Li, W., 2008. Enhanced preservation effects of sugar apple fruit by salicylic acid treatment during post-harvest storage. J. Sci. Food Agric. 88, 2693–2699.

Moller, I.M., 2001. Plant mitochondria and oxidative stress: electron transport, NADPH turnover, and metabolism of reactive oxygen species. Annu. Rev. Plant Physiol. Plant Mol. Biol. 52, 561–591.

Morris, Jr., S.M., 2009. Recent advances in arginine metabolism: roles and regulation of the arginases. Br. J. Pharmacol. 157, 922–930.

Neta-Sharir, I., Isaacson, T., Lurie, S., Weiss, D., 2005. Dual role for tomato heat shock protein 21: protecting photosystem II from oxidative stress and promoting color changes during fruit maturation. Plant Cell 17, 1829–1838.

Ojaghian, M.R., Almoneafy, A.A., Cui, Z.Q., Xie, G.-L., Zhang, J., Shang, C., Li, B., 2013. Application of acetyl salicylic acid and chemically different chitosans against storage carrot rot. Postharvest Biol. Technol. 84, 51–60.

Panchuk, I.I., Volkov, R.A., Schoffl, F., 2002. Heat stress- and heat shock transcription factor-dependent expression and activity of ascorbate peroxidase in *Arabidopsis*. Plant Physiol. 129, 838–853.

Pérez-Balibrea, S., Moreno, D.A., García-Viguera, C., 2011. Improving the phytochemical composition of broccoli sprouts by elicitation. Food Chem. 129, 35–44.

Pérez-Tortosa, V., López-Orenes, A., Martínez-Pérez, A., Ferrer, M.A., Calderón, A.A., 2012. Antioxidant activity and rosmarinic acid changes in salicylic acid-treated *Thymus membranaceus* shoots. Food Chem. 130, 362–369.

Promyou, S., Ketsa, S., van Doorn, W.G., 2012. Salicylic acid alleviates chilling injury in anthurium (*Anthurium andraeanum* L.) flowers. Postharvest Biol. Technol. 64, 104–110.

Qin, G.Z., Tian, S.P., Xu, Y., Wan, Y.K., 2003. Enhancement of biocontrol efficacy of antagonistic yeasts by salicylic acid in sweet cherry fruit. Physiol. Mol. Plant Pathol. 62, 147–154.

Qin, X., Xiao, H., Xue, C., Yu, Z., Yang, R., Cai, Z., Si, L., 2015. Biocontrol of gray mold in grapes with the yeast *Hanseniaspora uvarum* alone and in combination with salicylic acid or sodium bicarbonate. Postharvest Biol. Technol. 100, 160–167.

Rao, T.V.R., Gol, N.B., Shah, K.K., 2011. Effect of postharvest treatments and storage temperatures on the quality and shelf life of sweet pepper (*Capsicum annum* L.). Sci. Hortic. 132, 18–26.

Rinaldo, D., Mbéguié-A-Mbéguié, D., Fils-Lycaon, B., 2010. Advances on polyphenolics and their metabolism in sub-tropical and tropical fruit. Trend Food Sci. Technol. 21, 599–606.

Sala, J.M., 1998. Involvement of oxidative stress in chilling injury in cold-stored mandarin fruit. Postharvest Biol. Technol. 13, 255–261.

Sayyari, M., Babalar, M., Kalantari, S., Serrano, M., Valero, D., 2009. Effect of salicylic acid treatment on reducing chilling injury in stored pomegranates. Postharvest Biol. Technol. 53, 152–154.

Sayyari, M., Babalar, M., Kalantari, S., Martínez-Romero, D., Guillén, F., Serrano, M., Valero, D., 2011a. Vapour treatments with methyl salicylate or methyl jasmonate alleviated chilling injury and enhanced antioxidant potential during postharvest storage of pomegranates. Food Chem. 124, 964–970.

Sayyari, M., Castillo, S., Valero, D., Díaz-Mula, H.M., Serrano, M., 2011b. Acetyl salicylic acid alleviates chilling injury and maintains nutritive and bioactive compounds and antioxidant activity during postharvest storage of pomegranates. Postharvest Biol. Technol. 60, 136–142.

Sevillano, L., Sanchez-Ballesta, M.T., Romojaro, F., Flores, F.B., 2009. Physiological, hormonal and molecular mechanisms regulating chilling injury in horticultural species. J. Sci. Food Agric. 89, 555–573.

Shang, H., Cao, S., Yang, Z., Cai, Y., Zheng, Y., 2011. Effect of exogenous gamma-aminobutyric acid treatment on proline accumulation and chilling injury in peach fruit after long-term cold storage. J. Agric. Food Chem. 59, 1264–1268.

Shi, H.Y., Zhang, Y.X., 2014. Expression and regulation of pear 1-aminocyclopropane-1-carboxylic acid synthase gene (*PpACS1a*) during fruit ripening, under salicylic acid and indole-3-acetic acid treatment, and in diseased fruit. Mol. Biol. Rep. 41, 4147–4154.

Srivastava, M.K., Dwivedi, U.N., 2000. Delayed ripening of banana fruit by salicylic acid. Plant Sci. 158, 87–96.

Sun, J.-h., Chen, J.-y., Kuang, J.-f., Chen, W.-x., Lu, W.-j., 2010. Expression of sHSP genes as affected by heat shock and cold acclimation in relation to chilling tolerance in plum fruit. Postharvest Biol. Technol. 55, 91–96.

Sun, B., Yan, H., Zhang, F., Wang, Q., 2012. Effects of plant hormones on main health-promoting compounds and antioxidant capacity of Chinese kale. Food Res. Int. 48, 359–366.

Tareen, M.J., Abbasi, N.A., Hafiz, I.A., 2012. Postharvest application of salicylic acid enhanced antioxidant enzyme activity and maintained quality of peach cv. "Flordaking" fruit during storage. Sci. Hortic. 142, 221–228.

Tian, S., Qin, G., Li, B., Wang, Q., Meng, X., 2007. Effects of salicylic acid on disease resistance and postharvest decay control of fruit. Stewart Postharvest Rev. 3, 1–7.

Timperio, A.M., Egidi, M.G., Zolla, L., 2008. Proteomics applied on plant abiotic stresses: role of heat shock proteins (HSP). J. Proteom. 71, 391–411.

Todd, J.F., Paliyath, G., Thompson, J.E., 1990. Characteristics of a membrane-associated lipoxygenase in tomato fruit. Plant Physiol. 94, 1225–1232.

Torok, Z., Goloubinoff, P., Horvath, I., Tsvetkova, N.M., Glatz, A., Balogh, G., Varvasovszki, V., Los, D.A., Vierling, E., Crowe, J.H., Vigh, L., 2001. Synechocystis HSP17 is an amphitropic protein that stabilizes heat-stressed membranes and binds denatured proteins for subsequent chaperone-mediated refolding. Proc. Natl. Acad. Sci. USA 98, 3098–3103.

Tsai, C.J., Harding, S.A., Tschaplinshi, T.J., Lindroth, R.L., Yuan, Y., 2006. Genome-wide analysis of the structural genes regulating defense phenylpropanoid metabolism in *Populus*. New Phytol. 172, 47–62.

Tsuda, K., Sato, M., Glazebrook, J., Cohen, J.D., Katagiri, F., 2008. Interplay between MAMP-triggered and SA-mediated defense responses. Plant J. 53, 763–775.

Tsvetkova, N.M., Horvath, I., Torok, Z., Wolkers, W.F., Balogi, Z., Shigapova, N., Crowe, L.M., Tablin, F., Vierling, E., Crowe, J.H., Vigh, L., 2002. Small heat-shock proteins regulate membrane lipid polymorphism. Proc. Natl. Acad. Sci. USA 99, 13504–13509.

Valero, D., Diaz-Mula, H.M., Zapata, P.J., Castillo, S., Guillen, F., Martinez-Romero, D., Serrano, M., 2011. Postharvest treatments with salicylic acid, acetylsalicylic acid or oxalic acid delayed ripening and enhanced bioactive compounds and antioxidant capacity in sweet cherry. J. Agric. Food Chem. 59, 5483–5489.

Valero, D., Mirdehghan, S.H., Sayyari, M., Serrano, M., 2015. Vapor treatments, chilling, storage, and antioxidants in pomegranates. Processing and Impact on Active Components in Food. Academic Press, USA, pp. 189–196.

Van Loon, L., Rep, M., Pieterse, C., 2006. Significance of inducible defense-related proteins in infected plants. Annu. Rev. Phytopathol. 44, 135–162.

Vinson, J.A., Su, X., Zubik, L., Bose, P., 2001. Phenol antioxidant quantity and quality in foods: fruit. J. Agric. Food Chem. 49, 5315–5321.

Vlot, A.C., Dempsey, D.A., Klessig, D.F., 2009. Salicylic acid, a multifaceted hormone to combat disease. Ann. Rev. Phytopathol. 47, 177–206.

Wang, L.-J., Li, S.-H., 2006. Salicylic acid-induced heat or cold tolerance in relation to Ca^{2+} homeostasis and antioxidant systems in young grape plants. Plant Sci. 170, 685–694.

Wang, W., Vinocur, B., Shoseyov, O., Altman, A., 2004. Role of plant heat-shock proteins and molecular chaperones in the abiotic stress response. Trends Plant Sci. 9, 244–252.

Wei, Y., Liu, Z., Su, Y., Liu, D., Ye, X., 2011. Effect of salicylic acid treatment on postharvest quality, antioxidant activities, and free polyamines of asparagus. J. Food Sci. 76, 126–132.

Xu, W.P., Chen, K.S., Li, F., Zhang, S.L., 2000. Regulation of lipoxygenase on jasmonic acid biosynthesis in ripening kiwifruit. Acta Phytophysiol. Sin. 26, 507–514.

Xu, X., Chan, Z., Xu, Y., Tian, S., 2008. Effect of *Pichia membranaefaciens* combined with salicylic acid on controlling brown rot in peach fruit and the mechanisms involved. J. Sci. Food Agric. 88, 1786–1793.

Yamaguchi, T., Takamura, H., Matoba, T., Terao, J., 1998. HPLC method for evaluation of the free radical-scavenging activity of foods by using 1,1-diphenyl-2-picrylhydrazyl. Biosci. Biotechnol. Biochem. 62, 1201–1204.

Yang, Z., Cao, S., Zheng, Y., Jiang, Y., 2012. Combined salicyclic acid and ultrasound treatments for reducing the chilling injury on peach fruit. J. Agric. Food. Chem. 60, 1209–1212.

Yang, T., Peng, H., Whitaker, B.D., Jurick, W.M., 2013. Differential expression of calcium/calmodulin-regulated SlSRs in response to abiotic and biotic stresses in tomato fruit. Physiol. Plant. 148, 445–455.

Yao, H., Tian, S., 2005. Effects of pre- and post-harvest application of salicylic acid or methyl jasmonate on inducing disease resistance of sweet cherry fruit in storage. Postharvest Biol. Technol. 35, 253–262.

Yin, X.R., Zhang, Y., Zhang, B., Yang, S.L., Shi, Y.N., Ferguson, I.B., Chen, K.S., 2013. Effects of acetylsalicylic acid on kiwifruit ethylene biosynthesis and signaling components. Postharvest Biol. Technol. 83, 27–33.

Yu, T., Zheng, X.D., 2006. Salicylic acid enhances biocontrol efficacy of the antagonist *Cryptococcus laurentii* in apple fruit. J. Plant Growth Reg. 25, 166–174.

Yu, T., Chen, J., Chen, R., Huang, B., Liu, D., Zheng, X., 2007. Biocontrol of blue and gray mold diseases of pear fruit by integration of antagonistic yeast with salicylic acid. Int. J. Food Microbiol. 116, 339–345.

Zeng, K., Cao, J., Jiang, W., 2006. Enhancing disease resistance in harvested mango (*Mangifera indica* L. cv. "Matisu") fruit by salicylic acid. J. Sci. Food Agric. 86, 694–698.

Zhang, C., Tian, S., 2009. Crucial contribution of membrane lipids' unsaturation to acquisition of chilling tolerance in peach fruit stored at 0°C. Food Chem. 115, 405–411.

Zhang, Y., Chen, K., Zhang, S., Ferguson, I., 2003. The role of salicylic acid in postharvest ripening of kiwifruit. Postharvest Biol. Technol. 28, 67–74.

Zhang, J., Huang, W., Pan, Q., Liu, Y., 2005. Improvement of chilling tolerance and accumulation of heat shock proteins in grape berries (*Vitis vinifera* cv. Jingxiu) by heat pretreatment. Postharvest Biol. Technol. 38, 80–90.

Zhang, H., Ma, L., Wang, L., Jiang, S., Dong, Y., Zheng, X., 2008. Biocontrol of gray mold decay in peach fruit by integration of antagonistic yeast with salicylic acid and their effects on postharvest quality parameters. Biol. Control 47, 60–65.

Zhang, H., Ma, L., Turner, M., Xu, H., Zheng, X., Dong, Y., Jiang, S., 2010. Salicylic acid enhances biocontrol efficacy of *Rhodotorula glutinis* against postharvest Rhizopus rot of strawberries and the possible mechanisms involved. Food Chem. 122, 577–583.

Zhang, X., Shen, L., Li, F., Meng, D., Sheng, J., 2011. Methyl salicylate-induced arginine catabolism is associated with up-regulation of polyamine and nitric oxide levels and improves chilling tolerance in cherry tomato fruit. J. Agric. Food. Chem. 59, 9351–9357.

Zou, J., Liu, C., Liu, A., Zou, D., Chen, X., 2012. Overexpression of OsHsp17.0 and OsHsp23. 7 enhances drought and salt tolerance in rice. J. Plant Physiol. 169, 628–635.

9

CHITOSAN: PROPERTIES AND ROLES IN POSTHARVEST QUALITY PRESERVATION OF HORTICULTURAL CROPS

Swati Sharma*, **Kalyan Barman****, **Mohammed Wasim Siddiqui**[†]

*ICAR–National Research Centre on Litchi, Muzaffarpur, Bihar, India; **Bihar Agricultural University, Department of Horticulture (Fruit and Fruit Technology), Sabour, Bhagalpur, Bihar, India; †Bihar Agricultural University, Department of Food Science and Postharvest Technology, Sabour, Bhagalpur, Bihar, India

1 Introduction

Chitosan is a polysaccharide, which is extracted commercially by deacetylation of the chitin extracted from the exoskeleton of crustaceans such as shrimps (*Pandalus borealis*), crabs, fungal cell walls, etc. Chitosan, also called soluble chitin, is known chemically as poly-(β-1/4)-2-amino-2-deoxy-D-glucopyranose (Yogeshkumar et al., 2013). It is mainly subcategorized based upon its molecular weight, the degree of deacetylation, and the source from which it is obtained (Goy et al., 2009). The chitosan available commercially in markets is generally found to have less than 15% degree of acetylation and 100–1000 kDa molecular weight (Goy et al., 2009). Chitosan less than 50 kDa has a low molecular weight, between 50 and 150 kDa a medium molecular weight, and more than 150 kDa a high molecular weight. Chitosan is a β-1,4-polymer of glucose and glucosamine. The cellulose, chitin, and chitosan polymers are the most abundant natural polymers (Castro and Paulin, 2012). It is known that cellulose is the chief component of plant cells and chitin of fungi, insects, and crustaceans, while chitosan is found in fungal walls. Plant cells have many fewer glucosamine polymers but have β-glucanase and chitinase enzymes, which can lyse chitosan and chitin polymers. The presence of these hydrolytic enzymes in the plants without the occurrence of glucosamine polymers suggests that these enzymes might have

Eco-Friendly Technology for Postharvest Produce Quality. http://dx.doi.org/10.1016/B978-0-12-804313-4.00009-8
Copyright © 2016 Elsevier Inc. All rights reserved.

been retained as a protective mechanism for managing the attacks caused by insects and fungi. The chitosan polymer exhibits natural antimicrobial, biodegradable (Arvanitoyannis, 1999), environment friendly, biocompatible (Castro and Paulin, 2012), and film-forming properties (Aider, 2010; No et al., 2002; Zheng and Zhu, 2003; Terry and Joyce, 2004), and is nontoxic to mammals (Castro and Paulin, 2012). The chitosan polymer exhibits the potential to be used for maintaining the quality, safety, and enhancement of the postharvest life of horticultural and agricultural produce.

Chitosan is being widely used in different fields, which have various important applications ranging from agriculture, medicine, tissue and bone engineering, the food sector, cosmetics, textiles, pharmaceutical nanostructure materials, biotechnology, the paper industry, and also in wastewater treatment. Chitosan is a polysaccharide soluble in dilute organic acids and is suitable as a preservative coating for fruit (Jiang et al., 2005). The application of chitosan as a coating on horticultural commodities has shown immense potential to maintain the quality as well as extend the shelf life of several fruits such as litchi (Lin et al., 2011; Zhang and Quantick, 1997), longan (Jiang and Li, 2001), papaya (Ali et al., 2011), peach (Ma et al., 2013), mango (Cisse et al., 2015; Medeiros et al., 2012), table grapes, strawberries, and sweet cherries (Romanazzi, 2010), among many others. It is also used in agricultural fields for antimicrobial action and for using biological and safe approaches to attain sustainability in agricultural practices.

2 Properties of Chitosan

2.1 Biocompatibility, Biofunctionality, and Biodegradability

Biocompatibility is defined as the degree or intensity of damaging effects on interaction with the living organisms (Castro and Paulin, 2012). Chitosan shows better biocompatibility with mammals, particularly humans, since it is a naturally derived polysaccharide. The amino group in its structure undergoes protonation in acidic to neutral solutions below its pKa (~6.3) and results in chitosan becoming soluble and acting like a bioadhesive depending upon the pH of the solution, its molecular weight, and degree of acetylation. The N-acetylglucosamine unit of the chitosan polymer also occurs in hyaluronic acid and is structurally similar to various other important macromolecules; it also displays biocompatible and biofunctional properties. This is the main reason why the chitosan polymer is extensively used for several different applications and uses ranging from agricultural to pharmaceutical and medical fields, for example. Chitosan is an environmentally friendly polymer since it is derived naturally from deacetylation of chitin and is biodegradable based upon the degree of deacetylation. The United States Environmental Protection Agency (EPA, 2008) also reported that chitosan use will most probably not have any adverse influence on the environment (EPA-HQ-OPP-2007-0037 FRL-8392-6). It has been reported that higher deacetylated chitosan polymer degrades at a slower rate (Yogeshkumar et al., 2013). Moreover, it is reported that it can be degraded by various oxidation–reduction reactions and free radical reactions as well as by bacteria, fungi, other simple organisms, plants, as well as by humans. Enzymatic degradation of the chitosan polymer by lysozomes, chitinases, and some bacterial enzymes in vertebrates along with chemical degradation catalyzed by acids in the stomach has also been reported by different researchers.

2.2 Biosafety, Analgesic, and Antitumor Activity

The chitosan polymer is a biologically compatible natural material and has been approved for dietary applications in Japan, Italy, and Finland (Illum, 1998) and for use in wound dressings by the Food and Drug Administration (Wedmore et al., 2006). The chitosan polymer is generally used in agriculture for its antimicrobial properties to prevent losses due to decay and diseases both in pre- and postharvest stages (Bautista-Banos et al., 2006). Moreover, chitosan can increase yields, and is edible and biodegradable without having any adverse influences such as allergenic, mutagenic, or carcinogenic activities. This implies that the chitosan polymer can be used and is safe for application on food products and agricultural and horticultural commodities (Jianglian and Shaoying, 2013). However, the chitosan polymer represents structurally different chemical entities depending upon the source and the degree of acetylation because it might display different biodistribution, biodegradation, and toxicity levels. The toxicity of the chitosan polymer depends upon the degree of deacetylation and molecular weight. It also varies with the modifications made to it and the dose at which it is consumed. Besides, the small molecular weight chitosan polymer less than 10 kDa is known to be not significantly toxic. The chitosan polymer having a degree of deacetylation between 40 and 60% or a degree of trimethylation is supposed to be safe.

It has been reported by some workers that chitin and chitosan polymers display analgesic and antitumor activities (Castro and Paulin, 2012). The chitosan polymer has been observed to provide soothing and calming effects when applied to wounds. The antitumor activity of the chitosan polymer is applied in medical fields and is displayed by the stimulation of the immune system. Chito-oligomers, which are chitosan with a degree of polymerization less than 20, also exhibit antibacterial (Jeon et al., 2001), antitumor, and immune-enhancing influences (Jeon and Kim, 2002; Tian et al., 2010).

2.3 Antimicrobial Activity and Influences on Elicitation of Defense Mechanisms in Plant Tissues

Chitosan is a natural polymer with proven antimicrobial activity for which different antibacterial mechanisms have been proposed by various workers (Devlieghere et al., 2004; Goy et al., 2009; Dutta et al., 2011). The ionic surface interaction between the chitosan polymer and the microbes results in alterations in the plasma membrane, cell wall leakage, and death. It has been reported that the polycationic nature of the chitosan polymer in acidic solutions below pH 6.5 plays an important role in its antimicrobial activity since the positively charged amino groups of the chitosan polymer interact with negatively charged components in microbial cell membranes, thus altering their membrane barrier properties and resulting in leakage of intracellular contents. The second mechanism is the inhibition of the mRNA and protein synthesis through the penetration of chitosan polymer into the nuclei of the microorganisms. The other mechanisms may be by activating the defense processes in plant cells, forming an external barrier, chelating metals, and by suppression of the supply and assimilation of the essential nutrients to microbial growth. The antimicrobial activity of the chitosan molecule is also dependent upon molecular weight and degree of acetylation (Dutta et al., 2011; Kong et al., 2010; Liu et al., 2004). It has been previously recorded by different workers that the chitosan polymer having lower molecular weight and degree of acetylation has a higher efficacy on reducing and inhibiting the growth rates of microorganisms. Sometimes deviations in the antimicrobial activity of the chitosan polymer have been observed by different workers, which might be attributed to different reasons such as the differences in microbial status in reference to the particular species and cell age, intrinsic properties of the chitosan polymer, its physical state, and environmental conditions such as treatment time, temperature, pH, etc. However, it has been observed that the antimicrobial properties of chitosan showed an increase, with an increase in the degree of deacetylation, which might be due to an increase in the positive charge of the amino groups of the chitosan polymer (Hongpattarakere and Riyaphan, 2008; Takahashi et al., 2008). The broad-spectrum antibacterial activity of chitosan was first proposed by Allan (Allan and Hadwiger, 1979). The submicron chitosan polysaccharide triggers the induction of inherent defense responses of plants by strengthening the cell wall by accumulation of lignin and production of pathogenesis-related proteins and enzymes (Ali et al., 2014, 2015).

2.4 Molecular and Physical Properties of Chitosan

Chitosan and chitin are biopolymers that are obtained from the waste by-products remaining in edible crustaceans such as shrimps and crabs. Chitosan and chitin biopolymers are not always pure. The chitosan polymer often consists of about 20% of the N-acetyl glucosamine sugar residues of chitin while chitin often consists of about 20% of the glucosamine residues of chitosan (Hadwiger, 2013). Chitosan and chitin biopolymers are relatively water insoluble until they are broken down into oligomers with 7 degrees of polymerization (Castro and Paulin, 2012). The chitosan polymers longer than this become water soluble in solutions of pH ≤ 7. The physical properties of the chitosan polymer exert significant influence on its biological properties. The chitosan polymer must be properly dissolved to influence and display its antimicrobial and other biological activities like postharvest shelf-life enhancing properties. The physical structure of both cellulose and chitosan are based upon the β-1,4 linkages. The chitosan solution can be dried as transparent sheets, which look like cellophane. The chemical nature and biological properties of chitosan are different from chitin and cellulose polymers due to the presence of the amino groups, which are capable of binding with positively charged molecules.

3 Factors Affecting the Properties and Activities of the Chitosan Polymer

The antimicrobial as well as other biological activities of the chitosan polymer and its derivatives are dependent on many intrinsic and extrinsic factors, such as the pH and pKa of solution, microorganism species and cell age, the presence or absence of metal cations, molecular weight, and degree of deacetylation of chitosan polymer among others. The inherent biological properties of chitosan in addition to its ability to form coatings or films result in it being a highly appropriate packaging material for horticultural commodities and other foods. The antitranspirant activity of the chitosan polymer is due to abscisic acid-dependent stomatal closure and forming a thin film, which reduces transpirational loss. It also activates plants' inherent defense machinery against pathogens (Iriti et al., 2009). The mechanical, physicochemical, and color properties of chitosan-based coatings in combination with aloe vera gel coating in different proportions (Abras et al., 2012). They observed that 20% aloe vera gel incorporation into chitosan showed good results and improved mechanical properties.

Composite films were prepared by using chitosan polysaccharide and a commercial galactomannan, that is, tara gum, and their properties were studied. The composite films prepared using bulk chitosan exhibited higher antimicrobial properties while the films using chitosan nanoparticles showed lower moisture content of the films (Antoniou et al., 2015). The antimicrobial and rheological properties of the chitosan polymer are influenced by extraction conditions and exposure to humidity. Chitosan with different molecular weights and similar deacetylation degree showed similar high antimicrobial activity. They observed that the antimicrobial property of the chitosan polymer was enhanced at acidic pH. The 1600 kDa chitosan polymer with 82% degree of deacetylation showed superior rheological properties and high mechanical resistance. Thus it can be used for antimicrobial coating in many food products (Arancibia et al., 2015). Yoshida et al. (2014) prepared chitosan polymer and anthocyanin-based intelligent films that change color in different pH solutions and the mechanical properties of the films were maintained. The development of natural, biodegradable wax for coating of citrus fruit using carboxymethyl cellulose and chitosan bilayer was attempted by Arnon et al. (2014). It was found that composite coating was equally effective as the commercial wax in citrus. The bilayer coating on citrus fruit having carboxymethyl cellulose as an internal layer and chitosan as an external layer maintained the fruit quality for extended storage periods in comparison to synthetic waxes (Arnon et al., 2015).

The composite coating preparation, which consists of a bioactive compound such as essential oils along with chitosan dispersion, shows enhanced results in maintaining the physicochemical properties of fruits and inhibiting pathogenic microorganisms (Xing et al., 2011; Azeredo et al., 2011). The incorporation of essential oils to chitosan edible coating further enhances the postharvest life, which might be attributed to its prolonged antimicrobial activity. This is due to the continuous release of essential oil compounds over a long period of time on the surface of the food product during storage. The emulsifying properties of the chitosan polymer allow the assimilation of essential oils, permitting its homogeneous distribution, forming a thin and translucent edible coating. The submicron chitosan dispersion (1%) showed the maximum anthracnose disease reduction and vegetative growth and development in dragon fruit plants (Zahid et al., 2014). Thus the results reveal that submicron chitosan dispersion is a more effective antimicrobial agent and plant growth enhancer than the conventional chitosan solution treatments. The chemical modification of chitosan polysaccharide by introducing quaternary ammonium moieties into its structure enhances its antimicrobial activity. The results elucidated clearly that the quaternization of the derivatives onto the chitosan structure inhibited the microbial growth and can be used as antimicrobial agents in crop protection against microbial pathogens (Badawy et al., 2014).

The effectiveness of the chitosan coating can be enhanced by combining it with organic or inorganic compounds (Jianglian and Shaoying, 2013). The combination of chitosan coating with essential oil, organic acids, and other substances such as ethanol, wax, etc., improves fruit preservation. The chitosan combination with metal ions such as calcium, zinc, and cerium enhances firmness, maintains quality, extends postharvest life, and decreases pesticide residues in fruits. The combination of chitosan biopolymer treatment with inorganic nanomaterials such as nano-ZnO, nano-silicon, and nano-$CaCO_3$ has been found to be useful to reduce decay, enzymatic activity, malondialdehyde content, respiration rate, ascorbic acid content, and weight loss (Jianglian and Shaoying, 2013). The combination coating of chitosan polymer with biological control agents such as *Pseudomonas syringae* and *Metschnikowia fructicola* inhibits postharvest diseases.

The application of chitosan polymer in combination with postharvest treatments like heat and hypobaric treatment have also shown efficacy for postharvest quality maintenance and extension of shelf life of several fruits (Romanazzi et al., 2003). It is an effective nonchemical method for management of postharvest pests and diseases and to reduce the quality losses. The hypobaric and chitosan treatments are effective to control postharvest decay of different fruits. The chitosan coating treatment integrated with 1-methylcyclopropene and modified atmosphere packaging treatments reduces enzymatic activity and maintenance of fruit quality (Jianglian and Shaoying, 2013). Its application as nanoparticles can increase the efficiency of the treatment (Qi et al., 2004). Chitosan can be integrated with anthocyanin pigments for creation of an active and intelligent packaging for maintenance of food quality as well as to act as an indicator of food quality for consumers (Pereira et al., 2015). Further statistical tools such as response surface methodology can be used for standardization of various organic and inorganic components with chitosan for enhancing its efficacy (Azevedo et al., 2014).

4 Extraction Procedures and Structure of Chitosan

The extraction of chitin from the waste by-products of crustaceans consists of acid removal of calcium carbonate, which is known as demineralization. This is followed by removal of proteins, which is usually done by alkaline treatments (Castro and Paulin, 2012). The extracted chitin displays poor solubility and is hard and translucent physically. Chitin is hydrolyzed chemically by strong alkaline solution at high temperatures to produce the deacetylated form, which is known as chitosan after the percentage of acetylated amino groups is lowered to about 35–40%. Chitosan is a linear polysaccharide, which is composed of β-(1-4) linkages in 2-amino-2-deoxy-D-glucose components having their origin in chitin. It is a partially deacetylated polymer of N-acetyl-D-glucosamine and is water soluble. The chitosan polymer consists of randomly distributed β-(1-4)-linkages in D-glucosamine and N-acetyl-D-glucosamine. It is produced commercially by deacetylation of chitin. The degree of deacetylation in chitosan polymer available commercially ranges from 60 to 100% while the molecular weight is 38 and 20 kDa (Castro and Paulin, 2012; Aruldhason et al., 2012; Yogeshkumar et al., 2013) (Fig. 9.1).

5 Applications of Chitosan Polymer

The chitosan polymer exhibits several beneficial biological properties due to the positive charge on the glucosamine units. These properties render the chitosan polymer applicable in various diverse fields such as cosmetics, agriculture, the food industry, pharmaceuticals, biotechnology, and medicine (Benjakul et al., 2000; Liu et al., 2001; Ren et al., 2001). In agriculture, it is used particularly as edible coatings, and for antimicrobial, antioxidant, and preservative activities. It is also used as a soil modifier and immune response elicitor in plants. The chitosan polymer is also used in the textile industry because of its antimicrobial and moisture retention properties.

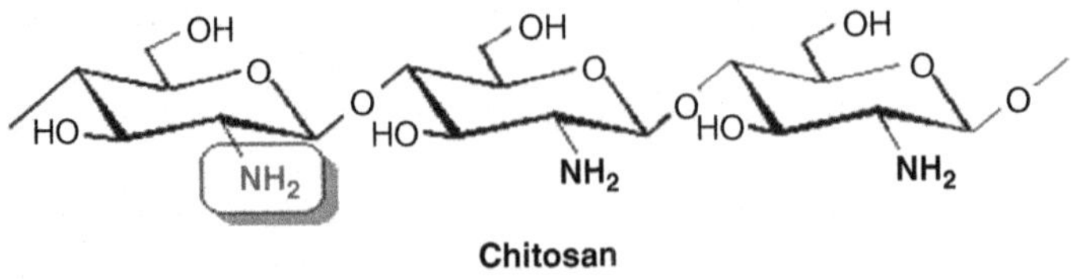

Chitosan

Figure 9.1 Structure of chitosan (Yogeshkumar et al., 2013).

6 Applications of Chitosan Polymer in Agriculture

The chitosan biopolymer is being put to several uses in agriculture. It is used as a treatment and/or coating for seeds of several crops such as wheat, maize, cotton, soybeans, and many other vegetables to enhance their growth and to act as a protectant against fungal infections and insect or nematode attacks. The antimicrobial properties of the chitosan polymer result in protection of seeds against diseases. Further, it induces innate defense responses in plants against insects and other pathogens. The use of chitosan for plants and horticultural commodities has been approved by the EPA. The chitosan polymer has been reported to increase photosynthetic rates, enhancing growth and development by higher nutrient uptake and assimilation. It also shows an increase in germination and sprouting percentage of seeds (Bautista-Banos et al., 2006; Yogeshkumar et al., 2013; Castro and Paulin, 2012; Hadwiger, 2013).

7 Horticultural and Food Applications

There is a growing demand by consumers for ecofriendly, biodegradable, safe, and natural packaging material. The chitosan polymer forms a semipermeable coating and enhances the postharvest life of fruits and vegetables by lowering the respiration and transpirational losses. The chitosan polymer offers plenty of advantages when used as a coating on horticultural products. It has unique properties such as nontoxicity, biodegradability, and antimicrobial and antioxidant activities. It acts as an ecofriendly, safe approach to manage the pathogenic microbes and insect pests. The chitosan polymer can be made in different forms such as films, gels, beads, and nanoparticles as well as being applied using a dip or spray. Chitosan polymer films due to their antimicrobial properties have potential for quality maintenance and postharvest life extension of various food and horticultural products.

It has been elucidated from the work of several researchers that the chitosan polymer causes reduction in the incidence and severity of both pre- and postharvest diseases on many horticultural crops (Bautista-Banos et al., 2006). The chitosan polymer displays increase in the synthesis and activities of a few enzymes such as glucanohydrolases and some phenolic compounds and phytoalexins, which also show antifungal properties. It has also been reported that it reduces the activity of polygalacturonases and pectin methyl esterase enzymes, thus maintaining the firmness of the fruit and reducing the decay percentage. It has potential for use as an agricultural and horticultural crop protection and food preservation polymer.

Chitosan coating on artichoke seeds enhances their germination percentage and growth and development. A decrease in fungal contamination of artichoke seeds was also observed. The chitosan polymer is also used as a clarifying agent for removal of pectin and carbohydrates from fruit juices to obtain clear juice free from suspensions. Juice clarification using the chitosan polymer has been done for various fruits such as apple, grape, lemon, orange, and pineapple juices (Chatterjee et al., 2004; Domingues et al., 2012; Nualkaekul et al., 2012). It has also been applied for increasing the bloom and enhancing the postharvest life of cut flowers.

Cruz-Romero et al. (2013) studied the antimicrobial activity of low and medium molecular weight chitosan and organic acids such as benzoic and sorbic acid against commercially available meat coatings. It was reported that both low and medium molecular weight chitosan polymer coatings displayed the highest antimicrobial activity against all the tested bacterial populations. It was also observed that the antimicrobial activity is dependent on the molecular weight of the chitosan polysaccharide. It is evident from the work of Qi et al. (2011) on minimally processed apple slices that chitosan polymer coatings effectively lowered enzymatic browning and maintained texture. The study by Lou et al. (2011) revealed that the acid-soluble chitosan polymer had potential to control the apricot fruit rot pathogenic microorganism *Burkholderia seminalis*. This might be because of membrane disruption and cell lysis. Chitosan polymer coating has been applied on several fruits to enhance the postharvest life and maintain their quality by reducing transpiration and respiration rates. It was recorded by Ma et al. (2014) that the treatment of chitosan solution or combination of 1-methycyclopropene and chitosan on aprium fruits reduced firmness loss, decay, respiration, and ethylene production rates. The effect of low and high molecular weight chitosan on asparagus was studied by Qiu et al. (2013). The results showed that 0.25% high molecular weight and 0.50% low molecular weight chitosan polymer-treated asparagus showed lower color changes, transpirational losses, and extended shelf life over other treatments or control during storage. Chitosan coating was found to be effective in controlling decay in tomato and citrus fruits (Liu et al., 2007; Chien et al., 2007a).

The gum of unripe bael fruits was processed with chitosan polymer to improve the film-forming attribute of the bael gum for use in modification of release rate of drugs and in processed food products (Jindal et al., 2013). The antifungal activities of cinnamon extract along with chitosan polymer showed significant delay in ripening and decay incidence (Win et al., 2007). Suseno et al. (2014) applied chitosan polymer of different degrees of deacetylation to Cavendish banana to study its effects on postharvest quality. The results revealed that the chitosan-coated banana fruit showed delay in the ripening process compared to control fruit. The weight and ascorbic acid loss showed a decrease with an increase in the concentration and degree of deacetylation of chitosan polysaccharide. The efficacy of lemongrass essential oil with chitosan as an edible coating for managing anthracnose in bell pepper was studied by Ali et al. (2014). The chitosan treatment at 1% and the lemongrass essential oil with chitosan treatment enhanced the antimicrobial activity. It was found that the quality of bell pepper fruits was maintained by these treatments. However, the chitosan treatment was found to be more effective for reduction of disease incidence and enhancing shelf life. Poverenov et al. (2014) investigated the influence of a composite chitosan–gelatin coating on the quality and shelf life of peppers. The composite coating exhibited a decrease in decay, maintained texture, and prolonged storage. The delay in ripening due to chitosan treatment might be due to the enhanced antioxidant ability of the fruit (Hong et al., 2012).

Agricultural produce is perishable and in particular most horticultural commodities have a very limited postharvest life. Fruits and vegetables are living organisms and exhibit continuous respiration and transpiration resulting in losses both physically and in quality. Edible coating, especially chitosan application, is a cheap, easy, and effective technique for avoiding moisture loss and reducing decay and respiration rate. Besides, it is biologically safe to use and has no toxicity issues. The chitosan polymer has been found to be very useful both in combination and as a single treatment. Several researchers across the world have been endeavoring to maintain the quality and enhance the postharvest life of horticultural produce. Tables 9.1 and 9.2 highlight the work done and the results obtained by various researchers using chitosan polymer-based treatments, alone or in combination, for postharvest quality maintenance, reduction of decay, and enhanced shelf life of various horticultural commodities.

Minimal processing of horticultural products is a prerequisite of the times to provide convenience for consumers. The minimally processed products exhibit a faster deterioration rate as compared to fresh produce due to the physical injuries, enzyme activities, and enhanced decay incidence and severity. Browning also occurs in some of the susceptible products resulting in

Table 9.1 Effect of Chitosan Polymer on the Quality, Safety, and Postharvest Life of Fruits

References	Treatment	Fruit	Beneficial Effects of Chitosan
Aquino et al. (2015)	Application of edible chitosan–cassava starch coatings containing essential oil mixtures enriched with *Lippia gracilis* Schauer genotype	Guava	Inhibition of the growth of the majority of bacteria
Cisse et al. (2015)	Functional chitosan (0.5, 1, and 1.5%) and lactoperoxidase system coatings	Mango cv. "Kent"	Reduced weight loss and delay in the decline in firmness and respiration rate
Shao et al. (2015)	Chitosan combined with clove oil	Citrus cv. "Miyagawawase"	1% chitosan alone can effectively contribute to the growth of green mold in citrus fruit
Waewthongrak et al. (2015)	Chitosan, cyclic lipopeptide antibiotics (CLPs), and *Bacillus subtilis* application	Citrus—mandarin	Protection of citrus fruit from the green mold pathogen *Penicillium digitatum*
Aloui et al. (2014)	Chitosan and locust bean gum with different citrus essential oils	Date var. "Deglet Nour"	Reduced conidial germination and *Aspergillus flavus* growth in dates
Elbarbary and Mostafa (2014)	Irradiated carboxymethyl chitosan solutions	Peach	Lower molecular weight carboxymethyl chitosan delayed spoilage and malondialdehyde content
Kou et al. (2014)	Chitosan (0.2%) and calcium chloride (2%) treatments	Pear cv. "Huang Guan"	Significant positive effect on the activities of nicotinamide adenine dinucleotide-dependent malate dehydrogenase and nicotinamide adenine dinucleotide phosphate-dependent malic enzyme both in pulp and peel
Liu et al. (2014)	Aqueous solutions of water (control), 40.0 mM ascorbic acid, 1.0% chitosan, and 40.0 mM ascorbic acid combined with 1.0% chitosan	Plum cv. "Sanhuali"	Maintained firmness, decreased color changes, and lowered respiration rate, PPO activity and malondialdehyde content.
Lopes et al. (2014)	Potassium silicate and chitosan application	Strawberry	64% lower gray mold rot by using chitosan

Table 9.1 Effect of Chitosan Polymer on the Quality, Safety, and Postharvest Life of Fruits (*cont.*)

References	Treatment	Fruit	Beneficial Effects of Chitosan
Lu et al. (2014)	0.2, 0.5, or 1% (w/v) chitosan solution	Satsuma orange	Severe inhibition of *P. digitatum* spore germination by 1% chitosan
Oliveira et al. (2014a)	Chitosan from *Mucor circinelloides*	Table grape	Controlled pathogenic fungi and maintained the postharvest quality of table grapes
Oliveira et al. (2014b)	Chitosan from *Cunninghamella elegans*	Table grape	Preserved the quality of grapes and controlled postharvest pathogenic fungi, particularly *B. cinerea* and *P. expansum*
Plainsirichai et al. (2014)	Chitosan (1, 2, and 3%) coating	Rose apple cv. "Tabtimchan"	Lowered PLW and disease incidence, maintained firmness
Uliana et al. (2014)	Pre- and postharvest chitosan application (0.5, 1.0, and 2%) spray and dip treatments, respectively	Raspberry cv. "Autumn Bliss"	Lower PLW, respiration rate, and decay, maintenance of firmness
Wang et al. (2014)	25 g L^{-1} in 1% (v/v) HCl chitosan solution	Jujube	Spore germination, germ tube length, and mycelial growth of *P. expansum* were significantly inhibited
Yang et al. (2014)	Blueberry leaf extracts (4, 8, and 12%) incorporated chitosan (2%) coatings and modified atmosphere packaging	Blueberry	Lowered decay rate and maintenance of high nutritional value
Zhang et al. (2014)	UV irradiation and coating with 1, 1.5, 2, and 2.5% chitosan	Jujube	Reduced decay incidence, respiration rate, loss in weight, malondialdehyde, and electrolyte leakage
Ali et al. (2013)	Conventional chitosan and submicron chitosan dispersions	Dragon fruit	Significant reduction of anthracnose and disease development, maintenance of quality
Gao et al. (2013)	Chitosan (1%), glucose (1%), and chitosan–glucose complex coating	Table grape cv. "Muscat Hamburg"	Inhibited senescence and postharvest diseases, delayed loss of total soluble solids, ascorbic acid, and titratable acidity
Gol et al. (2013)	CMC (1%), HPMC (1%), CMC (1%) + chitosan (1%), and HPMC (1%) + chitosan (1%)	Strawberry cv. "Camarosa"	Extension of shelf life and maintenance of fruit quality

(*Continued*)

Table 9.1 Effect of Chitosan Polymer on the Quality, Safety, and Postharvest Life of Fruits (*cont.*)

References	Treatment	Fruit	Beneficial Effects of Chitosan
Ma et al. (2013)	Chitosan and oligochitosan	Peach	Significant control of disease, delay in fruit softening and senescence
Romanazzi et al. (2013)	Chitosan (1%) in solution with acetic (1%), glutamic (1%), formic (1%), and hydrochloric acids (1%)	Strawberry	Controlled storage decay
Shi et al. (2013)	Chitosan/nano-silica hybrid film	Longan cv. "Shijia"	Extension of shelf life, reduced browning index, weight loss, malondialdehyde amount, and polyphenoloxidase activity
Wang and Gao (2013)	Chitosan (0.5, 1.0, and 1.5%)	Strawberry	Extension of shelf life, maintenance of quality and controlled decay
Hong et al. (2012)	0.5, 1.0, and 2.0% chitosan coatings	Guava cv. "Pearl"	Significant lowering of loss in firmness, weight, ascorbic acid, and titratable acidity
Medeiros et al. (2012)	Nanomultilayer coating of pectin and chitosan	Mango cv. "Tommy Atkins"	Extension of shelf life
Santos et al. (2012)	Coating composed of chitosan and *Origanum vulgare* L. essential oil	Grape cv. "Isabella"	Controlled postharvest pathogenic fungi in fruits, particularly *Rhizopus stolonifer* and *Aspergillus niger* in grapes
Yang et al. (2012)	Chitosan and oligochitosan	Peach	Spore germination and mycelial growth of *M. fructicola* were strongly inhibited by chitosan and oligochitosan treatments
Yu et al. (2012a)	Chitosan at different concentrations alone and in combination with a biocontrol yeast *Cryptococcus laurentii* and calcium chloride	Pear cv. "Shuijing"	The combination of chitosan at 0.5% and *C. laurentii* resulted in more effective mold control than chitosan or *C. laurentii* alone
Yu et al. (2012b)	1% chitosan film with 0.04% nano-silicon dioxide	Jujube	Reduction in decay, weight loss, malondialdehyde content, and respiration rate of the coated jujubes
Ali et al. (2011)	Chitosan (0.5, 1.0, 1.5, and 2.0%) coatings	Papaya cv. "Eksotika II"	Lower weight loss and color change, maintained firmness, prolonged storage life

Table 9.1 Effect of Chitosan Polymer on the Quality, Safety, and Postharvest Life of Fruits (*cont.*)

References	Treatment	Fruit	Beneficial Effects of Chitosan
Gonzalez et al. (2011)	HPMC or chitosan with and without bergamot essential oil	Table grape, cv. "Muscatel"	Chitosan containing bergamot oil showed the highest antimicrobial activity and the highest control of respiration rates with lower water loss during storage
Lin et al. (2011)	Chitosan (1%) solution	Litchi cv. "Heli"	Lesser respiration rate, sarcocarp temperature, polyphenol oxidase activity, and weight loss
Meng et al. (2010)	Chitosan (350 kDa) and oligochitosan (6 kDa) solutions	Pear	Strong inhibition of spore germination and mycelial growth of *Alternaria kikuchiana* and *Physalospora piricola*
Munoz et al. (2009)	Chitosan (0, 1, 1.5, 2, and 2.5%) solutions	Grapes	Reduced lesion size and lesion diameter of *Colletotrichum* sp.
Collin et al. (2008)	Citric acid and chitosan solution	Litchi cvs. "Red Kwai May" and "Wai Chee"	The red color of Kwai May was better preserved than the other cultivar
Meng et al. (2008)	Preharvest chitosan spray and/or postharvest chitosan coating treatments	Table grape	Maintenance of fruit quality and resistance to fruit decay
Chien et al. (2007a)	Low and high molecular weight chitosan	Tangor cv. "Murcott"	Low molecular weight chitosan exhibited greater antifungal resistance and better quality
Qiuping and Wenshui (2007)	1-Methylcyclopropene and chitosan coating 1.5 g/100 mL	Indian jujube cv. "Cuimi"	Senescence inhibition and extension of storage life
Ribeiro et al. (2007)	Starch carrageenan and chitosan coatings	Strawberry	Minimum PLW and microbial growth
Munoz et al. (2006)	1% calcium gluconate dips, 1.5% chitosan coating, or coating formulation containing 1.5% chitosan + 1% Calcium gluconate	Strawberry cv. "Camarosa"	No sign of fungal disease, decreased PLW, slow ripening
Vargas et al. (2006)	Chitosan–oleic acid coating	Strawberry cv. "Camarosa"	Enhanced antimicrobial activity and improved water vapor resistance

(Continued)

Table 9.1 Effect of Chitosan Polymer on the Quality, Safety, and Postharvest Life of Fruits (*cont.*)

References	Treatment	Fruit	Beneficial Effects of Chitosan
Caro and Joas (2005)	Chitosan and organic acids	Litchi cv. "Kwai Mi"	Response to acid chitosan treatment is partially dependent on pericarp water content, and treatments at higher pH (≥ 1) may be done if treatment and storage conditions are properly controlled
Jiang et al. (2005)	Chitosan (2%) solution	Litchi cv. "Huaizhi"	Delay in loss of anthocyanin content, decreased PPO activity, and partial inhibition of decay
Joas et al. (2005)	Chitosan and organic acids	Litchi cv. "Kwai Mi"	Lowest weight loss and better acidification of the pericarp
Ruoyi et al. (2005)	Chitosan coating and intermittent warming	Peach cv. "Zhong-huashoutao"	Maintenance of quality and extended shelf life
Galed et al. (2004)	Biorend, a compound whose active molecule is chitosan	Mandarin cv. "Fortune" and Orange cv. "Valencia"	Lower PLW and enhanced visual appearance
Bautista-Banos et al. (2003)	Chitosan and plant extracts	Papaya cv. "Maradol"	Chitosan at 2.0% and 3.0% had a fungicidal effect on *Colletotrichum gloeosporioides* and maintained greater firmness
Romanazzi et al. (2003)	Chitosan	Sweet cherry cv. "Ferrovia"	Significant reduction in brown rot, gray mold, and total rot
Jiang and Li (2001)	Chitosan (0.5, 1.0, and 2.0%) solutions	Longan cv. "Shixia"	Reduced respiration rate and weight loss, delayed rise in PPO enzyme activity and less decay
Reddy et al. (2000)	Preharvest chitosan sprays (2, 4, and 6 g L^{-1})	Strawberry cv. "Seascape"	Higher firmness, slow ripening, and lower decay
Zhang and Quantick (1997)	Chitosan solutions (1.0 or 2.0%)	Litchi cv. "Huaizhi"	Delayed changes in anthocyanin, flavonoid, and total phenolics content and partial inhibition of decay

Table 9.2 Effect of Chitosan Polymer on the Quality, Safety, and Postharvest Life of Vegetables

References	Treatment	Vegetable	Beneficial Effects of Chitosan
Chen et al. (2014)	Chitosan and methyl jasmonic acid	Cherry tomato	Reduced disease incidence and lesion diameter
Han et al. (2014)	Chitosan (0, 0.5, and 1.0%)	Sponge gourd	Lowered respiration rate and PLW, maintained firmness, phenolics, ascorbic acid and visual appearance
Alvarez et al. (2013)	Chitosan enriched with bioactive compounds and essential oils	Broccoli	Reduction in mesophilic and psychrotrophic microbial counts
Jiang et al. (2012)	Chitosan, glucose, and chitosan–glucose complex	Shiitake mushroom	Maintenance of firmness, lower respiration rate, decay, and extension of its postharvest life
Moreira et al. (2011)	Chitosan coating	Broccoli	Inhibition of yellowing and opening of florets
Xing et al. (2011)	Chitosan coating enriched with cinnamon oil	Sweet pepper	Decay below 5% and good sensory acceptability
Badawy and Rabea (2009)	Chitosan of different molecular weights	Tomato	Low disease incidence, high phenolics, PPO activity, and total protein content
Munoz et al. (2009)	Chitosan (0, 1, 1.5, 2, and 2.5%) solutions	Tomato	Reduced lesion size and lesion diameter of *Colletotrichum* sp.
Yongcai et al. (2009)	Chitosan (0.5 and 1.0%)	Potato	Effective control of dry rot of potato tuber. However, the chitosan treatment at 1% caused phytotoxicity to potato tuber
Xiaojuan et al. (2008)	Chitosan (0.25%)	Potato	Reduction in the lesion diameter and increased flavonoid contents and lignin in tissues
Liu et al. (2007)	Chitosan	Tomato	Inhibition of spore germination, germ tube elongation, and mycelia growth on gray mold and blue mold

spoilage of the products' appearance and quality, and impacting on price. It is very much required to maintain the appearance of fresh-cut produce, and chitosan as an edible coating has shown much potential to cause delay in spoilage rates and weight and quality loss while maintaining visual acceptability of the produce. Chitosan also exhibits high potential for clarification of fruit and vegetable juices and maintaining their consumer acceptance for a longer period of time by delaying the degradation of anthocyanin and other pigments. The most marked influences of chitosan are to prevent both enzymatic and nonenzymatic browning in the minimally processed horticultural products, clarification of various juices, and marked inhibition of spoilage causing pathogenic microorganisms. Table 9.3 reveals the influences of chitosan biopolymer on the various minimally processed products and juices as observed and recorded by different workers.

8 Conclusions

Chitosan is a unique natural biopolymer, which is available in abundance since it is obtained from waste crustacean products. It can play a tremendous role in crop protection at both pre- and postharvest stages to achieve sustainable agriculture using natural, safe compounds. The use of chitosan polymer as a clarifying agent, edible coating, and food packaging material during handling procedures after harvest, processing, and food packaging is very beneficial in maintaining the quality and enhancing the shelf life of produce. The beneficial influences of this biopolymer may further be enhanced by incorporating other natural compounds such as essential oils and other biological control agents with it. It may also be applied in combination with other treatments such as modified atmosphere or hypobaric storage.

It is required that future research studies should be aimed at elucidating the molecular mechanisms of the antimicrobial actions of the chitosan polymer and the development of resistance in bacteria on its use. The integration of the chitosan polymer with other natural pigments such as anthocyanins, etc., to create natural, antimicrobial, and biodegradable intelligent packaging, can be done for the convenience of consumers. It can also be applied as chitosan nanoparticles to enhance its effectiveness.

Table 9.3 Effect of Chitosan Polymer on the Quality, Safety, and Postharvest Life of Minimally Processed Products

References	Treatment	Minimally Processed Product	Beneficial Effects of Chitosan
Leceta et al. (2015)	Chitosan-based coatings	Ready to eat, MAP-packaged baby carrots	Delay in microbial spoilage, maintenance of color and texture
Velasco and Beltran (2014)	Acetic acid (1 and 2.5%) and chitosan coating	Peeled prickly pear (white and red)	Delayed weight loss, maintained firmness and color
Pushkala et al. (2013)	Chitosan-based powder coating technique using purified chitosan and chitosan lactate	Radish shreds	Lowering of PLW, respiration rate, TSS, and titratable acidity Lesser browning and microbial load
Domingues et al. (2012)	Chitosan, pH, and slow velocity speed and time	Passion fruit juice	Best result for passion fruit clarification
Nualkaekul et al. (2012)	Chitosan-coated alginate beads. Uncoated, single and double chitosan-coated beads	Pomegranate juice	Survival of the cells in simulated gastric solution (pH 1.5) was better
Pushkala et al. (2012)	Chitosan coating alone and in combination with citric acid	Shredded carrots	Lowered PLW, microbial activity, and minimal changes in pH, total acidity, TSS, and respiration rate. Better color retention
Varasteh et al. (2012)	Edible coatings as chitosan treatments (0, 1, and 2%)	Pomegranate arils cv. "Rabbab-e-Neyriz"	Delayed anthocyanin degradation and color deterioration
Pitak and Rakshit (2011)	Banana flour/chitosan composite films	Fresh-cut vegetables, asparagus, baby corn, and Chinese cabbage	Reduction of decay by *Staphylococcus aureus*
Xiao et al. (2010)	Combination of pure oxygen pretreatment and chitosan coating containing 0.03% rosemary extracts	Fresh-cut pears cv. "Huangguan"	Inhibition of PPO activity, softening, and weight loss, and enhanced shelf life
Xing et al. (2010)	Chitosan-based coating and MAP	Fresh-cut lotus root	Browning prevented, lowest PPO activity, and malondialdehyde content

(Continued)

Table 9.3 Effect of Chitosan Polymer on the Quality, Safety, and Postharvest Life of Minimally Processed Products (*cont.*)

References	Treatment	Minimally Processed Product	Beneficial Effects of Chitosan
Diana et al. (2009)	Chitosan solutions	Orange juice cv. "Navelina" and "Valencia Late"	Reduced enzymatic and nonenzymatic browning, control of spoilage during the storage time, extended quality and preserved ascorbic acid and carotenoids during storage up to chitosan (1 g L^{-1})
Simoes et al. (2009)	Chitosan (5 mL L^{-1}) in MAP	Carrot sticks cv. "Tino"	Quality maintenance and enhanced phenolic content
Vargas et al. (2009)	High molecular weight chitosan coating by immersion and vacuum method	Fresh-cut carrots cv. "Nantesa"	Coating application by vacuum pulse enhanced appearance and reduced PLW
Campaniello et al. (2008)	Chitosan solution (1%) and MAP with 80% O_2	Minimally processed strawberries	Prolonged quality and shelf life, inhibition of growth of microorganisms
Sangsuwan et al. (2008)	Commercial stretch film, chitosan/methyl cellulose film, and chitosan/ methylcellulose film incorporating vanillin	Fresh-cut cantaloupe and pineapple	Rapid reduction in the number of *Saccharomyces cerevisiae* yeast inoculated on cantaloupe and pineapple
Chien et al. (2007b)	Chitosan (0, 0.5, 1, or 2%) solutions	Sliced mango cv. "Irwin"	Maintenance of quality, inhibition of the growth of microorganisms, and extension of shelf life
Chatterjee et al. (2004)	Chitosan from shrimp shell	Fruit juices (apple, grape, lemon, and orange)	Significant increase in appearance and acceptability of the juices on a nine-point Hedonic scale
Dong et al. (2004)	Chitosan (0, 1, 2, or 3%) solutions	Peeled litchi fruit cv. "Huaizhi"	Lowered weight loss and PPO and peroxidase activities, effective maintenance of quality attributes and extension of shelf life

References

Abras, S.K., Azizi, M.H., Hamidy, Z., Fallah, N.B., 2012. Mechanical, physicochemical and color properties of chitosan based-films as a function of *Aloe vera* gel incorporation. Carbohyd. Polym. 87, 2058–2062.

Aider, M., 2010. Chitosan application for active bio-based films production and potential in the food industry: review. LWT—Food Sci. Technol. 43, 837–842.

Ali, A., Muhammad, M.T.M., Sijam, K., Siddiqui, Y., 2011. Effect of chitosan coatings on the physicochemical characteristics of Eksotika II papaya (*Carica papaya* L.) fruit during cold storage. Food Chem. 124, 620–626.

Ali, A., Zahid, N., Manickam, S., Siddiqui, Y., Alderson, P.G., Maqbool, M., 2013. Effectiveness of submicron chitosan dispersions in controlling anthracnose and maintaining quality of dragon fruit. Postharvest Biol. Technol. 86, 147–153.

Ali, A., Zahid, N., Manickam, S., Siddiqui, Y., Alderson, P.G., Maqbool, M., 2014. Induction of lignin and pathogenesis related proteins in dragon fruit plants in response to submicron chitosan dispersions. Crop Protect. 63, 83–88.

Ali, A., Noh, N.M., Mustafa, M.A., 2015. Antimicrobial activity of chitosan enriched with lemon grass oil against anthracnose of bell pepper. Food Packag. Shelf Life 3, 56–61.

Allan, C.R., Hadwiger, L.A., 1979. The fungicidal effect of chitosan on fungi of varying cell wall composition. Exp. Mycol. 3, 285–2878.

Aloui, H., Khwaldia, K., Licciardello, F., Mazzaglia, A., Muratore, G., Hamdi, M., Restuccia, C., 2014. Efficacy of the combined application of chitosan and locust bean gum with different citrus essential oils to control postharvest spoilage caused by *Aspergillus flavus* in dates. Int. J. Food Microbiol. 170, 21–28.

Alvarez, M.V., Ponce, A.G., Moreira, M.R., 2013. Antimicrobial efficiency of chitosan coating enriched with bioactive compounds to improve the safety of fresh cut broccoli. LWT—Food Sci. Technol. 50, 78–87.

Antoniou, J., Liu, F., Majeed, H., Zhong, F., 2015. Characterization of tara gum edible films incorporated with bulk chitosan and chitosan nanoparticles: a comparative study. Food Hydrocolloids 44, 309–319.

Aquino, A.B., Blank, A.F., Santana, L.C.L.A., 2015. Impact of edible chitosan-cassava starch coatings enriched with *Lippia gracilis* Schauer genotype mixtures on the shelf life of guavas (*Psidium guajava* L.) during storage at room temperature. Food Chem. 171, 108–116.

Arancibia, M.Y., Caballero, M.E.L., Guillen, M.C.G., Garcia, M.F., Martin, F.F., Montero, P., 2015. Antimicrobial and rheological properties of chitosan as affected by extracting conditions and humidity exposure. LWT—Food Sci. Technol. 60 (2), 802–810.

Arnon, H., Zaitsev, Y., Porat, R., Poverenov, E., 2014. Effects of carboxymethyl cellulose and chitosan bilayer edible coating on postharvest quality of citrus fruit. Postharvest Biol. Technol. 87, 21–26.

Arnon, H., Granit, R., Porat, R., Poverenov, E., 2015. Development of polysaccharides-based edible coatings for citrus fruits: a layer-by-layer approach. Food Chem. 166, 465–472.

Aruldhason, B., Pasiyappazham, R., Vairamani, S., Annaian, S., 2012. Extraction, characterization and in vitro antioxidative potential of chitosan and sulfated chitosan from cuttlebone of *Sepia aculeate* Orbigny. Asian Pacific J. Tropical Biomed. 2 (1), S334–S341.

Arvanitoyannis, I.S., 1999. Totally and partially biodegradable polymer blends based on natural and synthetic macromolecules: preparation, physical properties, and potential as food packaging materials. J. Macromol. Sci.—Rev. Macromol. Chem. Phy. 39, 205–271.

Azeredo, G.A., Stamford, T.L.M., Nunes, P.C., Neto, N.J.G., Oliveira, M.E.G., Souza, E.L., 2011. Combined application of essential oils from *Origanum vulgare* L. and *Rosmarinus officinalis* L. to inhibit bacteria and autochthonous microflora associated with minimally processed vegetables. Food Res. Int. 44, 1541–1548.

Azevedo, A.N., Buarque, P.R., Cruz, E.M.O., Blank, A.F., Alves, P.B., Nunes, M.L., Santana, L.C.L.A., 2014. Response surface methodology for optimisation of edible chitosan coating formulations incorporating essential oil against several foodborne pathogenic bacteria. Food Cont. 43, 1–9.

Badawy, M.E.I., Rabea, E.I., 2009. Potential of the biopolymer chitosan with different molecular weights to control postharvest gray mold of tomato fruit. Postharvest Biol. Technol. 51, 110–117.

Badawy, M.E.I., Rabea, E.I., Taktak, N.E.M., 2014. Antimicrobial and inhibitory enzyme activity of *N*-(benzyl) and quaternary *N*-(benzyl) chitosan derivatives on plant pathogens. Carbohyd. Polym. 111, 670–682.

Bautista-Banos, S., Lopez, M.H., Molina, E.B., Wilson, C.L., 2003. Effects of chitosan and plant extracts on growth of *Colletotrichum gloeosporioides*, anthracnose levels and quality of papaya fruit. Crop Prot. 22, 1087–1092.

Bautista-Banos, S., Hernandez-Lauzardo, A.N., Velazquez-del Valle, M.G., Hernandez-Lopez, M., Barka, E.A., Bosquez-Molina, E., Wilson, C.L., 2006. Chitosan as a potential natural compound to control pre and postharvest diseases of horticultural commodities. Crop Prot. 25, 108–118.

Benjakul, S., Visessanguan, W., Tanaka, M., Ishizaki, S., Suthidham, R., Sungpech, O., 2000. Effect of chitin and chitosan on gelling properties of surimi from barred garfish (*Hemir amphusfar*). J. Sci. Food Agric. 81, 102–108.

Campaniello, D., Bevilacqua, A., Sinigaglia, M., Corbo, M.R., 2008. Chitosan: antimicrobial activity and potential applications for preserving minimally processed strawberries. Food Microbiol. 25, 992–1000.

Caro, Y., Joas, J., 2005. Postharvest control of litchi pericarp browning (cv. Kwai Mi) by combined treatments of chitosan and organic acids. II. Effect of the initial water content of pericarp. Postharvest Biol. Technol. 38, 137–144.

Castro, S.P.M., Paulin, E.G.L., 2012. Is chitosan a new panacea? Areas of application. http://dx.doi.org/10.5772/51200.

Chatterjee, S., Chatterjee, S., Chatterjee, B.P., Guha, A.K., 2004. Clarification of fruit juice with chitosan. Process Biochem. 39, 2229–2232.

Chen, J., Zou, X., Liu, Q., Wang, F., Feng, W., Wan, N., 2014. Combination effect of chitosan and methyl jasmonate on controlling *Alternaria alternata* and enhancing activity of cherry tomato fruit defense mechanisms. Crop Prot. 56, 31–36.

Chien, P., Sheu, F., Lin, H., 2007a. Coating citrus (*Murcott tangor*) fruit with low molecular weight chitosan increases postharvest quality and shelf life. Food Chem. 100, 1160–1164.

Chien, P., Sheu, F., Yang, F., 2007b. Effects of edible chitosan coating on quality and shelf life of sliced mango fruit. J. Food Eng. 78, 225–229.

Cisse, M., Polidori, J., Montet, D., Loiseau, G., Collin, M.N.D., 2015. Preservation of mango quality by using functional chitosan-lactoperoxidase systems coatings. Postharvest Biol. Technol. 101, 10–14.

Collin, M.N.D., Ramarson, H., Lebrun, M., Self, G., Reynes, M., 2008. Effect of citric acid and chitosan on maintaining red colouration of litchi fruit pericarp. Postharvest Biol. Technol. 49, 241–246.

Cruz-Romero, M.C., Murphy, T., Morris, M., Cummins, E., Kerry, J.P., 2013. Antimicrobial activity of chitosan, organic acids and nano-sized solubilisates for potential use in smart antimicrobially-active packaging for potential food applications. Food Cont. 34, 393–397.

Devlieghere, F., Vermeulen, A., Debevere, J., 2004. Chitosan: antimicrobial activity, interactions with food components and applicability as a coating on fruit and vegetables. Food Microbiol. 21, 703–714.

Diana, A.B.M., Rico, D., Barat, J.M., Ryan, C.B., 2009. Orange juices enriched with chitosan: optimisation for extending the shelf-life. Innov. Food Sci. Emerg. Technol. 10, 590–600.

Domingues, R.C.C., Junior, S.B.F., Silva, R.B., Cardoso, V.L., Reis, M.H.M., 2012. Clarification of passion fruit juice with chitosan: effects of coagulation process variables and comparison with centrifugation and enzymatic treatments. Process Biochem. 47, 467–471.

Dong, H., Cheng, L., Tan, J., Zheng, K., Jiang, Y., 2004. Effect of chitosan coating on quality and shelf life of peeled litchi fruit. J. Food Eng. 64, 355–358.

Dutta, J., Tripathi, S., Dutta, P.K., 2011. Progress in antimicrobial activities of chitin, chitosan and its oligosaccharides: a systematic study needs for food applications. Food Sci. Technol. Int. 18 (1), 3–34.

Elbarbary, A.M., Mostafa, T.B., 2014. Effect of gamma-rays on carboxymethyl chitosan for use as antioxidant and preservative coating for peach fruit. Carbohyd. Polym. 104, 109–117.

EPA, 2008. Environmental Protection Agency review decision of chitosan EPA-HQ-OPP-2007-0037 FRL-8392-6 in the Federal Register/vol. 73, No. 248/ Wednesday, Dec. 24, 2008/Notices.

Galed, G., Valle, M.E.F., Martínez, A., Heras, A., 2004. Application of MRI to monitor the process of ripening and decay in citrus treated with chitosan solutions. Magn. Reson. Imag. 22, 127–137.

Gao, P., Zhu, Z., Zhang, P., 2013. Effects of chitosan–glucose complex coating on postharvest quality and shelf life of table grapes. Carbohyd. Polym. 95, 371–378.

Gol, N.B., Patel, P.R., Rao, T.V.R., 2013. Improvement of quality and shelf-life of strawberries with edible coatings enriched with chitosan. Postharvest Biol. Technol. 85, 185–195.

Gonzalez, L.S., Pastor, C., Vargas, M., Chiralt, A., Martinez, C.G., Chafer, M., 2011. Effect of hydroxyl propyl methyl cellulose and chitosan coatings with and without bergamot essential oil on quality and safety of cold-stored grapes. Postharvest Biol. Technol. 60, 57–63.

Goy, R.C., Britto, D., Assis, O.B.G., 2009. A review of the antimicrobial activity of chitosan. Assis Polimeros: Ciencia e Tecnol. 19 (3), 241–247.

Hadwiger, L.A., 2013. Plant science review: multiple effects of chitosan on plant systems: solid science or hype. Plant Sci. 208, 42–49.

Han, C., Zuo, J., Wang, Q., Xu, L., Zhai, B., Wang, Z., Dong, H., Gao, L., 2014. Effects of chitosan coating on postharvest quality and shelf life of sponge gourd (*Luffa cylindrica*) during storage. Sci. Hortic. 166, 1–8.

Hong, K., Xie, J., Zhang, L., Sun, D., Gong, D., 2012. Effects of chitosan coating on postharvest life and quality of guava (*Psidium guajava* L.) fruit during cold storage. Sci. Hortic. 144, 172–178.

Hongpattarakere, T., Riyaphan, O., 2008. Effect of deacetylation conditions on antimicrobial activity of chitosans prepared from carapace of black tiger shrimp (*Penaeus monodon*). Songklanakarin J. Sci. Technol. 30, 1–9.

Illum, L., 1998. Chitosan and its use as a pharmaceutical excipient. Pharm. Res. 15, 1326–1331.

Iriti, M., Picchi, V., Rossoni, M., Gomarasca, S., Ludwig, N., Gargano, M., Faoro, F., 2009. Chitosan antitranspirant activity is due to abscisic acid-dependent stomatal closure. Environ. Exper. Bot. 66, 493–500.

Jeon, Y.J., Kim, S.K., 2002. Antitumor activity of chitosan oligosaccharides produced in ultrafiltration membrane reactor system. J. Microbiol. Biotechnol. 12, 503–507.

Jeon, Y.J., Park, P.J., Kim, S.K., 2001. Antimicrobial effect of chito oligosaccharides produced by bioreactor. Carbohyd. Polym. 44, 71–76.

Jiang, Y., Li, Y., 2001. Effects of chitosan coating on postharvest life and quality of longan fruit. Food Chem. 73, 139–143.

Jiang, Y., Li, J., Jiang, W., 2005. Effects of chitosan coating on shelf life of cold-stored litchi fruit at ambient temperature. LWT 38, 757–761.

Jiang, T., Feng, L., Li, J., 2012. Changes in microbial and postharvest quality of shiitake mushroom (*Lentinus edodes*) treated with chitosan–glucose complex coating under cold storage. Food Chem. 131, 780–786.

Jianglian, D., Shaoying, Z., 2013. Application of chitosan based coating in fruit and vegetable preservation: a review. J. Food Process. Technol. 4, 5.

Jindal, M., Kumar, V., Rana, V., Tiwary, A.K., 2013. Physico-chemical, mechanical and electrical performance of bael fruit gum-chitosan IPN films. Food Hydrocolloids 30, 192–199.

Joas, J., Caro, Y., Ducamp, M.N., Reynes, M., 2005. Postharvest control of pericarp browning of litchi fruit (*Litchi chinensis* Sonn cv Kwai Mi) by treatment with chitosan and organic acids. I. Effect of pH and pericarp dehydration. Postharvest Biol. Technol. 38, 128–136.

Kong, M., Chen, X.G., Xing, K., Park, H.J., 2010. Antimicrobial properties of chitosan and mode of action: a state of the art review. Int. J. Food Microbiol. 144, 51–63.

Kou, X., Wang, S., Zhang, Y., Guo, R., Wu, M., Chen, Q., Xue, Z., 2014. Effects of chitosan and calcium chloride treatments on malic acid-metabolizing enzymes and the related gene expression in post-harvest pear cv "Huang guan". Sci. Hortic. 165, 252–259.

Leceta, I., Molinaro, S., Guerrero, P., Kerry, J.P., Cab, K., 2015. Quality attributes of map packaged ready-to-eat baby carrots by using chitosan-based coatings. Postharvest Biol. Technol. 100, 142–150.

Lin, B., Du, Y., Liang, X., Wang, X., Wang, X., Yang, J., 2011. Effect of chitosan coating on respiratory behavior and quality of stored litchi under ambient temperature. J. Food Eng. 102, 94–99.

Liu, X.F., Guan, Y.L., Yang, D.Z., Li, Z., Yao, K.D., 2001. Antibacterial action of chitosan and carboxymethylated chitosan. J. Appl. Polym. Sci. 79 (7), 1324–1335.

Liu, H., Du, Y., Wang, X., Sun, L., 2004. Chitosan kills bacteria through cell membrane damage. Int. J. Food Microbiol. 95 (2), 147–155.

Liu, J., Tian, S., Meng, X., Xu, Y., 2007. Effects of chitosan on control of postharvest diseases and physiological responses of tomato fruit. Postharvest Biol. Technol. 44, 300–306.

Liu, K., Yuan, C., Chen, Y., Li, H., Liu, J., 2014. Combined effects of ascorbic acid and chitosan on the quality maintenance and shelf life of plums. Sci. Hortic. 176, 45–53.

Lopes, U.P., Zambolim, L., Costa, H., Pereira, O.L., Finger, F.L., 2014. Potassium silicate and chitosan application for gray mold management in strawberry during storage. Crop Prot. 63, 103–106.

Lou, M., Zhu, B., Muhammad, I., Li, B., Xie, G., Wang, Y., Li, H., Sun, G., 2011. Antibacterial activity and mechanism of action of chitosan solutions against apricot fruit rot pathogen *Burkholderia seminalis*. Carbohyd. Res. 346, 1294–1301.

Lu, L., Liu, Y., Yang, J., Azat, R., Yu, T., Zheng, X., 2014. Quaternary chitosan oligomers enhance resistance and biocontrol efficacy of *Rhodosporidium paludigenum* to green mold in satsuma orange. Carbohyd. Polym. 113, 174–181.

Ma, Z., Yang, L., Yan, H., Kennedy, J.F., Meng, X., 2013. Chitosan and oligochitosan enhance the resistance of peach fruit to brown rot. Carbohyd. Polym. 94, 272–277.

Ma, L., Cao, J., Xu, L., Zhang, X., Wang, Z., Jiang, W., 2014. Effects of 1-methylcy-clopropene in combination with chitosan-oligosaccharides on post-harvest quality of aprium fruits. Sci. Hortic. 179, 301–305.

Medeiros, B.G.S., Pinheiro, A.C., Cunha, M.G.C., Vicente, A.A., 2012. Development and characterization of a nano multilayer coating of pectin and chitosan—evaluation of its gas barrier properties and application on "Tommy Atkins" mangoes. J. Food Eng. 110, 457–464.

Meng, X., Li, B., Liu, J., Tian, S., 2008. Physiological responses and quality attributes of table grape fruit to chitosan preharvest spray and postharvest coating during storage. Food Chem. 106, 501–508.

Meng, X., Yang, L., Kennedy, J.F., Tian, S., 2010. Effects of chitosan and oligochitosan on growth of two fungal pathogens and physiological properties in pear fruit. Carbohyd. Polym. 81, 70–75.

Moreira, M.R., Roura, S.I., Ponce, A., 2011. Effectiveness of chitosan edible coatings to improve microbiological and sensory quality of fresh cut broccoli. LWT—Food Sci. Technol. 44, 2335–2341.

Munoz, P.H., Almenar, E., Ocio, M.J., Gavara, R., 2006. Effect of calcium dips and chitosan coatings on postharvest life of strawberries (*Fragaria* x *ananassa*). Postharvest Biol. Technol. 39, 247–253.

Munoz, Z., Moret, A., Garces, S., 2009. Assessment of chitosan for inhibition of *Colletotrichum* sp. on tomatoes and grapes. Crop Prot. 28, 36–40.

No, H.K., Park, N.Y., Lee, S.H., Meyers, S.P., 2002. Antibacterial activity of chitosans and chitosan oligomers with different molecular weights. Int. J. Food Microbiol. 74 (1–2), 65–72.

Nualkaekul, S., Lenton, D., Cook, M.T., Khutoryanskiy, V.V., Charalampopoulos, D., 2012. Chitosan coated alginate beads for the survival of micro encapsulated *Lactobacillus plantarum* in pomegranate juice. Carbohyd. Polym. 90, 1281–1287.

Oliveira, C.E.V., Magnani, M., Sales, C.V., Pontes, A.L.S., Takaki, G.M.C., Stamford, T.C.M., Souza, E.L., 2014a. Effects of post-harvest treatment using chitosan from *Mucor circinelloides* on fungal pathogenicity and quality of table grapes during storage. Food Microbiol. 44, 211–219.

Oliveira, C.E.V., Magnani, M., Sales, C.V., Pontes, A.L.S., Takaki, G.M.C., Stamford, T.C.M., Souza, E.L., 2014b. Effects of chitosan from *Cunninghamella elegans* on virulence of post-harvest pathogenic fungi in table grapes (*Vitis labrusca* L.). Int. J. Food Microbiol. 171, 54–61.

Pereira, V.A., Arruda, I.N.Q., Stefani, R., 2015. Active chitosan/PVA films with anthocyanins from *Brassica oleraceae* (red cabbage) as time-temperature indicators for application in intelligent food packaging. Food Hydrocolloids 43, 180–188.

Pitak, N., Rakshit, S.K., 2011. Physical and antimicrobial properties of banana flour/chitosan biodegradable and self sealing films used for preserving fresh-cut vegetables. LWT—Food Sci. Technol. 44, 2310–2315.

Plainsirichai, M., Leelaphatthanapanich, S., Wongsachai, N., 2014. Effect of chitosan on the quality of Rose Apples (*Syzygiumagueum* Alston) cv. Tabtim Chan stored at an ambient temperature. APCBEE Proc. 8, 317–322.

Poverenov, E., Zaitsev, Y., Arnon, H., Granit, R., Tuvia, S.A., Perzelan, Y., Weinberg, T., Fallik, E., 2014. Effects of a composite chitosan–gelatin edible coating on postharvest quality and storability of red bell peppers. Postharvest Biol. Technol. 96, 106–109.

Pushkala, R., Parvathy, K.R., Srividya, N., 2012. Chitosan powder coating, a novel simple technique for enhancement of shelf life quality of carrot shreds stored in macro perforated LDPE packs. Innov. Food Sci. Emerg. Technol. 16, 11–20.

Pushkala, R., Raghuram, P.K., Srividya, N., 2013. Chitosan based powder coating technique to enhance phytochemicals and shelf life quality of radish shreds. Postharvest Biol. Technol. 86, 402–408.

Qi, L., Xu, Z., Jiang, X., Hu, C., Zou, X., 2004. Preparation and antibacterial activity of chitosan nanoparticles. Carbohyd. Res. 339, 2693–2700.

Qi, H., Hu, W., Jiang, A., Tian, M., Li, Y., 2011. Extending shelf-life of Fresh-cut "Fuji" apples with chitosan-coatings. Innov. Food Sci. Emerg. Technol. 12, 62–66.

Qiu, M., Jiang, H., Ren, G., Huang, J., Wang, X., 2013. Effect of chitosan coatings on postharvest green asparagus quality. Carbohyd. Polym. 92, 2027–2032.

Qiuping, Z., Wenshui, X., 2007. Effect of 1-methylcyclopropene and/or chitosan coating treatments on storage life and quality maintenance of Indian jujube fruit. LWT 40, 404–411.

Reddy, M.V.B., Belkacemi, K., Corcuff, R., Castaigne, F., Arul, J., 2000. Effect of pre-harvest chitosan sprays on post-harvest infection by *Botrytis cinerea* and quality of strawberry fruit. Postharvest Biol. Technol. 20, 39–51.

Ren, H., Endo, H., Hayashi, T., 2001. Antioxidative and antimutagenic activities and polyphenol content of pesticide-free and organically cultivated green vegetable using water-soluble chitosan as a soil modifier and leaf surface spray. J. Sci. Food Agric. 81, 1426–1432.

Ribeiro, C., Vicente, A.A., Teixeira, J.A., Miranda, C., 2007. Optimization of edible coating composition to retard strawberry fruit senescence. Postharvest Biol. Technol. 44, 63–70.

Romanazzi, G., 2010. Chitosan treatment for the control of postharvest decay of table grapes, strawberries and sweet cherries. Fresh Prod. 4, 111–115.

Romanazzi, G., Nigro, F., Ippolito, A., 2003. Short hypobaric treatments potentiate the effect of chitosan in reducing storage decay of sweet cherries. Postharvest Biol. Technol. 29, 73–80.

Romanazzi, G., Feliziani, E., Santini, M., Landi, L., 2013. Effectiveness of postharvest treatment with chitosan and other resistance inducers in the control of storage decay of strawberry. Postharvest Biol. Technol. 75, 24–27.

Ruoyi, K., Zhifang, Y., Zhaoxin, L., 2005. Effect of coating and intermittent warming on enzymes, soluble pectin substances and ascorbic acid of *Prunus persica* (cv. Zhonghuashoutao) during refrigerated storage. Food Res. Int. 38, 331–336.

Sangsuwan, J., Rattanapanone, N., Rachtanapun, P., 2008. Effect of chitosan/methyl cellulose films on microbial and quality characteristics of fresh-cut cantaloupe and pineapple. Postharvest Biol. Technol. 49, 403–410.

Santos, N.S.T., Aguiar, A.J.A.A., Oliveira, C.E.V., Sales, C.V., Silva, S.M., Silva, R.S., Stamford, T.C.M., Souza, E.L., 2012. Efficacy of the application of a coating composed of chitosan and *Origanum vulgare* L. essential oil to control *Rhizopus stolonifer* and *Aspergillus niger* in grapes (*Vitis labrusca* L.). Food Microbiol. 32, 345–353.

Shao, X., Cao, B., Xu, F., Xie, S., Yu, D., Wang, H., 2015. Effect of postharvest application of chitosan combined with clove oil against citrus green mold. Postharvest Biol. Technol. 99, 37–43.

Shi, S., Wang, W., Liu, L., Wu, S., Wei, Y., Li, W., 2013. Effect of chitosan/nano-silica coating on the physicochemical characteristics of longan fruit under ambient temperature. J. Food Eng. 118, 125–131.

Simoes, A.D.N., Tudela, J., Allende, A., Puschmann, R., Gil, M.I., 2009. Edible coatings containing chitosan and moderate modified atmospheres maintain quality and enhance phytochemicals of carrot sticks. Postharvest Biol. Technol. 51, 364–370.

Suseno, N., Savitri, E., Sapei, L., Padmawijaya, K.S., 2014. Improving shelf-life of Cavendish banana using chitosan edible coating. Proc. Chem. 9, 113–120.

Takahashi, T., Imai, M., Suzuki, I., Sawai, J., 2008. Growth inhibitory effect on bacteria of chitosan membranes regulated with deacetylation degree. Biochem. Eng. J. 40, 485–491.

Terry, L.A., Joyce, D.C., 2004. Elicitors of induced disease resistance in postharvest horticultural crops: a brief review. Postharvest Biol. Technol. 32, 1–13.

Tian, M., Chen, F., Ren, D., Yu, X., Zhang, X., Zhong, R., Wana, C., 2010. Preparation of a series of chitooligomers and their effect on hepatocytes. Carbohyd. Polym. 79 (1), 137–144.

Uliana, J.V.T., Fargoni, G.P., Geerdink, G.M., Kluge, R.A., 2014. Chitosan applications pre- or postharvest prolong raspberry shelf-life quality. Postharvest Biol. Technol. 91, 72–77.

Varasteh, F., Arzani, K., Barzegar, M., Zamani, Z., 2012. Changes in anthocyanins in arils of chitosan-coated pomegranate (*Punica granatum* L. cv. Rabbab-e-Neyriz) fruit during cold storage. Food Chem. 130, 267–272.

Vargas, M., Albors, A., Chiralt, A., Martinez, C.G., 2006. Quality of cold-stored strawberries as affected by chitosan–oleic acid edible coatings. Postharvest Biol. Technol. 41, 164–171.

Vargas, M., Chiralt, A., Albors, A., Martinez, C.G., 2009. Effect of chitosan-based edible coatings applied by vacuum impregnation on quality preservation of fresh-cut carrot. Postharvest Biol. Technol. 51, 263–271.

Velasco, C.E.O., Beltran, J.A.G., 2014. Postharvest quality of peeled prickly pear fruit treated with acetic acid and chitosan. Postharvest Biol. Technol. 92, 139–145.

Waewthongrak, W., Pisuchpen, S., Leelasuphakul, W., 2015. Effect of *Bacillus subtilis* and chitosan applications on green mold (*Penicilium digitatum* Sacc.) decay in citrus fruit. Postharvest Biol. Technol. 99, 44–49.

Wang, S.Y., Gao, H., 2013. Effect of chitosan-based edible coating on antioxidants, antioxidant enzyme system, and postharvest fruit quality of strawberries (*Fragaria* x *ananassa* Duch.). LWT—Food Sci. Technol. 52, 71–79.

Wang, L., Wu, H., Qin, G., Meng, X., 2014. Chitosan disrupts *Penicillium expansum* and controls postharvest blue mold of jujube fruit. Food Cont. 41, 56–62.

Wedmore, I., McManus, J.G., Pusateri, A.E., Holcomb, J.B., 2006. A special report on the chitosan-based hemostatic dressing: experience in current combat operations. J. Trauma 60, 655–658.

Win, N.K.K., Jitareerat, P., Kanlayanarat, S., Sangchote, S., 2007. Effects of cinnamon extract, chitosan coating, hot water treatment and their combinations on crown rot disease and quality of banana fruit. Postharvest Biol. Technol. 45, 333–340.

Xiao, C., Zhu, L., Luo, W., Song, X., Deng, Y., 2010. Combined action of pure oxygen pretreatment and chitosan coating incorporated with rosemary extracts on the quality of fresh-cut pears. Food Chem. 121, 1003–1009.

Xiaojuan, S., Yang, B.I., Yongcai, L.I., Ruifeng, H., Yonghong, G.E., 2008. Postharvest chitosan treatment induces resistance in potato against *Fusarium sulphureum*. Agric. Sci. China 7 (5), 615–621.

Xing, Y., Li, X., Xu, Q., Jiang, Y., Yun, J., Li, W., 2010. Effects of chitosan-based coating and modified atmosphere packaging (MAP) on browning and shelf life of fresh-cut lotus root (*Nelumbo nucifera* Gaerth). Innov. Food Sci. Emerg. Technol. 11, 684–689.

Xing, Y., Li, X., Xu, Q., Yun, J., Lu, Y., Tang, Y., 2011. Effects of chitosan coating enriched with cinnamon oil on qualitative properties of sweet pepper (*Capsicum annuum* L.). Food Chem. 124, 1443–1450.

Yang, L.U., Zhang, J.L., Bassett, C.L., Meng, X.H., 2012. Difference between chitosan and oligochitosan in growth of *Monilinia fructicola* and control of brown rot in peach fruit. LWT—Food Sci. Technol. 46, 254–259.

Yang, G., Yue, J., Gong, X., Qian, B., Wang, H., Deng, Y., Zhao, Y., 2014. Blueberry leaf extracts incorporated chitosan coatings for preserving postharvest quality of fresh blueberries. Postharvest Biol. Technol. 92, 46–53.

Yogeshkumar, G.N., Atul, S.G., Yadav, A.V., 2013. Chitosan and its applications: a review of literature. Int. J. Res. in Pharma. Biomed. Sci. 4 (1), 312–331.

Yongcai, L.I., Xiaojuan, S., Yang, B.I., Yonghong, G.E., Yi, W., 2009. Antifungal activity of chitosan on *Fusarium sulphureum* in relation to dry rot of potato tuber. Agric. Sci. China 8 (5), 597–604.

Yoshida, C.M.P., Maciel, V.B.V., Mendonça, M.E.D., Franco, T.T., 2014. Chitosan biobased and intelligent films: monitoring pH variations. LWT—Food Sci. Technol. 55, 83–89.

Yu, T., Yu, C., Chen, F., Sheng, K., Zhou, T., Zunun, M., Abudu, O., Yang, S., Zheng, X., 2012a. Integrated control of blue mold in pear fruit by combined application of chitosan, a biocontrol yeast and calcium chloride. Postharvest Biol. Technol. 69, 49–53.

Yu, Y., Zhang, S., Ren, Y., Li, H., Zhang, X., Di, J., 2012b. Jujube preservation using chitosan film with nano-silicon dioxide. J. Food Eng. 113, 408–414.

Zahid, N., Ali, A., Manickam, S., Siddiqui, Y., Alderson, P.G., Maqbool, M., 2014. Efficacy of curative applications of submicron chitosan dispersions on anthracnose intensity and vegetative growth of dragon fruit plants. Crop Prot. 62, 129–134.

Zhang, D., Quantick, P.C., 1997. Effects of chitosan coating on enzymatic browning and decay during postharvest storage of litchi (*Litchi chinensis* Sonn.) fruit. Postharvest Biol. Technol. 12, 195–202.

Zhang, S., Yu, Y., Xiao, C., Wang, X., Lei, Y., 2014. Effect of ultraviolet irradiation combined with chitosan coating on preservation of jujube under ambient temperature. LWT—Food Sci. Technol. 57, 749–754.

Zheng, L.Y., Zhu, J.F., 2003. Study on antimicrobial activity of chitosan with different molecular weights. Carbohyd. Polym. 54, 527–530.

SUBJECT INDEX